OXFORD REVISION GUID

GCSE

SCIENCE

through diagrams

George Bethell

Oxford University Press

Oxford University Press,
Great Clarendon Street, Oxford OX2 6DP

Oxford New York
Athens Auckland Bangkok Bogota Bombay
Buenos Aires Calcutta Cape Town Dar es Salaam
Delhi Florence Hong Kong Istanbul Karachi
Kuala Lumpur Madras Madrid Melbourne
Mexico City Nairobi Paris Singapore
Taipei Tokyo Toronto Warsaw

and associated companies in
Berlin Ibadan

Oxford is a trade mark of Oxford University Press

First published 1997

School edition ISBN 0 19 914705 1
Bookshop edition ISBN 0 19 914706 X

A CIP catalogue record for this book is available from the British Library.

Acknowledgements:
We are grateful to the following Examination Boards for permission to use GCSE examinations questions and specimen questions (Sp = specimen):

Questions (including all multiple choice questions) have been provided by **London Examinations**, a division of Edexcel Foundation. Edexcel Foundation, London Examinations accepts no responsibility whatsoever for the accuracy or method of working in the answers given. **MEG**: questions from MEG reproduced by kind permission of the Midland Examining Group. The Midland Examining Group bears no responsibility for the example answers to questions taken from its past question papers which are contained in this publication. **NICCEA**: questions from NICCEA are reproduced with the permission of the Northern Ireland Council for the Curriculum, Examinations and Assessment. The Northern Ireland Council for the Curriculum, Examinations and Assessment bears no responsibility for the example answers to questions taken from its past question papers which are contained in this publication. **SEG**: questions from SEG are reproduced with the kind permission of the Southern Examining Group. The Southern Examining Group bears no responsibility for the example answers to questions taken from its past question papers which are contained in this publication. **WJEC**: questions from WJEC are reproduced with the kind permission of the Welsh Joint Education Committee. The Welsh Joint Education Committee bears no responsibility for the example answers to questions taken from its past question papers which are contained in this publication.

All answers are the responsibility of the author.

Typeset and illustrated by Hardlines, Charlbury, Oxford
Printed and bound in Great Britain

CONTENTS

How to use this book

This book is arranged into three main sections:
SECTION 1: EXAMINATIONS AND REVISION
SECTION 2: SUBJECT CONTENT
SECTION 3: QUESTIONS

USING SECTION 1: EXAMINATIONS AND REVISION

- Read the **GCSE SCIENCE EXAMINATIONS** table to identify:
  your examination
  how it is examined
  the types of examination papers
  the styles of questions
- Work out a revision programme using the **REVISION TIMETABLE** and place copies around your home.
- Use the **REVISION PATHWAYS** to help you navigate easily through your planned revision programme.
- Read **HOW TO REVISE** for some general guidelines on successful revision techniques.
- Remind yourself how to answer questions by reading the **MODEL ANSWERS**.

USING SECTION 2: SUBJECT CONTENT

- Use a copy of your syllabus to identify those pages you need to revise as part of your revision programme.
- Mark your revision pages on the **CHECKLISTS** and on the **REVISION PATHWAYS** with a highlighter pen.
- Each time you revise a page tick it off on the **CHECKLISTS/PATHWAYS**.
- Use highlighter pens to identify key words and concepts on individual pages.
- Colour in parts of the diagrams to help you to remember them more easily.
- Use pages from this book to test yourself with a friend.

USING SECTION 3: QUESTIONS

- With this section you can:
  follow your progress
  build your confidence in answering questions
  identify your strengths and weaknesses
  choose questions from the ***Foundation*** or ***Higher*** tiers

VARIETY AND STYLES OF EXAMINATION QUESTION

The examination papers set by the different examination groups are likely to contain three styles of questions: **Multiple choice**; **Short answers/Structured questions**; **Free response/Long questions**.

MULTIPLE CHOICE QUESTIONS

This type of question is usually done on a special Multiple Choice answer form which is computer marked.

Even if your particular examination does not include Multiple Choice questions they provide useful examination level questions to work through. They also help you to focus on small sections of the syllabus. Also they are useful to help identify areas of weakness or confusion.

Each question gives you four (or some examinations: five) alternatives. Only one is correct. Your task is to select the correct one.

how to answer them

- *CHOOSE ONLY ONE ANSWER*: Select just one answer for each question – if more than one has been selected the question will be marked wrong.
- *WATCH THE TIME*: Keep an eye on the clock. You will be able to answer some questions immediately you have finished reading them, others may take several minutes to work out. Nevertheless, as a rough guide check that halfway through the examination you are approximately halfway through the paper.
- *ELIMINATE INCORRECT ANSWERS*: If the correct answer isn't obvious then eliminate those answers you know to be incorrect. Select an answer. Then mark the question on your question sheet with a star or asterisk so that you can identify it as a question to return to towards the end of the examination.
- *ANSWER ALL THE QUESTIONS*: At the end of the examination don't leave any multiple choice questions unanswered – if all else fails guess!

Before filling in the form you should know:

- how to indicate which answer you have selected
- what to do if you want to change your answer

All this is explained on the form itself but you may feel happier if you have already seen one or used one prior to the exam itself. Your teacher will almost certainly have some examples from previous years that you can have a look at.

Typical example:

1. Which of the following types of radiation is NOT part of the electromagnetic spectrum?
A infrared radiation
B ultraviolet radiation
C sound waves
D radio waves

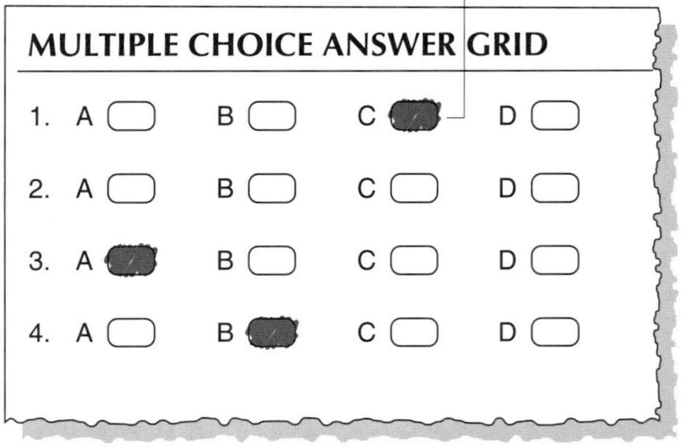

HINT: Check carefully the types of examination questions you will have to answer

SHORT ANSWER/STRUCTURED QUESTIONS

This type of question is usually completed on the exam paper itself. Extended, wordy answers are not wanted here. Answers should be short, concise and complete (You may need answers from early parts of the question later on.)

Typical example:

1. The radioactive isotope carbon-14($^{14}_{6}C$) is used for carbon dating. It has a half life of 5730 years.

   (a) What is an isotope?

   ....

   ....

   (2 marks)

   (b) What is meant by the phrase 'half life of 5730 years'

   ....

   ....

   (2 marks)

how to answer them

- *ANSWER THE QUESTION*: if the question says state, then don't explain. If it says calculate, then show the calculation, don't just write the answer. Answer the question the way it asks to be answered.
- *GIVE FULL ANSWERS*: Give answers as fully as you can in the space provided. As a general rule if an answer is worth two marks there should be two pieces of information in your answer. If there are three or four lines provided for the answer then a one-word answer is unlikely to be sufficient.
- *SHOW ALL YOUR WORKING*: You have worked hard to revise so show the examiner how you arrive at your answers. Show all your working out; write down equations in symbols; substitute in your values and then work out your final answers. The working out is often worth more than the answer itself.
- *TIME YOURSELF*: Well before the exam, work out approximately how much time there is per mark on the paper. If the paper is 1 hour long and there are 120 marks available then 1 minute is equivalent to 2 marks. Use this as a guide to how much time you should spend on each question or part question.
- *TAKE YOUR TIME*: Be aware if you are on time-target or not, and don't panic. Remember, it is often much better to answer many questions partly than to fully answer only a few.
- *CHECK YOUR ANSWERS*: When you think you have finished and completed as much of the paper as you can stop and collect your thoughts. Now, read your answers again carefully to confirm that there are no omissions and that you really have written what you wanted to.

FREE RESPONSE/LONG QUESTIONS

This type of question is less common than it used to be but there are some papers where this style is still used.

These types of questions require extended answers. You must judge how much or how little is required. A good exam technique is particularly important here if you are to gain the maximum number of marks.

Typical example:

1. Explain the advantages and disadvantages of using renewable sources of energy, such as wind energy. Compare these advantages and disadvantages with those of using non-renewable sources of energy such as coal. (7 marks)

how to answer them

In addition to those suggestions given for Short Answer /Structured Questions:

- *KNOW WHAT IS REQUIRED*: Read the question carefully to ensure that you know precisely what the question is looking for. Incorrect interpretations with this type of question can mean losing a lot of marks.
- *PLAN YOUR ANSWER*: Sketch a plan of attack before tackling the question properly: will making some notes help you set out the answer more logically; are diagrams going to be useful? But, this is not an art exam so don't make diagrams too elaborate – and remember labels.
- *BE especially AWARE OF THE TIME*: Longer questions take much more time and effort to correct if you stray off your time-target.

COURSEWORK

The four skill areas that will be assessed through coursework are:

1 Your ability to plan an experiment

- Can you plan a fair/safe practical procedure using the appropriate apparatus?
- Can you predict the outcome of your experiment based on scientific knowledge?

2 Your ability to obtain evidence (the accuracy of your observations and/or measurements)

- Can you use the appropriate apparatus to make accurate measurements or observations?
- Can you record clearly and accurately your observations and measurements?

3 Your ability to analyse your evidence and to draw conclusions from it.

- Can you construct appropriate diagrams, charts, graphs – to process your data?
- Can you draw conclusions from your results and then link these with other scientific knowledge and your prediction?

4 Your ability to evaluate your evidence

- Can you recognise measurements and observations that don't fit a pattern or that might be 'faulty'?
- Can you explain why they arose and suggest changes in your experiment to improve the reliability of your observations or extend your enquiry.

As part of your course your teacher will assess your experimental and investigative skills. You will have many opportunities throughout your course to practise and improve these skills. Your teacher will tell you when the skills are to be tested and will make clear what proof you need to provide to demonstrate the level of your expertise.

Coursework very often has deadlines to achieve throughout the course. It may not be possible to hand work in late and be credited with marks towards your final examination. Check with your teacher.

NOTE: There are marks available for accurate spelling, punctuation, and grammar. Be sure to bear this in mind when you provide any written work.

A final thought – examiners want you to do well. By setting out your answers in a clear, complete and logical fashion you will help them to help you.

GCSE Science examinations - (double award)

EXAM GROUP/ SYLLABUS	TIER/ GRADES	PAPERS	time	weighting%	QUESTION STYLES
EDEXCEL					
MODULAR SCIENCE (1531)	FOUNDATION GG-CC	10 modules		25%	Multiple choice
		PAPER 1F	(1½h)	25%	Structured and free
		PAPER 2F	(1½h)	25%	response questions
		COURSEWORK		25%	
	HIGHER DD-A*A*	10 MODULES		25%	Multiple choice
		PAPER 1H	(2h)	25%	Structured and free
		PAPER 2H	(2h)	25%	response questions
		COURSEWORK		25%	
COMBINED SCIENCE (1524)	FOUNDATION GG-CC	PAPER IF	(1½h)	25%	Structured questions
		PAPER 2F	(1½h)	25%	Structured questions
		PAPER 3F	(1½h)	25%	Structured questions
		COURSEWORK		25%	
	HIGHER DD-A*A*	PAPER 1H	(1½h)	25%	Structured questions
		PAPER 2H	(1½h)	25%	Structured questions
		PAPER 3H	(1½h)	25%	Structured questions
		COURSEWORK		25%	
MEG					
CO-ORDINATED SCIENCE (1794)	FOUNDATION GG-CC	PAPER 1	(1½h)	50%	Structured questions
		PAPER 3	(1½h)	25%	Structured questions
		COURSEWORK		25%	
	HIGHER DD-A*A*	PAPER 2	(1½h)	50%	Structured questions
		PAPER 4	(1½h)	25%	Structured questions
		COURSEWORK		25%	
SUFFOLK SCIENCE (1777)	FOUNDATION GG-CC	PAPER 1	(1½h)	50%	Structured questions
		PAPER 3	(¾h)	25%	Structured questions
		COURSEWORK		25%	
	HIGHER DD-A*A*	PAPER 2	(1¾h)	50%	Structured questions
		PAPER 4	(1h)	25%	Structured questions
		COURSEWORK		25%	
SALTERS' SCIENCE (1774)	FOUNDATION GG-CC	PAPER 1	(2h)	} 75%	Structured questions
		PAPER 2	(2h)		Structured questions
		COURSEWORK		25%	
	HIGHER DD-A*A*	PAPER 1	(2¼h)	} 75%	Structured questions
		PAPER 2	(2¼h)		Structured questions
		COURSEWORK		25%	
NEAB					
CO-ORDINATED SCIENCE (1201)	FOUNDATION GG-CC	PAPER 1F	(1½h)	25%	Structured questions
		PAPER 2F	(1½h)	25%	Structured questions
		PAPER 3F	(1½h)	25%	Structured questions
		COURSEWORK		25%	
	HIGHER DD-A*A*	PAPER 1H	(1½h)	} 75%	Structured questions
		PAPER 2H	(1½h)		Structured questions
		PAPER 3H	(1½h)		Structured questions
		COURSEWORK		25%	
MODULAR SCIENCE (1206)	FOUNDATION GG-CC	6 MODULES		25%	Multiple choice
		PAPER 1F	(1½h)	25%	Structured questions
		PAPER 2F	(1½h)	25%	Structured questions
		COURSEWORK		25%	
	HIGHER DD-A*A*	6 MODULES		25%	Multiple choice
		PAPER 1H	(1½h)	25%	Structured questions
		PAPER 2H	(1½h)	25%	Structured questions
		COURSEWORK		25%	
NICCEA					
MODULAR SCIENCE	FOUNDATION GG-CC	3 MODULES		25%	Short answers
		PAPER 1	(1½h)	16.66%	Structured questions
		PAPER 2	(1½h)	16.66%	Structured questions
		PAPER 3	(1½h)	16.66%	Structured questions
		COURSEWORK		25%	
	HIGHER DD-A*A*	3 MODULES		25%	Short questions
		PAPER 1	(1½h)	16.66%	Structured questions
		PAPER 2	(1½h)	16.66%	Structured questions
		PAPER 3	(1½h)	16.66%	Structured questions
		COURSEWORK		25%	
NON MODULAR SCIENCE	FOUNDATION GG-CC	PAPER 1	(1½h)	25%	} Short answers and structured questions
		PAPER 2	(1½h)	25%	
		PAPER 3	(1½h)	25%	
		COURSEWORK		25%	
	HIGHER DD-A*A*	PAPER 1	(1¾h)	25%	} Short answers and structured questions
		PAPER 2	(1¾h)	25%	
		PAPER 3	(1¾h)	25%	
		COURSEWORK		25%	

HINT: Use a highlighter pen to identify your examination papers.

EXAM GROUP/ SYLLABUS	TIER/ GRADES	PAPERS:	time	weighting%	QUESTION STYLES
SEG					
MODULAR SCIENCE (2630)	FOUNDATION GG-CC	9 MODULES		25%	Multiple choice
		PAPER 2F	(1½h)	25%	} Short, structured, and free response questions
		PAPER 3F	(1½h)	25%	
		COURSEWORK		25%	
	HIGHER DD-A*A*	9 MODULES		25%	Multiple choice
		PAPER 4H	(2h)	25%	} Short, structured, and free response questions
		PAPER 5H	(2h)	25%	
		COURSEWORK		25%	
NON MODULAR SCIENCE (2610)	FOUNDATION GG-CC	PAPER 2	(1½h)	25%	} Short, structured, and free response questions
		PAPER 3	(1½h)	25%	
		PAPER 4	(1½h)	25%	
		COURSEWORK		25%	
	HIGHER DD-A**	PAPER 5	(1½h)	25%	} Short, structured, and free response questions
		PAPER 6	(1½h)	25%	
		PAPER 7	(1½h)	25%	
		COURSEWORK		25%	
WJEC					
MODULAR SCIENCE	FOUNDATION GG-CC	7 MODULES		25%	Structured questions
		PAPER 1F	(1½h)	20%	} Short, structured and free response questions
		PAPER 2F	(1½h)	30%	
		COURSEWORK		25%	
	HIGHER DD-A*A*	7 MODULES		25%	Structured questions
		PAPER 1H	(2h)	20%	} Short, structured, and free response questions
		PAPER 2H	(2h)	30%	
		COURSEWORK		25%	
NON MODULAR SCIENCE (2610)	FOUNDATION GG-CC	PAPER 1	(1¼h)	25%	} Short, structured, and free response questions
		PAPER 2	(1⅓h)	25%	
		PAPER 3	(1⅓h)	25%	
		COURSEWORK		25%	
	HIGHER DD-A*A*	PAPER 4	(1⅔h)	25%	} Short, structured, and free response questions
		PAPER 5	(1⅔h)	25%	
		PAPER 6	(1⅔h)	25%	
		COURSEWORK		25%	

SINGLE AWARD SCIENCE

All examining groups offer science courses which lead to a single grade GCSE certification in the range G to A*. Students taking the foundation tier papers will be able to achieve a single grade G to C. Students taking the higher tier papers will be able to achieve a single grade D to A*.

The assessment of these courses is very similar to those for the Double Award science but written papers may be shorter in duration or there may be fewer papers/modules taken.

The assessment weightings for Single Award science are identical to those for the Double Award science: written papers 75%, coursework 25%.

EXAMINATION GROUPS

EDEXCEL
London Examinations
Stewart House
32 Russell Square
London WC1B 5DN

MIDLAND EXAMINING GROUP (MEG)
Syndicate Buildings
1 Hills Road
Cambridge CB1 2EU

NORTHERN EXAMINATIONS AND ASSESSMENT BOARD (NEAB)
31-33 Springfield Avenue
Harrogate
North Yorkshire HG1 2HW

NORTHERN IRELAND COUNCIL FOR THE CURRICULUM, EXAMINATIONS AND ASSESSMENT (NICCEA)
Beechill House
42 Beechill Road
Belfast BT8 4RS

SOUTHERN EXAMINING GROUP (SEG)
Stag Hill House
Guildford
Surrey GU2 5XJ

WELSH JOINT EDUCATION COMMITTEE (WJEC)
245 Western Avenue
Cardiff CF5 2YX

Model answers

Knowing the correct answer to a question is often not enough to get you full marks in an examination. To demonstrate to an examiner the full extent of your ability and understanding you must show how you arrived at your answer.

It is important to remember that an examiner is trying to give you as many marks as possible. The way in which examination papers are worded and set out can give you valuable clues to obtaining maximum marks.

Typical example:

1. Write down two differences between the properties of alpha radiation and gamma radiation.

(2 marks)

TYPICAL ANSWERS:

Answer A:

Alpha radiation is affected by magnetic fields. Gamma radiation is unaffected by magnetic fields.

Gamma radiation is highly penetrating. Alpha radiation has a low penetrating power.

Comment: This answer will receive full marks as the candidate has done what the question asked. He/she has given two differences.

Answer B:

Alpha radiation is affected by magnetic fields.

Gamma radiation is highly penetrating.

Comment: This answer may receive no marks as the candidate has not fully answered the question. He/she has not given differences between the properties of the two radiations.

NOTE: The question asks for two differences and there are two marks to be awarded. It is likely that one mark will be awarded for each difference. Do not leave the answer blank if you only know one, you may still gain one mark for one difference.

Typical example:

2. Calculate the pd across the ends of a 33 Ω resistor when a current of 0.2 A passes through it.

....

....

....(3 marks)

TYPICAL ANSWERS:

Answer A:

Using V = I x R ✓

V = 0.2 x 33 ✓

V = 4.6 volts X

Comment: This candidate has shown that he/she understands the science of this question even though the final answer is incorrect. He/she is likely to be awarded two of the three marks for stating the equation correctly and for inserting the values correctly.

Answer B:

6.6V

Comment: This candidate is likely to receive full marks - for the correct answer only. But had the answer been wrong no marks would have been given although the candidate might have understood fully the material being tested.

NOTE: In extended length questions it is quite possible you will need answers from earlier parts of the question to help you complete later parts of the question.

Answer C:

Using V = I x R

V = 0.2 x 33

V = 6.6 volts

Comment: This answer is certain to be awarded all three marks. It demonstrates clearly how the candidate has arrived at his or her answer.

NOTE: The question has provided three lines in which to answer the question. Use this 'space' information as a guide to the amount of space likely to be needed for the answer-in this case 3 lines, and the equation needed three lines to complete. Examination papers are set out with space to answer questions in the way the examiner wants the answer presented: in order to help you gain maximum marks!

Also, the question says 'Calculate' and not 'State' the answer - so you need to show the calculation.

How to revise

There is no one method of revising which works for everyone. It is therefore important to discover the approach that suits you best. The following rules may serve as general guidelines.

GIVE YOURSELF PLENTY OF TIME

Leaving your revision until the last minute reduces your changes of success. There are very few people who can revise everything 'the night before' and still do well in an examination the next day. You need to plan your revision timetable for some weeks before the examinations start.

PLAN YOUR REVISION TIMETABLE

Plan your revision timetable well before the examinations start. Once you have done this, follow it – don't be sidetracked. Stick your timetable somewhere prominent where you will keep seeing it – or better still put several around your home!!!!

RELAX

You will be working very hard revising. It is as important to give yourself some free time to relax as it is to work. So, build some leisure time into your revision timetable.

ASK OTHERS

Friends, relatives, teachers will be happy to help if you ask them. Go and talk to them if you are having any difficulties – don't just give up on something that is causing you a problem. And don't forget your parents too!

FIND A QUIET CORNER

Find the conditions in which you can revise most efficiently. Many people think they can revise in a noisy, busy atmosphere – most cannot! And don't try and revise in front of the television – it doesn't generally work. Revision in a distracting environment is very inefficient.

LET THE CHECKLISTS/PATHWAYS HELP YOU

Use the Checklists and Pathways. When you have completed a topic, mark it off. You can also mark off topics you already feel confident about. That way you won't waste time revising unnecessarily.

MAKE SHORT NOTES, USE COLOURS...

As you read through your work or your textbooks make brief notes of the key ideas and facts as you go along. But be sure to concentrate on understanding the ideas rather than just memorizing the facts. Use colours and highlighters to help you.

PRACTISE ANSWERING QUESTIONS

As you finish revising each topic try answering some questions. At first you may need to refer to your notes or textbooks. As you gain confidence you will be able to attempt questions unaided, just as you will in the exam.

GIVE YOURSELF A BREAK

When you are working, work for perhaps an hour then reward yourself with a short break for 15 to 20 minutes while you have a coffee or cola ... then go back for another period of revision.

Revision pathways 1

- **LIVING THINGS**
  - Characteristics A1
    - Humans: systems and processes A2, A3, A6, A7, A8, A9, A10, A11, A12, A13, A14
      - Humans: control and protection A13, A14, A15, A16, A17, A18, A19
    - Plants: structures and processes A2, A4, A5, A20, A21, A22, A23
- **VARIATION AND INHERITANCE**
  - Cells, genes and chromosomes A24, A26, A27, A28
    - Variation, selection and evolution A25, A28, A29, A30, A31

- **ELECTRICITY**
  - Static electricity C1
  - Current electricity C2, C3, C4, C5, C6, C7, C8, B14
    - Electromagnetism C9, C10, C11, C12, C13

- **ATOMS AND MOLECULES**
  - Structure of atoms and molecules B2, B3, B4, B26
    - Structure of materials B1, B5, B9, B10
    - **PERIODICITY**
      - The periodic table B25, B26
        - Groups B27, B28, B29
          - Transition elements B30

- **PLANET EARTH**
  - The Earth in space C36, C37, C38, C39
    - Structure of the Earth B22, B23, B24, C29
      - **MATERIALS FROM THE EARTH**
        - Hydrocarbons B6, B7, B8, B9
        - Metals B10, B11, B12, B13, B14
    - The atmosphere A37, A38, B20, B21
    - Earth as a habitat A32, A33, A34, A35, A36, A37, A38, B37

- **CHEMICAL REACTIONS**
  - Formulae and equations B15, B16, B17, B18
  - Types of reaction B31, B32, B35, B36, B37, B38, B39
    - Rates of reaction B33, B34, A7, B19

Revision pathways 2

FORCES, WORK AND ENERGY

- Forces and their effects C14, C15, C16, C17, C18
- Force, work and energy C19, C20
  - Motion and kinetic energy C20, C21, C22, C23
- Energy transfer and efficiency C31, C32, C13, B10

WAVES AND RADIATION

- Waves C24, C25, C26
  - Sound C24, C28
  - Electromagnetic spectrum C30
    - Light C25, C26, C27, A12
  - Nuclear radiation B2, C33, C34, C35

Construct your own pathways here:

Have you timetabled your favourite TV programme?

Revision Timetable

Subject: ....

Week beginning: ....

Week no: .... Exam in: .... weeks!

Have you remembered to take a break?

	Monday	Tuesday	Wednesday	Thursday	Friday	Saturday	Sunday	*notes*
morning								
afternoon								
evening (don't work too late!)								

Is your favourite music playing quietly in the background?

End of day check: more work needed on?

1. ....
2. ....
3. ....

Timetable check: extra topics for next week?

1. ....
2. ....
3. ....

Have you given yourself time to go to the cinema or to a disco?

Biology checklist

LIFE PROCESSES AND LIVING THINGS

Page	Topic	Revised ✔	See also ...
13	A1 – Characteristics of living things		
14	A2 – Cells: building blocks of life		C34
15	A3 – Cells, tissues, organs and organ systems		
16	A4 – Organs in plants – roots, stems, leaves and flowers		
17	A5 – Diffusion, osmosis and active transport		B1
18	A6 – Human digestive system		
19	A7 – Digestive processes		B34
20	A8 – Blood and the human circulatory system		
21	A9 – Respiration		
22	A10 – Breathing, gaseous exchange and respiration		
23	A11 – The senses		
24	A12 – The human eye		C26
25	A13 – The nervous system		
26	A14 – The endocrine system		
27	A15 – Hormones and sexual reproduction		
28	A16 – Homeostasis 1: controlling body temperature		
29	A17 – Homeostasis 2: controlling water content		
30	A18 – The body's defence systems		
31	A19 – Substance abuse		
32	A20 – Photosynthesis		
33	A21 – Water uptake and transpiration in plants		
34	A22 – Mineral requirements of plants		
35	A23 – Hormones and plant growth		
36	A24 – Chromosomes, genes and cell division		
37	A25 – Variation and mutation		C34
38	A26 – Genes and inherited characteristics		
39	A27 – X and Y chromosomes		
40	A28 – Sexual and asexual reproduction		
41	A29 – Selective breeding and genetic engineering		
42	A30 – Variation, natural selection and evolution		
43	A31 – Evolution: the evidence		B22, B23
44	A32 – Habitats, communities and populations		
45	A33 – Impact of humans on the environment		B21
46	A34 – Food chains and ecological pyramids		
47	A35 – Energy flow in ecosystems		
48	A36 – Managing food production		B37
49	A37 – The nitrogen cycle		
50	A38 – The carbon cycle		B7

A1 – Living things: their characteristics

The biosphere is made up of living and non-living things. Plants and animals are living things because they have these characteristics:

RESPIRATION: this is the process which releases energy from food. Plants and animals need energy for movement, growth and repair. Respiration usually needs oxygen:

food + oxygen → energy + water + carbon dioxide

GROWTH: plants and animals grow from a single cell until they are adults. Animals usually stop growing at this stage but trees and other plants can keep growing until they cannot get enough nutrients from their surroundings.

MOVEMENT: animals use energy to move around in search of food, water, warmth, and safety. Most plants are fixed by their roots. They move towards light, water, and nutrients by growth. This is much slower than animal **locomotion**.

NUTRITION: plants and animals need food for energy and growth. Green plants make their own food from carbon dioxide and water by photosynthesis. Animals cannot make their own food so they eat organic food made by plants.

EXCRETION: nutrition and other processes produce waste material that cannot be used. Animals get rid of waste gases from their lungs. They also excrete dissolved waste in sweat and urine.Unused solid material is removed (egested) as faeces. Plants accumulate waste products in their leaves. These are excreted when the leaves fall from the plant.

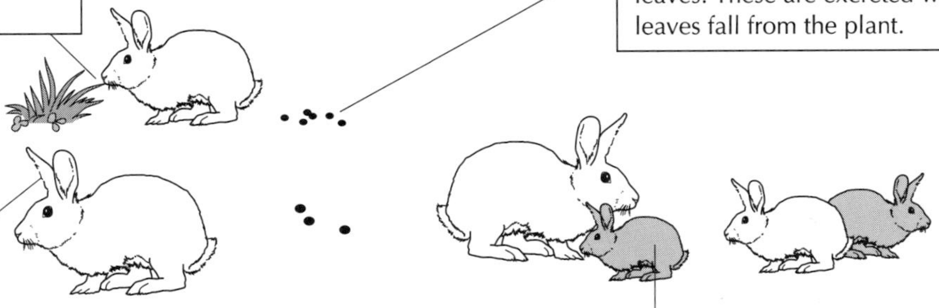

SENSITIVITY: all living things can sense and react to changes in the environment. Animals react to temperature, light, sound, smell, taste, and physical stimuli like being jabbed with a pin! Plants react by growing towards light, away from gravity. Some carnivorous plants react quickly when touched by an insect.

REPRODUCTION: all living things can make new organisms like themselves. Simple organisms such as bacteria do this by splitting in half (**asexual reproduction**). Complex plants and animals reproduce **sexually** to produce fertilized eggs or seeds.

A2 – Cells: building blocks of life

Living things are made of cells. Many of the chemical reactions which keep organisms alive (metabolic functions) take place in cells.

COMMON FEATURES OF CELLS

All cells (with a few exceptions) have these three things:

Cell membrane: a thin 'skin' which surrounds the cell contents. It controls the passage of dissolved substances into and out of the cell.

Cytoplasm: the contents of the cell (except for the nucleus). It is made up of water and dissolved substances. It also contains small structures (**organelles**) where chemical reactions take place.

Nucleus: the 'control centre' of the cell. It contains the genetic material (**DNA**) which carries the instructions that control the structure and activities of the cell. (Red blood cells do not have nuclei.)

PLANT CELL FEATURES

Cell wall: a rigid (stiff) cell wall made of cellulose. This gives support. As a result, plant cells are fairly regular in shape. Water and dissolved substances can pass through the **permeable** cell wall.

Vacuole: the large, permanent vacuole contains water and dissolved substances (**cell sap**). This helps to maintain pressure in the cells.

Chloroplasts: these contain **chlorophyll** and the **enzymes** needed for photosynthesis. They are found in the cells of green plants.

Stored food (starch): photosynthesis produces glucose (sugar). This is converted into **starch** and stored in the cytoplasm.

PLANT CELL

ANIMAL CELL

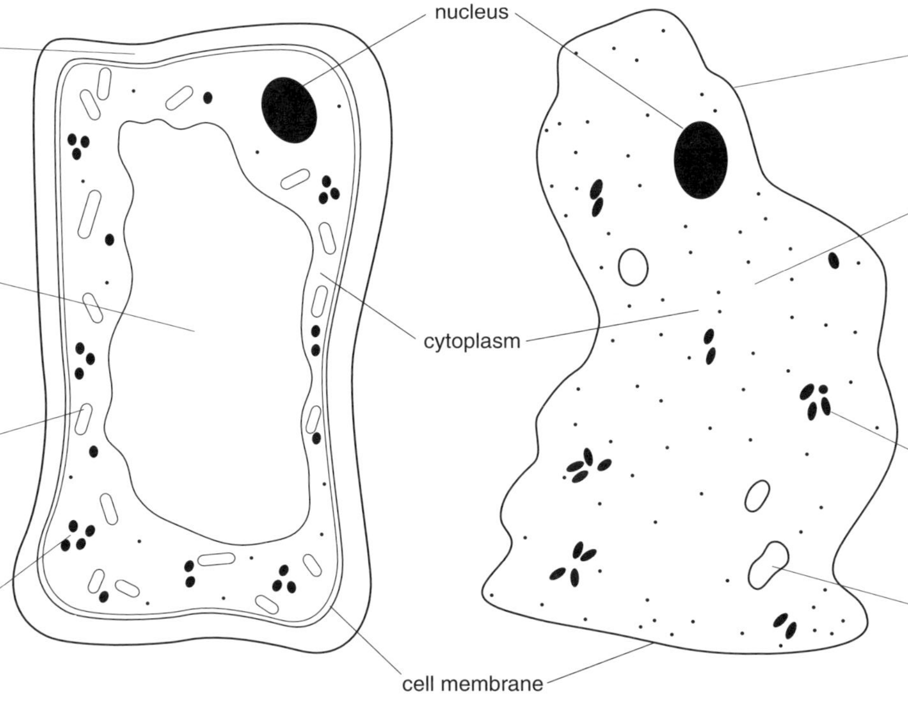

ANIMAL CELL FEATURES

Irregular shape: animal cells do not have a rigid cell wall so they are irregular in shape.

Denser cytoplasm: animal cells contain more dissolved substances and more organelles than plant cells. For example, animal cells contain more of the rod-like structures called **mitochondria** where respiration takes place. This is so they can release lots of energy quickly for fast movement.

Stored food (glycogen): carbohydrates are stored as glycogen in animal cells.

Vacuoles: animal cells may have several small, temporary vacuoles. These can be for digestion or the excretion of excess water.

A3 – Cells, tissues, organs and organ systems

Multicellular plants and animals contain many different types of cell. Each type of cell is designed for a particular function. Cells are organized to form tissues, organs, and organ systems. In a healthy **organism**, all the systems work together.

SPECIALIZED CELLS
A specialized cell is designed to do a particular job.

- Nerve cells have long fibres to carry messages.
- Muscle cells can contract and relax.
- Red blood cells carry oxygen around the body. They contain **haemoglobin** which can combine with oxygen.

TISSUES
Large numbers of specialized cells together make up **tissue**.

Muscle, blood and nerves are all tissues.

Blood tissue contains red cells for carrying oxygen, white cells for destroying harmful bacteria, and **platelets** to cause clotting in cuts.

NB Arteries and veins are usually thought of as organs as they consist of several tissue layers.

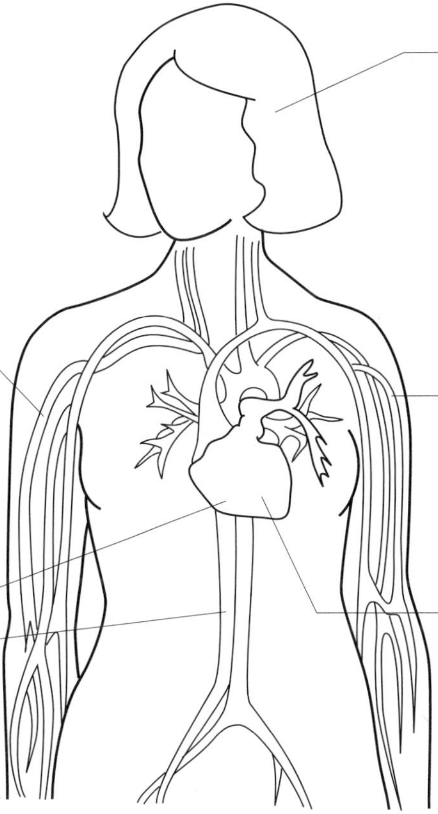

ORGANS
Various tissues together make up an **organ**. Each organ has its own specific job. The heart, the stomach and the brain are all organs.

The **heart** has to pump blood around the body. It is made up of **muscle tissue**, **blood vessels** and **nerves**.

ORGAN SYSTEMS
Various organs together make up an **organ system**. For example, the **circulatory system** carries blood to all parts of the body. It is made up of the heart, the arteries, the veins, the capillaries and, of course, the blood.

ORGANISM
Various organ systems together make up an **organism**.

You are a human organism. You have:

- a respiratory system
- a digestive system
- a circulatory system
- a nervous system
- an endocrine system

A4 – Organs in plants – roots, stems, leaves and flowers

The organs in plants contain specialized cells organized to carry out particular functions.

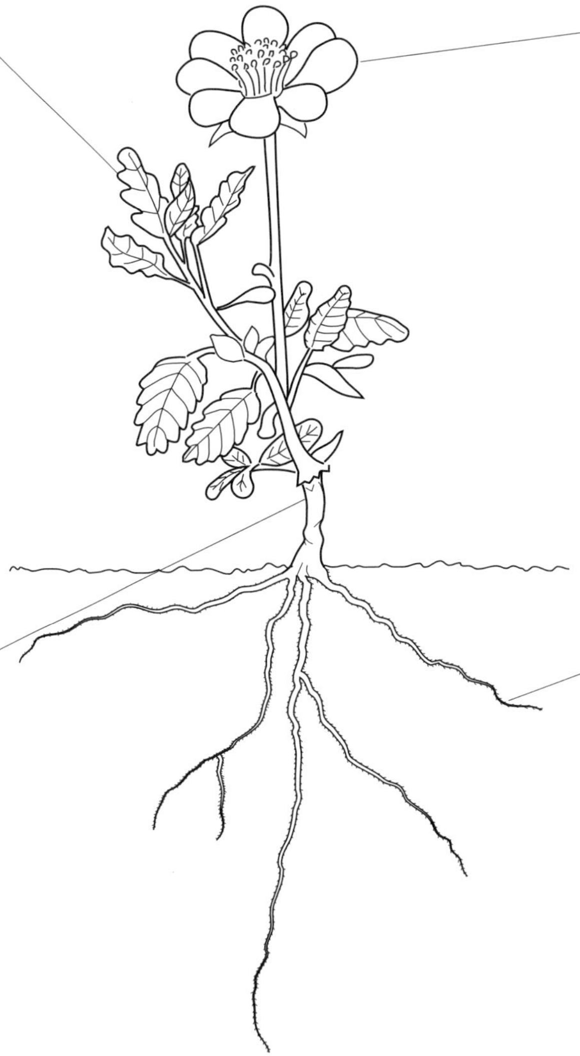

LEAF FUNCTIONS:
- to make food by photosynthesis
- to store food as starch
- to control the rate of water loss from the plant

Specialized cells include:
- **palisade cells for photosythesis**. These are long, cylinder-shaped cells, packed closely together. They have many **chloroplasts** which contain chlorophyll for photosynthesis.
- **guard cells**. These are 'sausage-shaped' cells which surround the stomata (pores) in the leaf surface. When full of water, the guard cells open the pore: when there is little water, the guard cells shrink and close the pore.

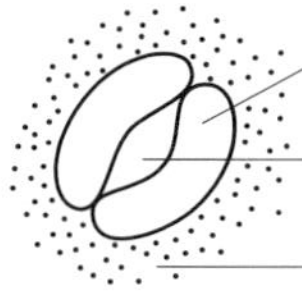

FLOWER FUNCTION:
- to produce seeds by sexual reproduction

Specialized parts include:
- male sexual organs (**stamens**)
- female sexual organ (**carpel**)

The stamen's anther produces **pollen** which contains the male sex cells.

In the carpel, the ovary produces the **ovule** which contains the female sex cell.

When fertilized, the ovule turns into a seed.

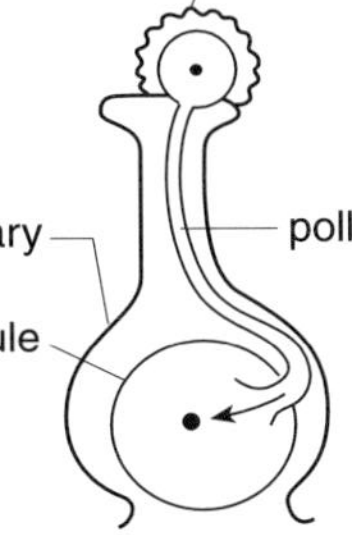

STEM FUNCTIONS:
- to support the plant
- to transport water, nutrients and dissolved minerals around the plant

Specialized structures include:
- phloem to carry amino acids and sugars up and down the stem
- xylem to carry water and mineral salts up the stem
- xylem vessels have strong, thick walls for support in woody plants

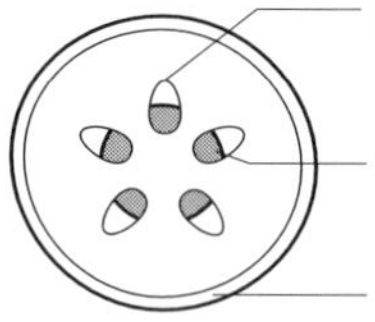

ROOT FUNCTIONS:
- to support the plant by anchoring it in the soil
- to take in nutrients and water from the soil
- to store food as starch in the winter (some plants only)

Specialized parts include:
- long, thin root hairs for taking in water and dissolved mineral salts
- xylem vessels to take water and minerals up the plant
- phloem vessels to take nutrients to the growing tips of the roots

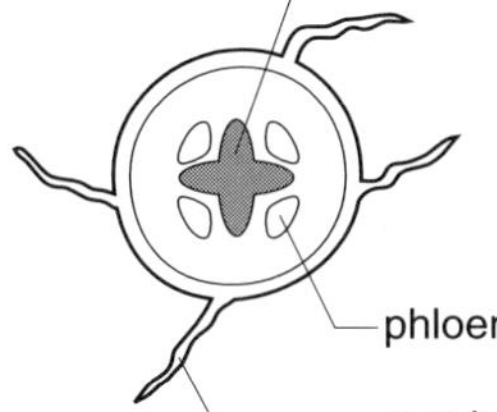

A5 – Diffusion, osmosis, and active transport

These are the three main mechanisms that living things use to move substances in and out of cells.

DIFFUSION: the movement of particles from a region of high concentration to one of low concentration.

Diffusion takes place because all the particles in gases and liquids are constantly moving. Small, light particles diffuse more quickly than large heavy ones. Diffusion is faster at high temperatures.

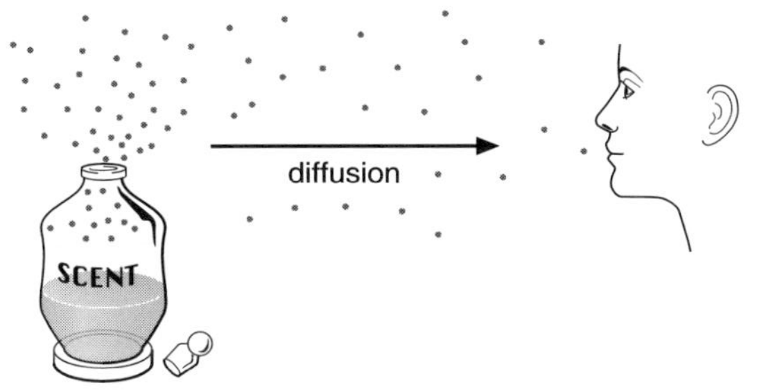

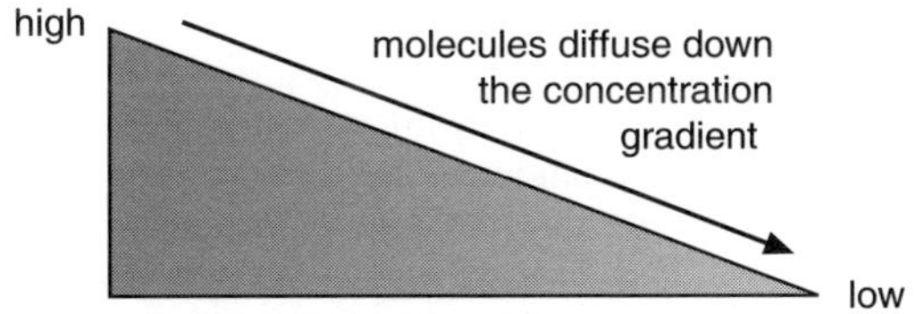

In the air sacs of the lungs, oxygen molecules diffuse into the blood where the concentration of oxygen is low. Carbon dioxide molecules diffuse from the blood into the lungs. Carbon dioxide is then exhaled.

OSMOSIS: the diffusion of water across a selectively permeable membrane (s.p.m.).

Osmosis takes place because the water molecules can easily pass through the s.p.m.. Large molecules (e.g. glucose) try to diffuse the other way but they are not able to pass through the cell membrane.

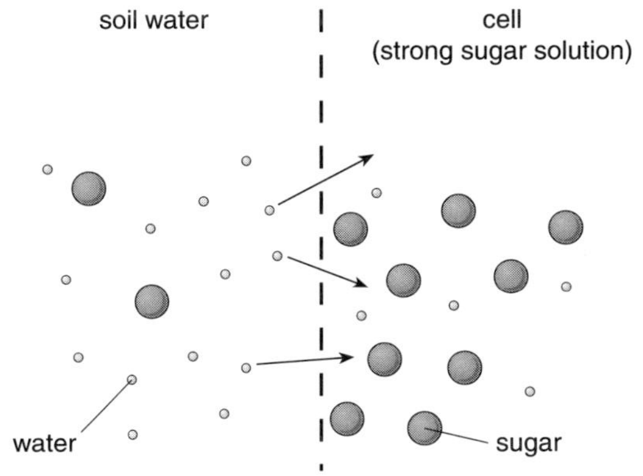

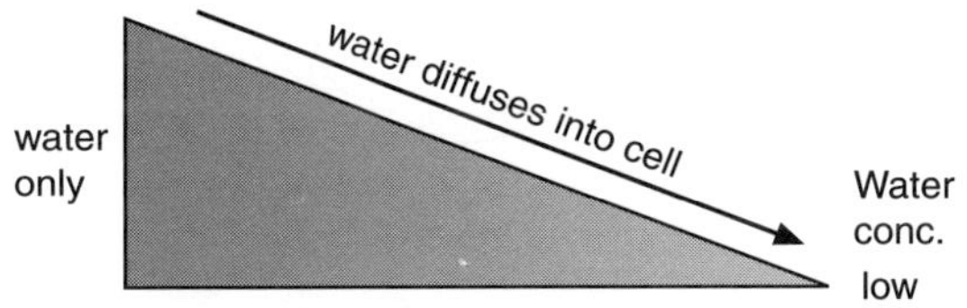

Water from the soil moves into the root hair cells of a plant by osmosis. Sugar molecules in the plant cells cannot diffuse out because the cell membrane is permeable to water but not to sugar molecules.

ACTIVE TRANSPORT: the movement of molecules from a region of low concentration, across a selectively permeable membrane, to a region of high concentration.

Because this is against the concentration gradient, some extra energy is needed. This comes from respiration.

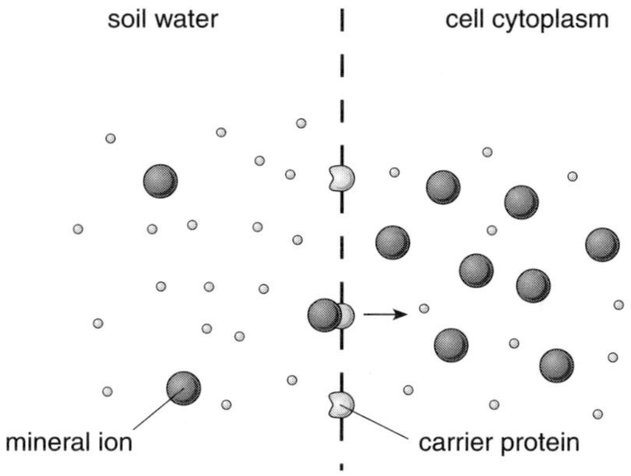

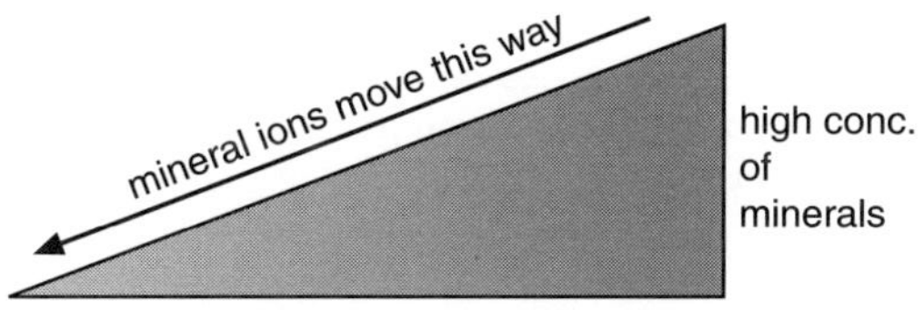

To get mineral ions into the root cells, the plant has to move them across the cell membrane. The mineral ion binds to a special carrier protein in the membrane which changes shape and then carries the molecule into the cell. This needs energy.

A6 – Human digestive system

Digestion is the breaking down of large food molecules into small ones so that they can be absorbed into the bloodstream.

THE DIGESTIVE SYSTEM

Food is digested in the **alimentary canal**. This is a long tube which starts at the mouth, runs through the stomach and intestines and finishes at the anus.

Food is broken down with the help of digestive juices which contain special chemicals called **enzymes**.

The digestive system is the alimentary canal plus all the organs which secrete digestive juices into it.

DEALING WITH FOOD

There are four stages in the way we deal with food:

1 **Ingestion** – getting food into the body ('eating')

2 **Digestion** – breaking complex food molecules down into smaller molecules

3 **Absorption** – absorbing small molecules from the alimentary canal into the bloodstream so they can be transported around the body

4 **Egestion** – getting rid of food which could not be digested (e.g. dietary fibre) by passing it as faeces

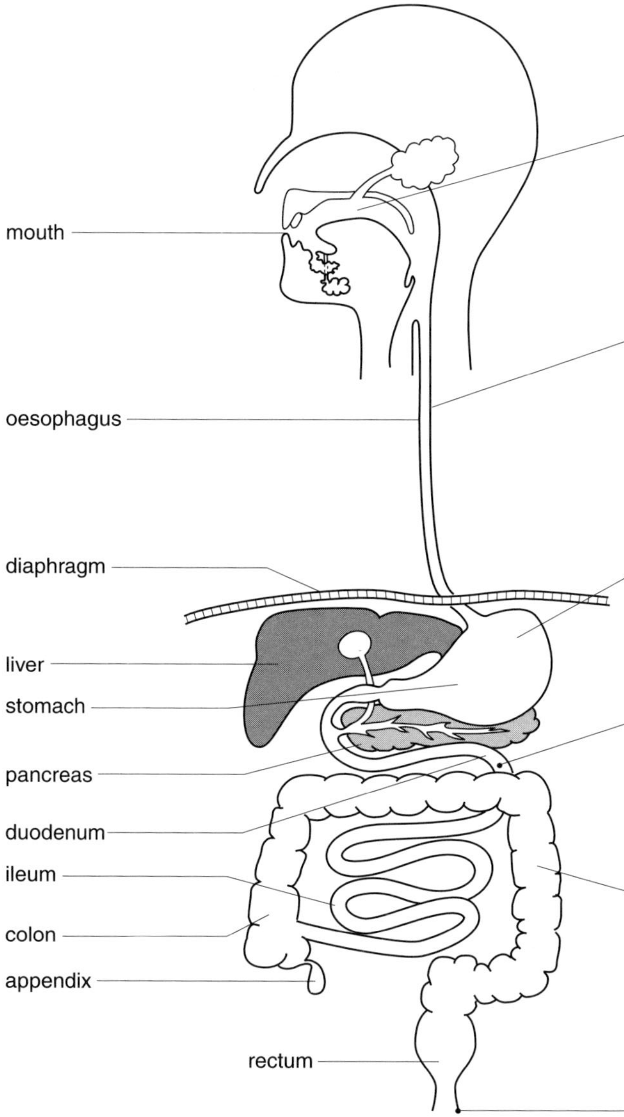

Mouth – Digestion starts here! The teeth cut and grind the food, which is mixed with saliva. The enzyme salivary amylase breaks starch down into maltose (sugar).

Oesophagus – lumps of moist, chewed-up food are carried to the stomach by muscle movements. This is called **peristalsis**.

Stomach - the stomach is like a sack. Here the enzyme **pepsin** breaks big proteins down into small proteins (**polypeptides**). This can take several hours.

Small intestine – this is made up of the **duodenum** and the **ileum**. Here more digestive juices are added. Starches, fats, proteins, and complex sugars are broken down into simpler molecules.

Fully digested food is absorbed into the bloodstream.

Large intestine – this is made up of the **colon** and the **rectum**. Only undigested food reaches here. Water absorbed.

Anus – undigested solid food is passed out as **faeces**.

A7 – Digestive processes

Large food molecules are broken down in our digestive system mostly by chemical reactions. The products are **absorbed** into the body.

ENZYMES AT WORK

Enzymes are **catalysts**. They speed up the reactions which break down large food molecules, e.g. carbohydrates, proteins and fats.

Enzyme molecules have special shapes. Reactions occur more easily when a food molecule 'locks on' to the **active site of the enzyme**.

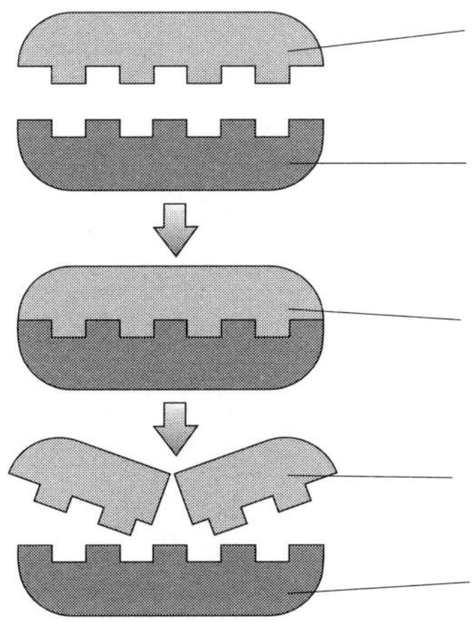

The enzymes in our bodies work best at about 37°C. Some, like those found in the stomach, work best in acid conditions (pH2). Those found in the duodenum need an alkaline environment (pH8).

Enzyme (where found)	**Action**
pepsin (stomach)	proteins → polypeptides (small proteins)
amylase (duodenum)	carbohydrates → maltose (sugar)
lipase (small intestine)	fats and oils → fatty acids and glycerol

ABSORPTION IN THE SMALL INTESTINE

The wall of the small intestine has millions of tiny finger-shaped structures called **villi**. These give a huge surface area for absorbing digested food easily.

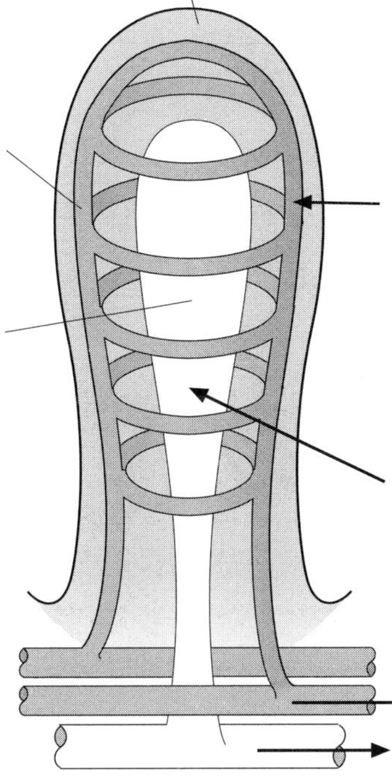

DIGESTED FOOD AND THE LIVER

The liver is the largest organ in the human body. It is like a 'chemical factory'. It processes digested food and other substances in the blood. Its main functions are:

- storing vitamins, minerals and glycogen
- producing special chemicals, e.g. bile for digestion
- processing unwanted substances from the blood, e.g. alcohol is removed from the blood by the liver
- generating heat to keep the body's internal temperature at 37°C

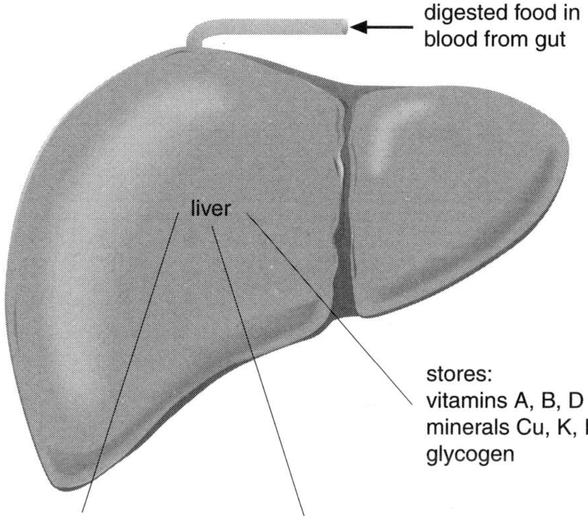

A8 – Blood and the human circulatory system

Blood tissue transports vital substances around the body.
It also plays an essential part in protecting the body from damage and disease.

BLOOD TISSUE

Spinning blood in a centrifuge separates the plasma from the cells.

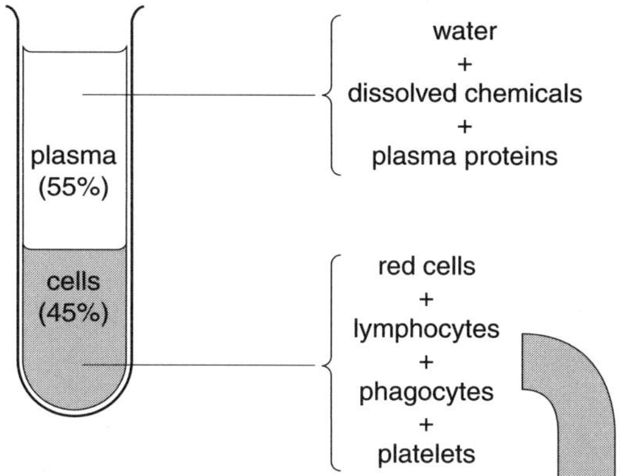

THE FUNCTIONS OF BLOOD CELLS

Red blood cells carry oxygen by combining it with **haemoglobin**.

Lymphocytes fight disease by producing **anti-bodies** which destroy dangerous microbes or mark them for attack by phagocytes.

Phagocytes fight disease by **engulfing** dangerous microbes.

Platelets are cell fragments. They help **clotting**, preventing blood loss and infection.

THE HEART

Blood is pumped around the body by a muscular pump called the **heart**.

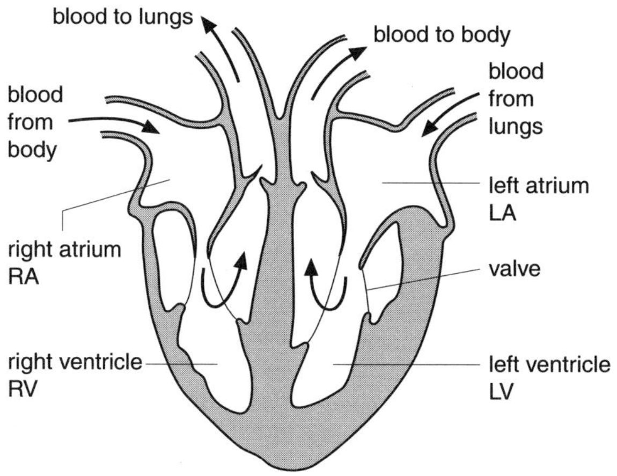

- Blood in the RV is pumped to the lungs where it is oxygenated.
- Blood from the lungs flows back into the LA and then into the LV.
- Blood in the LV is pumped through the body (except for the lungs).
- Blood returns to the heart where it enters the RA.

Blood passes through the heart twice for each trip around the body. We call this **double circulation**.

Valves in the heart prevent blood from being pushed up into the atria when the heart 'beats'.

THE HUMAN CIRCULATORY SYSTEM

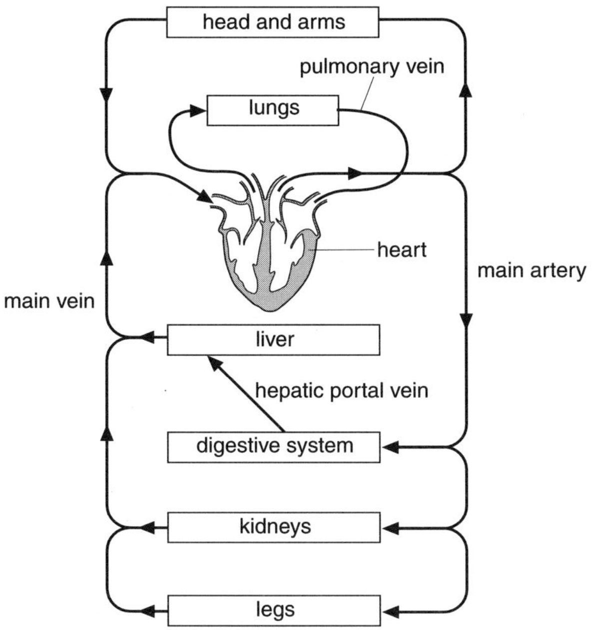

- **Arteries** carry blood **away** from the heart. Blood in arteries has more oxygen than blood in veins – except for the pulmonary artery and veins which go to and from the lungs!
- **Arteries** have thick walls to withstand higher blood pressure.
- **Veins** have thinner walls but have valves to stop blood flowing 'backwards'.
- **Veins** carry blood back to the heart.
- **Capillaries** reach all tissues and organs.

A9 – Respiration

Respiration is the process whereby food is broken down to release energy. **All** living things respire. They need energy for:

- mechanical work (movement of muscles, movement, etc.)
- growth and repair (by cell division)
- chemical work (active transport and chemical building in plants and animals)
- production of heat needed for **metabolic** (life) processes

AEROBIC RESPIRATION

In most organisms, respiration uses **oxygen**. This is called **aerobic respiration**.

The chemical reactions are complex but we can summarize aerobic respiration in this equation:

ANAEROBIC RESPIRATION

In some organisms, e.g. yeast, respiration takes place without oxygen. This is **anaerobic respiration**.

Notice that **energy** is released.

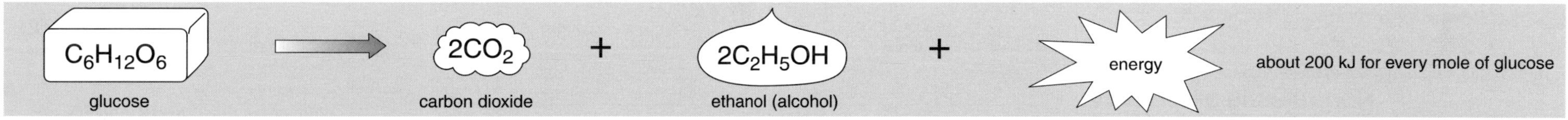

In anaerobic respiration, one of the products is **alcohol**. We call this process **fermentation**. It is used for making alcoholic drinks (brewing), and for making alcohol as a fuel. Fermentation is also used in baking bread – the carbon dioxide makes the dough 'rise'.

ENERGY STORAGE

Some of the energy from respiration can be stored by making a molecule called **ATP** (**adenosine triphosphate**).

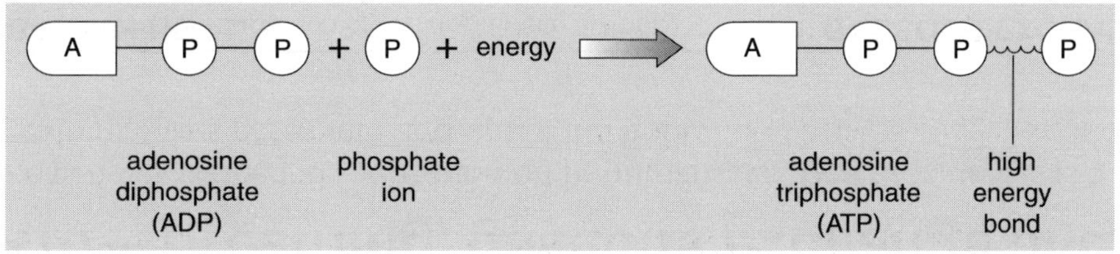

RELEASING ENERGY

When cells need to release energy quickly ATP is broken down.

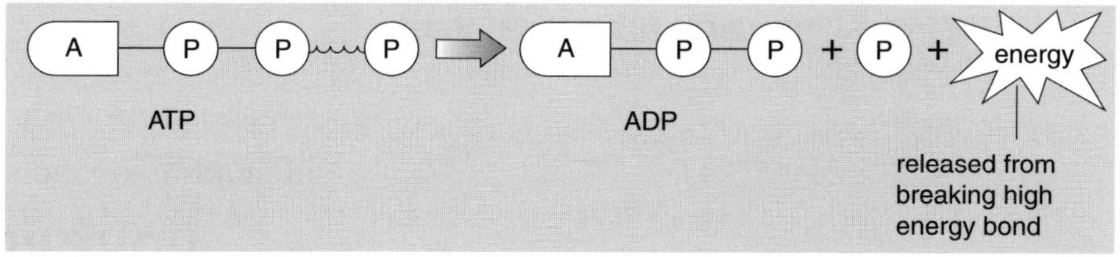

A10 – Breathing, gaseous exchange and respiration

Oxygen gas is needed for respiration in humans. Carbon dioxide gas is a waste product of respiration. Breathing takes gases into and out of the body.

BREATHING: the action of drawing air into the body (inhaling) and pushing air and waste gases out (exhaling).

Breathing in:
- muscles between the ribs contract, causing the chest to expand
- diaphragm flattens, increasing the volume of the chest and reducing gas pressure in the lungs
- air enters the lungs
- inhaled air has about **21% oxygen** and 0.03% carbon dioxide

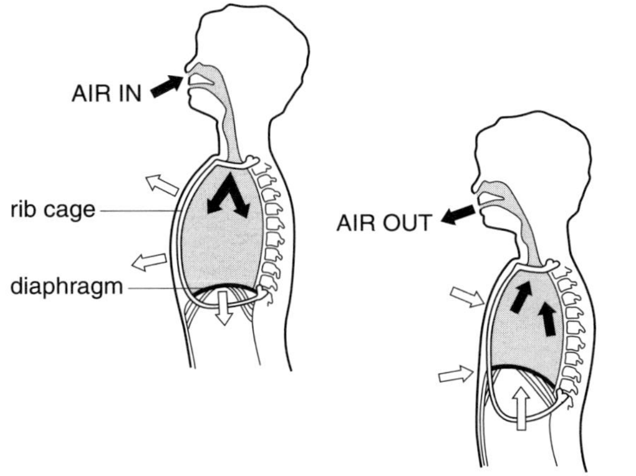

Breathing out:
- muscles between the ribs relax
- diaphragm raised up, decreasing the volume of the chest cavity and increasing gas pressure in the lungs
- air 'pushed' out of the lungs
- exhaled air has about **4% carbon dioxide**, 17% oxygen, and is saturated with water vapour

GASEOUS EXCHANGE: the movement of oxygen from inhaled air into the blood and the movement of carbon dioxide from the blood into the airways of the lungs.

The airways of the lungs get smaller and smaller as they divide. The **bronchioles** end in thousands of tiny air sacs called **alveoli**. These have thin, moist walls so that gases can pass in and out easily.

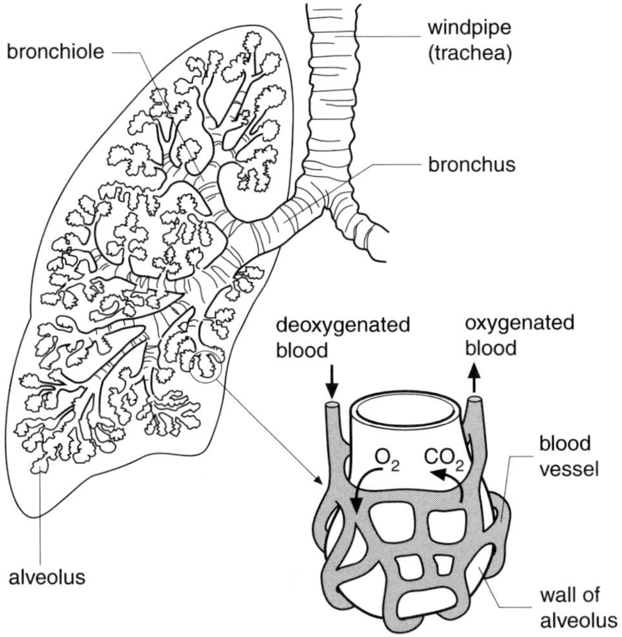

Each **alveolus** is covered by thin capillaries. Oxygen diffuses into the blood where it is taken up by red blood cells. Carbon dioxide diffuses from the blood into the alveolus, ready to be exhaled.

RESPIRATION IN HUMANS: We usually respire aerobically, using oxygen to release energy from our food.

AEROBIC RESPIRATION

glucose + oxygen → carbon dioxide + water + energy

ANAEROBIC RESPIRATION

When the cells have no oxygen available they can respire **anaerobically**.

glucose → lactic acid + energy

In plants, the waste product of anaerobic respiration is alcohol. In animals it is **lactic acid**.

After exercise oxygen is needed for recovery!

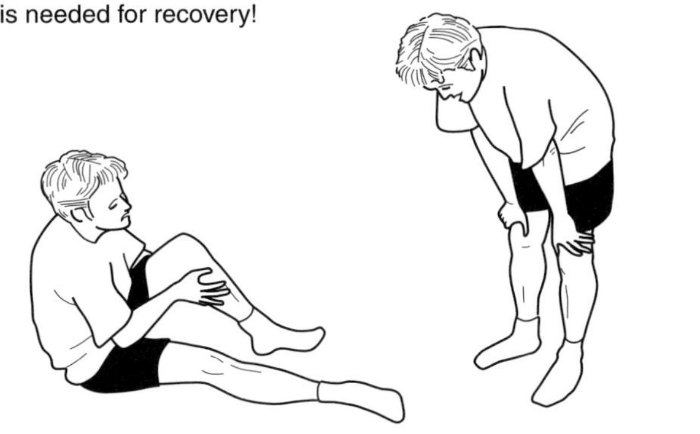

During sport or strenuous activity, muscle cells can run out of oxygen. They then start to respire anaerobically. The lactic acid produced builds up in the muscles and can cause painful 'cramps' until you have taken in enough oxygen to break down the lactic acid and repay the **oxygen debt**.

A11 – The senses

Our sense organs contain receptors which respond to chemical or physical stimuli. Receptors send messages to the central nervous system so we can respond. The five senses are: touch, smell, hearing, taste and sight (see A12–The eye).

TOUCH: The skin contains receptors which are sensitive to pressure and temperature. Some give the sensation of pain.

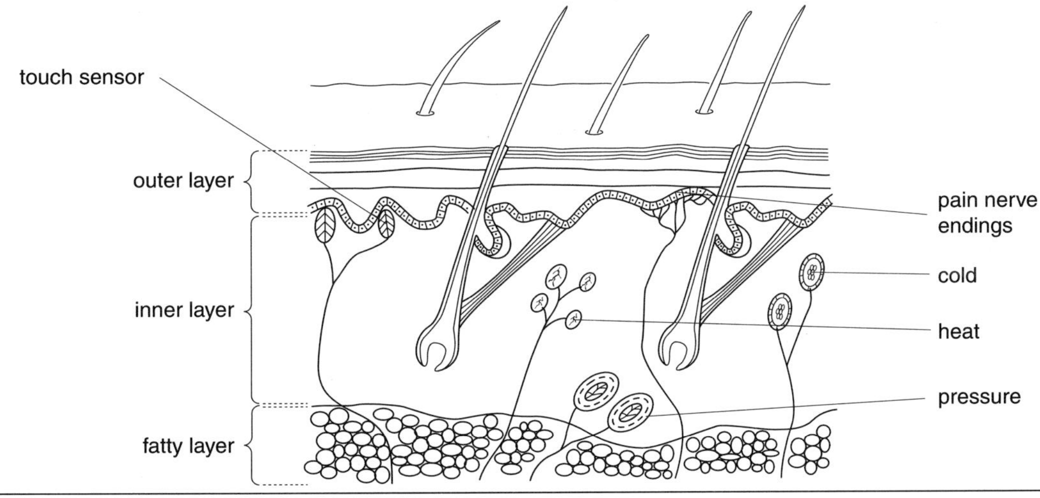

SMELL: The nasal cavity contains smell receptors which are sensitive to dissolved chemicals.

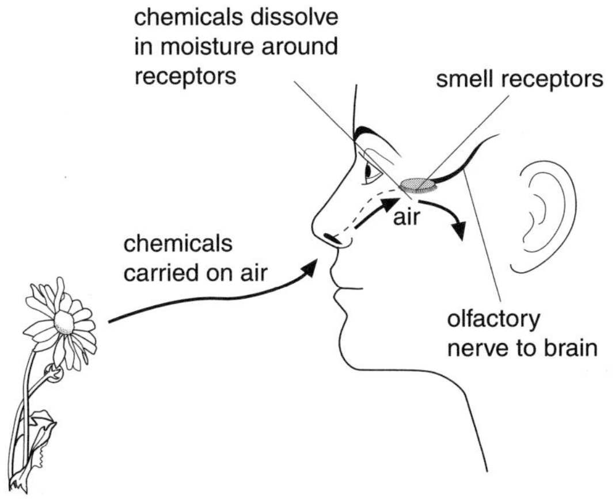

HEARING:

- The ear responds to **pressure waves** (sound waves) in the air.
- The wave makes the **ear drum** vibrate. Vibrations are passed on through tiny bones to the **oval window**.
- The oval window vibrates, sending vibrations through a liquid in a coiled tube called the **cochlea**.
- Receptors in the cochlea send messages to the brain.

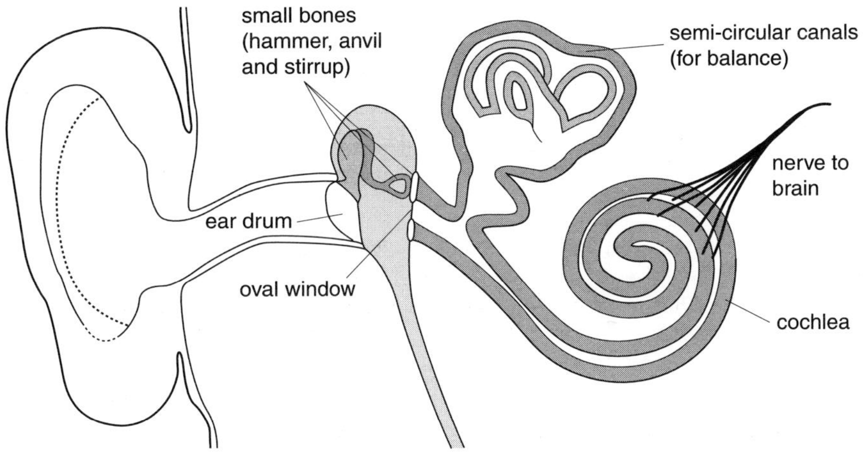

TASTE: The tongue has **taste buds** which are sensitive to dissolved chemicals. Different parts of the tongue detect different tastes. There are four tastes.

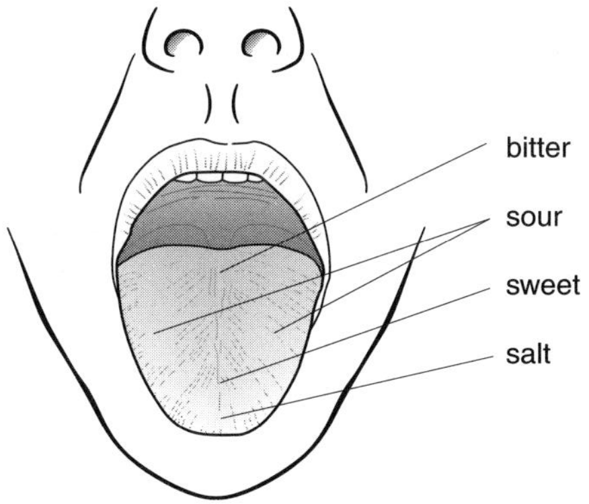

A12 – The human eye

The eye is a sense organ. The specialized cells of the retina are sensitive to the intensity (brightness) and frequency (colour) of light.

PARTS OF THE EYE

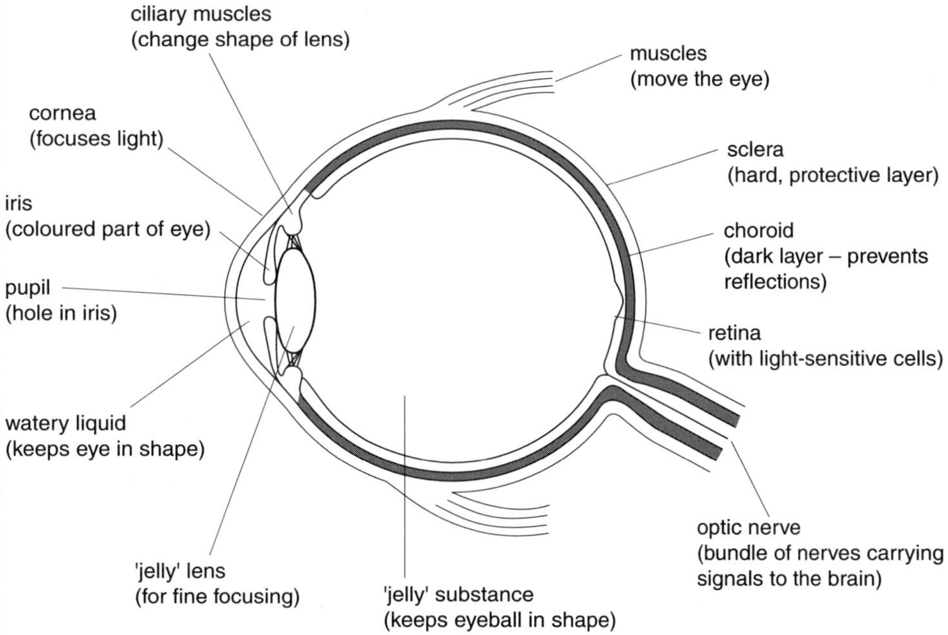

ADAPTING FOR BRIGHTNESS

Bright light

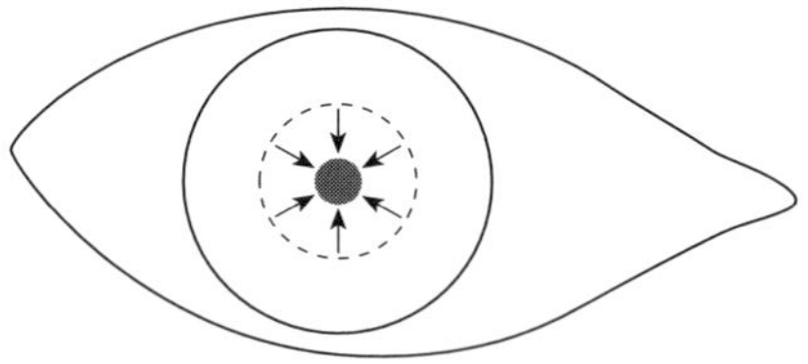

- circular muscles in iris contract
- pupil is made smaller
- less light enters the eye
- the retina is protected

Dim light

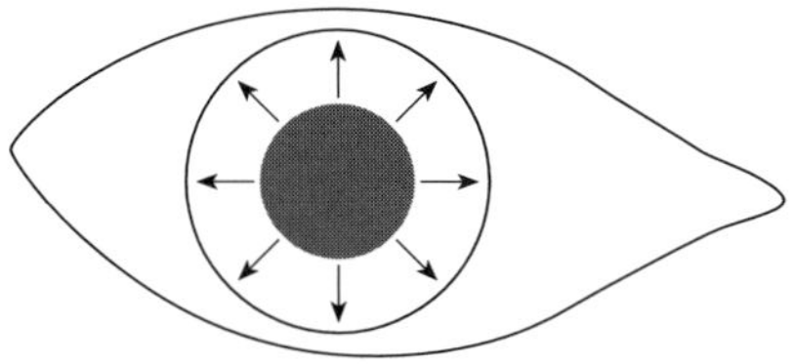

- radial muscles in iris contract
- pupil is made larger
- more light enters the eye
- vision is possible even in dim light

FORMING AN IMAGE

- The cornea refracts (bends) light from the object.
- The lens refracts the light a bit more to focus it.
- A small, upside-down (inverted) image forms on the retina.

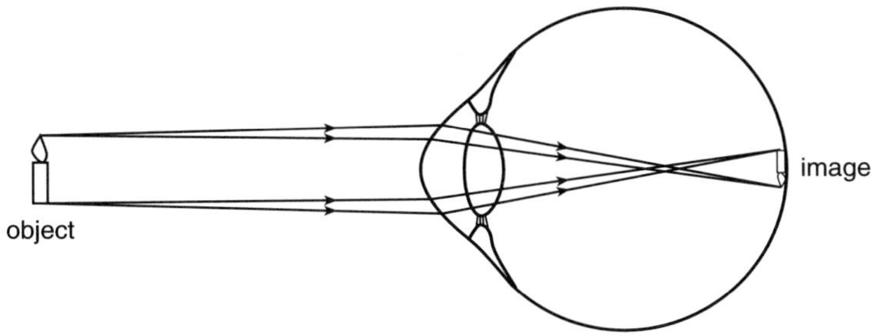

Rods: specialized cells in the retina – very sensitive to light. Form black and white images even in dim light.

Cones: specialized cells in the retina – sensitive to red, blue and green light. Form detailed coloured images in bright light.

ACCOMMODATION: the eye can focus on far away objects and those nearby.

Close object

- ciliary muscles contract
- ligaments relax
- lens becomes 'fat'
- light refracted a lot
- light is focused on the retina

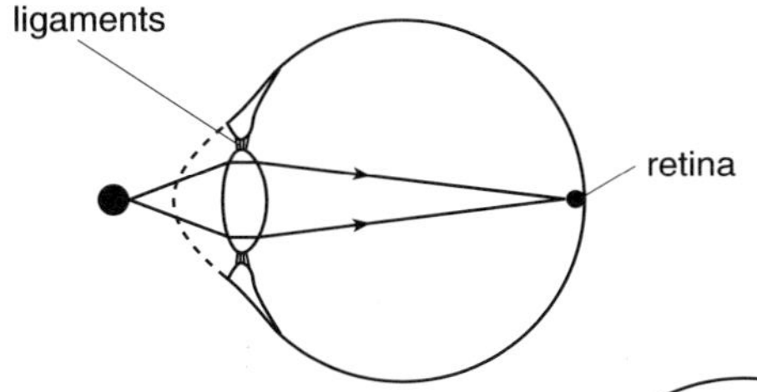

Distant object

- ciliary muscles relax
- ligaments get tight
- lens pulled into thin shape
- light refracted less
- light is focused on the retina

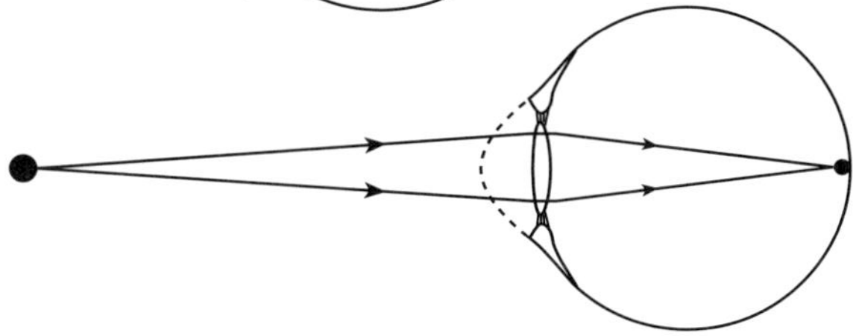

A13 – The nervous system

The nervous system, together with the hormone system, co-ordinates all the functions of the body.

The **central nervous system** is made up of the brain and the spinal cord. Thousands of nerves connected to the central nervous system carry electrical impulses to and from all parts of the body.

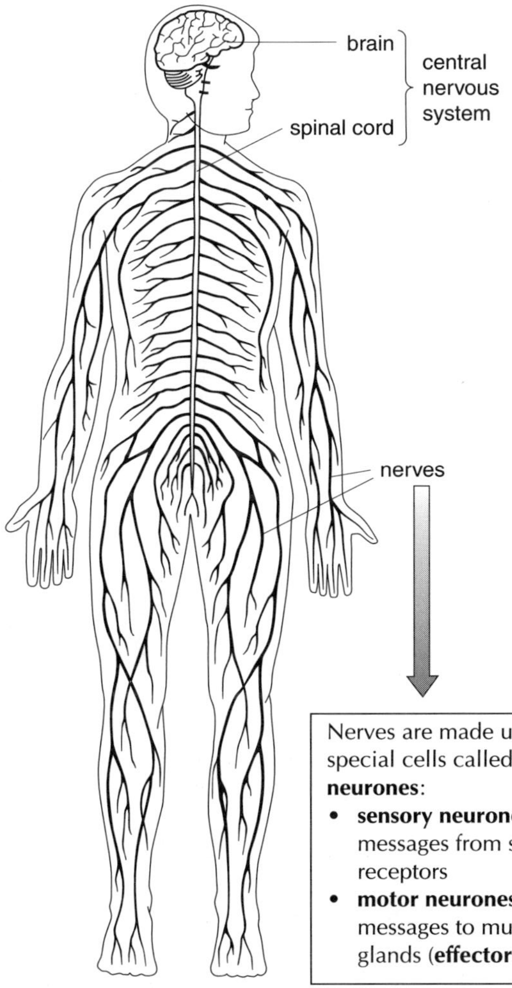

Nerves are made up of special cells called **neurones**:

- **sensory neurones:** carry messages from sense receptors
- **motor neurones** carry messages to muscles and glands (**effectors**)

Nerve cells are adapted to carry messages as electrical impulses.

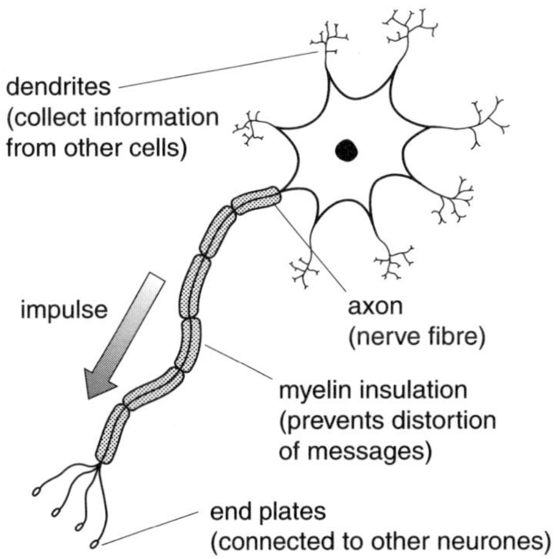

Synapses link neurones.

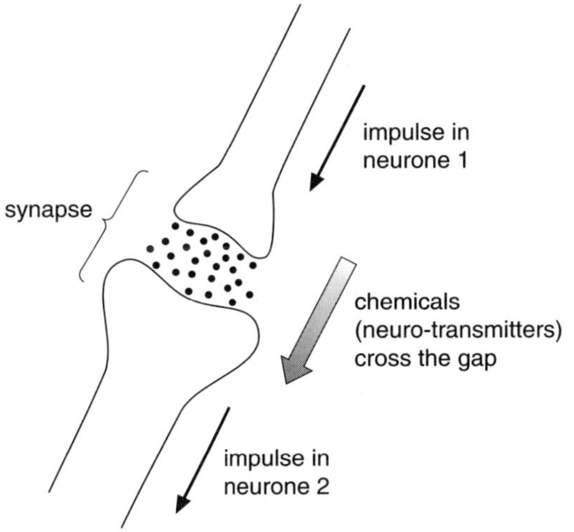

REFLEX ACTIONS

A reflex action is a rapid, automatic response to a stimulus which is potentially harmful. For example, you automatically pull your hand away from a very hot object because otherwise your skin would be damaged. The pathway for messages in a reflex action is called a **reflex arc**.

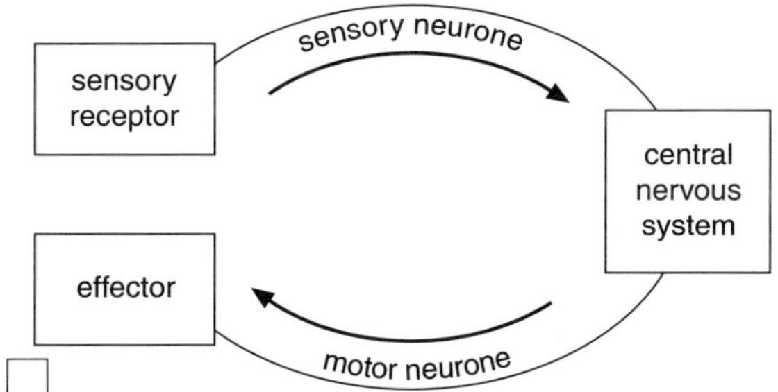

Example: The pupil's response to a bright light is an example of a reflex action.

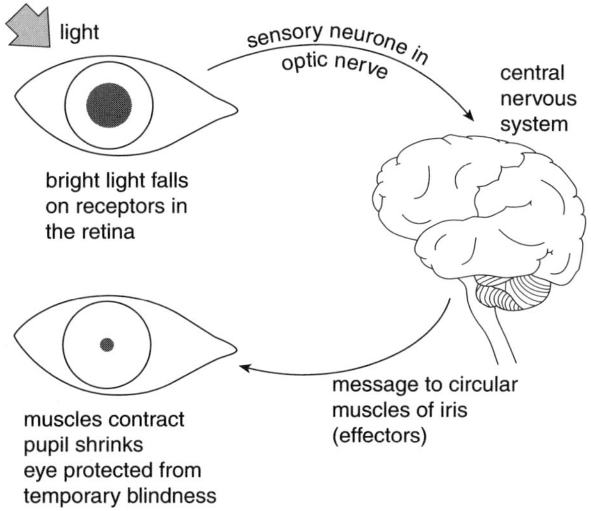

A14 – The endocrine system

The endocrine system uses chemical 'messengers' called **hormones** to co-ordinate the response of organs to stimuli and changes in the environment.

The **endocrine system** is made up of **glands** which can release special chemicals called hormones into the blood stream. Detectors on body organs, e.g. the heart, detect changes in the level of hormones in the blood. When the hormone level changes, the organ responds.

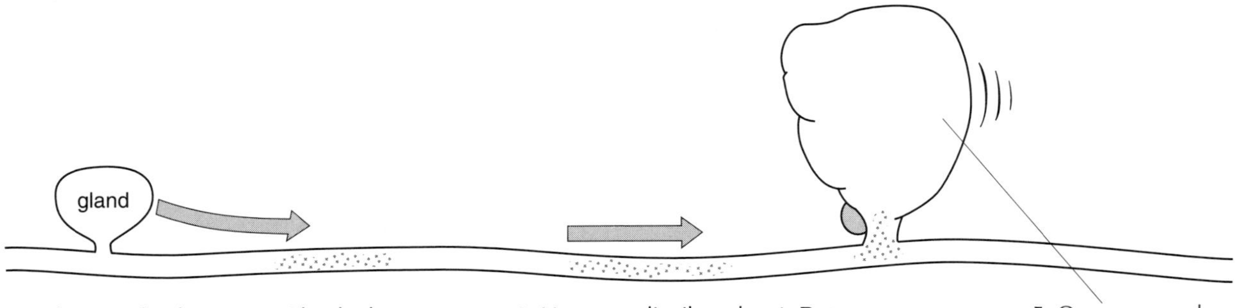

1 Endocrine gland responds to change in environment

2 Gland releases hormone

3 Hormone distributed throughout the body

4 Detector on organ senses change in hormone level

5 Organ responds e.g. heart beats faster

GLANDS, HORMONES AND THEIR FUNCTIONS

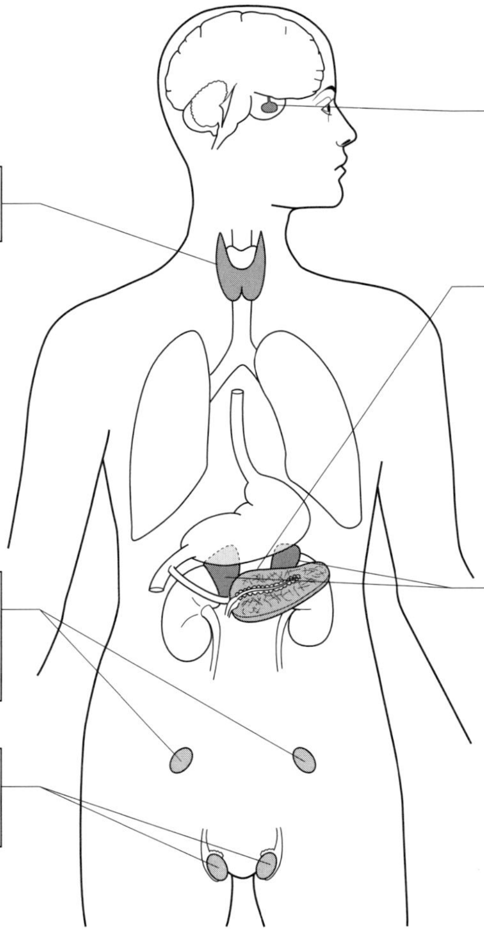

Pituitary: called the '**master gland**' because it produces several important hormones and controls the activity of other glands.

Thyroid: produces thyroxine which controls growth.

Pancreas: produces insulin which controls the level of sugar in the blood.

Diabetes is a disease where the body cannot control the blood sugar level properly. Diabetes sufferers have to control their diet carefully. Some have to inject themselves with insulin.

Adrenal glands: produce adrenalin where there is danger. This prepares the body for fighting or running away (**fight** or **flight** response).

Ovaries: in females the ovaries produce **oestrogen** and **progesterone**. These cause changes at puberty and control the menstrual cycle.

Testes: in males, the testes produce **testosterone** which causes changes at pubery.

Comparing the nervous system with the endocrine system

	What detects change? (receptor)	**What is the 'messenger'?**	**How is the message carried?**	**What responds? (effector)**
Nervous system	sensory receptors	electrical impulse	nerves – very fast	a muscle or a cell
Endocrine system	gland (via brain and bloodstream)	chemical (hormone)	bloodstream – slower	one or more organs

A15 – Hormones and sexual reproduction

Hormones control the development of the reproductive system at puberty.

MALE REPRODUCTIVE SYSTEM

At puberty, hormones from the pituitary gland start the development of the sex organs. **Testosterone**, produced by the testes, keeps the development going.

- penis grows
- testes grow
- sperm produced
- testosterone released

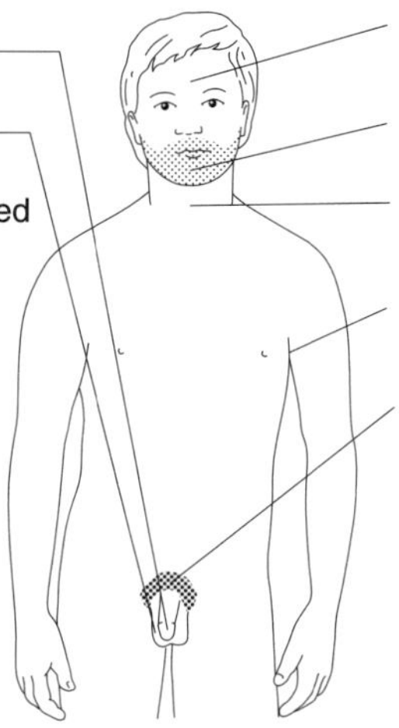

Secondary sexual characteristics are controlled by **testosterone**.

FEMALE REPRODUCTIVE SYSTEM

At puberty, hormones from the pituitary gland control the development of the sex organs.

- ovaries grow
- eggs develop
- female hormones released
- menstrual cycle starts

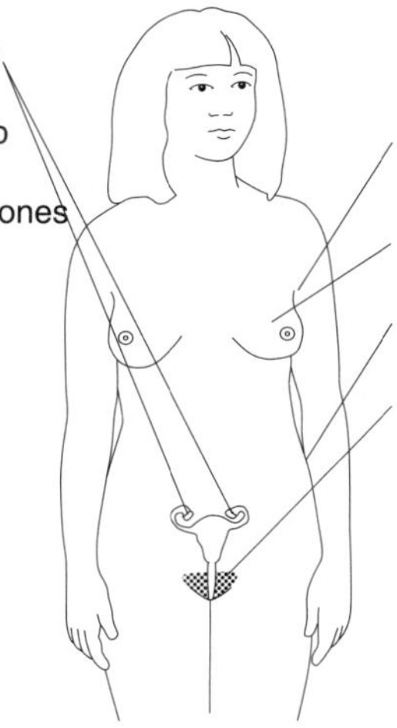

Secondary sexual characteristics are controlled by **oestrogen** produced by the ovaries.

HORMONES CONTROL THE MENSTRUAL CYCLE

During the menstrual cycle, hormones from the pituitary gland co-ordinate the preparation of the uterus for pregnancy and stimulate the release of a mature egg (ovum) at the right time for fertilization.

Progesterone keeps the uterus lining intact **if** the woman is pregnant.

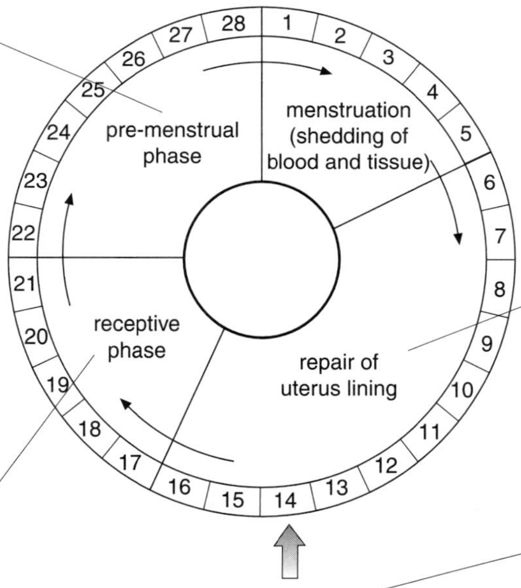

Oestrogen repairs the lining of the uterus. Oestrogen production is stimulated by **follicle stimulating hormone** (**FSH**) from the pituitary gland.

Progesterone keeps the lining of the uterus ready for implantation of a fertilized ovum and pregnancy.

ovum released

Luteinizing hormone (**LH**) stimulates an ovary to release a mature ovum.

ARTIFICIAL CONTROL

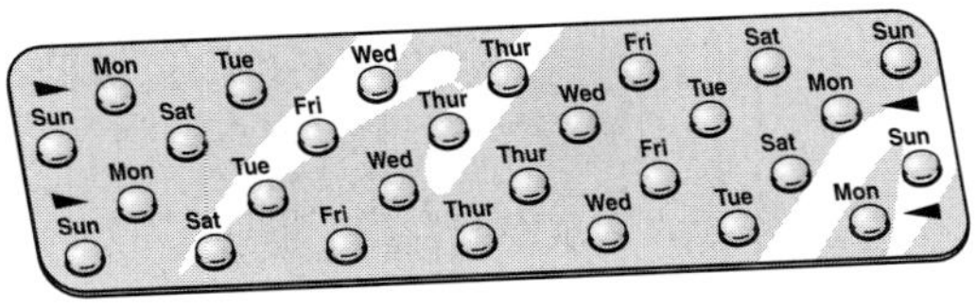

The oral contraceptive pill contains progesterone and/or oestrogen. These tell the pituitary gland not to release luteinizing hormone (LH) and so the ovary does not release an ovum. Ovulation stops.

A16 – Homeostasis 1: controlling body temperature

Homeostasis is the process whereby the body adjusts to changes to keep essential internal conditions steady.

Many of the body's systems work best under specific chemical and physical conditions. To keep things in a steady state, the body uses a system of **detectors** and **actuators**. The detectors detect changes inside the body. The actuators then bring about changes in the opposite direction in order to restore equillibrium. Keeping the body's internal temperature at 37°C is a good example of **homeostasis**.

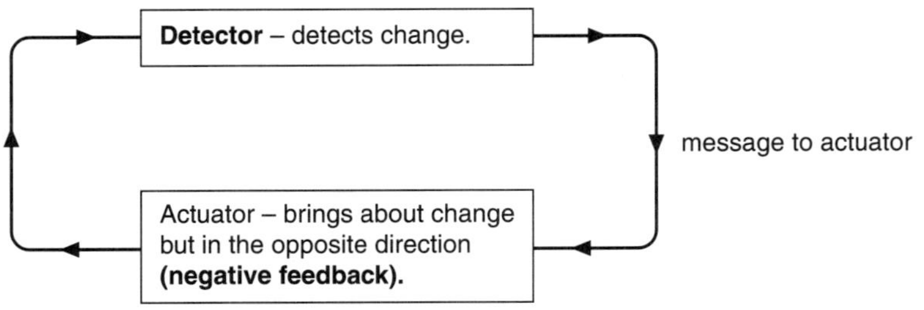

BODY TOO HOT ...

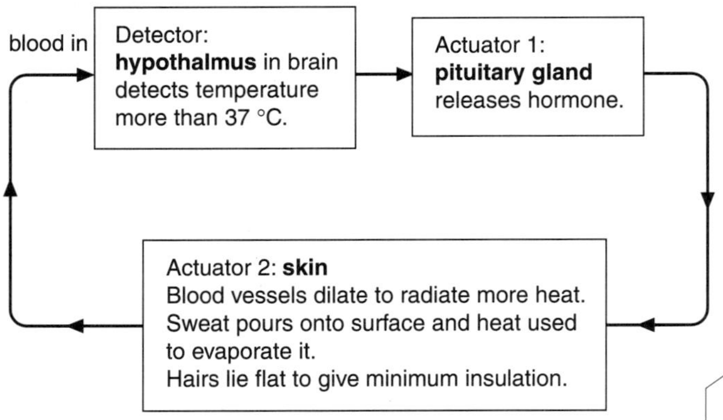

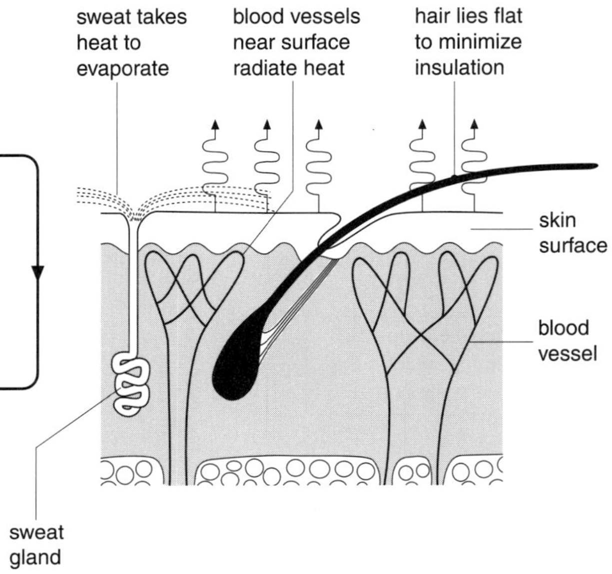

BODY TOO COLD ...

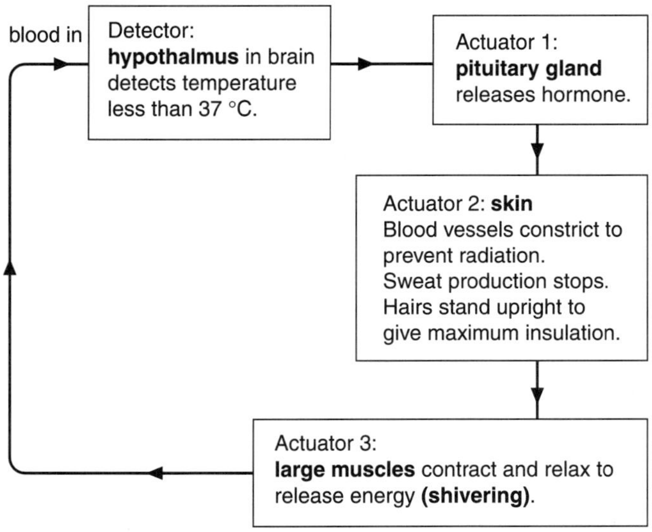

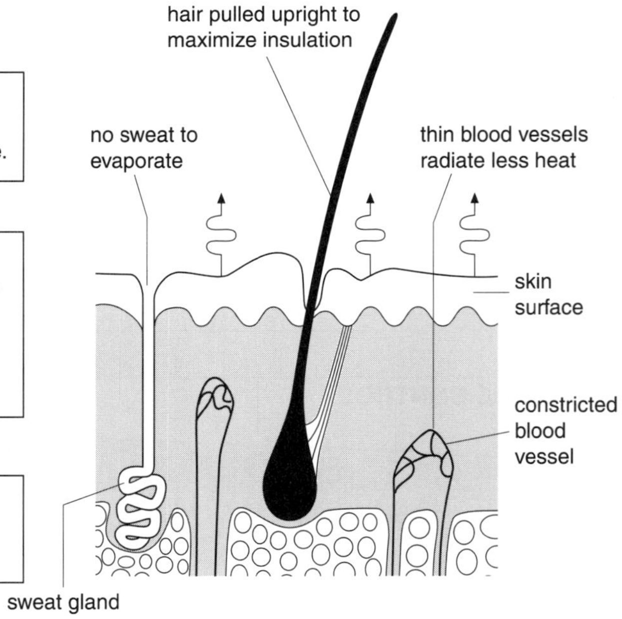

A17 – Homeostasis 2: controlling water content

The control of the body's water content is another example of homeostasis.

The level of water in the blood is detected by the **hypothalmus**. If there is not enough water, the hypothalmus tells the pituitary gland to produce the hormone **ADH** (**anti-diuretic hormone**). This tells the kidneys to allow more water to be absorbed back into the blood.

As the water level in the blood rises, the pituitary gland is told to release less ADH. The kidneys do not re-absorb so much water and so more water passes to the bladder.

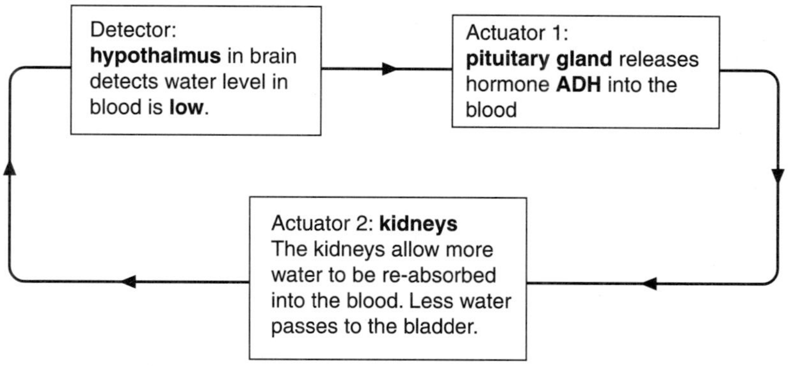

WATER CONTROL IN THE KIDNEYS

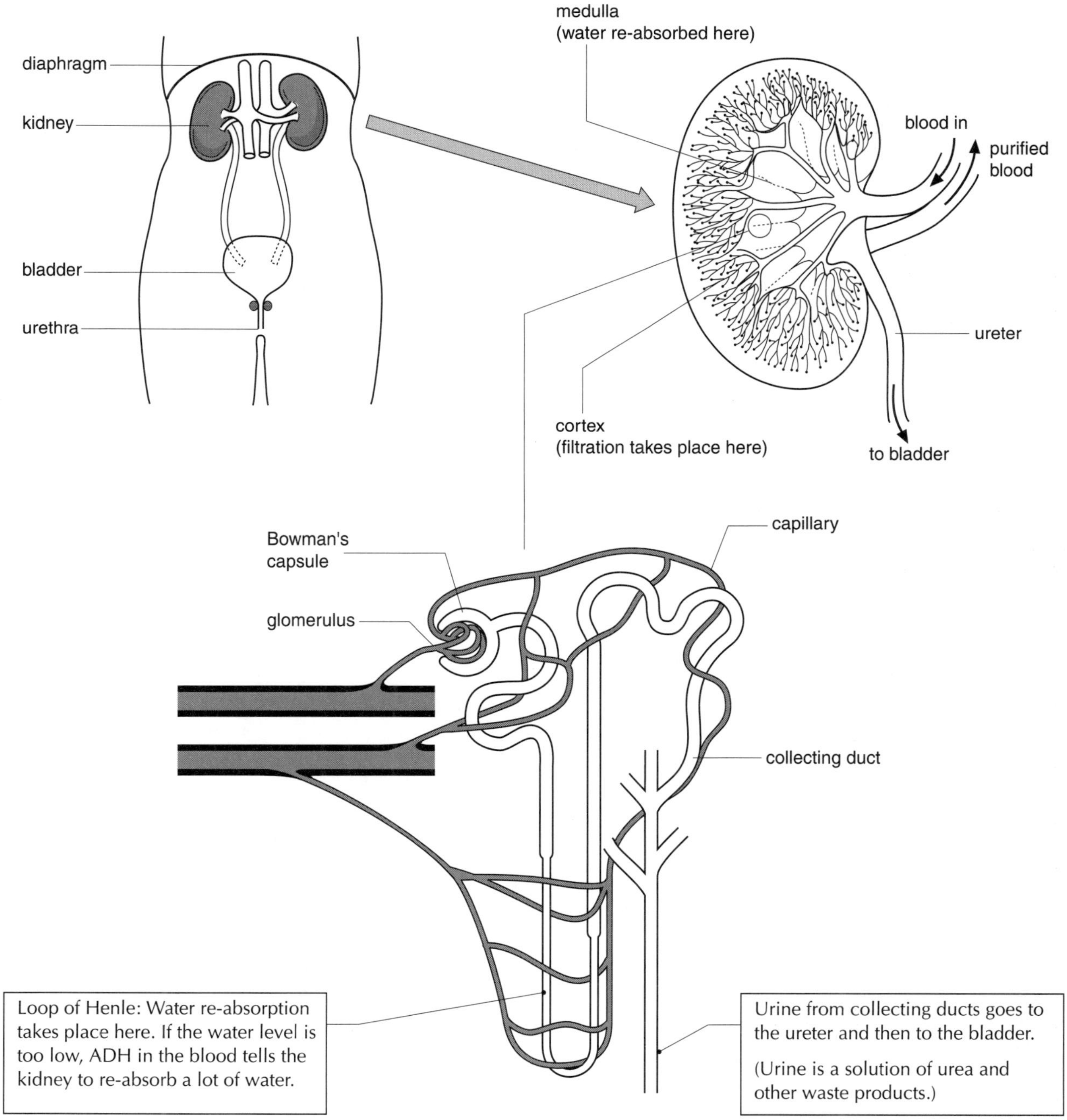

A18 – The body's defence systems

The skin and the blood are very important in preventing infections and disease.

Micro-organisms that infect the body or cause disease are called **pathogens**. Some pathogens just compete for nutrition with body cells. Other pathogens attack and destroy healthy cells.

Some pathogens produce **toxins** (poisons).

Most diseases are caused by **viruses**, **bacteria**, or **fungi**.

Pathogen type	Examples of diseases
virus 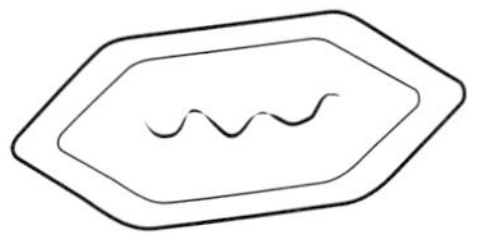	influenza (flu), colds measles mumps AIDS
bacterium 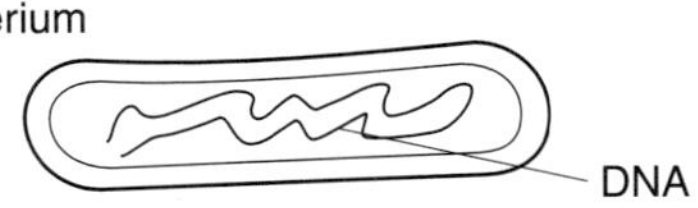	pneumonia gonorrhea syphilis
fungus 	athlete's foot ringworm thrush

SKIN AND BLOOD: PROTECTING THE BODY

The **skin** forms a barrier against water and pathogens.

An oily substance called **sebum** makes the skin waterproof and also slows the growth of microbes.

If the skin is cut, **clotting** prevents blood loss and further infection.

Blood platelets and blood proteins (e.g. fibrinogen) produce **fibres** which trap red blood cells. This blocks the cut.

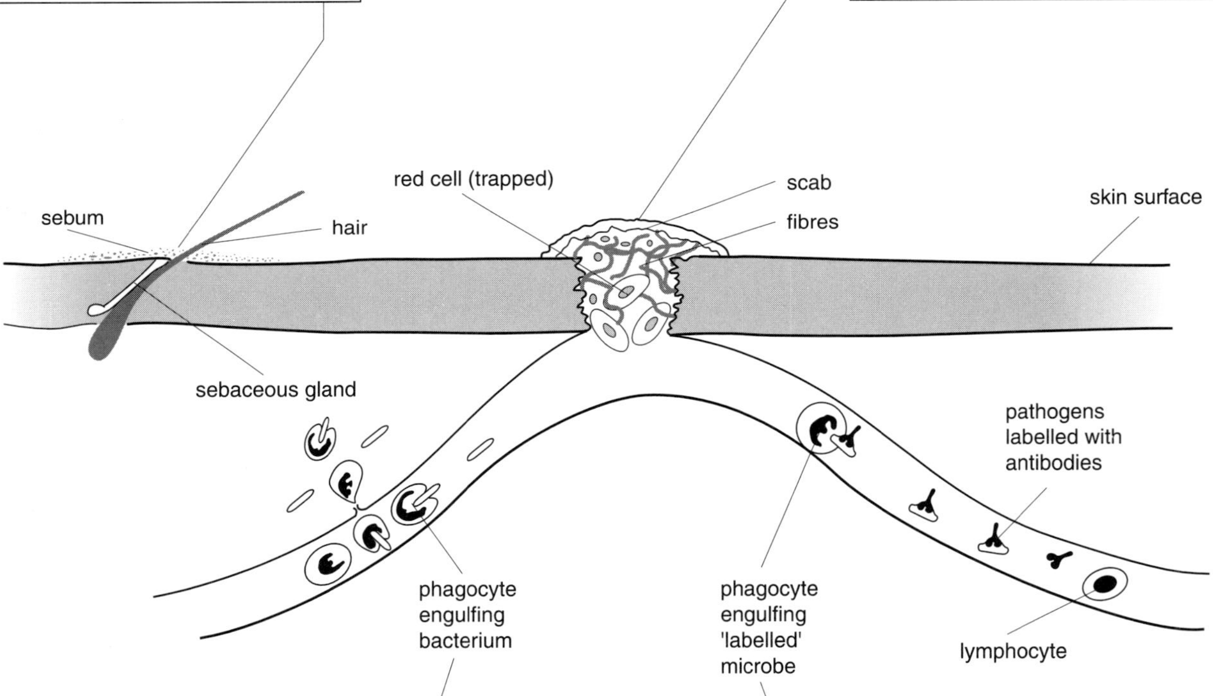

White blood cells called **phagocytes** engulf harmful microbes and digest them.

Phagocytes can squeeze through capillary walls to digest pathogens in tissues.

White blood cells called **lymphocytes** produce **antibodies**. These stick to pathogens, labelling them as dangerous. Phagocytes then engulf the pathogens.

Each type of 'germ' needs a different antibody.

A19 – Substance abuse

Substances taken into the body can have harmful effects.

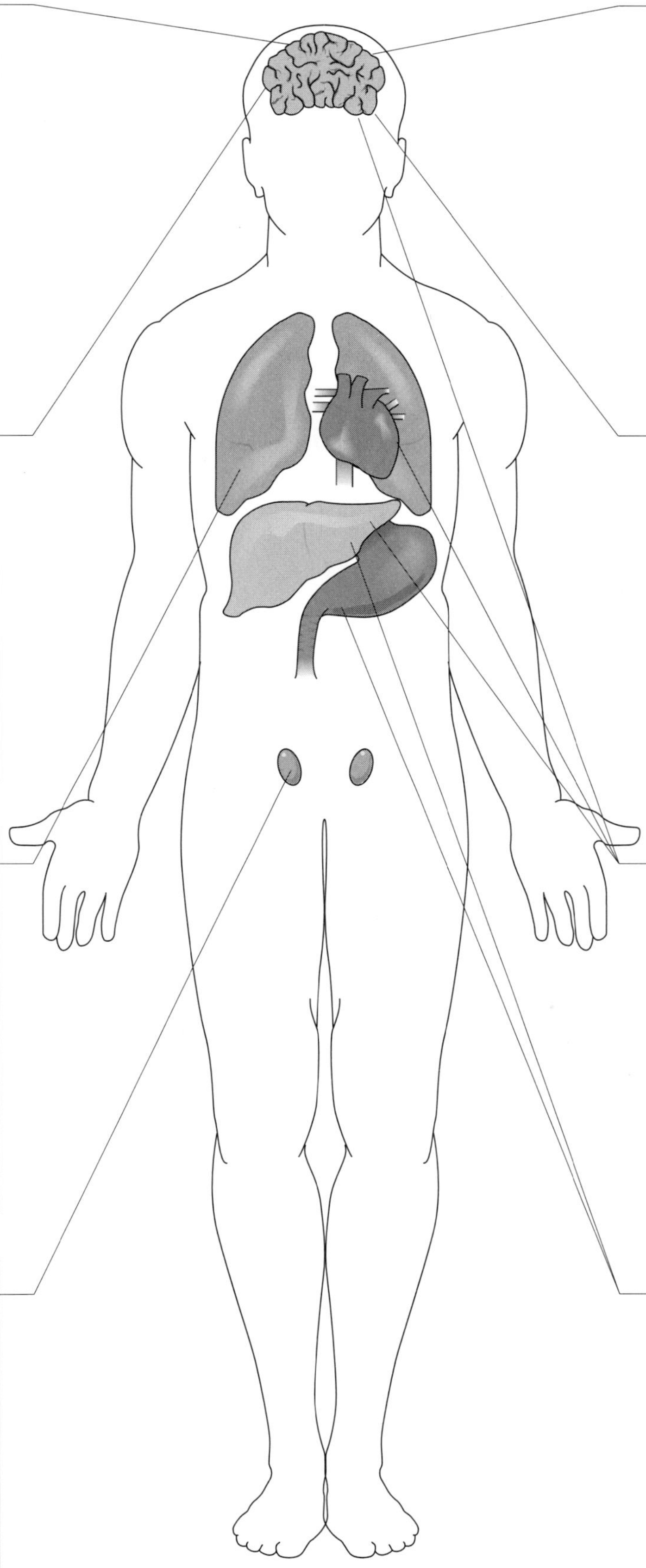

STIMULANTS

Amphetamines ('uppers') and cocaine are addictive.

Users experience depression and exhaustion when the effects wear off.

DEPRESSANTS

Barbiturates ('downers') and heroin cause lethargy, loss of self-control, mental and physical deterioration.

There is a serious danger of overdose, leading to coma and death.

TOBACCO

Nicotine is addictive.
Tar from cigarette smoke contains chemicals which cause cancer. It damages the cilia in the lungs, leading to infection and breathing difficulties including **bronchitis** and **emphysema**.

STEROID HORMONES

Hormones for increasing athletic performance and muscle development can inhibit natural production of sex hormones. This leads to sterility, disruption of the menstrual cycle, and loss of sexual desire.

HALLUCINOGENS

Cannabis and LSD ('acid') cause confusion, lack of co-ordination and distortion of perception of space and time.

There is a serious danger of accidents and, especially with LSD, overdose.

SOLVENTS

Fumes from glues and lighter fluid cause damage to brain cells, leading to mental confusion and memory loss.

Excessive intake or vomiting can lead to suffocation.

ALCOHOL

Alcohol is a depressant. It affects judgement and self-control. This can cause accidents, especially when driving.

Excessive alcohol intake can cause **hepatitis** (liver inflammation) or **cirrhosis** (permanent liver scarring).

It can lead to higher blood pressure and make **coronary heart disease** more likely.

PAIN KILLERS

Aspirin and paracetamol are useful drugs but when taken in excess they are dangerous.

Paracetamol can lead to liver failure and death.

Aspirin can cause bleeding of the stomach.

A20 – Photosynthesis

Green plants make their food from non-living materials: carbon dioxide from the air and water from the soil.

EQUATION FOR PHOTOSYNTHESIS

Photosynthesis is a series of complicated reactions controlled by enzymes. We can represent it by this summary equation:

$$6CO_2 + 6H_2O \xrightarrow[\text{chlorophyll}]{\text{sunlight}} C_6H_{12}O_6 + 6O_2$$

carbon dioxide + water → glucose + oxygen

TESTING FOR PHOTOSYNTHESIS

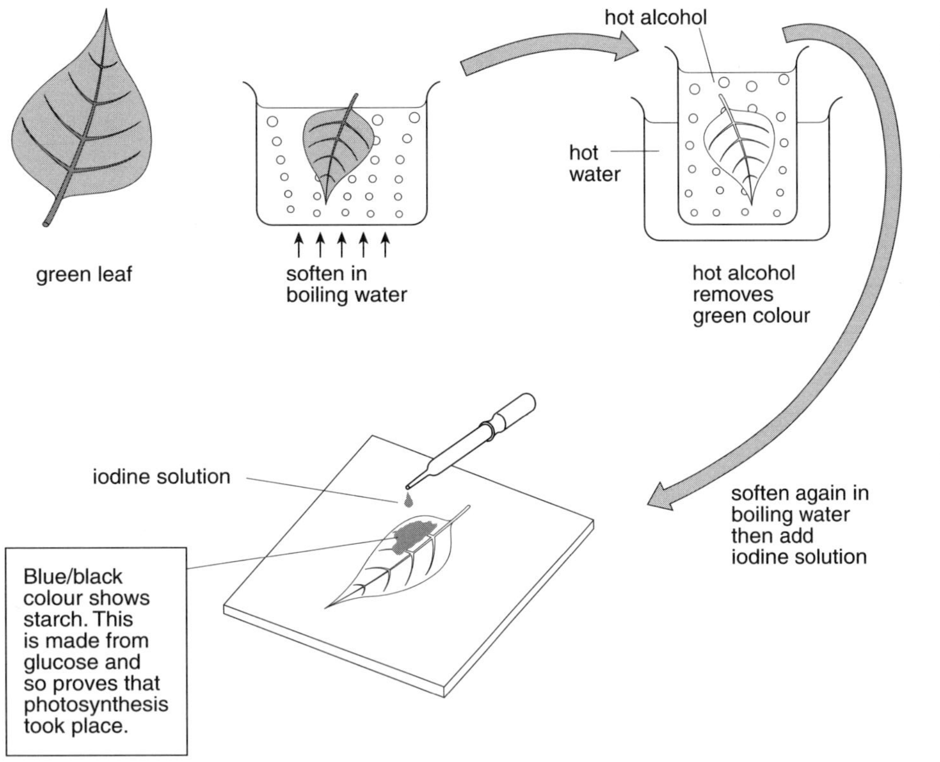

LEAVES ARE SPECIALLY ADAPTED FOR PHOTOSYNTHESIS

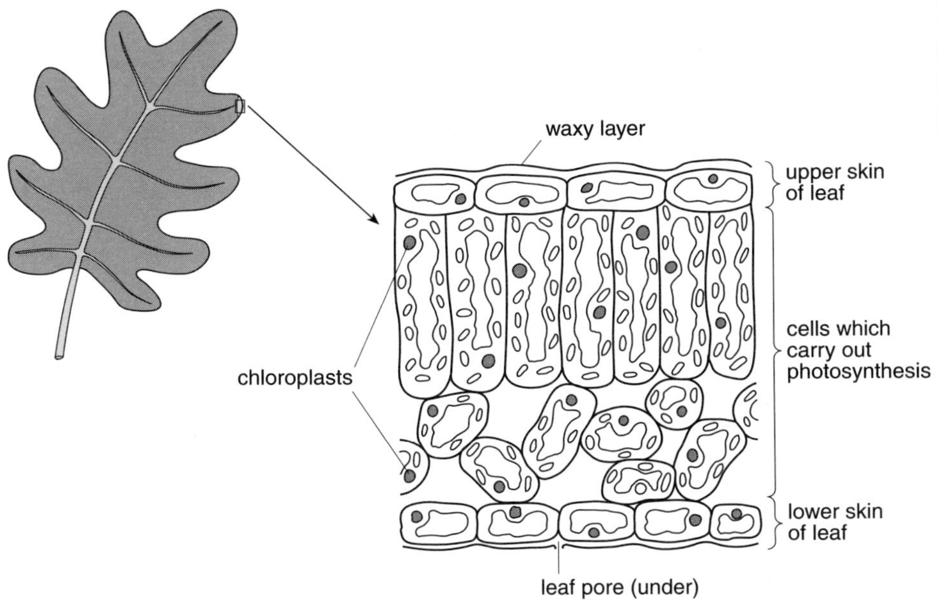

- Most leaves are flat. This gives maximum area for collecting sunlight.
- The cells which do most of the photosynthesis are shaped like cylinders. These are packed closely together just under the leaf's surface to give maximum photosynthesis.
- The cells in the upper layers have many chloroplasts. These contain the chlorophyll essential for photosynthesis.

FACTORS AFFECTING THE RATE OF PHOTOSYNTHESIS

1. **Light** – more light increases the rate of photosynthesis but only up to a limit.
2. **Carbon dioxide concentration** – greater concentration of CO_2 increases the rate of photosynthesis but only up to a limit.
3. **Temperature** – the enzymes which control photosynthesis have an optimum working temperature. If it gets too cold the enzymes slow down but if it gets too hot the enzymes are destroyed.

A21 – Water uptake and transpiration in plants

Plants need water for chemical reactions including photosynthesis. They also use water to transport minerals and food products around the plant.

WATER FLOW THROUGH A PLANT

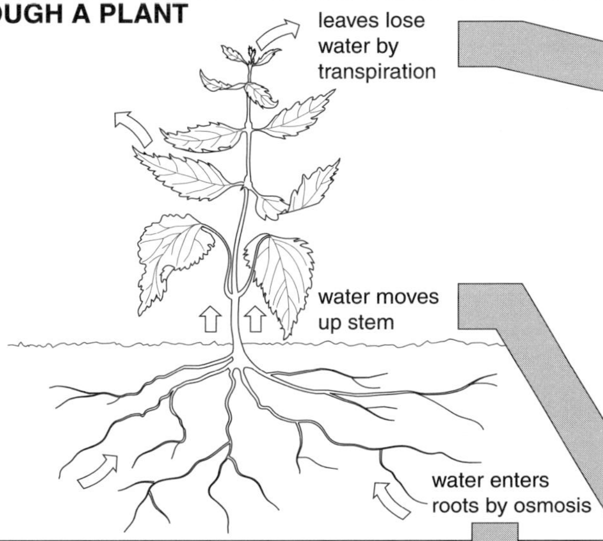

TRANSPIRATION IS CONTROLLED BY STOMATA

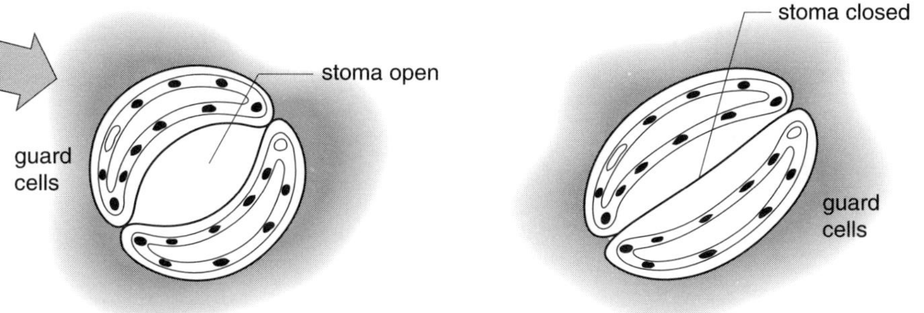

Guard cells swollen with water.
Stoma (pore) is held open.
Water can be lost through the stoma.

Guard cells limp with lack of water.
Stoma (pore) is closed.
Little water is lost through the stoma.

- Transpiration is faster on hot, windy, dry days.
- Transpiration is slower on cold, still, damp (humid) days.

WATER ENTERS THE PLANT THROUGH THE ROOTS

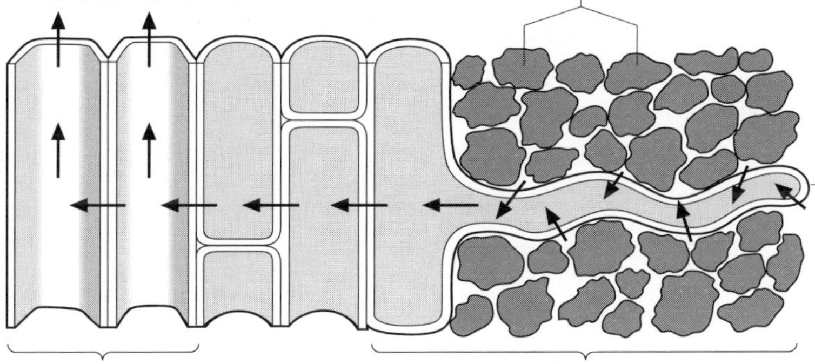

WATER MOVES UP THE PLANT THROUGH THE VASCULAR BUNDLE

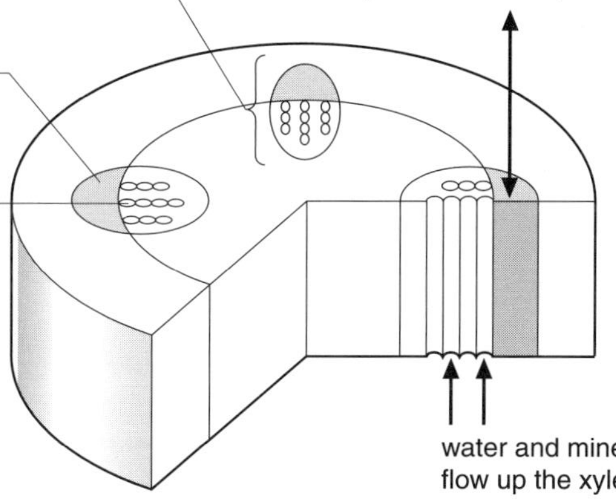

A22 – Mineral requirements of plants

Plants need minerals from the soil in order to grow properly. Without them plants develop **mineral deficiency symptoms.**

Plants need the following elements:

Nitrogen (N) **Phosphorus (P)** **Potassium (K)** **Magnesium (Mg)** **Sulphur (S)** **Calcium (Ca)**

They also need small quantities of these trace elements:

Manganese (Mn) **Copper (Cu)** **Iron (Fe)** **Boron (B)**

When crops are harvested, minerals are lost from the soil. Farmers can replenish these by adding a natural fertilizer such as compost or a chemical fertilizer.

Lack of nitrogen

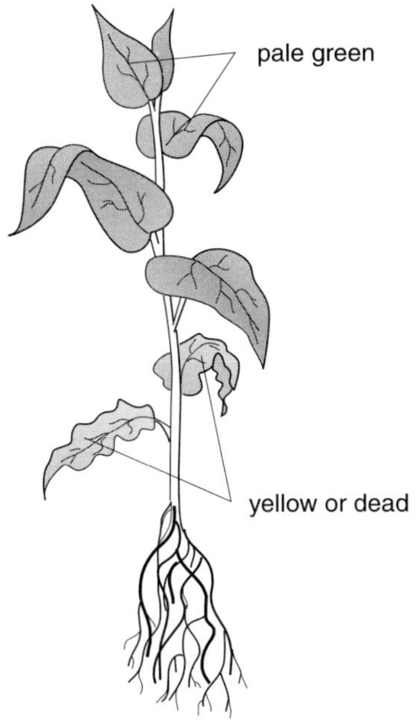

Weak stem and pale green/yellow leaves.

Nitrogen is needed for good growth. It is sometimes called the 'leaf maker'.

Lack of phosphorus

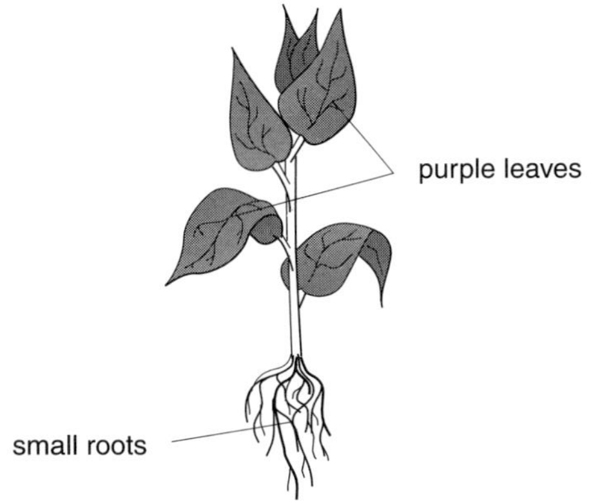

Poor root growth and purple leaves.

Phosphorus is sometimes called the 'root maker'.

Lack of potassium

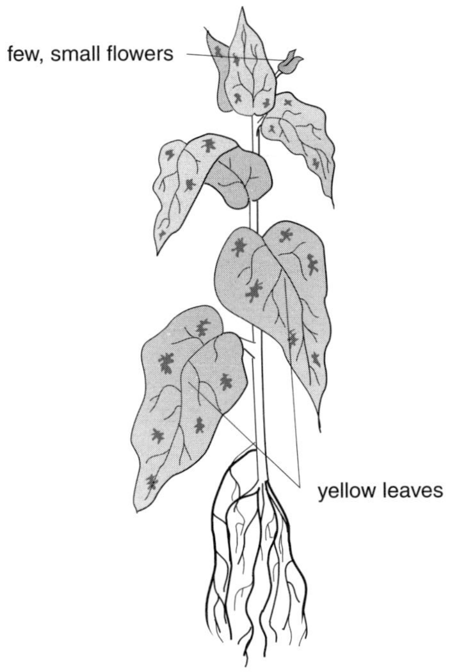

Poor flower and fruit growth. The leaves are yellow with dead spots.

Potassium is sometimes called the 'fruit and flower maker'.

Lack of magnesium

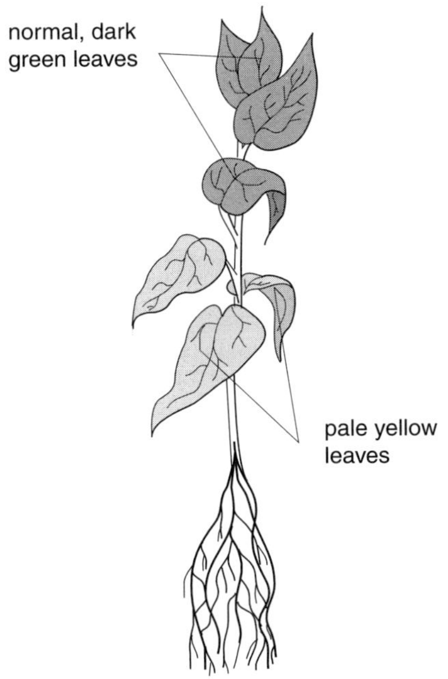

The upper leaves are normal and green. The lower leaves are pale green/yellow. (This is very common in tomato plants.) Magnesium is used to make chlorophyll.

A23 – Hormones and plant growth

Groups of plant hormones called auxins control the growth of shoots and roots.

PHOTOTROPISM

Plant shoots grow towards light. This is called phototropism. Phototropism is caused by auxins produced in the shoot tip. The auxins promote growth but are deactivated or destroyed by light.

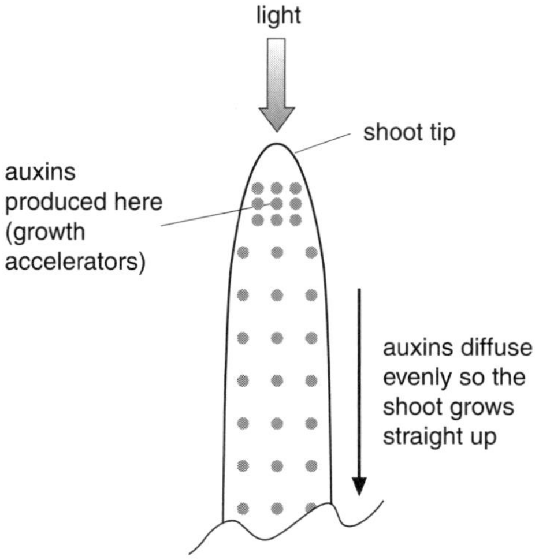

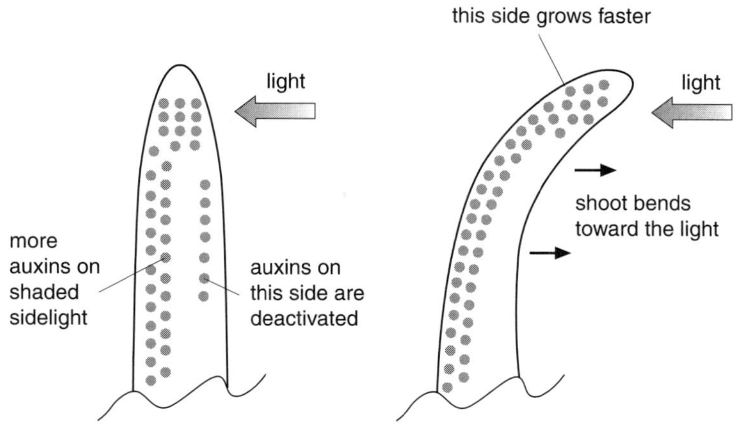

GEOTROPISM

Plant roots grow downwards in the direction of the pull of gravity. This is called geotropism. Geotropism is caused by auxins produced in the root tip. Root auxins slow down growth (i.e. opposite to the effect of shoot auxins).

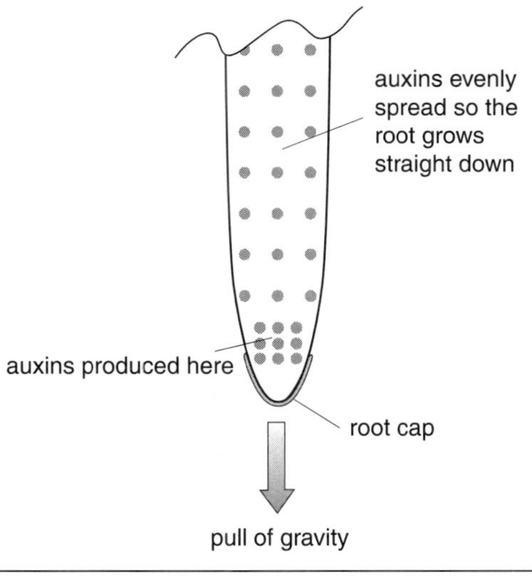

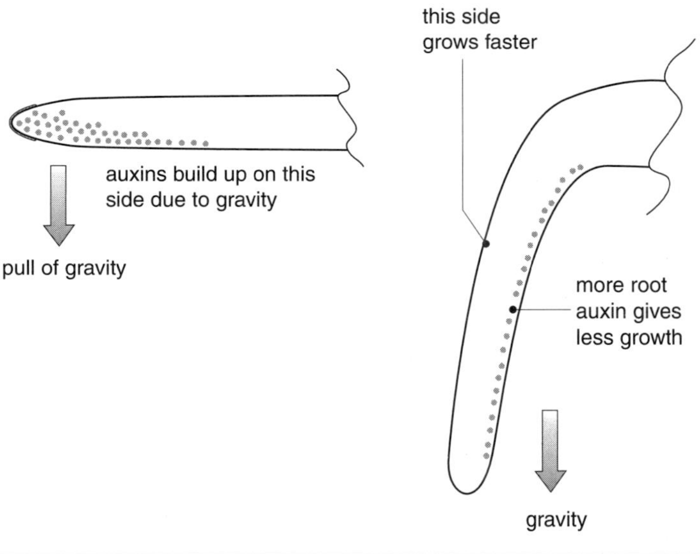

USING PLANT HORMONES

Hormone rooting powders can promote root growth in plant cuttings.

Selective weed killers are absorbed by broad-leaved weeds but narrow-leaved grasses and cereal crops absorb less. Hormones cause the weeds to grow so quickly that they wither and die.

A24 – Chromosomes, genes and cell division

The 'instructions' to make an organism are contained within the DNA inside the cell.

DNA, CHROMOSOMES AND GENES

DNA (deoxyribonucleic acid) is a long complex molecule shaped like a double helix. The two halves are linked by chemical bases adenine (A), cytosine (C), guanine (G) and thymine (T). The order in which the bases appear makes up the genetic code.

A group of bases which controls a particular characteristic is called a **gene**. A chromosome is a long, coiled DNA molecule which, in humans, contains up to 4000 genes! We can represent chromosomes like this:

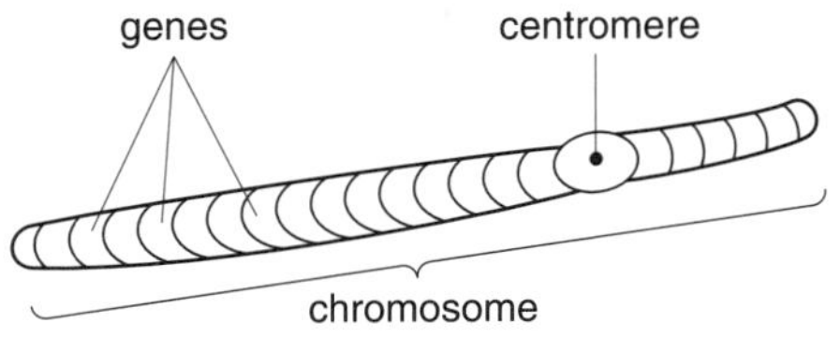

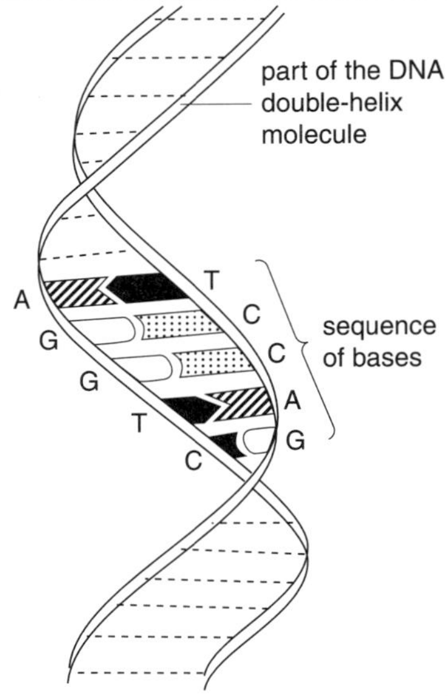

MITOSIS – CELL DIVISION BY COPYING

In order for an organism to grow, cells have to divide. Before they split they have to copy the genetic material inside. This is called **mitosis**.

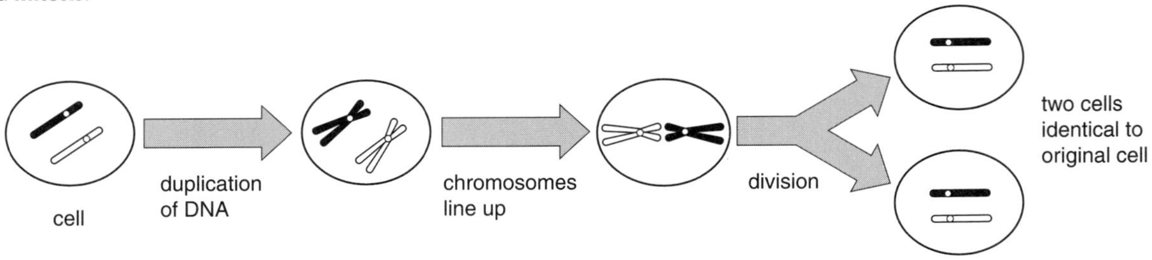

MEIOSIS – CELL DIVISION TO MAKE GAMETES (in animals)

All cells divide by mitosis but sex cells (gametes), i.e. sperm and ova, are made by **meiosis**.

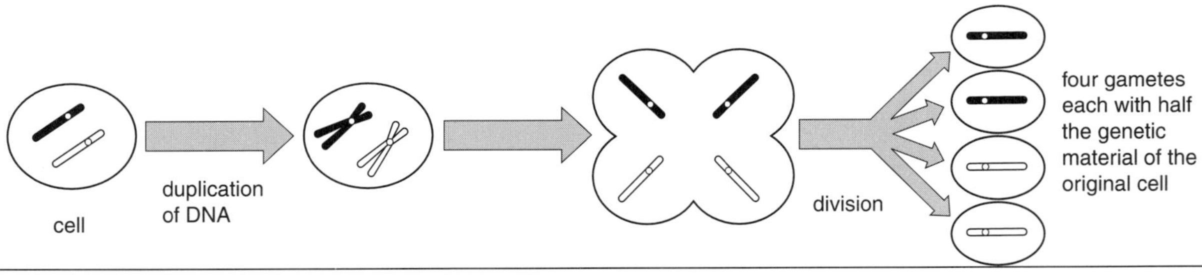

FERTILIZATION – JOINING GAMETES

At fertilization, the gametes fuse to give cells with a complete set of chromosome pairs.

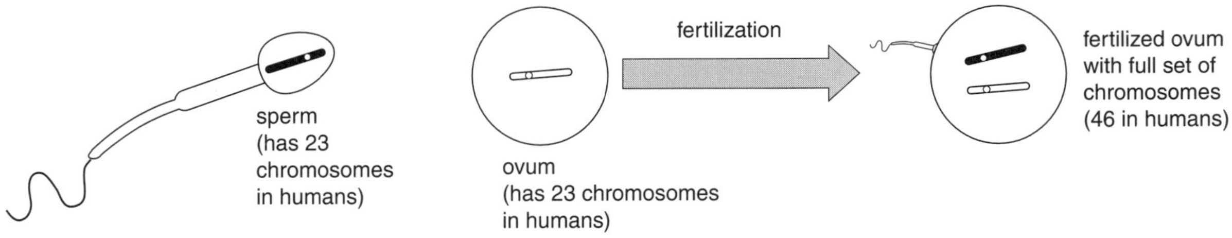

A25 – Variation and mutation

Individuals in a species are all different. This variation is very important. Evolution works by selecting advantageous variations

CONTINUOUS VARIATIONS: characteristics which can have any value. Examples are height and body weight. Continuous variations are due to the genetic code and also to **environmental factors**, e.g. your height depends on the genes you inherited and your diet while you are growing.

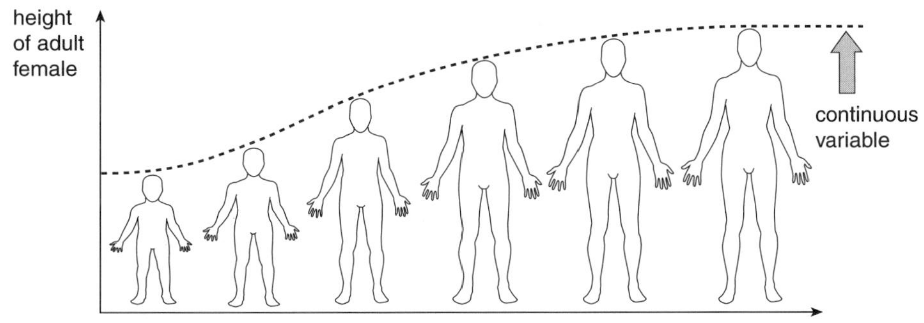

DISCONTINUOUS VARIATIONS: Characteristics which have only a limited number of variations, e.g. male or female, ears with or without lobes, etc. These variations are controlled almost entirely by genes.

HOW DO VARIATIONS OCCUR?

During meiosis

When cells are preparing to split, some genetic material can be transferred from one chromosome to another. This is called **crossing over**.

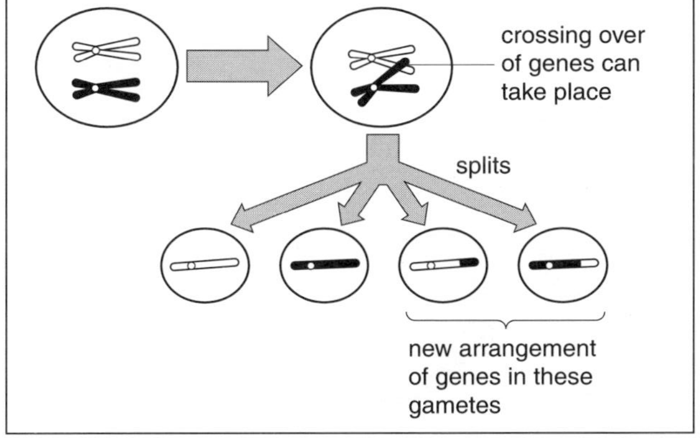

During fertilization

When gametes are formed there are many ways of combining the chromosomes which the ovum or sperm will carry. Then, at fertilization, any sperm can fertilize the egg so there are millions of different combinations in the fertilized ovum.

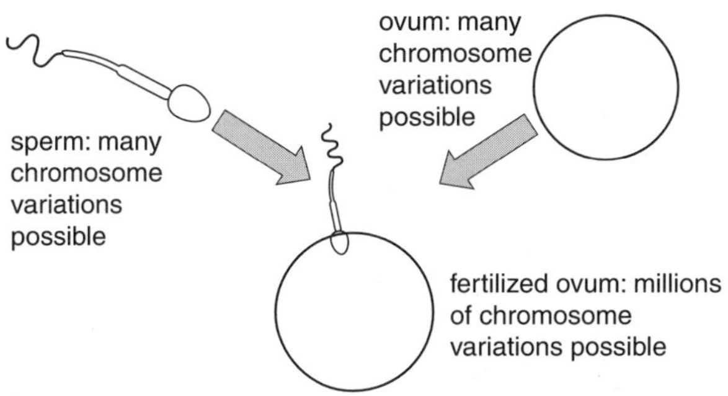

Due to environmental factors

Some chemicals and types of radiation can alter the genetic material inside cells. This causes **mutant genes**. If changes occur in the gametes, it is possible that the mutant gene will be inherited.

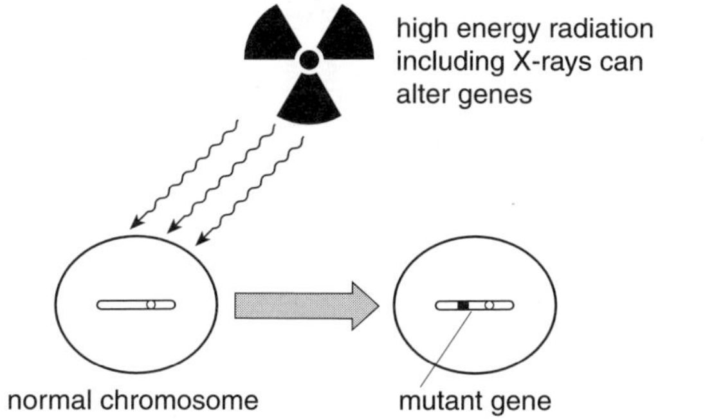

A26 – Genes and inherited characteristics

A chromosome has groups of chemicals called **genes** arranged along its length. These genes control inherited characteristics.

GENES

Our chromosomes contain the genes which determine our hair colour, eye colour, skin colour and many other characteristics. At fertilization, genes from the sperm pair up with genes from the ovum. The **pair of genes** controls the characteristic which will develop. **Dominant genes** show up when they are paired with **recessive genes**.

Dominant characteristics	Recessive characteristics
brown hair	blond hair
brown eyes	blue eyes
ears with lobes	ears without lobes
straight nose	turned-up nose
projecting chin	receding chin

MONOHYBRID INHERITANCE

In a monohybrid cross, both parents are **homozygous** for a particular characteristic – the two genes in a pair are the same.

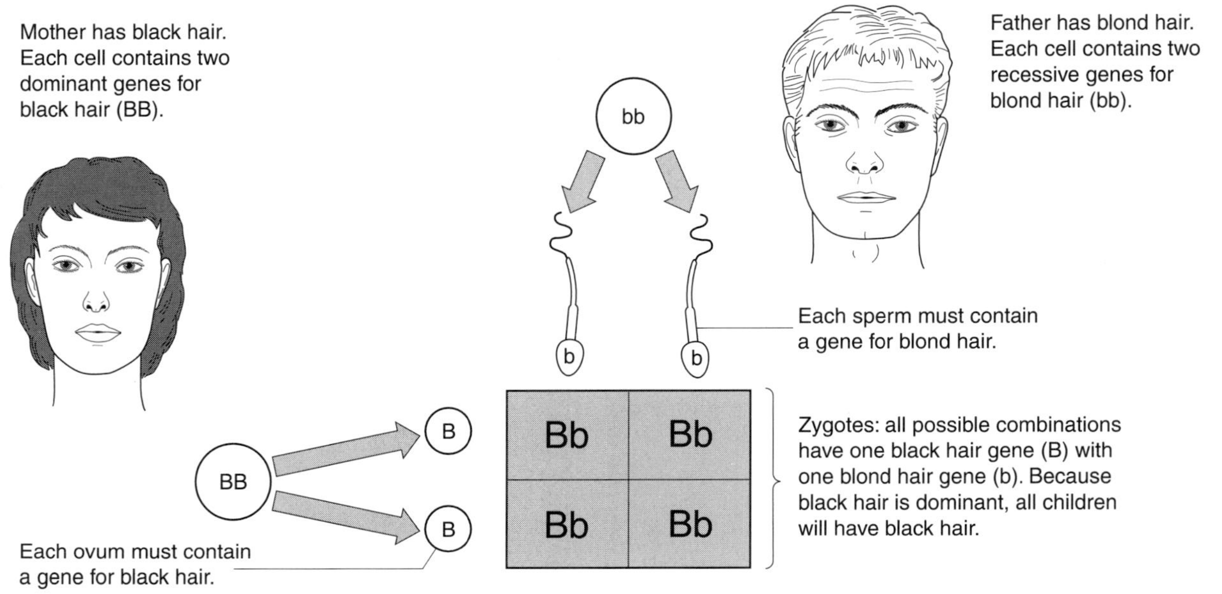

HETEROZYGOUS CROSS

In this case both parents are **heterozygous** for a particular characteristic – the two genes in a pair are different: one is dominant and the other is recessive.

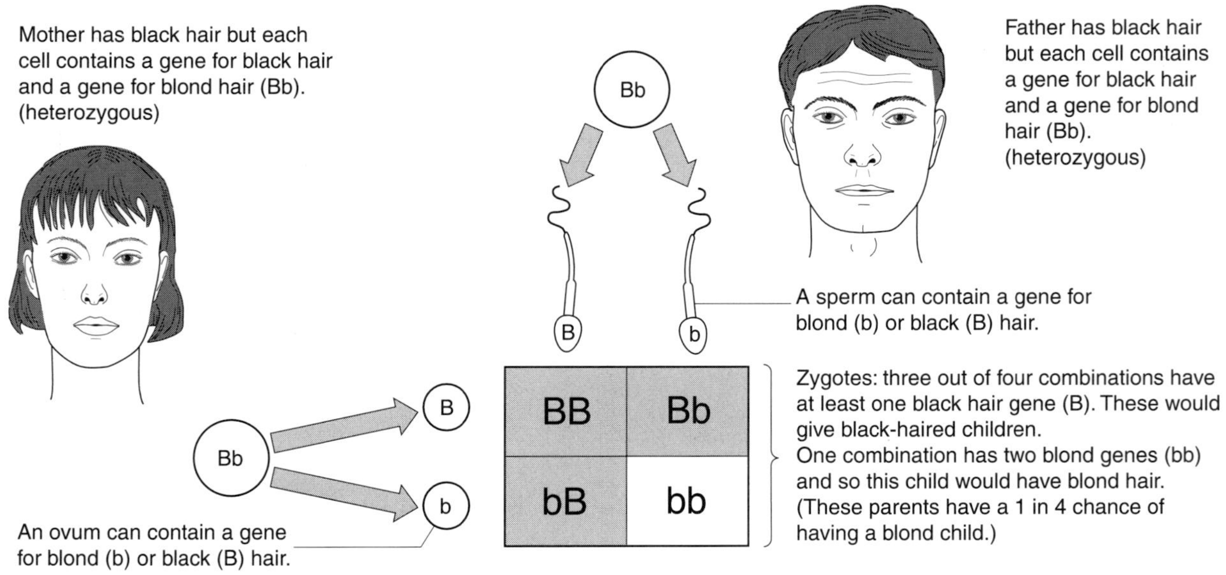

A27 – X and Y chromosomes

Human eggs and sperm contain 23 chromosomes. At fertilization 22 matched pairs are formed. The 23rd pair determines the sex of the baby.

SEX INHERITANCE – BOY OR GIRL?

In women, the 23rd pair of chromosomes is made up of two X chromosomes. When meiosis takes place, all the ova produced contain an X chromosome.

In men, the 23rd pair of chromosomes is made up of an X chromosome and a shorter Y chromosome. When meiosis takes place, half the sperm contain an X chromosome and half contain a Y chromosome.

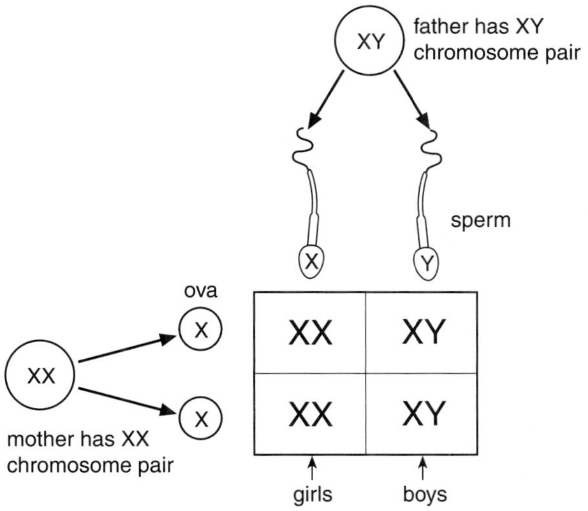

SEX-LINKED INHERITANCE

The Y chromosome cannot match all the genes on the X chromosome because it is much shorter. If the X chromosome from the mother carries a gene for an inherited disease like colour blindness (X^n) then her male children may be colour blind. A female child would be unlikely to be colour blind because a normal vision gene (X^N) on her inherited X chromosome would be dominant. However, she could pass the gene on to her sons – she is a **carrier**.

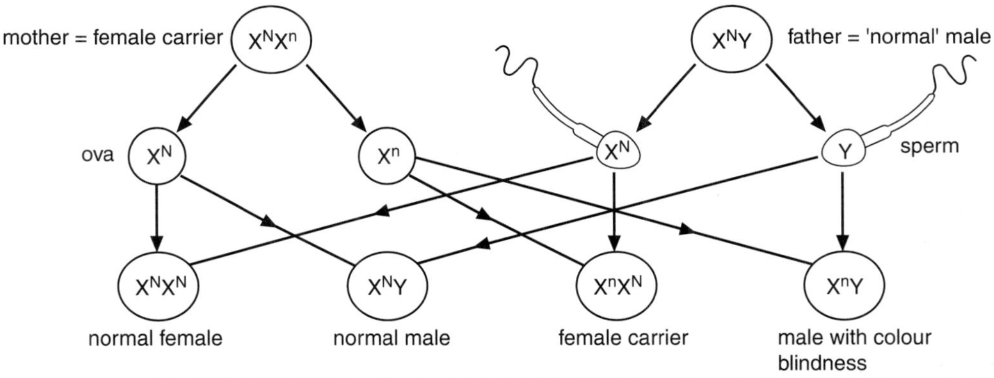

INHERITED DISORDERS

Disorder	Problem caused by ...	Symptoms
Haemophilia	The recessive gene for haemophilia is held on the X chromosome so it is a sex-linked disorder (like colour blindness).	Blood does not produce clotting agent. Serious problems may arise from cuts and internal injuries.
Cystic fibrosis	A recessive gene but not sex-linked. Inherited if both parents pass on the gene.	Congested lungs and airways, poor digestion, and sterility – often fatal
Sickle-cell anaemia	Gene mutation occurs when part of the DNA is altered.	Red blood cells contain faulty haemoglobin and so cannot transport oxygen – a very painful disease.
Down's syndrome	Chromosome mutation. If the ovum has an extra chromosome and if that chromosome belongs to the 21st pair, then Down's syndrome results.	Abnormal mental development and physical development (e.g. heart abnormalities)

A28 – Sexual and asexual reproduction

Sexual reproduction involves the fusion of gametes. The resulting offspring are not the same as their parents.

SEXUAL REPRODUCTION

Sexual reproduction involves the fusion of male and female gametes. At fertilization, the nuclei of the sex cells fuse, sharing their genetic material. The resulting offspring are not the same as the parents.

Animals

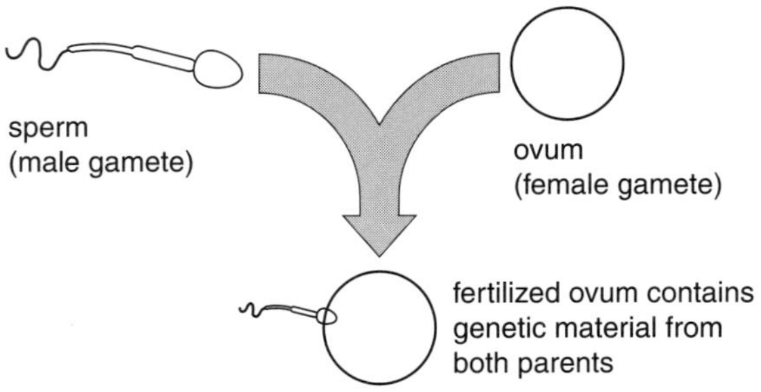

Plants

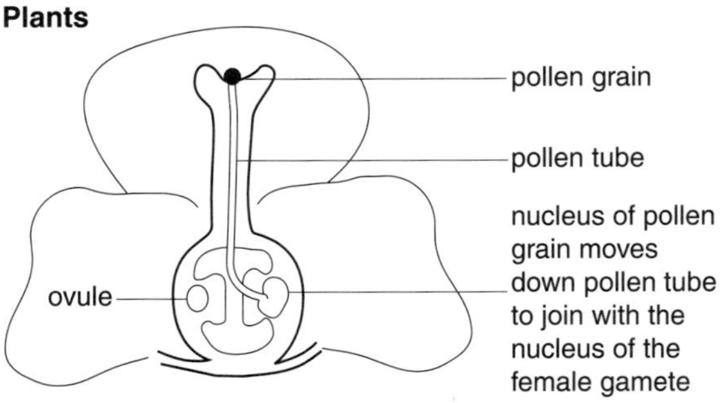

ASEXUAL REPRODUCTION

Asexual reproduction does not involve gametes. Because there is no sharing of genetic material, the offspring are identical to the parent organism.

Animals

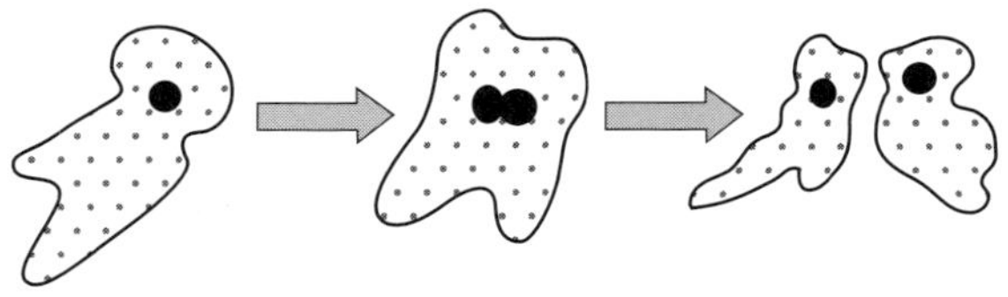

Simple organisms like this amoeba can reproduce by splitting in two (**binary fission**). The two new amoeba are genetically identical to the 'parent'.

Plants

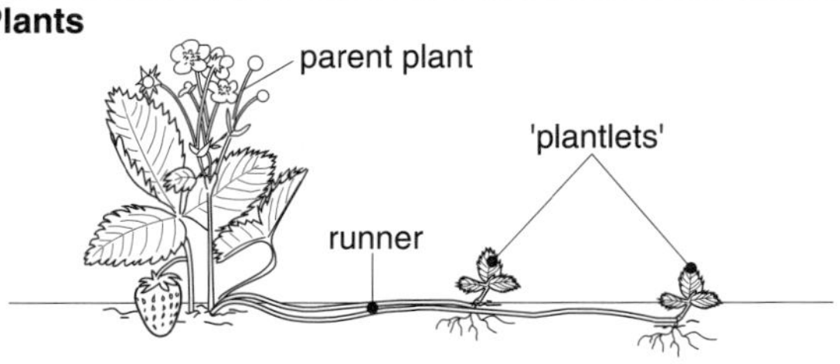

This strawberry plant can send out a 'runner'. Each small plant will root and become a separate plant, genetically identical to the 'parent'.

(Note that the strawberry plant can also reproduce sexually by producing seeds.)

CLONING

Cloning is the artificial production of many identical plants or animals. One method of cloning animals fertilizes an egg outside of the female (*in vitro* fertilization).

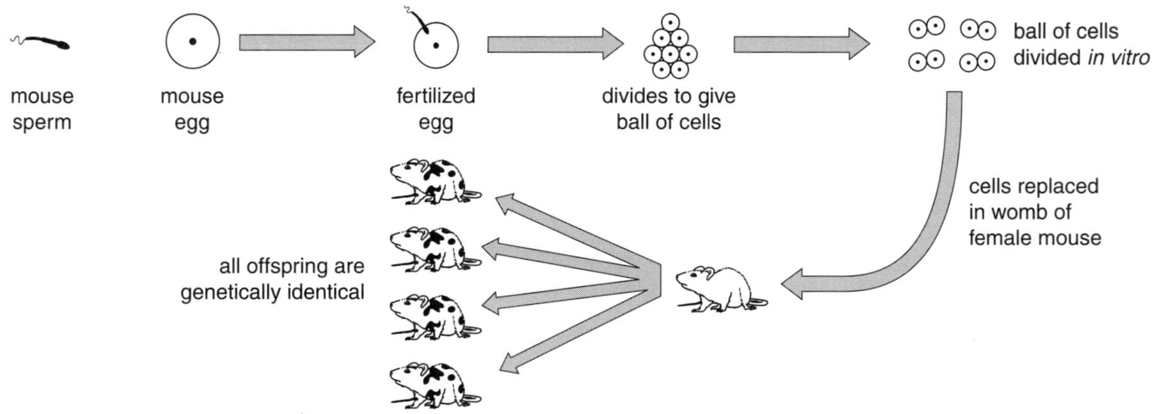

Uses of cloning:

1 Making identical plants and animals for use in controlled scientific research.
2 Making identical copies of animals and plants which are good for agriculture.
3 Making large numbers of rare and expensive plants, e.g. propagating orchids.
4 Increasing the chances of having a baby for couples who have difficulty conceiving.

A29 – Selective breeding and genetic engineering

Selective breeding and genetic engineering are methods we can use to produce plants and animals better suited to our purposes.

SELECTIVE BREEDING

For hundreds of years farmers have been breeding animals and plants to give greater productivity. By selecting parents with desired characteristics and mating them, there is a better chance of the offspring having those characteristics. For example, if a champion stallion (male horse) is mated with a champion mare (female horse) the foals (young horses) are likely to be fast runners.

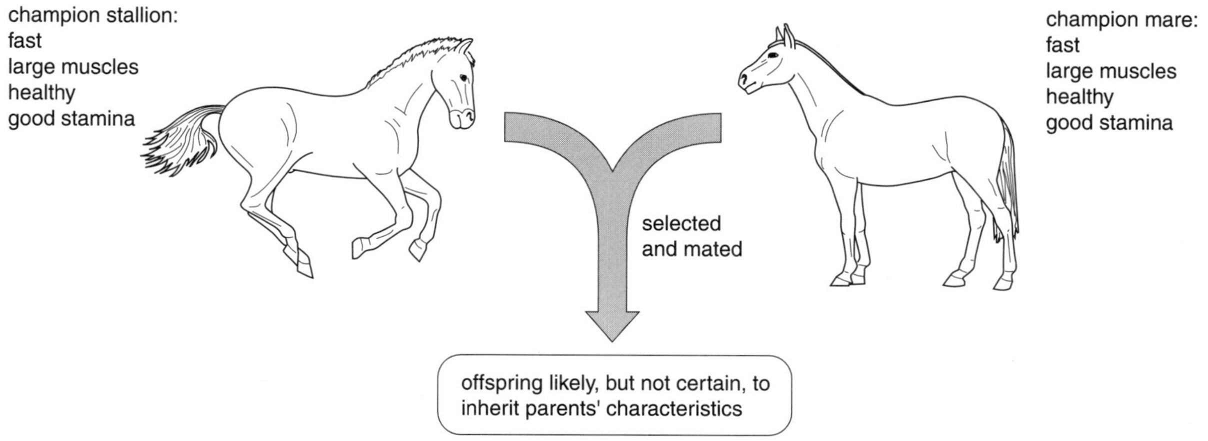

Selective breeding has been very successful but it is slow and unpredictable.

GENETIC ENGINEERING

Genetic engineers can identify single genes in the DNA of a plant or animal. They can then 'cut' that gene out and introduce it into other cells for duplication. The example below shows how genetic engineering can make insulin for use by people with diabetes.

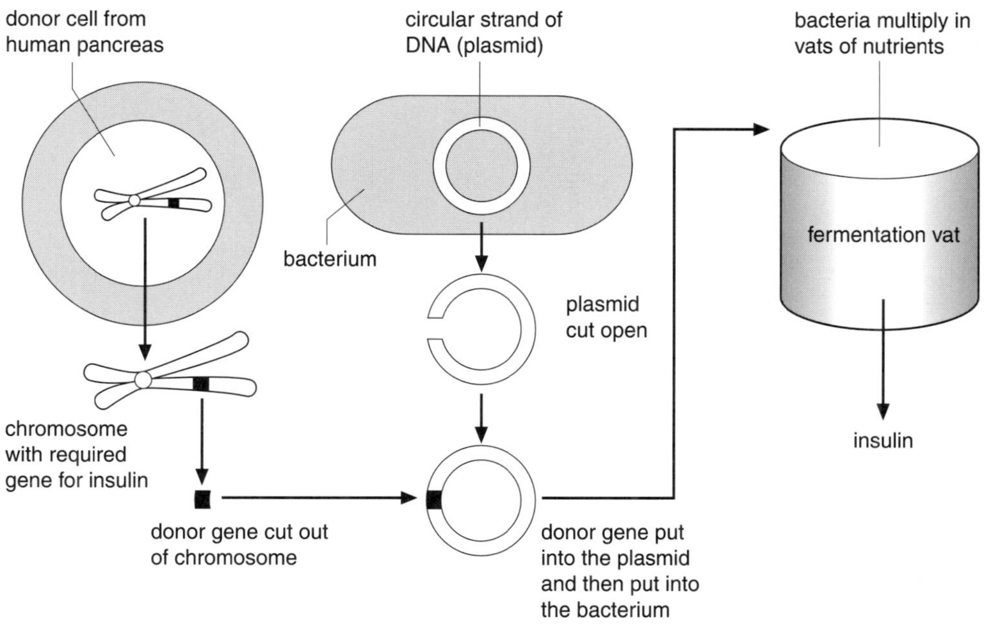

POTENTIAL USES OF GENETIC ENGINEERING

- Production of important medical products, e.g. insulin, human growth hormone, blood clotting agent (Factor 8)
- Gene therapy for inherited diseases, e.g. cystic fibrosis
- Plants which can resist frost and disease, or which can produce bigger fruit with more flavour
- Animals which produce more milk or meat and which are resistant to common diseases

A30 – Variation, natural selection and evolution

Species evolve because only those organisms that are well adapted to their environment can survive and reproduce. Organisms which are poorly adapted are more likely to die without reproducing and passing on their genes. Species' isolation lead to separate gene pools which then diverge into new species.

SEXUAL REPRODUCTION CAUSES:

Over-production
Organisms produce more offspring than can possibly survive, e.g. one oak tree may produce 10 000 acorns, one moth may lay 500 eggs.

Variation
Sexual reproduction gives offspring which are different from their parents and different from each other.

These peppered moths show variation in their colouring. Some are light and others are dark.

ENVIRONMENTAL RESISTANCE INCLUDES:

Competition for food
Limited food supplies mean that individuals have to compete for their food within their own species and with other species

Predation
Many animals are food for other animals! To be able to survive they must be able to run away, frighten their attackers, fight back or hide. **Camouflage** helps animals to hide from predators.

These moths are competing for the same food (nectar). Predators (birds) will eat them!

NATURAL SELECTION MEANS:

Survival of the fittest
Only well adapted organisms will survive and reproduce. Those that are poorly adapted will be more likely to die. Weak or poorly camouflaged individuals will be easier for predators to kill.

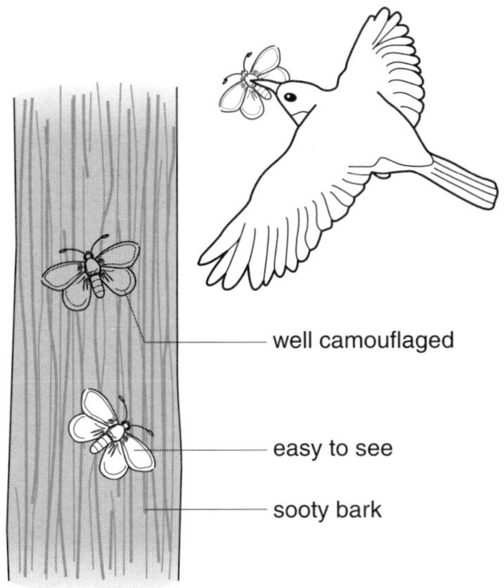

Dark peppered moths are well camouflaged on dark, soot-covered trees in industrial areas.

Light peppered moths are well camouflaged on trees covered in silvery-green lichen which grows best where the air is clear.

EVOLUTION:

Since the well adapted stand a better chance of reproducing, advantageous characteristics are passed on. This gradually changes the species.

For example, cheetahs have evolved into very fast runners because faster cheetahs are better at catching their prey.

Gazelles have evolved into fast, agile runners because faster runners are more likely to escape their predators, e.g. cheetahs!

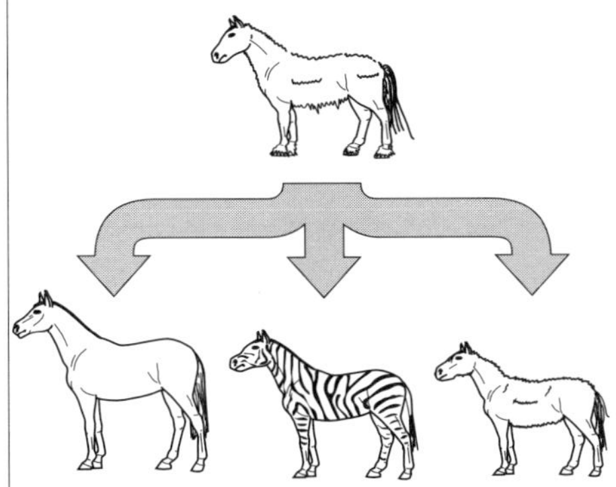

Horses, zebras and donkey all share a common recent ancestor. It was recognizably donkey-like.

A31 – Evolution: the evidence

Darwin's theory of evolution is supported by evidence from the fossil record, the anatomical structure of animals, and the geographical distribution of species. The further back in time you go the 'simpler' the organisms are.

FOSSILS

Fossils are the remains of plants and animals (many no longer existing) preserved in the rocks of the Earth's crust.

Using fossils we can study the organisms which were alive millions of years ago, many of which are now **extinct**.

By looking for similarities between fossils and existing plants and animals we can build theories of how modern species evolved from common ancestors.

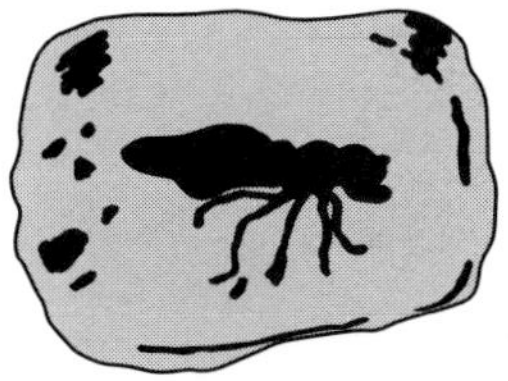

fossilized mosquito trapped in amber (fossilized tree resin)

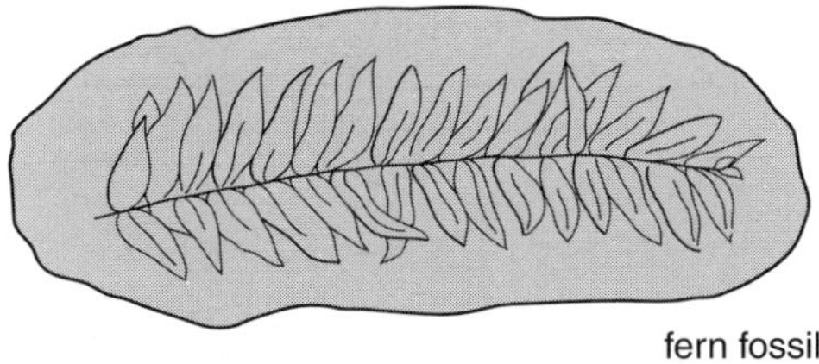

fern fossilized in coal (about 300 million years old

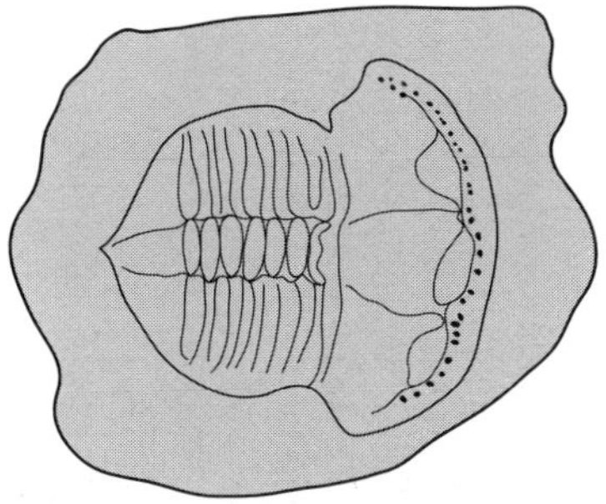

trilobite fossil: trilobites lived on the sea bed about 500 million years ago

ANATOMY

The skeletons of different species of mammals have similar structures even though they have different functions. This suggests that they evolved from a common ancestor.

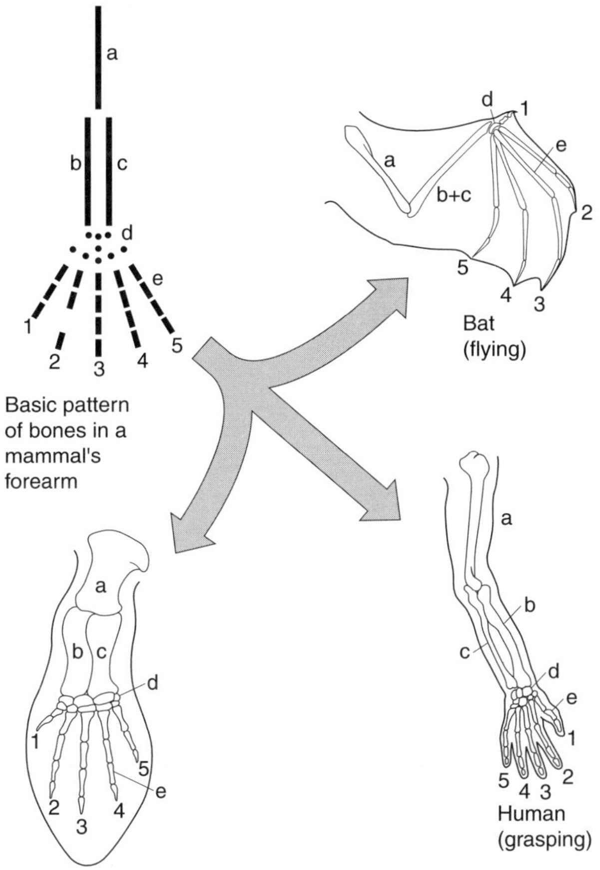

Basic pattern of bones in a mammal's forearm

Bat (flying)

Human (grasping)

Whale (swimming)

GEOGRAPHICAL DESTRIBUTION

Geographical or environmental changes may split a species into several groups. If these groups remain isolated for a very long time, they may evolve in different ways. Eventually they may form separate species.

Charles Darwin found several species of finch on the Galapagos Islands in the Pacific Ocean. He suggested that they had evolved from mainland finches by **natural selection**. Each species is well adapted to use a particular source of food.

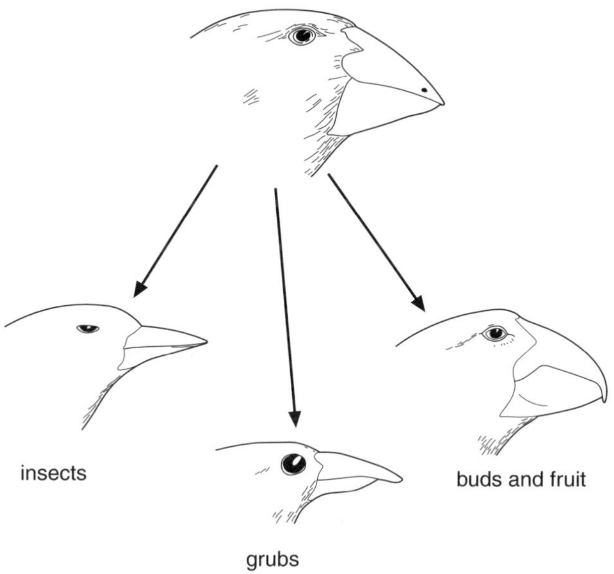

Mainland finches have beaks adapted for seed-eating.

Finches on the islands have evolved different beaks which are well adapted to eating other foods.

A32 – Habitats, communities and populations

In natural habitats, many species of plants and animals live and interact together.

HABITAT

The place where an animal or plant lives is its **habitat**. A habitat provides food, shelter and space for all the organisms within it to live and reproduce.

This is a woodland habitat.

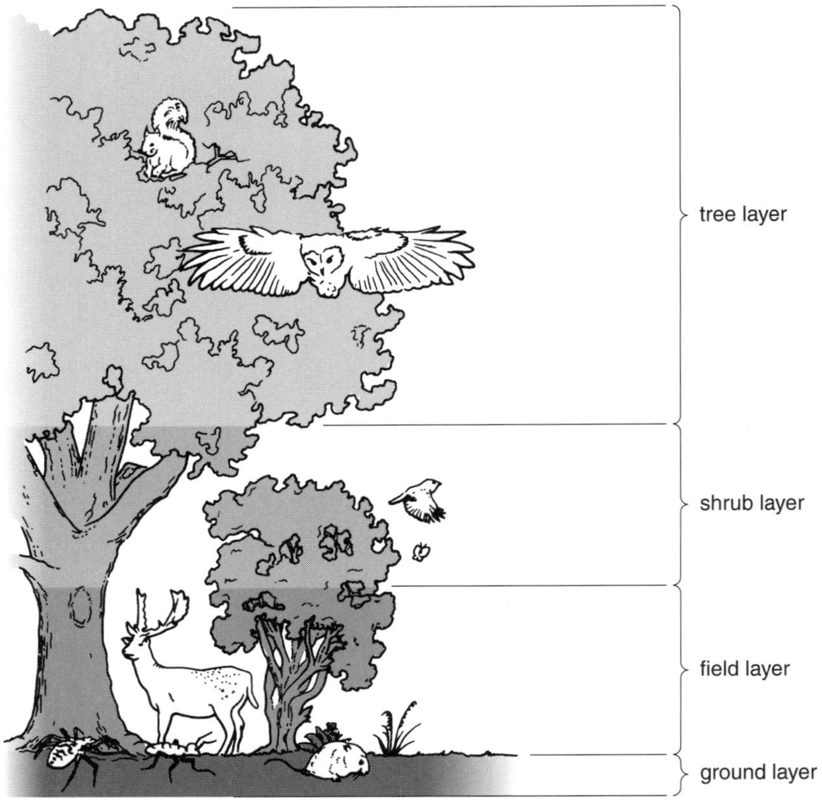

COMMUNITIES

Several species of plants and animals live and interact in this habitat. They form a **community**.

Each organism is adapted for life within its part of the habitat. For example, squirrels are well adapted for climbing and eating nuts in the tree layer. Woodland flowers are well adapted for growing and flowering under tall, deciduous trees.

POPULATIONS

All the individuals of the same species in a habitat make up a **population**. Under ideal conditions plants and animals reproduce quickly and the population grows 1. However, the habitat can only produce a certain amount of food. This will limit the size of the population 2. If the population damages the habitat too much, the numbers may start to fall 3.

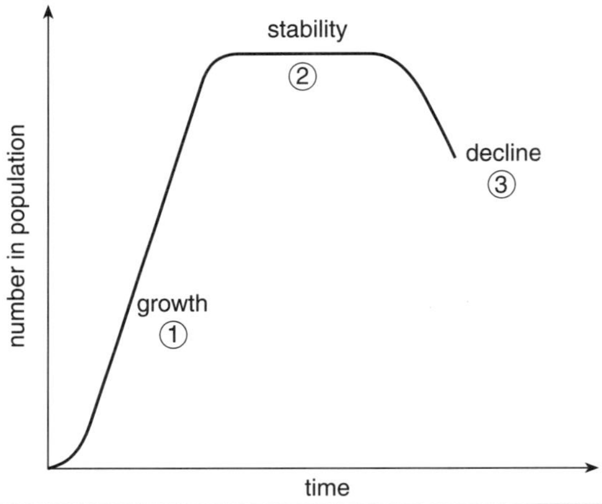

PREDATOR–PREY RELATIONSHIP

In the community there will be food chains where one animal (**predator**) eats another animal (**prey**). For example, foxes eat rabbits. If there are many rabbits the fox population will grow. This will reduce the rabbit population so there will be less food for foxes and so the number of foxes will start to fall again. This allows the number of rabbits to increase and so on.

The populations of predator and prey rise and fall typically as shown.

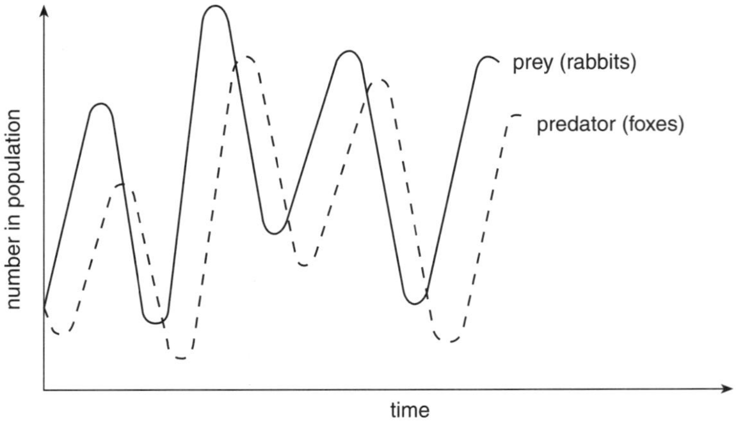

A33 – Impact of humans on the environment

We now know that human activities can have a major impact on the environment.

GLOBAL WARMING

Greenhouse gases (e.g. carbon dioxide, methane, CFCs) keep heat in and reflect it back to Earth. Greenhouse gases from industry may be causing global warming. This could cause:

- greater climatic extremes (high winds and heavy storms)
- melting of ice caps, causing seas to rise and flood low-lying land
- greater evaporation from soils, causing crop losses

DAMAGE CAUSED BY EXCESSIVE USE OF PESTICIDES

Some pesticides cause damage when they enter the food chain because the chemicals accumulate in the bodies of the higher predators.

Accumulation of pesticide

pesticide in water
microscopic water plants
small animals, e.g. water fleas
small fish
larger fish
grebe (fish-eating water fowl)

POLLUTION FROM SEWAGE AND FERTILIZERS

Sewage and fertilizers from farmland can enter lakes and rivers. The nutrients (nitrates and phosphates) make the algae in the water grow rapidly. Other plants are smothered and die.

Bacteria use up oxygen from the water and so fish and other animals die.
This process is called **eutrophication**.

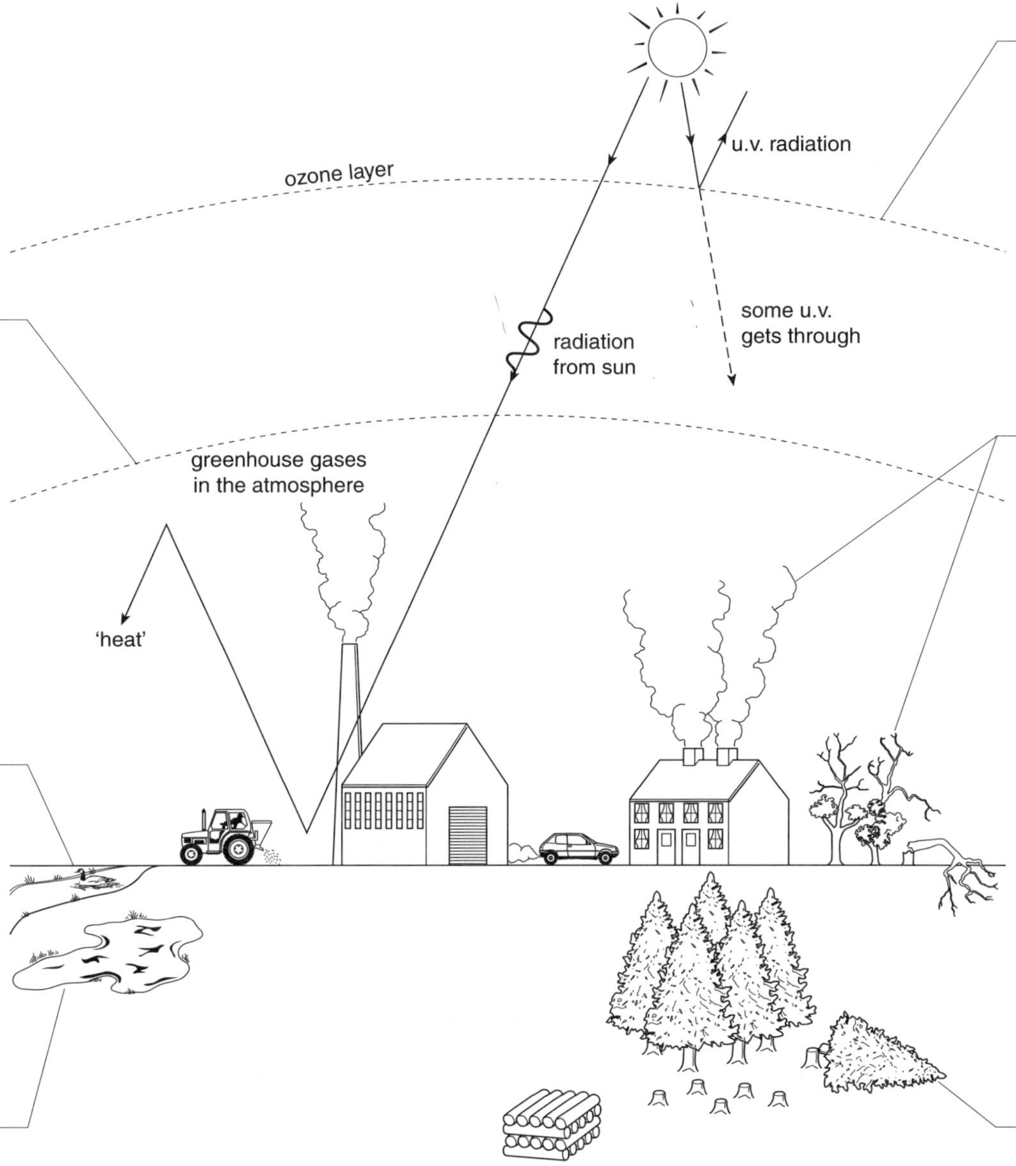

DAMAGE TO THE OZONE LAYER

Ozone protects us from ultraviolet radiation from the sun. The ozone layer is being broken down by chlorine gas produced by chlorofluorocarbons (CFCs) used in aerosols and in refrigerators.

Depletion of the ozone layer lets in more ultraviolet radiation. This causes:

- more skin cancer
- more cataracts of the eye
- more DNA mutation

ACID RAIN

Combustion of fossil fuels in industry, homes, and car engines produces sulphur dioxide and gaseous oxides of nitrogen. When these dissolve in water, acids are formed. This falls as acid rain.

Acid rain makes the soil acid. This damages plant roots and takes essential minerals from the soil. Poisonous chemicals are also released. Plants and trees may be killed. Acid rain and chemicals washed from the soil enter rivers and lakes. This kills fish and other aquatic animals.

HABITAT DESTRUCTION

Clearing woodlands, forests, swamps and wetlands in order to create more land for farming or building may destroy the natural habitats of rare plants and animals. Some may be lost forever.

Deforestation also increases soil erosion by removing tree roots which held the soil. In some countries this leads to flooding and mud slides.

A34 – Food chains and ecological pyramids

Food chains show how food (and energy) is passed between organisms.
An ecological pyramid shows how many plants or animals are in each link of the food chain.

A FOOD CHAIN

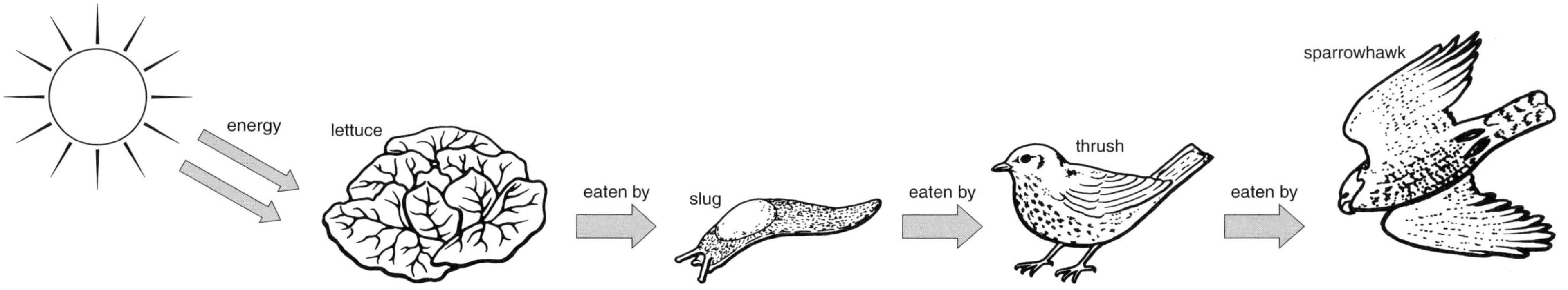

The Sun
The Sun is the ultimate source of energy in the food chain.

Producer
Green plants trap energy from the sun through photosynthesis. They produce sugars and starches.

First-order consumer
Herbivores eat green plants.

Second-order consumer
Carnivores eat other animals.

Third-order consumer
This carnivore is at the top of the food chain.

ECOLOGICAL PYRAMIDS

Pyramid of numbers

This shows the number of organisms in each link of the food chain. In this case, 1000 grass plants are needed to feed twenty rabbits which, in turn, support one fox.

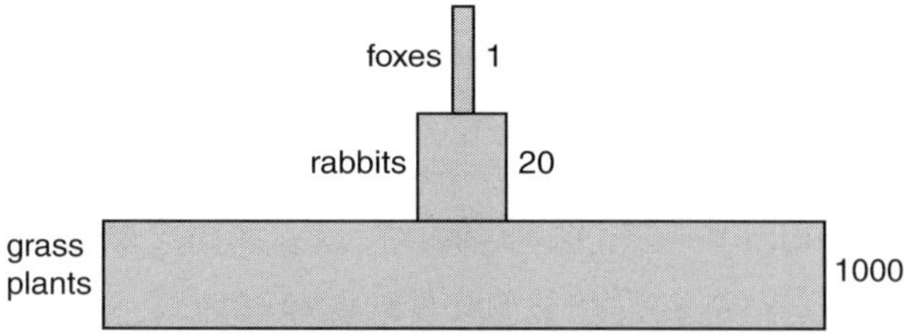

Another pyramid of numbers

Some food chains have pyramids of numbers that do not look like pyramids! This one shows that one oak tree can feed thousands of caterpillars. These feed twenty small birds. Finally, hundreds of fleas live by feeding off the birds.

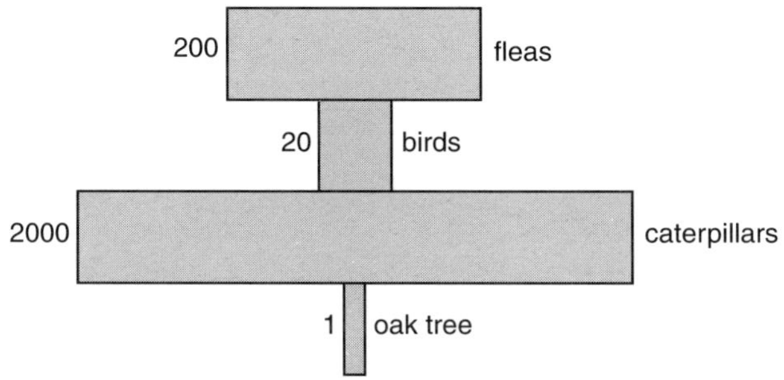

Pyramid of biomass

Sometimes we want to know about the **mass** of organisms that make up each level of the food chain. This one shows that 10 000 kg of oak tree supports a much smaller mass of insects. The mass of the birds is even smaller and, finally, the mass of the fleas is very small. This looks like a true pyramid.

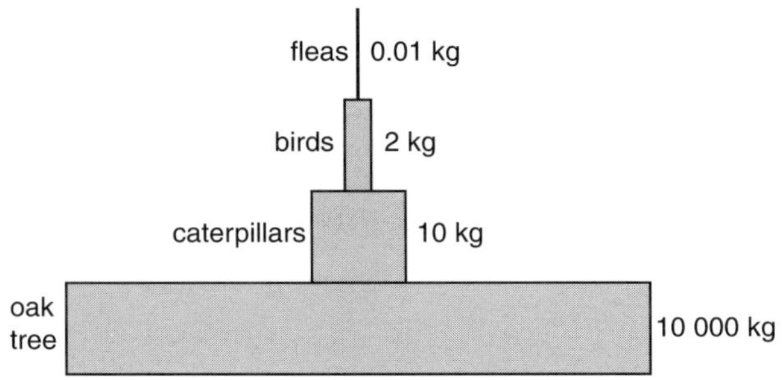

A35 – Energy flow in ecosystems

Carbon, nitrogen and water circulate in the environment but energy does not.
Lots of energy comes from the Sun but only a proportion is trapped in our food chains.

ENERGY FLOW IN A FOOD CHAIN

Energy comes from the Sun. Unfortunately, about 98% is lost by reflection or is used to evaporate water and heat up the soil. Only 2% gets trapped by the **producer**.

The producer uses some of the energy it receives for respiration. Of all the energy trapped by the plant, only about 10% can be passed on.

The first-order consumer uses some energy for respiration. It also loses some in its urine and faeces. It can only pass on about 10% of the energy it received to the next level of the food chain

The second-order consumer also uses some energy for respiration and loses some in its urine and faeces. It can only pass on about 10% of the energy it received to the next level of the food chain.

This level of the food chain only receives a very, very small proportion of the energy which originally came from the Sun.

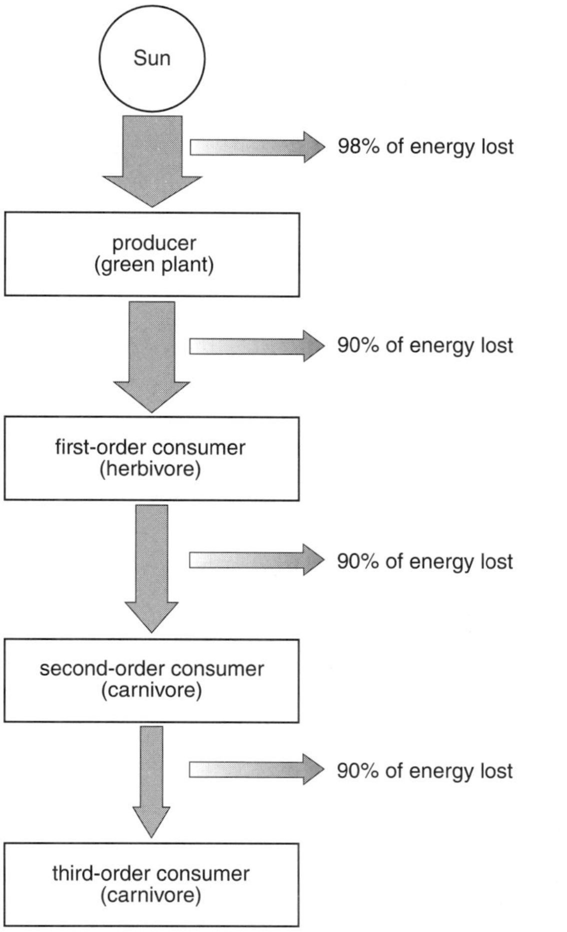

ENERGY FLOW IN A FOOD CHAIN

Some people eat beef from bullocks fed on grass.
The food chain is:

grass → **bullock** → **human**

Of the 1 000 000 kJ of energy which falls on one square metre of grass in a year, only about 100 kJ are available for humans.

It is much more efficient to grow wheat and rice for food rather than farming animals. This is because plants are at the first level of the food chain.

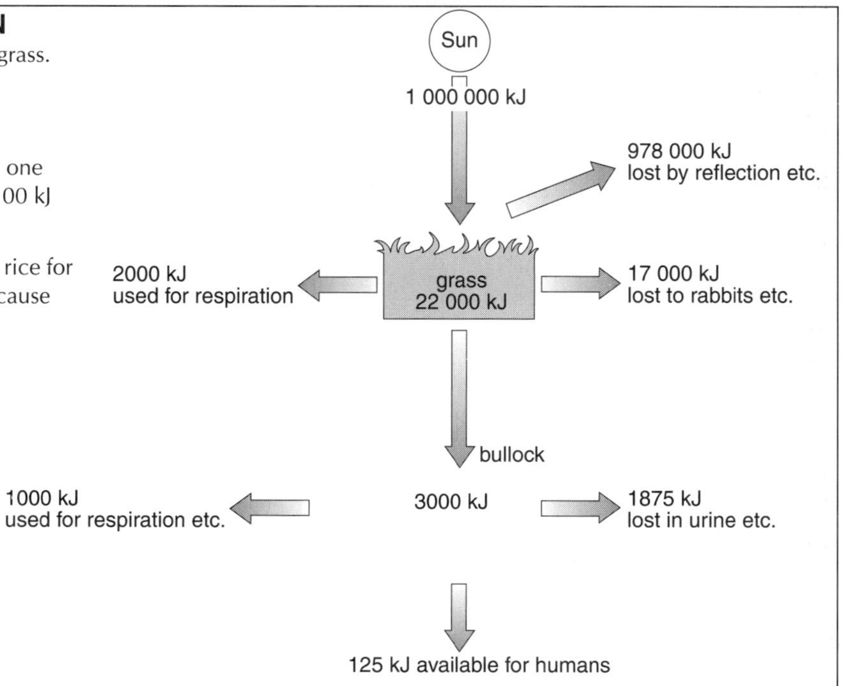

A36 – Managing food production

As the human population grows it is becoming increasingly important to produce large quantities of high quality food efficiently.

WEED CONTROL
Weeds compete with crops for nutrients in the soil and for light. They can be controlled by hand weeding or spraying with **herbicides**. The herbicides are absorbed by broad-leaved weeds but not by narrow-leaved plants.

PEST CONTROL
Some insects feed off crops and damage plants. They can be controlled by spraying with **insecticides**. Some pests can be controlled by **biological control**. Predators are introduced to eat the pests but not the plants (e.g. ladybirds eat aphids). Some plants are attacked by fungi. These can be controlled by spraying with a **fungicide**.

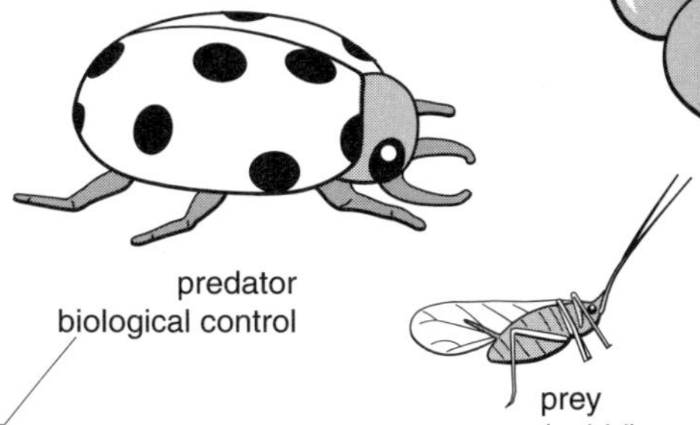

GOOD HUSBANDRY
Animals are more productive when they are healthy. Animals can be vaccinated against disease. They can also be treated with antibiotics when they get a bacterial infection.

Vitamin and mineral supplements can be added to their feed.

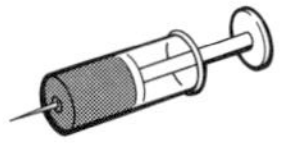

IRRIGATION
Crops can be grown under dry conditions by artificial watering.

CROP PROTECTION
Bad weather can destroy crops or prevent them from ripening. Plants can be protected by growing them in a greenhouse or under cloches.

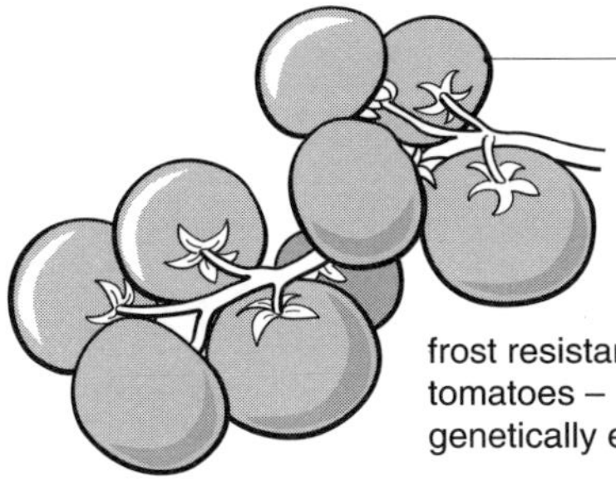

IMPROVING CROPS AND LIVESTOCK
Better plants and animals can be produced by selective breeding or by genetic engineering.

Growth can be controlled by injecting animals with hormones.

SOIL IMPROVEMENT
For maximum crop yields, soil must contain nutrients. It must also hold enough water for the plants to grow, but must not be too wet.

Soil can be improved by:

- installing drains in wet fields
- digging in organic material (compost etc.)
- adding organic fertilizer (including manure)
- adding inorganic fertilizers
- adding lime to neutralize acid soils.

INTENSIVE FARMING
Some animals (e.g. 'battery hens') are reared in intensive farming units. Many animals are kept close together in cages or pens. They are given plenty of food and warmth but they cannot move around freely.

Intensively farmed animals (e.g. pigs) grow quickly so production costs are low.

Fish can be intensively farmed in tanks.

A37 – The nitrogen cycle

All living things need nitrogen to make proteins.

Nitrogen in the air
About 80% of the air is nitrogen gas but plants and animals cannot use this directly. Plants get nitrogen from nitrogen compounds in the soil. Animals get nitrogen by eating plant protein.

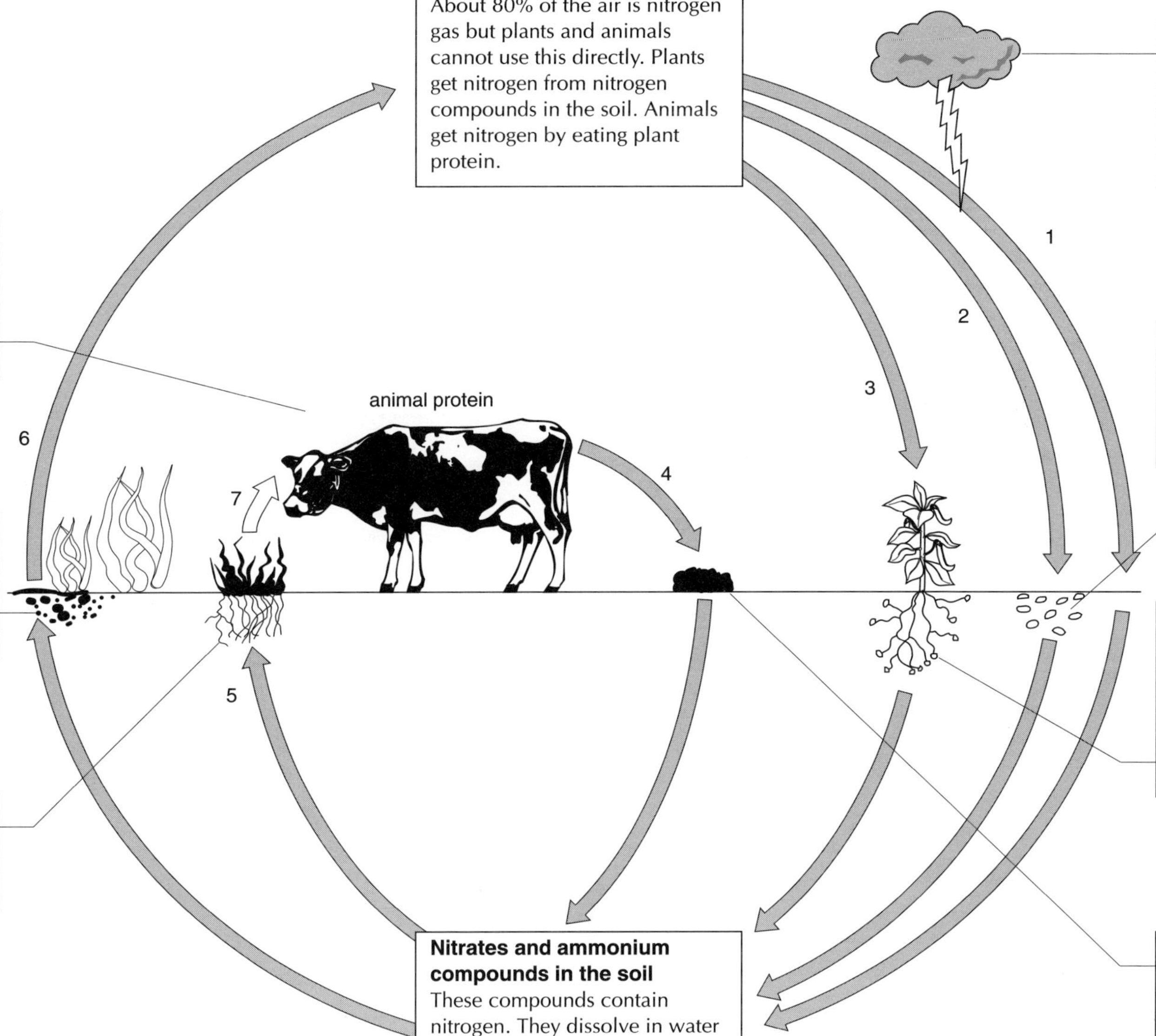

1 Lightning
Nitrogen and oxygen react when energy from lightning heats the air. The soluble nitrogen compounds formed are washed into the soil by rain.

2 Nitrogen-fixing bacteria in soil
Some bacteria can take nitrogen gas directly from the air and turn it into nitrogen compounds.

3 Nitrogen-fixing bacteria in legumes
Legumes are plants with 'lumps' or nodules on their roots which contain nitrogen-fixing bacteria. Peas, beans and clover are all legumes.

4 Nitrifying bacteria
Dead plants and animals, faeces and urine contain complex nitrogen compounds. Decomposers (nitrifying bacteria and fungi) break these down.

Nitrates and ammonium compounds in the soil
These compounds contain nitrogen. They dissolve in water in the soil. They are then taken up by plant roots.

5 Plant protein
Plants use nitrates and ammonium salts from the soil to make protein.

6 Denitrifying bacteria in water-logged soil
In very wet soil, denitrifying bacteria break down nitrates and release nitrogen back into the air.

7 Animal protein
Herbivores eat plant protein and make animal protein. Nitrogen from the atmosphere is now 'locked up' in this animal protein.

A38 – The carbon cycle

All living things need carbon. It is used in photosynthesis and found in energy-producing foods.

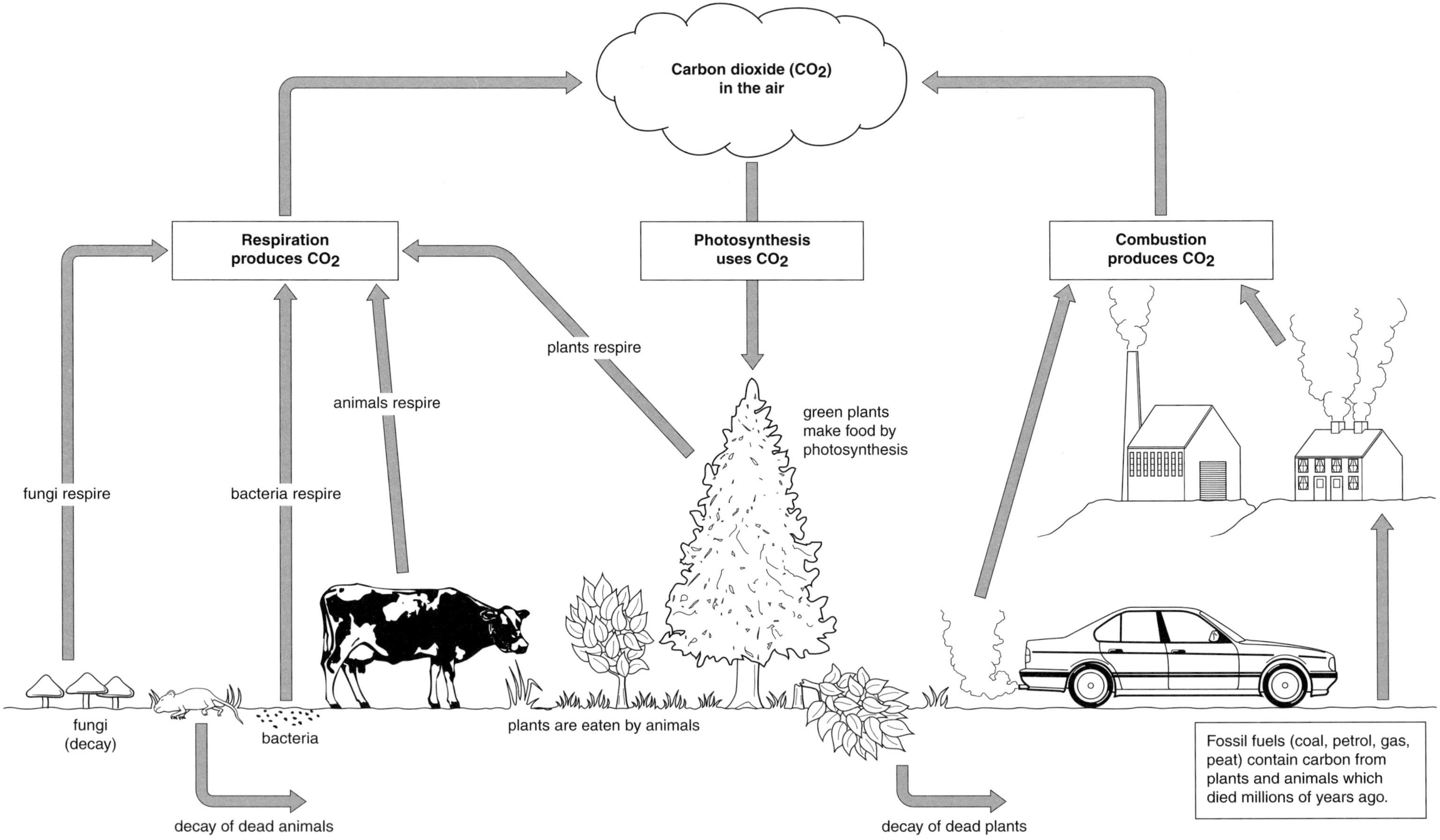

Chemistry checklist

MATERIALS AND THEIR PROPERTIES

Page	Topic	Revised ✔	See also ...
52	B1 – The particle model for solids, liquids and gases		C17
53	B2 – Atoms and sub-atomic particles		C33
54	B3 – Making molecules 1: ionic bonding		C1
55	B4 – Making molecules 2: covalent bonding		
56	B5 – Structures of molecular solids		
57	B6 – Oil and its distillation		
58	B7 – Combustion of hydrocarbons		A33
59	B8 – Alkanes and alkenes		
60	B9 – Cracking and polymerization		
61	B10 – Metals: structure and properties		C31
62	B11 – Reactions of metals 1		
63	B12 – Reactions of metals 2		
64	B13 – Extracting metals		
65	B14 – Electrolysis and processing metals		
66	B15 – Writing formulae and equations 1		
67	B16 – Writing formulae and equations 2		
68	B17 – Moles and reacting masses		
69	B18 – Finding masses and formulae		
70	B19 – Molar volume of gases and concentrations of solutions		
71	B20 – Evolution of the atmosphere		
72	B21 – Maintaining the atmosphere		A37, A38
73	B22 – The rock cycle		
74	B23 – Types of rock		A31, C35
75	B24 – The Earth's structure and tectonic plates		C29
76	B25 – The periodic table of elements		
77	B26 – Electronic structure of atoms		
78	B27 – Group 1: the alkali metals		
79	B28 – Group 7: the halogens		
80	B29 – Group 0: the noble gases		
81	B30 – The transition elements		
82	B31 – Acids		
83	B32 – Neutralization		
84	B33 – Rates of reaction		
85	B34 – Enzymes and their uses		A7
86	B35 – Reversible reactions		
87	B36 – Making ammonia: the Haber process		
88	B37 – Fertilizer production		A33, A36, A37
89	B38 – Exothermic and endothermic reactions		
90	B39 – Breaking and making bonds		

B1 – The particle model for solids, liquids and gases

The particle model helps us to explain many of the physical and chemical properties of materials.

In the particle model, all materials are made up of small particles which are moving about. (It is also called the **kinetic theory**.) The arrangement of particles and their movement is very different in the three **physical states**: solid, liquid and gas.

SOLID

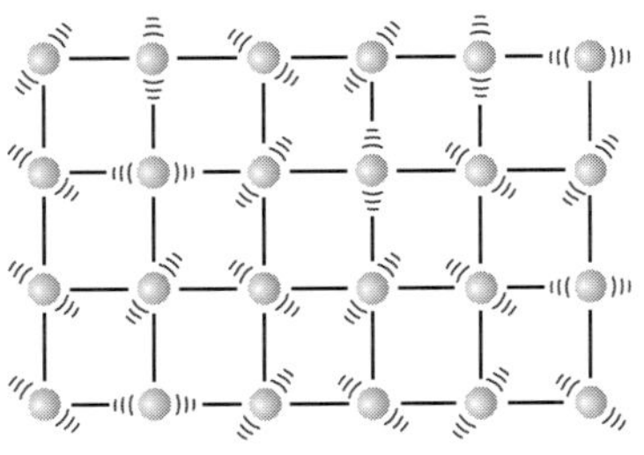

Solids have definite shapes (e.g. crystals). The particles are held in position. They just vibrate.

LIQUID

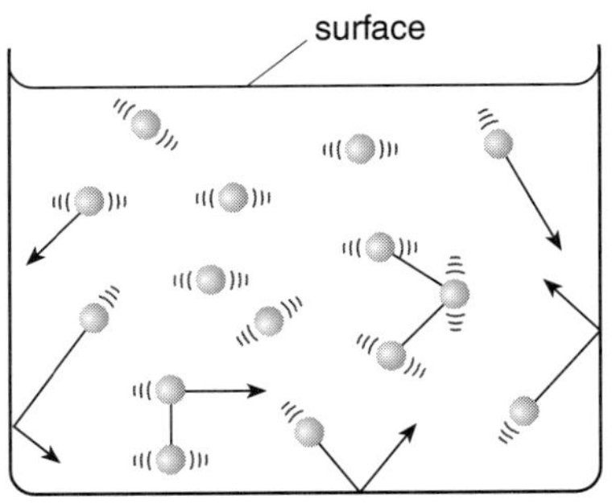

Liquids can **flow**. They fill a container up to a certain level. The particles attract each other but are free to move about beneath the surface. They collide with other particles and with the walls of the container.

GAS

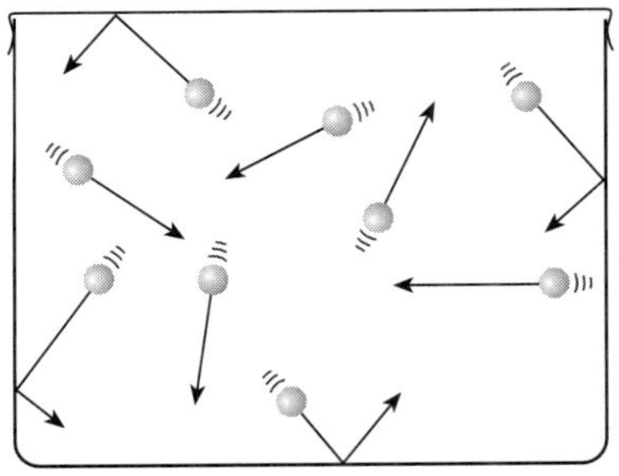

A gas completely fills its container. The particles are free to move about. They collide with the walls and with other particles.

The gas is much less dense than either the solid or the liquid.

Particles move faster if they are given more thermal energy (heat). If solids are given enough energy, they melt. If liquids are given enough energy, they boil.

SOLID **LIQUID** **GAS**

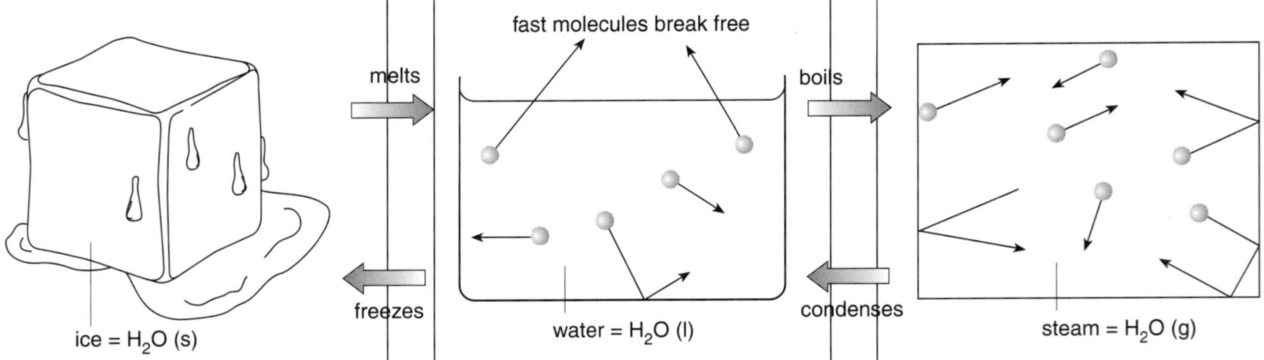

As the solid is heated the particles vibrate more vigorously. When they have enough energy they break away from each other.

The solid **melts**.

As the liquid is heated the particles move faster. Those that have enough energy can break away from the surface.

The liquid eventually **boils**.

As the gas is heated the particles move faster. Because they are moving faster, collisions with the wall create greater pressure.

Note that when the state changes, each particle remains the same. This is a **physical change**.

In a **chemical change**, new particles (molecules) are created. Physical changes are easy to reverse. Reversing chemical changes is usually more difficult.

B2 – Atoms and sub-atomic particles

Elements are made up of very small particles called atoms. Atoms are made up of even smaller sub-atomic particles.

All elements are made up of tiny particles called **atoms**. A diamond this size contains about 20 000 000 000 000 000 000 000 atoms!

Inside atoms there is a very small, dense **nucleus**. The nucleus is positively charged.

Negatively charged electrons move around the nucleus. Because they move so fast and in such complicated orbits we think of them as being like a '**cloud**'.

The charge on the electrons balances the charge on the nucleus: the atom is **neutral**.

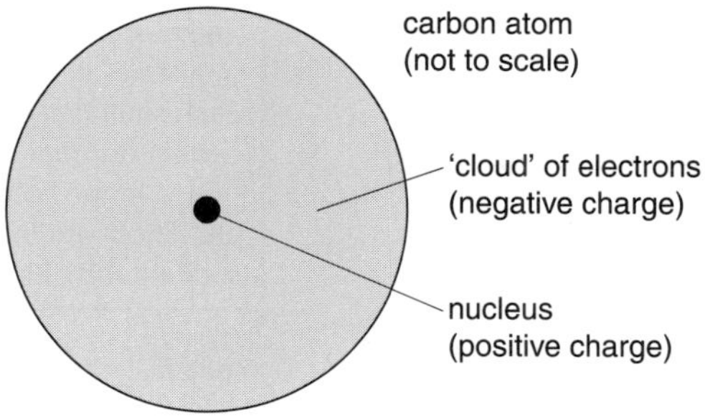

Inside the nucleus there are two types of particle: **protons** and **neutrons**. Protons are positively charged. Neutrons have no charge (neutral).

This carbon atom has six protons and six neutrons in its nucleus.

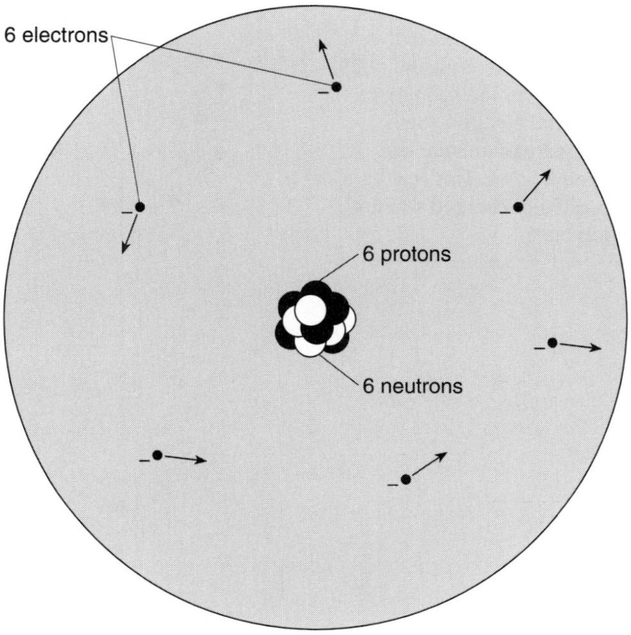

PROPERTIES OF SUB-ATOMIC PARTICLES

particle	mass	electrical charge
electron	nearly 0	negative (–1)
proton	1 atomic mass unit (amu)	positive (+1)
neutron	1 atomic mass unit (amu)	neutral (0)

NOTATION FOR ATOMS

$$^{23}_{11}\mathrm{Na}$$

mass number (or nucleon number) = number of particles (protons + neutrons) in the nucleus

symbol = chemical symbol for the element

atomic number (or Z-number) = number of protons in the nucleus

This atom has 23 particles in the nucleus. (11 protons + 12 neutrons)

This is a sodium atom. (The symbol for sodium is Na.)

This atom has 11 protons in the nucleus. (**All** sodium atoms have 11 protons.)

ISOTOPES

Some elements have different forms of atom called **isotopes**. They have the same number of protons but different numbers of neutrons. This affects their physical properties.

Isotope: carbon-12

$$^{12}_{6}\mathrm{C}$$

6 protons + 6 neutrons

'normal'

Isotope: carbon-14

$$^{14}_{6}\mathrm{C}$$

6 protons + 8 neutrons

'radioactive'

B3 – Making molecules 1: ionic bonding

Molecules are made up of two or more atoms held together.

The element sodium reacts with the element chlorine to produce the compound sodium chloride ('salt'). To form a sodium chloride molecule, one sodium atom has to bond to one chlorine atom.

$$\mathbf{Na + Cl \rightarrow NaCl}$$

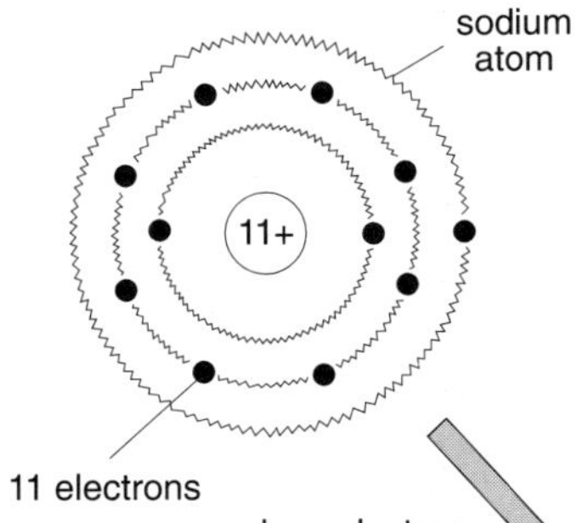

The electrons in **atoms** are arranged in a series of energy levels or **shells**. Each shell can only hold up to a certain number of electrons: 2 in the first, 8 in the second, 8 in the third, etc. These are the structures of the sodium and chlorine atoms.

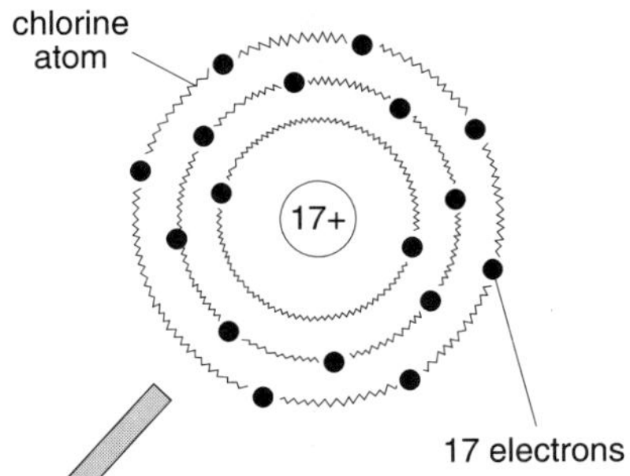

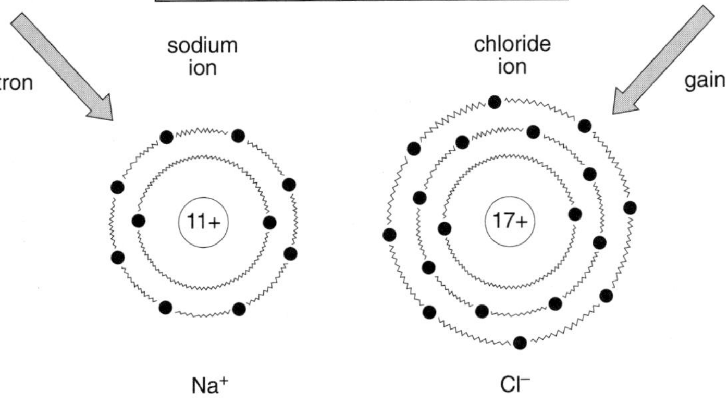

The outer electron of the sodium atom is easily lost. This leaves the sodium with full electron shells but with an unbalanced charge of +1. **This is a positively charged sodium ion Na^+.**

The chlorine atom can easily accept an extra electron into its outer shell. This gives full electron shells but with an unbalanced charge of –1. **This is a negatively charged chloride ion Cl^-.**

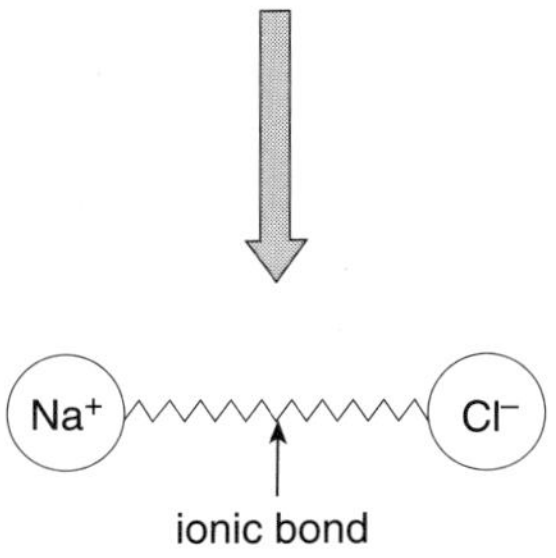

Opposite electrical charges attract. There is an electrostatic force holding the ions together. **This is an ionic bond.**

When sodium chloride molecules form they cluster together. They pack themselves neatly into a huge crystal lattice.

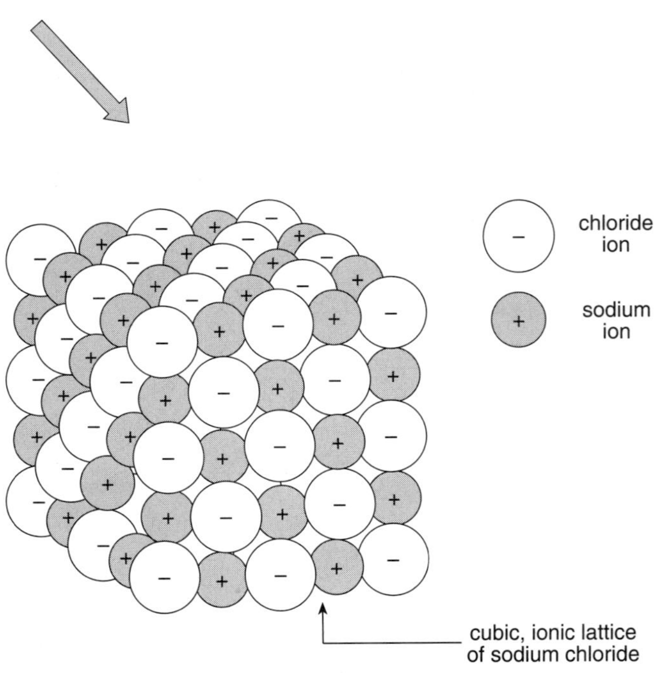

Properties of ionic solids
- They are usually built from the +ve ions of a metal and the –ve ions of a non-metal.
- They form crystals with regular shapes (salt is cubic).
- They are hard and brittle.
- They melt at high temperatures.
- They *do not* conduct electricity when solid.
- They *do* conduct electricity when melted or dissolved in water.
- They dissolve in water.

B4 – Making molecules 2: covalent bonding

The bonds in some molecules are made by 'sharing' electrons between atoms. These are called covalent bonds.

COVALENT BONDS IN ELEMENTS

When atoms of two non-metals react, they both need to gain electrons to fill their electron shells. They do this by 'sharing' an electron in a **covalent bond**. The simplest example is that of two hydrogen atoms bonding to make a hydrogen molecule:

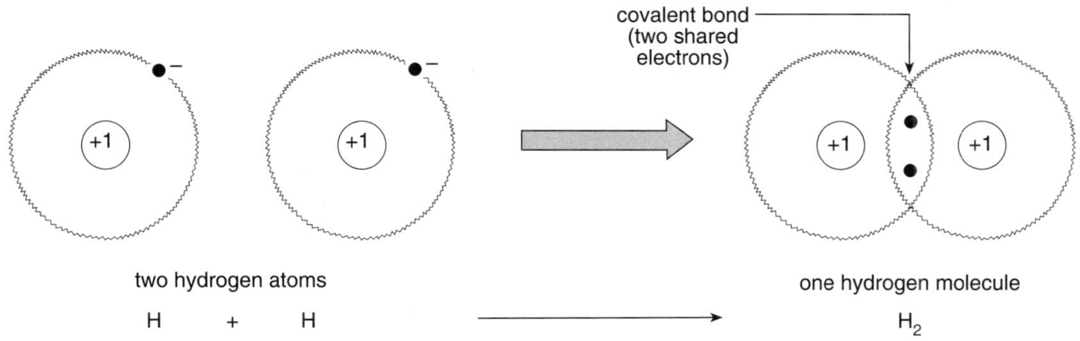

Hydrogen gas is made up of molecules containing two atoms. The formula for hydrogen gas is H_2. Chlorine (Cl_2), nitrogen (N_2) and oxygen (O_2) are all diatomic gases.

COVALENT BONDS IN COMPOUNDS

Compounds have molecules made up of atoms of different elements. Covalent compounds have atoms held together by covalent bonds.

Hydrogen chloride

One hydrogen atom shares an electron with a chlorine atom. The hydrogen fills its outer shell with 2 electrons and the chlorine fills its shell with 8 electrons.

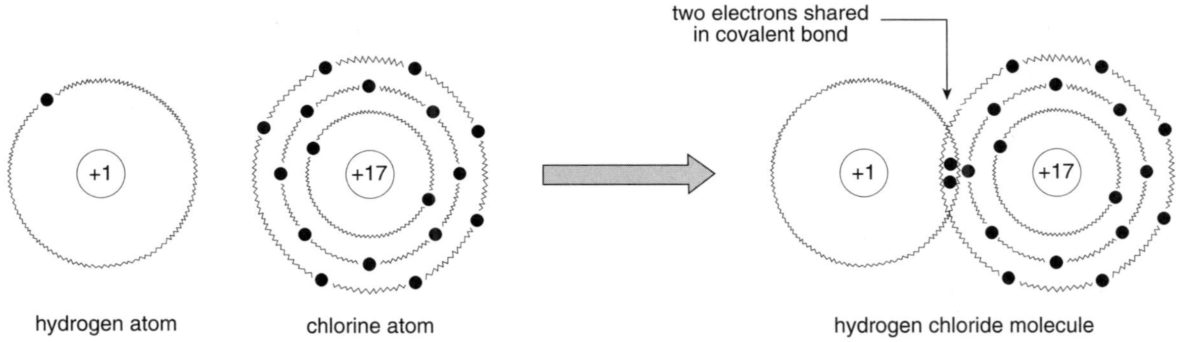

Water

In water, one oxygen molecule shares electrons with two hydrogen atoms. All reach full shells and are bonded together. The molecule is $\mathbf{H_2O}$.

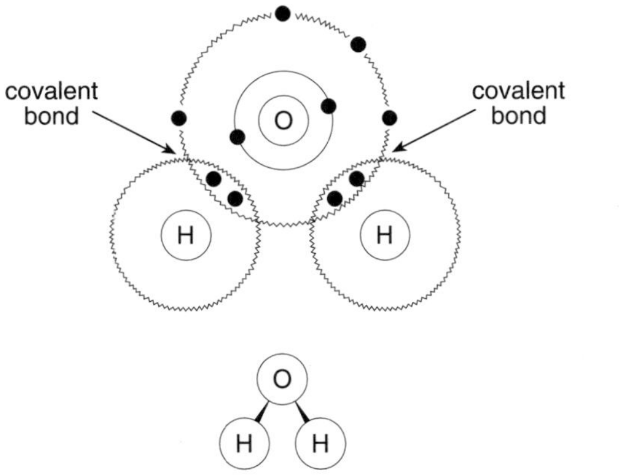

Ammonia

In ammonia, one nitrogen atom has to share electrons with three hydrogen atoms to fill its outer electron shell with 8 electrons. The molecule is $\mathbf{NH_3}$.

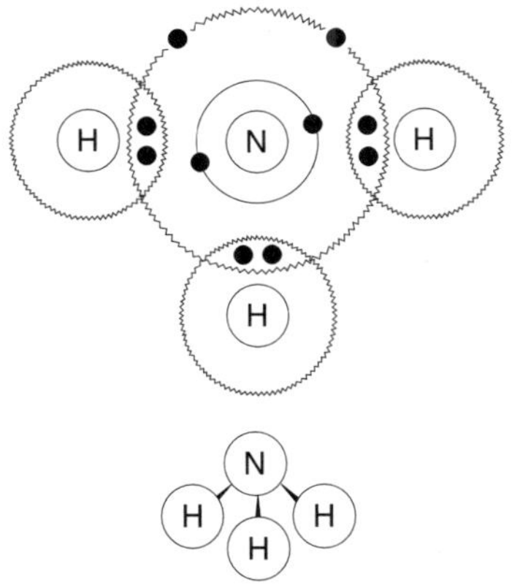

B5 – Structures of molecular solids

Molecules held together by covalent bonds may be held together in giant crystalline structures.

Covalent bonds within molecules are very strong. The forces of attraction between molecules may be very weak.

Carbon dioxide is a simple molecular substance which is a gas at room temperature and pressure. The forces between CO_2 molecules are very weak.

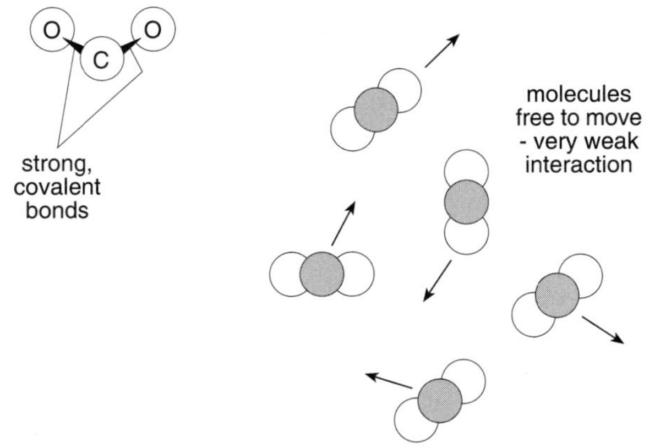

Iodine molecules have covalent bonds. The weak forces between the I_2 molecules hold them in a regular crystalline lattice. However, when heated, the iodine molecules break away easily.

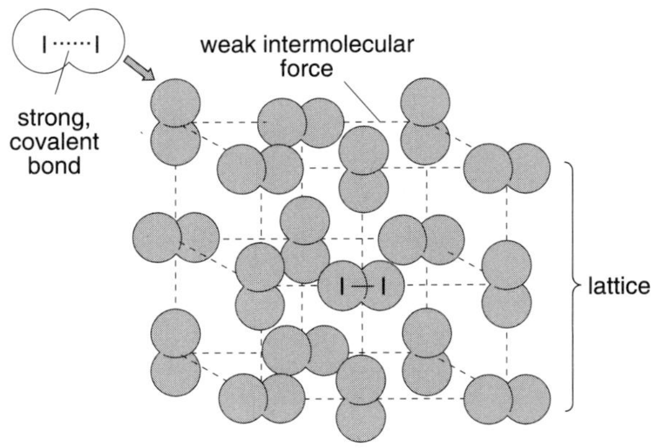

Some molecular solids are arranged so that all the atoms are held by covalent bonds in a **giant crystal lattice**.

Diamonds are giant lattices of carbon atoms bonded together. Each carbon atom is bonded to four others by covalent bonds.

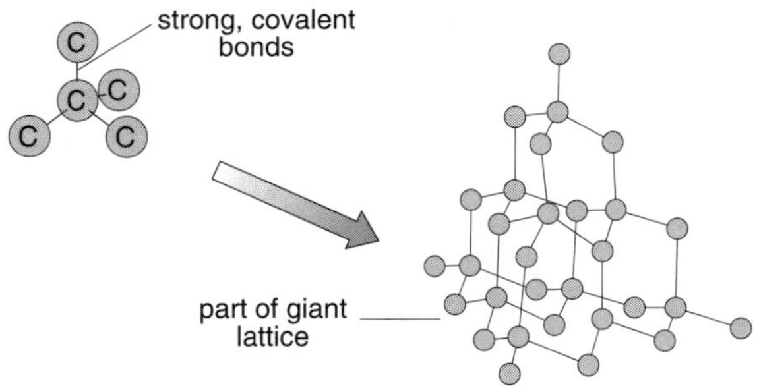

Properties:
- Very hard – the hardest known.
- Very high melting point (3550°C).
- Good insulator - no free charges to conduct electricity.

Graphite is a different form of carbon. It has very different properties from those of diamond because of the way its carbon atoms are bonded and arranged.

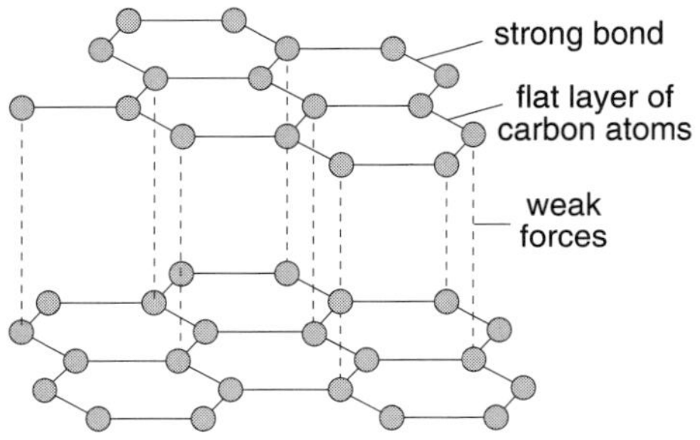

Properties:
- Soft – useful as a lubricant – because layers slip over one another.
- Good conductor – electrons in the weak bonds can move and conduct electricity.

Properties of simple molecular substances
(e.g. oxygen, carbon dioxide, bromine, iodine)

- They have low melting points and boiling points.
- Most are either gases or liquids at room temperature.
- Some are solids which melt easily.
- They do not conduct electricity.

Properties of substances with giant molecular structures
(e.g. silicon dioxide (quartz), carbon (diamond))

- They are solids with very high boiling points.
- They are hard and brittle.
- They do not conduct electricity.

B6 – Oil and its distillation

Oil is an important non-renewable resource. It is used for fuel and for making plastics and chemicals.

WHAT IS 'CRUDE OIL'?

- Oil is a mixture of saturated hydrocarbons.
- Hydrocarbon molecules have carbon and hydrogen atoms bonded together.
- The properties of a particular hydrocarbon depend on the number of carbon atoms and how they are arranged.

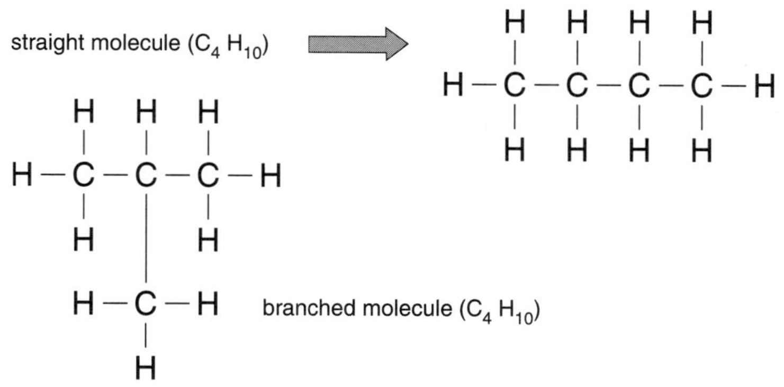

HOW WAS OIL FORMED?

- Oil was made from the bodies of microscopic plants and animals that lived in the seas millions of years ago.
- As sediment was laid down over the decaying organisms, high pressure and heat turned them into oil.
- Oil seeped through porous rocks but in some places it got trapped under folded 'domes' of hard rock. These oil and gas 'fields' are tapped by oil companies.

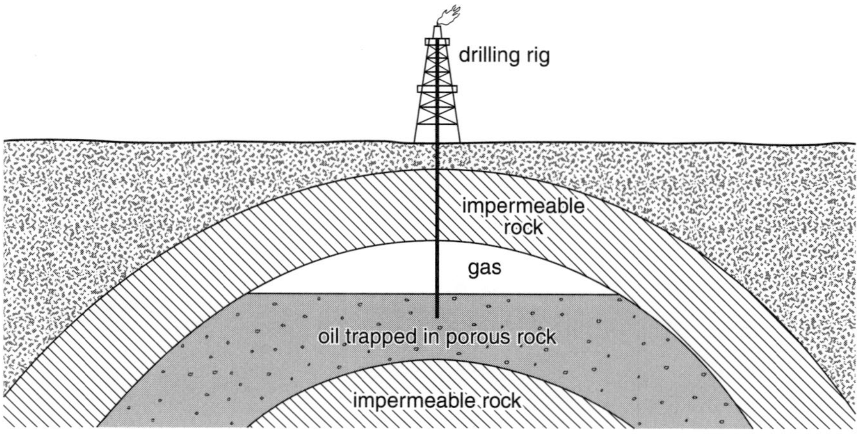

SEPARATING OIL: FRACTIONAL DISTILLATION

The hydrocarbons in crude oil have different boiling points. They can be separated using **fractional distillation**. Hot oil is pumped into the bottom of a tower. Hydrocarbons with lower boiling points move further up the tower before they condense. Different **fractions** are tapped off at different levels.

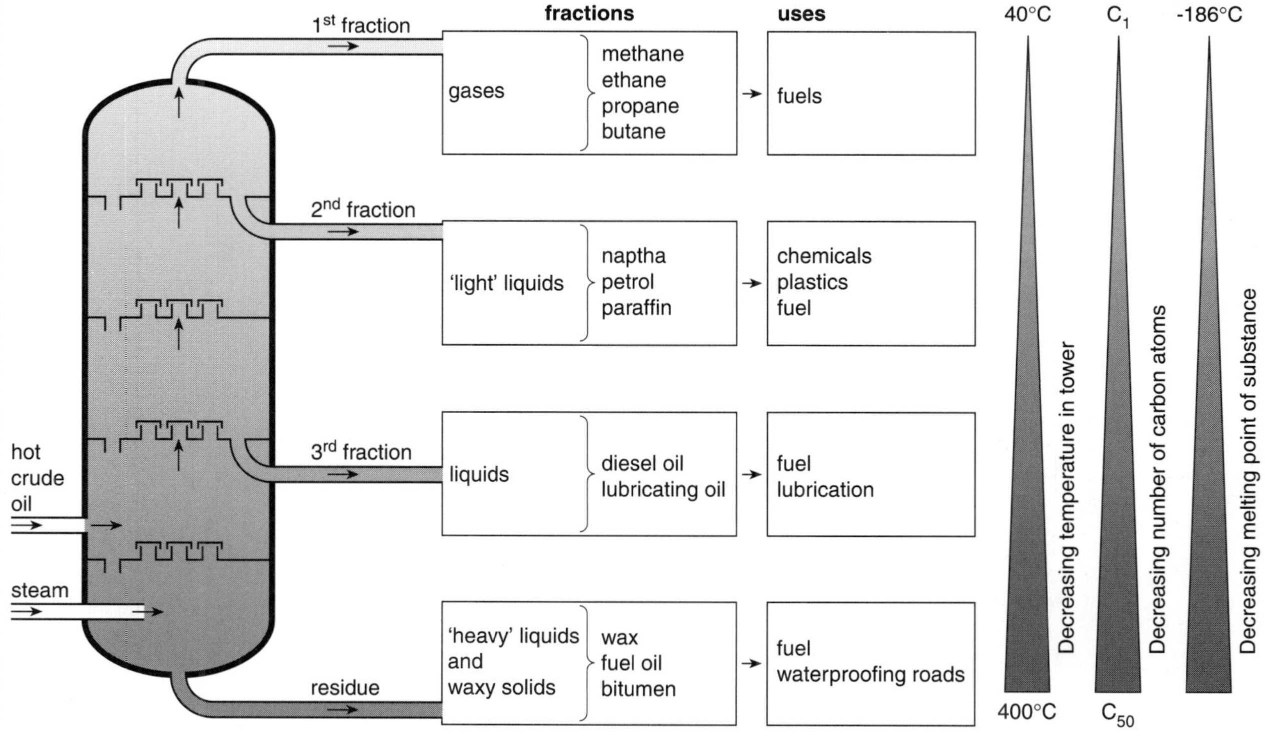

B7 – Combustion of hydrocarbons

Hydrocarbons from oil and natural gas are important fuels.
They are used in heating systems and in engines.

NATURAL GAS AS A FUEL

Many hydrocarbons are used as fuels because they burn in oxygen to release energy. We say that the combustion of hydrocarbons is **exothermic**. When a hydrocarbon burns in plentiful oxygen, the products are carbon dioxide and water (as a gas). These are colourless, odourless, tasteless and non-toxic. However, carbon dioxide is a **greenhouse gas** and so adds to global warming.

Natural gas is almost pure methane (CH_4). The equation for the complete combustion of methane is:

$$CH_4\,(g) + 2O_2\,(g) \rightarrow CO_2\,(g) + 2H_2O\,(g) + \textbf{energy}$$

methane (gas)	+	oxygen (gas)	→	carbon dioxide (gas)	+	water (gas)	+	698 kJ for every mole (16 g) of methane

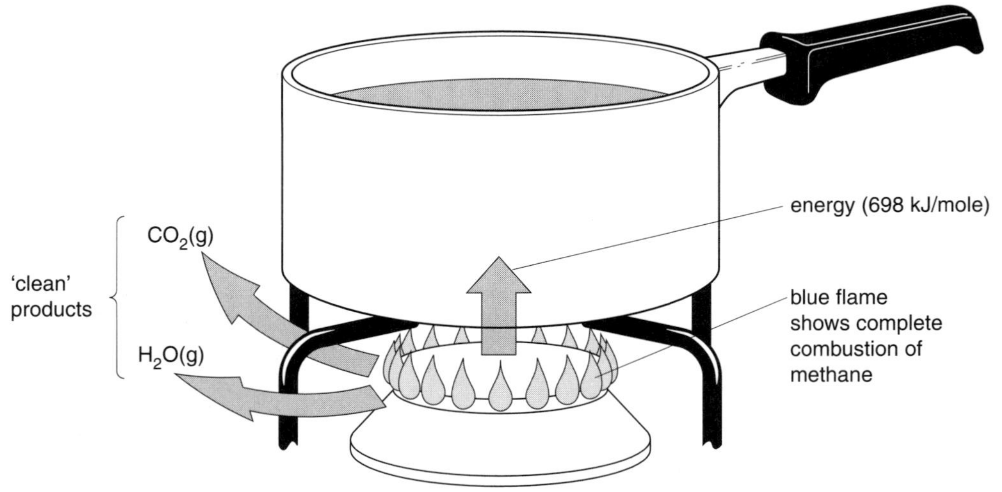

INCOMPLETE COMBUSTION

If there is not enough oxygen to burn the hydrocarbon completely, carbon monoxide (CO) gas is produced. Carbon monoxide is colourless and odourless but it is dangerous to breathe and can cause death by asphyxiation (suffocation). It reacts with the haemoglobin in red blood cells, preventing them from carrying oxygen. It is very dangerous to use a gas heater in a room without good ventilation or to run a car engine in a closed garage.

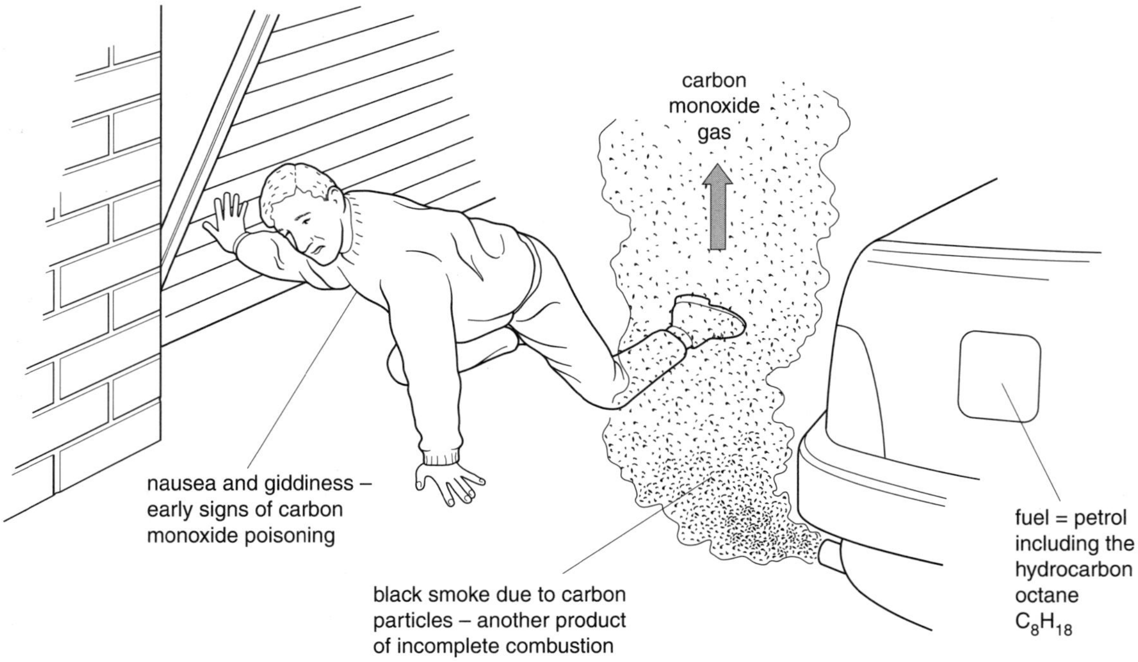

B8 – Alkanes and alkenes

Alkanes and alkenes make up two 'families' of hydrocarbons. They differ in the way their carbon atoms are bonded together.

ALKANES – A 'FAMILY' OF SATURATED HYDROCARBONS

What are alkanes?

Alkanes are **saturated** hydrocarbons. Each carbon atom is joined to four carbon or hydrogen atoms by single, covalent bonds.

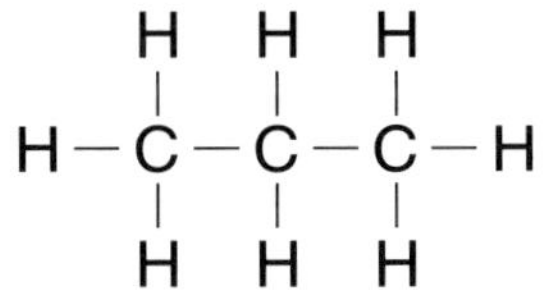

propane

Formulae

methane CH_4

ethane C_2H_6

propane C_3H_8

butane C_4H_{10}

general C_nH_{2n+2}

add $-CH_2$ each time

Physical properties

The alkanes form a homologous series. The physical properties change gradually as the number of carbon atoms increases.

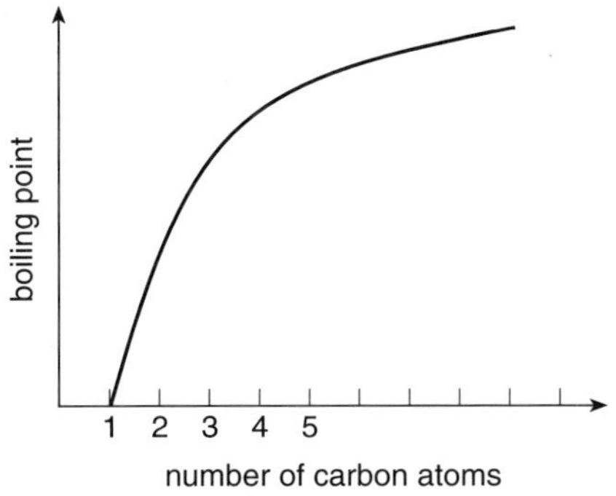

Chemical properties

The alkanes are not generally very reactive but they burn well in oxygen.

$$C_3H_8 + 5O_2 \rightarrow 3CO_2 + 4H_2O + \text{energy}$$

ALKENES – A 'FAMILY' OF UNSATURATED HYDROCARBONS

What are alkenes?

Alkenes are **unsaturated** hydrocarbons. Two carbon atoms are joined by a double covalent bond.

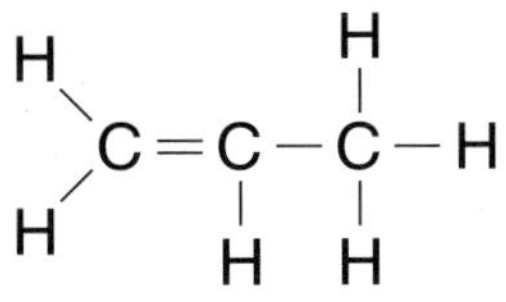

propene

Formulae

ethane C_2H_4

propane C_3H_6

butane C_4H_8

general C_nH_{2n}

add $-CH_2$ each time

The alkenes form a homologous series. Their physical properties change gradually as the number of carbon atoms increases.

Chemical properties

The carbon–carbon double bond makes alkenes more reactive than alkanes. The double bond can be 'opened' and other atoms added. These are **addition reactions**.

With hydrogen: when heated over a nickel catalyst, extra hydrogen is added, making an alkane.

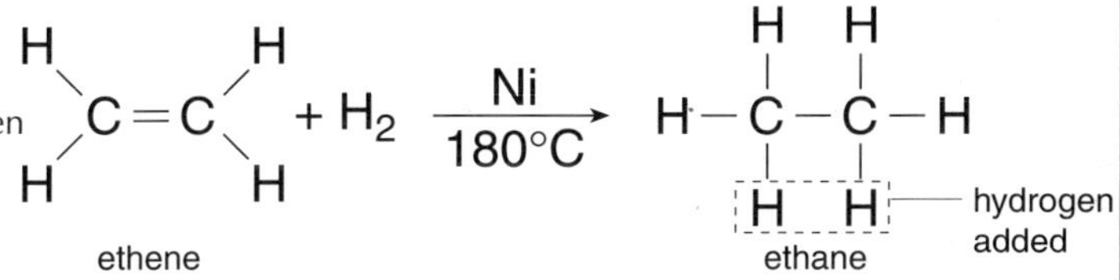

With bromine: when shaken with bromine water, the orange colour of the bromine disappears as the bromine reacts with the alkene.

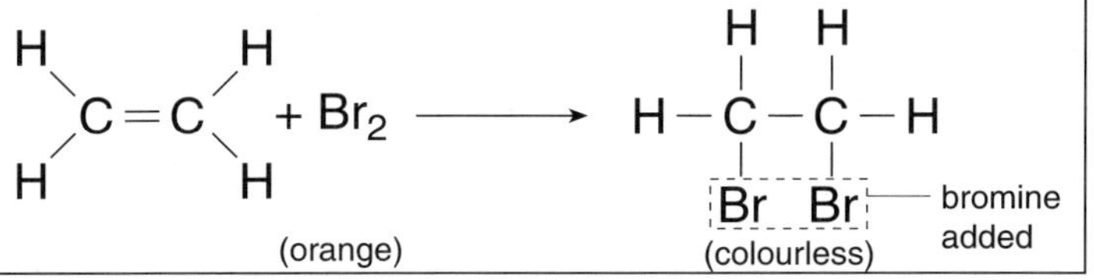

B9 – Cracking and polymerization

Long molecules from crude oil can be made into more valuable shorter molecules by cracking. Small molecules can be linked together to make useful **polymers**.

CRACKING: Distillation of crude oil separates the hydrocarbons into fractions. There is a big demand for the 'petrol' fraction but not so much for the others. Cracking breaks long chain molecules into shorter chains.

decane ($C_{10}H_{22}$)

heat at very high temperature for short time **(thermal cracking)**
or
heat over a catalyst **(catalytic cracking)**

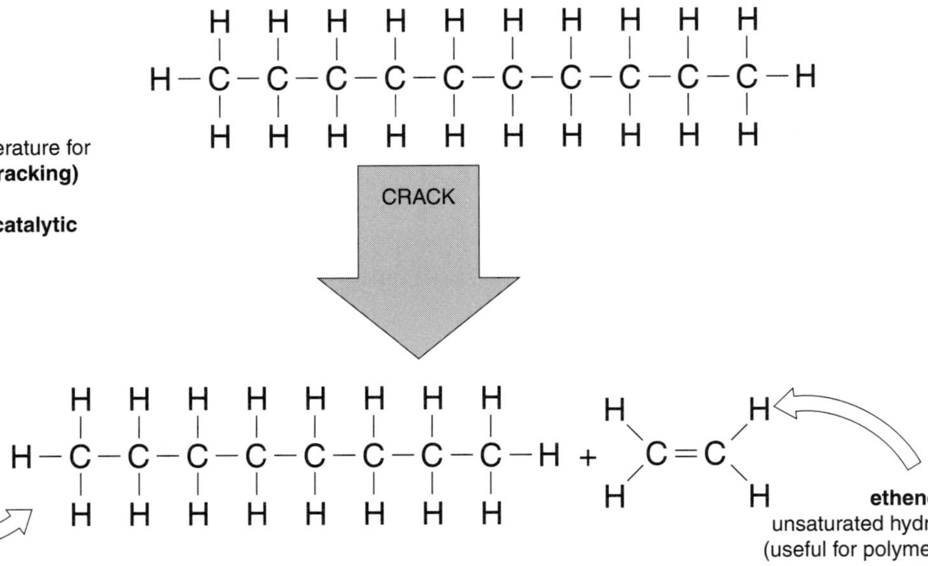

octane (C_8H_{18})
valuable for use in petrol

ethene (C_2H_4)
unsaturated hydrocarbon
(useful for polymerization)

Polymerization: When heated under pressure or in the presence of a catalyst, the double bonds in small alkene molecules are broken. Single bonds form to make very long molecules. Some of these are very useful plastics.

ethene (C_2H_4)
simple alkene molecule
the monomer (basic unit) for making polyethene (polythene)

heat at very high temperature
under great pressure
or
heat over a catalyst

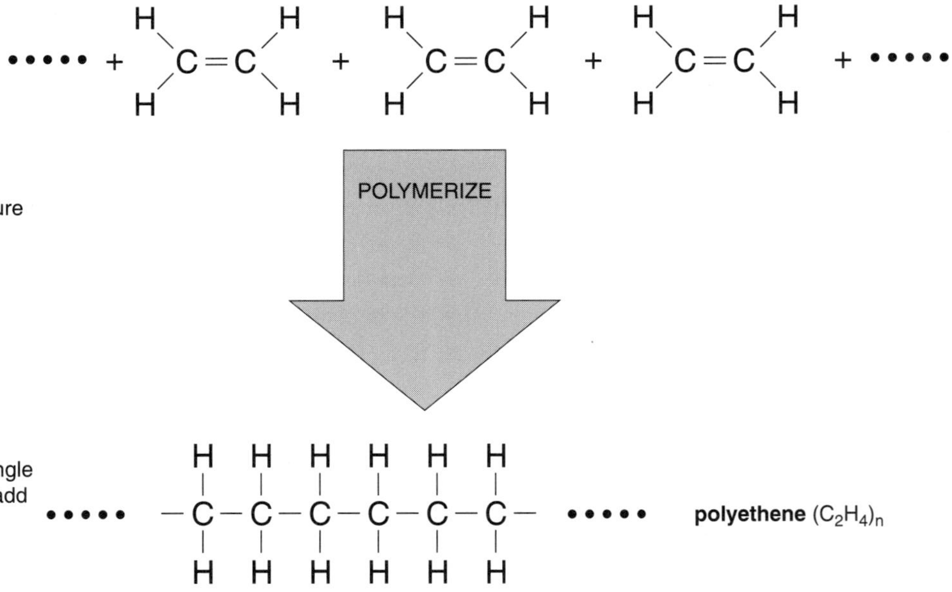

The double bonds break and single bonds re-form. The monomers add together. This is **addition polymerization**.

polyethene $(C_2H_4)_n$

Name of polymer	Monomer used	Uses of polymer
polyethene (polythene)	ethene (C_2H_4)	plastic bags, sheeting, bottles
polyvinyl chloride (pvc)	chloroethene (vinyl chloride) (C_2H_3Cl)	bottles, hoses, pipes, raincoats
polystyrene	styrene (C_8H_8)	insulating foams, cups, packaging

B10 – Metals: structure and properties

The physical properties of metals make them very important materials.

PHYSICAL PROPERTIES OF METALS

- good thermal conductivity
- reflective when polished
- good electrical conductivity
- ductile (can be drawn into wires)
- malleable (can be shaped and beaten into sheets)

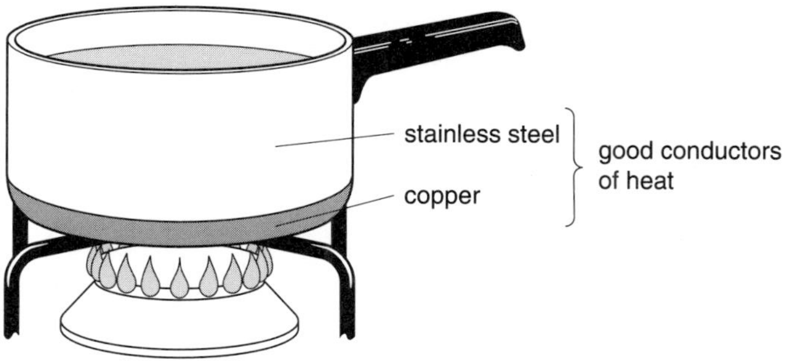

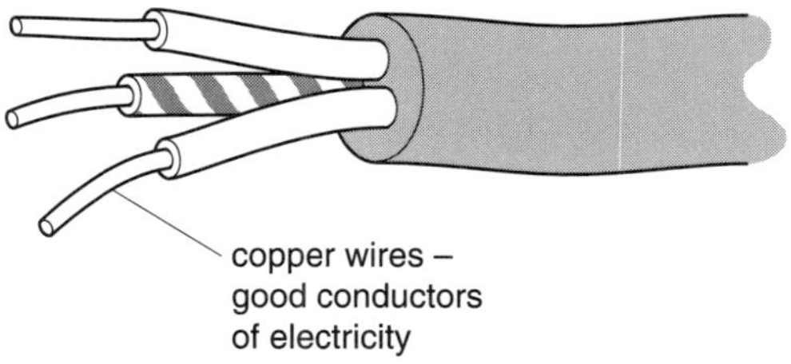

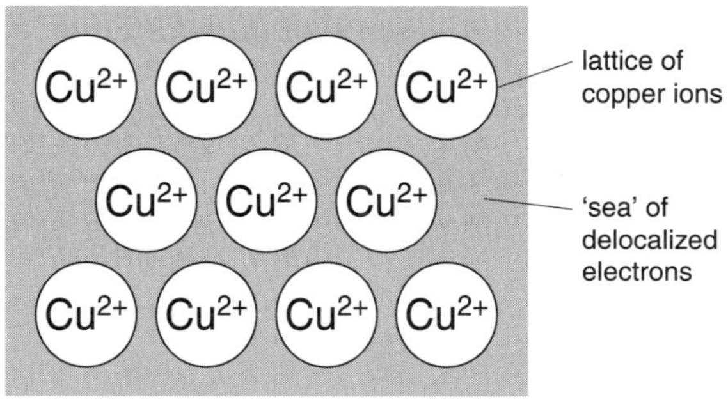

STRUCTURE OF METALS

Metal atoms form positive ions by losing electrons.

The ions are closely packed together in a regular lattice.

Around the ions there is a 'sea' of delocalized electrons.

The electrons are free to move.

ELECTRICAL CONDUCTIVITY

When a voltage is applied across a metal, the negatively charged electrons can drift through the metal lattice.

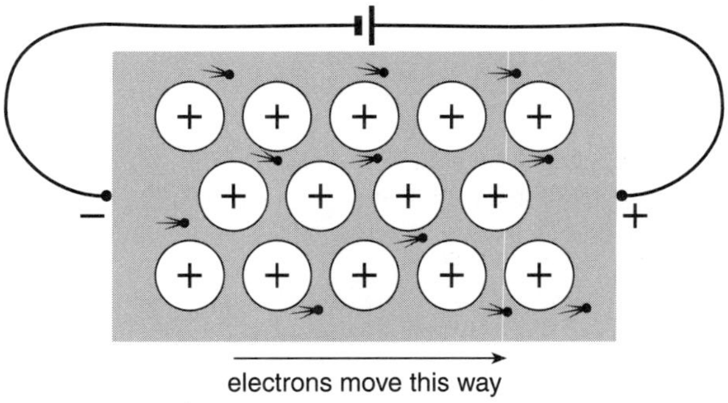

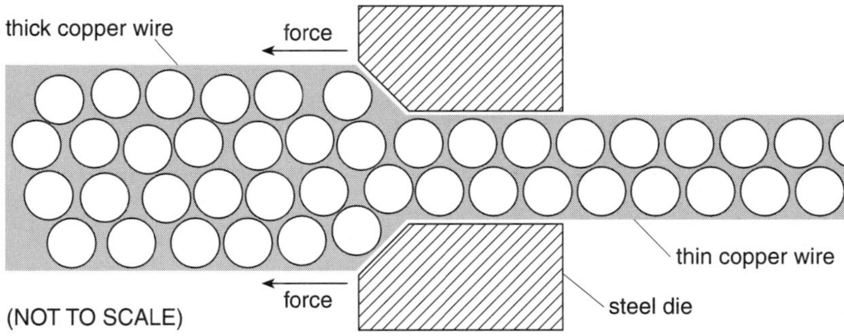

MALLEABILITY AND DUCTILITY

When forces are applied to a metal, the layers of ions in the lattice slide over each other. This allows metals to be drawn into wires or hammered into shape (malleability). If the metal does not lose its strength during this process it is said to be ductile.

B11 – Reactions of metals 1

Metals react with oxygen, acids, and water in characteristic ways. Some metals are much more reactive than others.

REACTIONS WITH OXYGEN

Some metals burn easily in oxygen to form oxides. Others react only if the metal is heated strongly.

If the metal oxide dissolves in water it forms an alkaline solution (pH>7).

Magnesium burns in air with a brilliant, white light. Magnesium oxide is left.

magnesium	+	oxygen	→	magnesium oxide
2Mg	+	**O_2**	→	**2MgO**
(shiny metal)		(colourless gas)		(white, flaky powder)

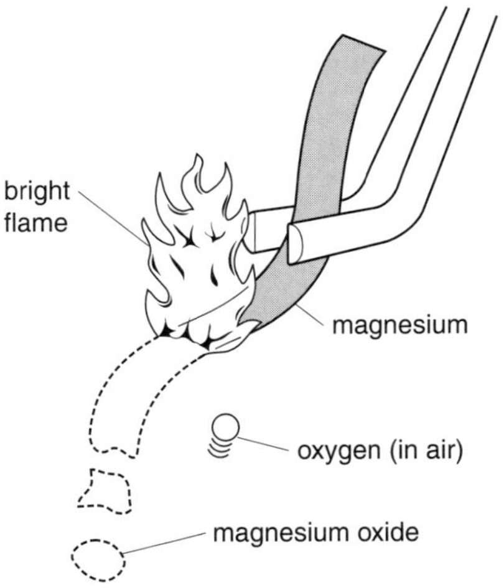

Metals that burn easily in air		Metals that react with oxygen when heated strongly		Metal that does not react with oxygen when heated strongly
sodium	magnesium	iron	copper	gold
← increasing reactivity				

REACTIONS WITH HYDROCHLORIC ACID

Some metals react with cold, dilute hydrochloric acid. Others react only if the acid is concentrated.

When metals react with acids, hydrogen gas is given off.

metal + acid → hydrogen + metal salt

Magnesium reacts with cold, dilute hydrochloric acid. Bubbles of hydrogen gas are given off. The salt formed is magnesium chloride.

magnesium	+	hydrochloric acid	→	hydrogen	+	magnesium chloride
Mg	+	**2HCl**	→	**H_2**	+	**$MgCl_2$**

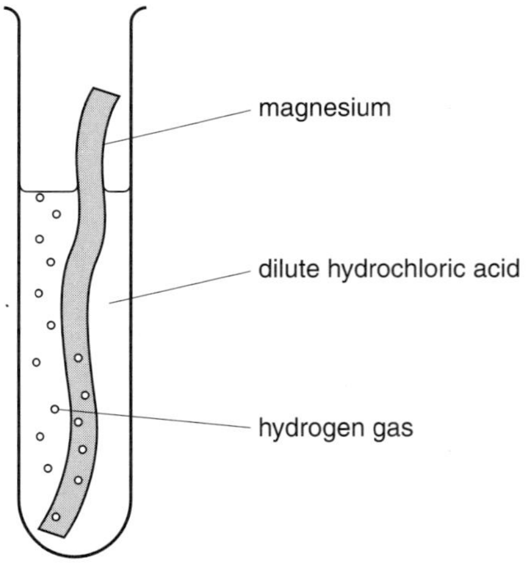

Metals that react vigorously with cold, dilute hydrochloric acid		Metals that react slowly with dilute hydrochloric acid		Metals that react with concentrated hydrochloric acid	Metals that do not react even with concentrated hydrochloric acid	
sodium	magnesium	zinc	iron	lead	copper	gold
← increasing reactivity						

B12 – Reactions of metals 2

We can place the metals in order of their reactivity. This is a reactivity series.

REACTIONS WITH WATER

Some metals react vigorously with cold water. Others react only when heated in steam. When they react they give off hydrogen gas.

Sodium metal reacts vigorously with cold water. Hydrogen gas is given off. An alkaline solution of sodium hydroxide is also produced.

sodium + water → hydrogen + sodium hydroxide solution

$$2Na + 2H_2O \rightarrow H_2 + 2NaOH\ (aq)$$

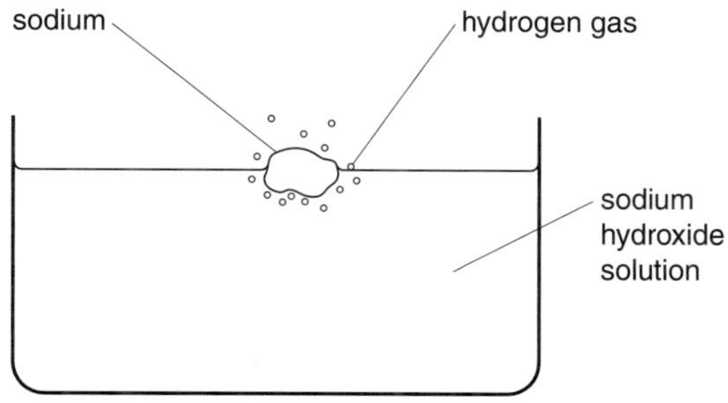

Metals that react vigorously with cold water	Metals that react with cold water	Metals that react slowly with steam	Metals that do not react with steam
potassium sodium	calcium magnesium	zinc iron	copper gold

← increasing reactivity
reactivity series

COMPETITION BETWEEN METALS

When two metals 'compete' in a chemical reaction, the outcome depends on the positions of the metals in the reactivity series.

- A reactive metal will take the oxygen from the oxide of a less reactive metal.
- A reactive metal will displace a less reactive metal from a solution of its salt.

Competing for oxygen

When iron powder is heated with copper oxide, a reaction starts. The iron 'takes' the oxygen from the copper oxide. Copper metal is left.

The more reactive iron has **reduced** the copper oxide.

iron + copper(II) oxide → iron(II) oxide + copper

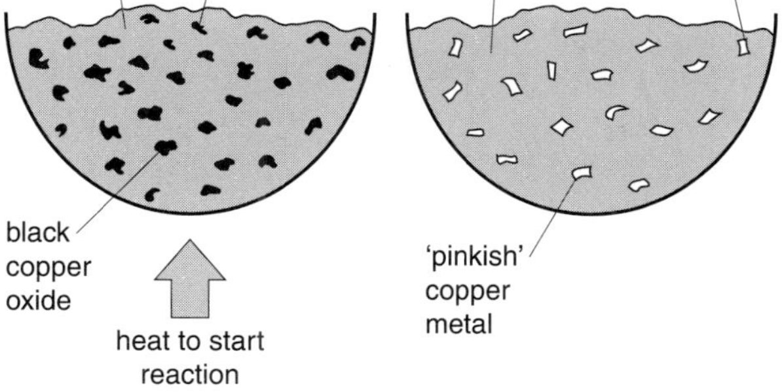

Displacement reactions

When copper wire is placed in silver nitrate solution, a reaction takes place. Crystals of silver metal appear and the solution turns blue as copper nitrate is formed. The more reactive copper has **displaced** the silver from the silver nitrate solution.

copper + silver nitrate solution → silver + copper nitrate solution

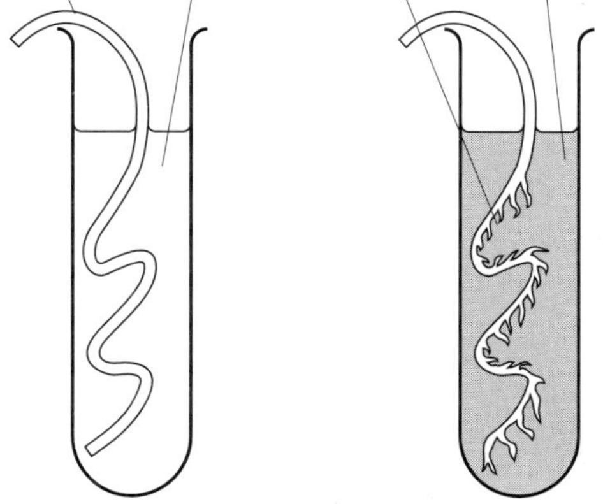

B13 – Extracting metals

Most metals are found in the rocks of the Earth's crust combined with other elements. These are the ores from which we extract pure metals.

Most metals are too reactive to be found as elements in the Earth. Gold and silver (and sometimes copper) are found as pure metals but the other metals have to be extracted from their compounds (**ores**).

The method of extracting a metal from its ore depends on the reactivity of the metal. In general, the more reactive the metal, the more difficult (and expensive) it is to extract.

Reactivity	Metal	Method of Extraction
very reactive	Potassium	Electrolysis of molten compound
	Sodium	
	Calcium	
	Magnesium	
	Aluminium	
	Zinc	Heat with carbon in a blast furnace
	Iron	
	Copper	Heat the ore in air
unreactive	Gold	Found as a pure metal

EXTRACTION OF IRON

Iron is found as the ore **haematite**. This is mainly iron(III) oxide.

Because iron is not a very reactive metal, iron oxide can be reduced by heating it with carbon.

In the blast furnace, coke (carbon) and limestone (calcium carbonate) produce carbon dioxide:

$$C + O_2 \rightarrow CO_2$$

$$CaCO_3 \rightarrow CaO + CO_2$$

The carbon dioxide reacts with coke to give carbon monoxide:

$$CO_2 + C \rightarrow 2CO$$

The carbon monoxide then reduces the iron oxide:

$$3CO + Fe_2O_3 \rightarrow 2Fe + 3CO_2$$

Molten iron is run off from the bottom of the furnace.

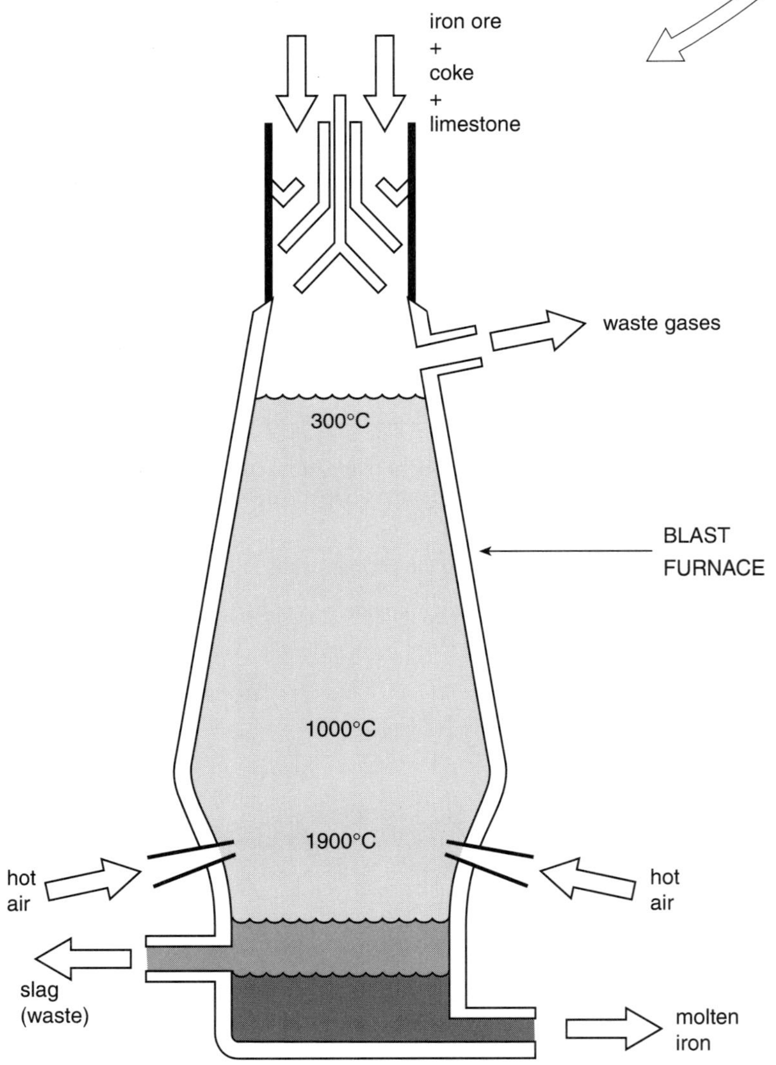

B14 – Electrolysis and processing of metals

Reactive metals are extracted by electrolysis of their molten compounds. Impure metals can be purified by electrolysis.

EXTRACTION OF ALUMINIUM BY ELECTROLYSIS

Bauxite is the main ore of aluminium. It is mainly aluminium oxide with impurities of sand and iron oxide.

The ore is purified to give pure aluminium oxide (alumina). This is then dissolved in cryolite (Na_3AlF_6) at about 950°C.

The alumina/cryolite solution has an electric current passed through it in an electrolysis cell.

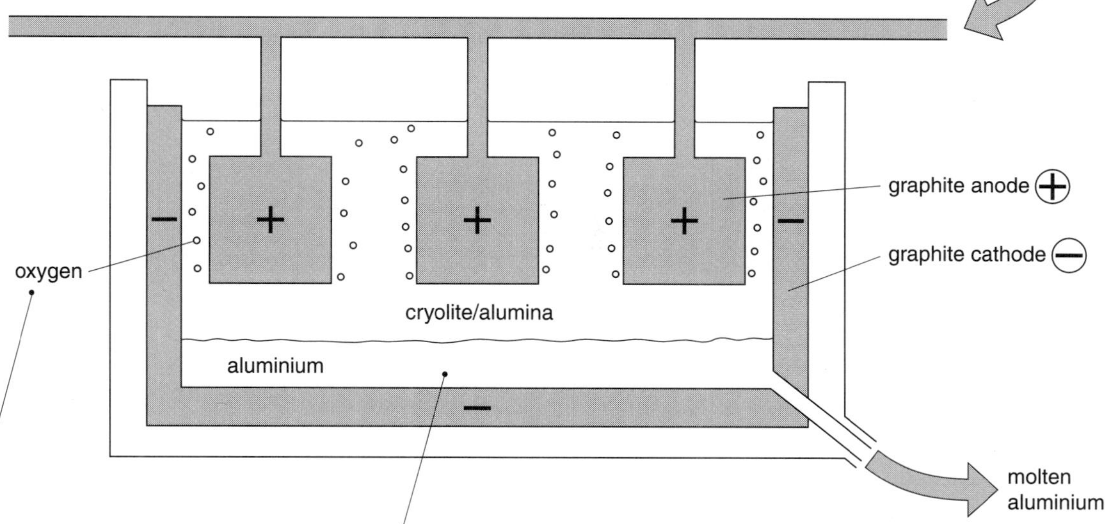

At the anodes, oxygen ions give up their spare electrons to become atoms. Oxygen gas is released.

$$2O^{2-} - 4e^- \rightarrow O_2$$

(ions lose electrons to become atoms)

Aluminium ions are positively charged. They move to the negative electrodes (cathodes). At the cathode, the ions pick up electrons and become aluminium atoms.

$$Al^{3+} + 3e^- \rightarrow 3Al$$

(ions gain electrons to become atoms)

The heating of the cryolite and the electrolysis takes a great deal of energy. Extracting aluminium is therefore very expensive.

Recycling scrap aluminium is much cheaper.

PURIFICATION OF COPPER BY ELECTROLYSIS

Copper is produced by heating its ore (copper sulphide) in oxygen. The copper produced is impure. It is purified by electrolysis.

Cathode (–ve)
pure copper

copper ions from solution gain electrons to become atoms

$$Cu^{2+} + 2e^- \rightarrow Cu$$

cathode is plated with pure copper

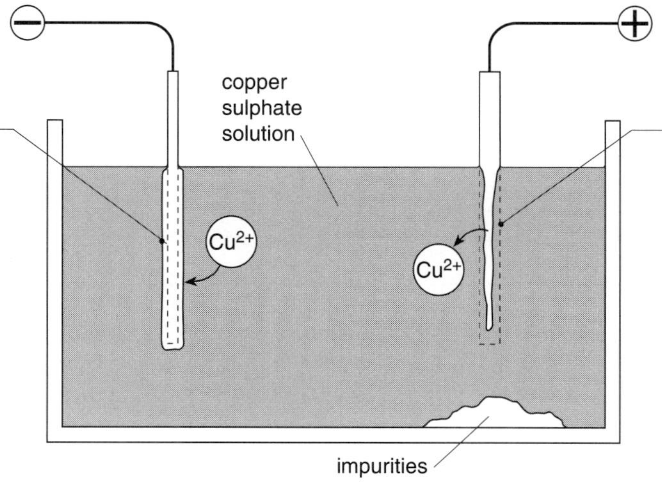

Anode (+ve)
impure copper

copper atoms lose electrons to become ions and move into solution

$$Cu - 2e^- \rightarrow Cu^{2+}$$

anode dissolves: impurities fall to bottom of electrolysis cell

B15 – Writing formulae and equations 1

The formula of a compound tells us what elements it contains and in what proportions.

MOLECULAR FORMULAE

- Molecules are made up of atoms held together by bonds.
- In most compounds, the molecule contains a positive ion bound to a negative ion.
- Ions join together in the right proportions to make neutral molecules.
- The formula of a compound tells us what elements it contains. It also tells us how many atoms there are in each molecule.

Common positive ions		Common negative ions	
Name	**Formula**	**Name**	**Formula**
hydrogen	H^+	chloride	Cl^-
potassium	K^+	oxide	O^{2-}
sodium	Na^+	hydroxide	OH^-
calcium	Ca^{2+}	carbonate	CO_3^{2-}
magnesium	Mg^{2+}	nitrate	NO_3^-
copper(I)	Cu^+	sulphate	SO_4^{2-}
copper(II)	Cu^{2+}		
iron(II)	Fe^{2+}		
iron(III)	Fe^{3+}		
aluminium	Al^{3+}		

Sodium ions have one positive charge Na^+.

Chloride ions have one negative charge Cl^-.

In sodium chloride (salt) one Na^+ is joined to one Cl^- ion.

The formula is NaCl.

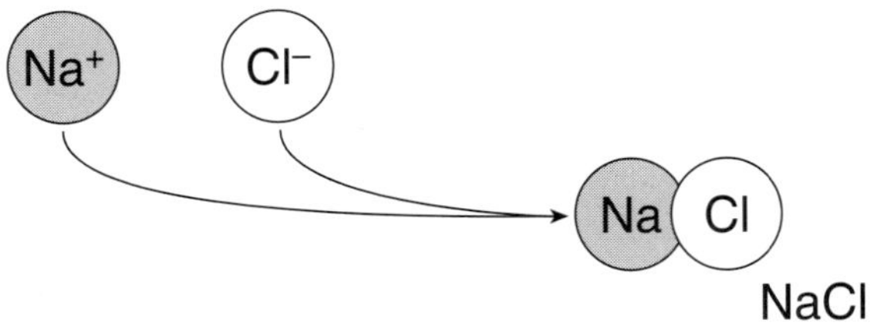

Hydrogen ions have one positive charge H^+.

Oxide ions have two negative charges O^{2-}.

In hydrogen oxide (water) two H^+ ions are joined to one O^{2-} ion.

The formula is H_2O.

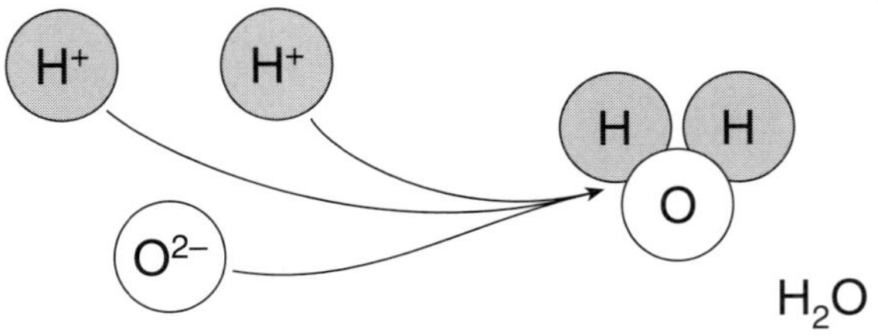

Aluminium ions have three positive charges Al^{3+}.

Oxide ions have two negative charges O^{2-}.

In aluminium oxide two aluminium ions are joined to three oxide ions.

The formula is Al_2O_3.

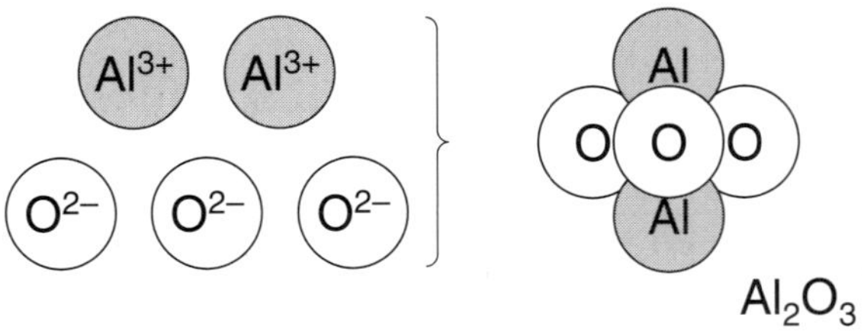

SYMBOLS OF STATE

State symbols tell you whether a chemical is a solid (*s*), a liquid (*l*), or a gas (*g*). There is also a symbol (*aq*) to tell you that the chemical is dissolved in water.

Example:

copper(II) carbonate	+	sulphuric acid	$\rightarrow$	carbon dioxide	+	copper sulphate	+	water
$CuSO_4(s)$	+	$H_2SO_4(aq)$	$\rightarrow$	$CO_2(g)$	+	$CuSO_4(aq)$	+	$H_2O(l)$

B16 – Writing formulae and equations 2

An equation tells what happens when a chemical reaction takes place. It tells us about the **reactants** and the products, and about the quantities involved.

WRITING A BALANCED EQUATION

1 Start with a word equation describing the reactants and the products.

hydrogen reacts with oxygen to form water (hydrogen oxide)

2 Write the equation using chemical symbols.

$$H_2 + O_2 \Rightarrow H_2O$$

3 Check that you have the same number of atoms of each element on both sides of the equation.

Left side: two H and two O — *Right side: two H and one O*

not balanced!

4 If necessary, balance the equation.

$$2H_2 + O_2 \Rightarrow 2H_2O$$

Left side: four H and two O — *Right side: four H and two O*

balanced!

BALANCING EQUATIONS IN ELECTROLYSIS

A direct electric current splits water into hydrogen and oxygen.

We can write equations for what happens at the electrodes.

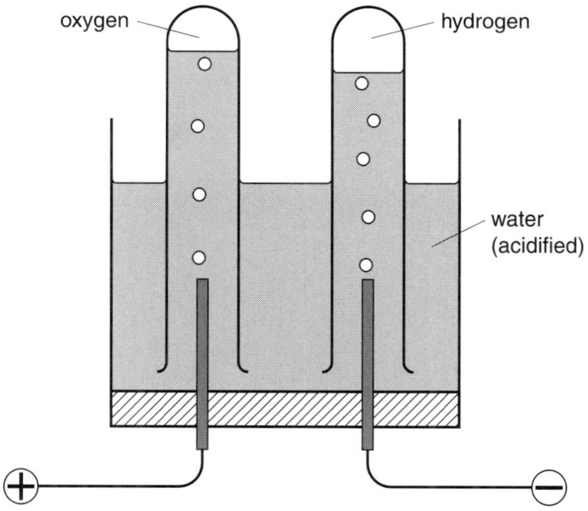

At the anode (+)

Each oxygen ion gives up two electrons to become an atom.

$$O^{2-} - 2e^- \rightarrow O$$

But to release one oxygen molecule (O_2) at the anode we need two ions to give up their electrons.

$$2O^{2-} - 4e^- \rightarrow O_2$$

At the cathode (–)

Each hydrogen ion takes one electron to become an atom.

$$H^+ + e^- \rightarrow H$$

But to release one hydrogen molecule (H_2) at the anode we need two ions to gain electrons.

$$2H^+ + 2e^- \rightarrow H_2$$

$$2O^{2-} - 4e^- \rightarrow O_2 \ : \ 4H^+ + 4e^- \rightarrow 2H_2$$

In the cell, the number of electrons taken in at the anode must balance the number of electrons given out at the cathode. We must balance the electrode reactions.

Notice that the electric current produces *one* volume of oxygen and *two* volumes of hydrogen.

B17 – Moles and reacting masses

An equation tells about the number of atoms involved in a reaction. We often need to know about the masses of the reactants and the products.

RELATIVE ATOMIC MASSES

The atoms of different elements have different masses. The **Relative Atomic Mass** (**RAM**) tells us what the mass of an atom is compared with a standard carbon-12 (^{12}C) atom. The table gives relative masses for some common elements.

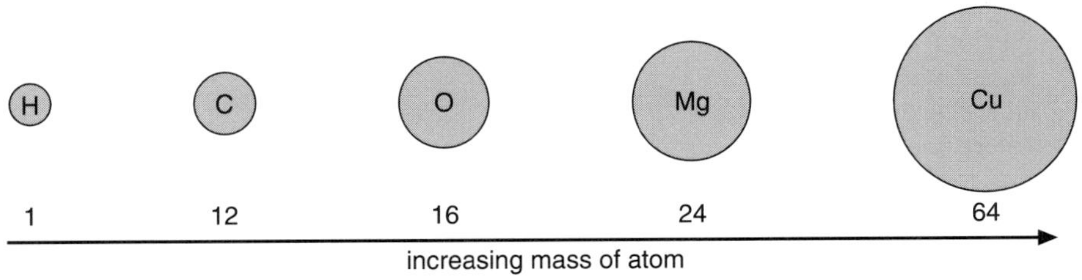

Element	RAM	Element	RAM
hydrogen (H)	1	sulphur (S)	32
carbon (C)	12	chlorine (Cl)	35.5
oxygen (O)	16	iron (Fe)	56
sodium (Na)	23	copper (Cu)	64
magnesium (Mg)	24	iodine (I)	127

RELATIVE MOLECULAR MASSES

To work out the relative mass of a molecule (**RMM**), you have to know its formula. Then you just add up the relative masses for all the atoms in the molecule.

hydrogen H_2 — RMM = 2 × 1 = 2

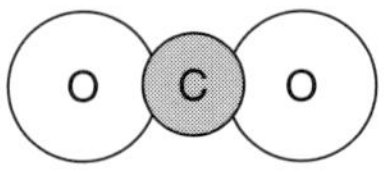

carbon dioxide CO_2 — RMM = 12 + (2 × 16) = 44

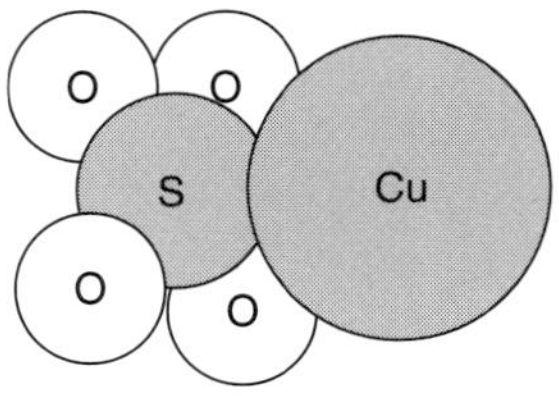

copper(II) sulphate $CuSO_4$ — RMM = 64 + 32 + (4 × 16) = 160

THE MOLE

A chemical equation tells us about the **numbers** of particles taking part in a reaction. The **mole** is the unit which is used for counting particles.

$$2Mg + O_2 \longrightarrow 2MgO$$ (balanced equation)

One mole of a substance contains 6 × 10^{23} atoms or molecules.

2 moles of magnesium + 2 mole of oxygen → 2 moles of magnesium oxide

One mole of a substance has a mass equal to the RMM in grams.

(2 × 24)g   (2 × 16)g   (2 × (24 + 16)g

Mass is conserved in chemical reactions.

48g of magnesium + 32g of oxygen → 80g of magnesium oxide

B18 – Finding masses and formulae

We can use moles and relative molecular masses to calculate the masses of reactants and products in a reaction. If we know the reacting masses, we can find the formula of a compound.

CALCULATING MASSES IN A REACTION

Example:

Methane (CH_4) burns in oxygen to produce carbon dioxide and water.

If we burn 48 g of methane how much CO_2 will be produced?

How much oxygen will be used in the reaction?

Write a balanced equation for the reaction.	CH_4	+	$2O_2$	$\longrightarrow$	CO_2	+	$2H_2O$
Write the number of moles for each substance.	1 mole		2 moles		1 mole		2 moles
	(12 + 4)		2 × (2 × 16)		12 + (2 × 16)		2 × ((2 × 1) + 16)
Use the relative molecular mass of each substance to calculate the reacting masses.	16 g	+	64 g	$\longrightarrow$	44 g	+	36 g
Divide by 16 to find what would happen with just 1 g of methane.	1 g	+	4 g	$\longrightarrow$	2.75 g	+	2.25 g
Now find what would happen with 48 g of methane by multiplying by 48.	48 g CH_4	reacts with	192 g O_2	to give $\longrightarrow$	132 g CO_2	+	108 g H_2O

FINDING A FORMULA

We can calculate the formula of a compound if we know the masses of the substances that produced it.

In the following example, magnesium burns in oxygen to produce magnesium oxide. We weigh the magnesium used and the magnesium oxide produced. We can then find the mass of oxygen used in the reaction.

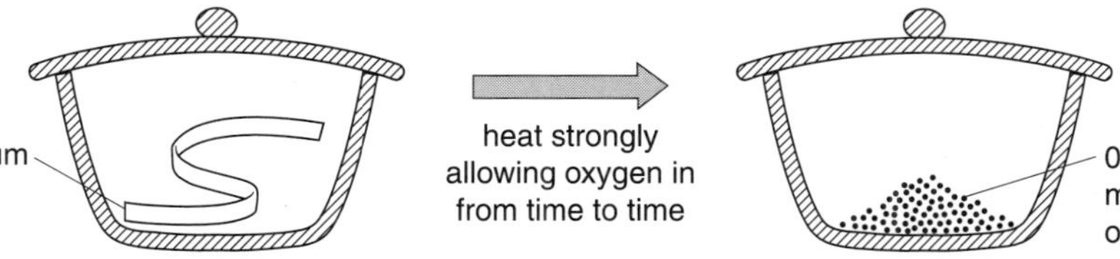

	magnesium (Mg) RAM = 24	oxygen (O) RAM = 16
1 Write down the reacting masses.	0.48 g	0.80 – 0.48 = 0.32 g
2 Find the number of moles by dividing by the RMM for each reactant.	$\frac{0.48}{24} = 0.02$	$\frac{0.32}{16} = 0.02$
3 Find the ratio of moles by dividing by the smallest value to give a whole number.	$\frac{0.02}{0.02} = 1$	$\frac{0.02}{0.02} = 1$
4 Write down the formula of the compound. This gives the proportion of atoms to each other.	MgO	

B19 – Molar volume of gases and concentrations of solutions

One mole of any gas occupies the same volume at the same temperature and pressure.
The concentration of a solution is expressed as the number of moles of solute dissolved in 1 litre (1 dm^3) of solvent.

MOLAR VOLUME OF GASES

One mole of **any** gas contains 6×10^{23} particles. At room temperature and atmospheric pressure (r.t.p), these particles take up 24 dm^3 of space. Therefore, when gases are involved in reactions, we can convert moles to volumes.

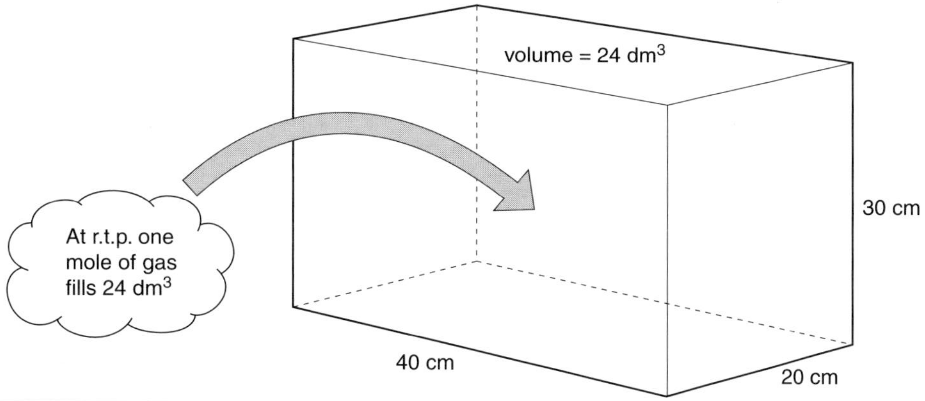

BURNING METHANE

1	Write a balanced equation.	$CH_4(g) + 2O_2(g) \rightarrow CO_2(g) + 2H_2O(g)$
2	Write the amount of each substance in moles.	**1 mole 2 moles → 1 mole 2 moles**
3	Write the mass of each substance using the RMM.	**16 g 64 g → 44 g 36 g**
4	Write the volumes of any gases.	**1 vol. 2 vols. → 1 vol. 2 vols.**
5	Write the volumes of any gases at r.t.p.	**24 dm^3 48 dm^3 24 dm^3 …**
6	Draw a conclusion.	***When 16 g of methane burns it uses 48 dm^3 of oxygen and produces 24 dm^3 of carbon dioxide at room temperature and atmospheric pressure. (The 'water' produced is a gas initially because of the heat produced by the reaction.)***

CONCENTRATION OF SOLUTIONS

The concentration of a solution tells you how much solute is dissolved in a given volume of solvent. Concentrations are measured in units of **mol/l** (moles per litre) or **mol/dm^3** (1 litre = 1 dm^3).

Concentration in moles per litre is also called **molarity** (**M**). A molar solution (**1 M**) is one in which 1 mole of solid is dissolved in 1 litre (1 dm^3) of solvent.

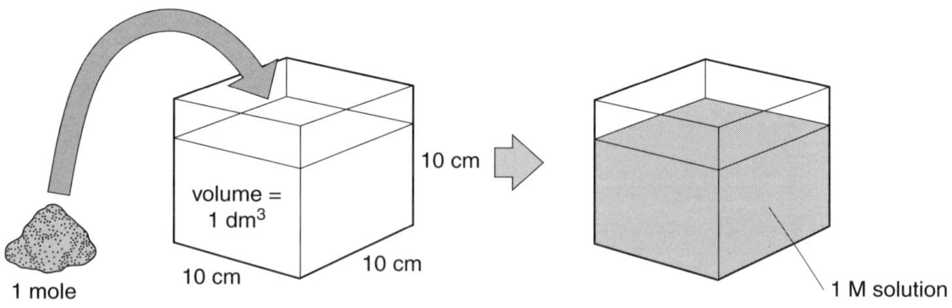

MAKING SODIUM CHLORIDE SOLUTION OF KNOWN CONCENTRATION

1	Write the molecular formula of the solute (solid) and calculate the RMM.	NaCl RMM = 23 + 35.5 = 58.5
2	Write a statement for a solution of concentration 1M (1 mol/l).	**1 M sodium chloride solution contains 58.5 g of sodium chloride dissolved in 1 dm^3 of water.**
3	Calculate how much solute is needed for a given concentration.	**0.2 M sodium chloride solution needs $58.5 \times 0.2 = 11.7$ g of NaCl in 1 dm^3 of water.**
4	Calculate how much solute is needed for a given volume of solvent.	**0.25 dm^3 of 0.2 M sodium chloride solution needs 11.7 g $\times$ 0.25 = 2.925 g of NaCl in 0.25 dm^3 of water.**

B20 – Evolution of the atmosphere

The gases in our atmosphere are essential for life. The composition of the atmosphere has evolved over millions of years and is maintained by complex biological and chemical processes.

ABOUT 5000 MILLION YEARS AGO ...

Gas particles from around the Sun formed a 'ball' under the attraction of gravity. This became the Earth.

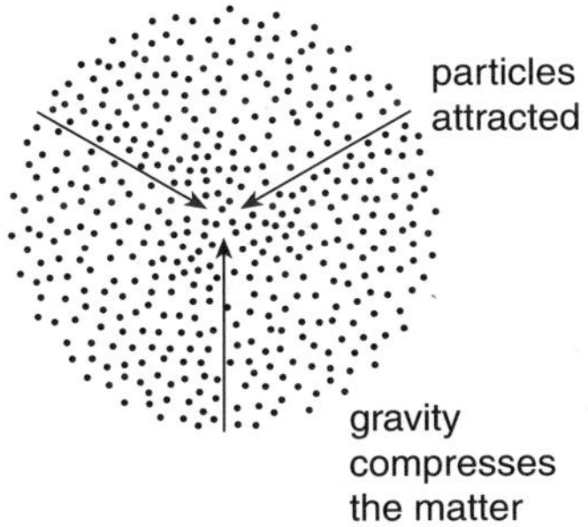

ABOUT 4500 MILLION YEARS AGO ...

Violent volcanic activity. Water vapour, carbon dioxide, sulphur dioxide, nitrogen and other gases produced – this was the early atmosphere.

ABOUT 3500 MILLION YEARS AGO ...

As the Earth cooled, water vapour **condensed**. The water fell as rain and formed the first oceans and seas.

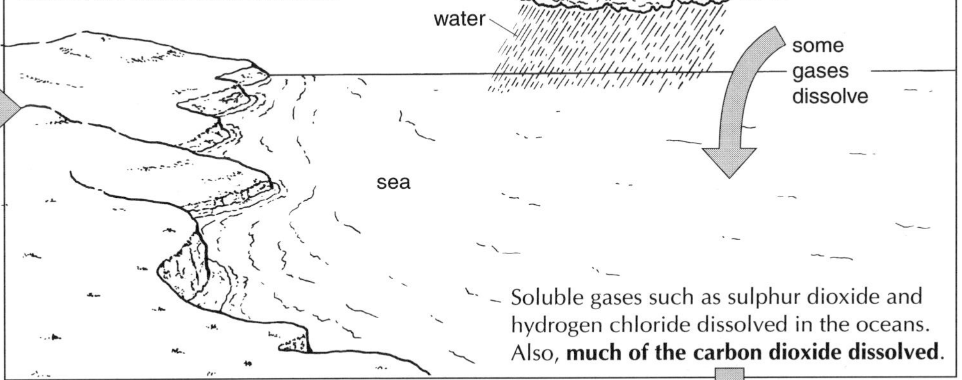

Soluble gases such as sulphur dioxide and hydrogen chloride dissolved in the oceans. Also, **much of the carbon dioxide dissolved**.

ABOUT 2200 MILLION YEARS AGO ...

The first green plants appeared. They **photosynthesized**. This used CO_2 from the atmosphere and released, for the first time, **oxygen** gas.

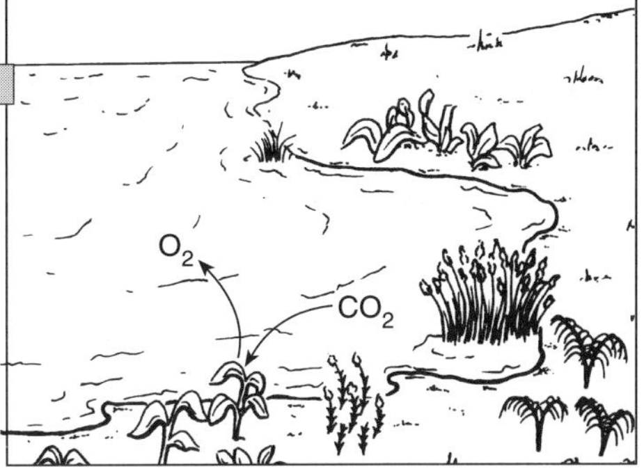

ABOUT 500 MILLION YEARS AGO ...

The first animals appeared. Respiration in animals and in plants used oxygen and released carbon dioxide

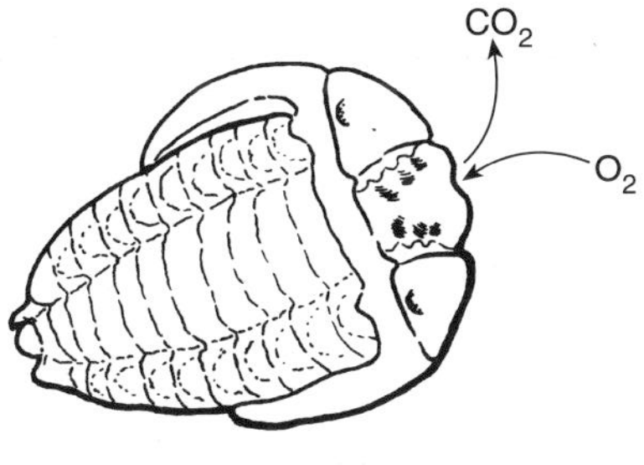

Present atmosphere:

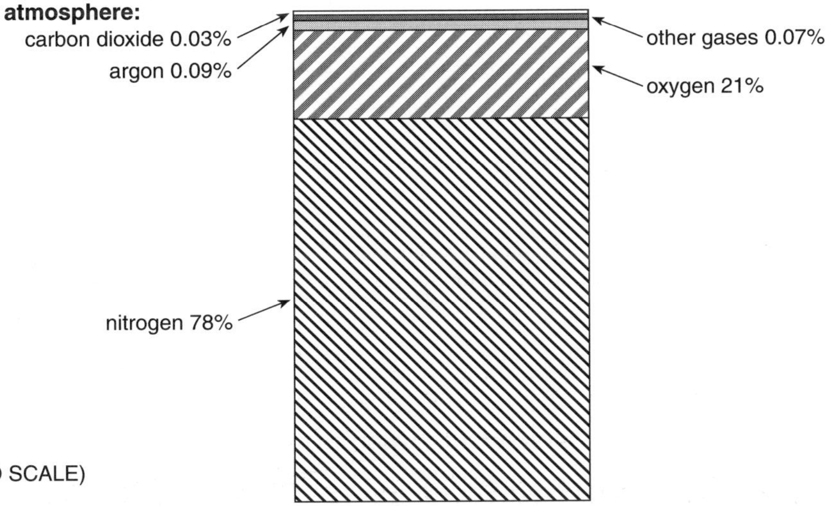

(NOT TO SCALE)

B21 – Maintaining the atmosphere

The balance of gases in our atmosphere is maintained by biological and chemical processes. Human activities can make damaging changes.

MAINTAINING THE ATMOSPHERE

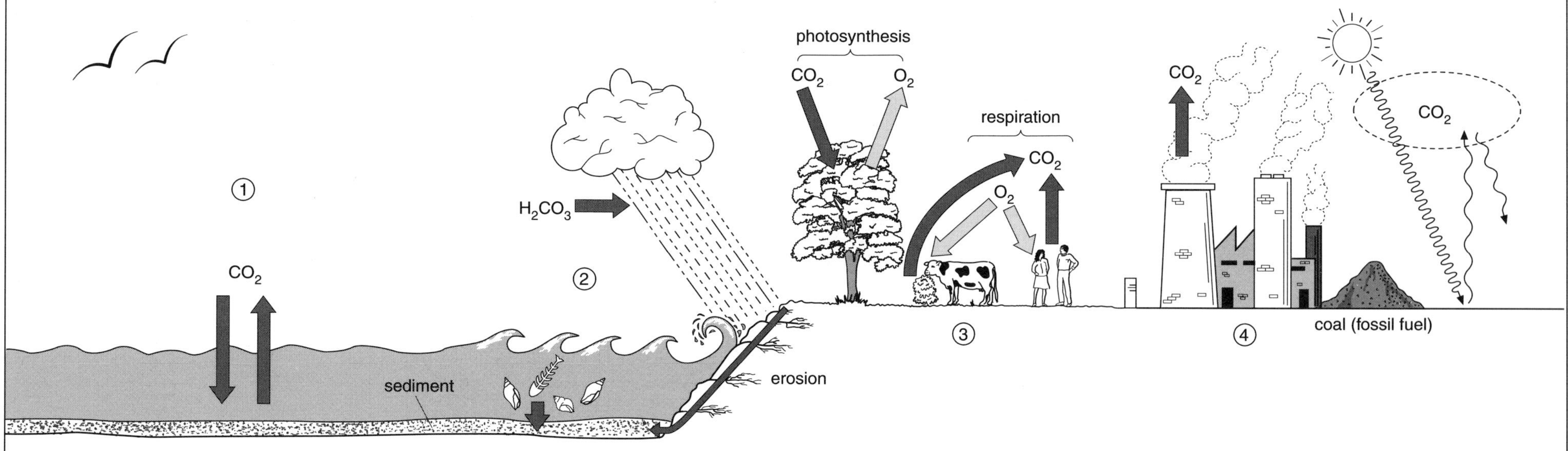

1 Carbon dioxide and the oceans
The sea absorbs much of the CO_2 in our atmosphere. CO_2 is absorbed across the surface of the seas and oceans. If the CO_2 levels in the air rise, the rate of absorption into the sea increases.

In recent years, much of the CO_2 released by burning fossil fuels has been absorbed by the oceans. (See Global warming.)

See also:
The carbon cycle (A38) and
The nitrogen cycle (A37)

2 Erosion and sedimentary rocks
Carbon dioxide dissolves in rainwater to form carbonic acid. This reacts with some minerals in rocks to form hydrogencarbonates (H_2CO_3) and carbonates. Insoluble carbonates, including calcium carbonate ($CaCO_3$) from the shells of marine animals, are deposited on the sea bed. In this way, carbon dioxide from the atmosphere becomes 'locked up' in sedimentary rocks such as limestone.

3 Photosynthesis and respiration
Green plants use CO_2 in **photosynthesis**. It is used, with water, to produce carbohydrates. Animals eat the sugars and starch produced by plants. Carbon from the atmosphere therefore becomes 'locked up' in the biomass.

Photosynthesis releases oxygen into the atmosphere.

Animals and plants use oxygen from the air for respiration. Carbon dioxide is released back into the air.

4 Global warming
Burning fossil fuels releases huge quantities of CO_2 into the atmosphere. CO_2 allows short wavelength radiation from the Sun to pass through but it 'traps' radiation of longer wavelengths emitted by the Earth. This is the **greenhouse effect**.

The greenhouse effect may raise the Earth's temperature by several degrees in the future. **Global warming may** cause:

- **flooding** as polar ice caps melt
- **crop failure** as climate changes
- **desertification** of some areas
- **violent storms** as parts of the atmosphere heat faster than others.

B22 – The rock cycle

New rocks are constantly being made under the surface of the Earth. Old rocks are eroded.

MOUNTAIN BUILDING
The huge pressure generated inside the Earth continually lifts newer rocks towards the surface. In some places the rocks fold to build huge mountain ranges.

WEATHERING AND EROSION
Rocks on the surface are broken up by:
- repeated heating by the Sun and cooling
- water expanding in cracks when it freezes
- chemical attack by rainwater with CO_2 dissolved in it (carbonic acid).

Rocks are worn away by water running over them and by the action of wind. This produces small particles which are **transported** by rivers.

The energy for weathering and erosion comes from the Sun.

IGNEOUS ROCKS
Molten rock (magma) from deep within the Earth cools as it nears the surface. It solidifies to form **igneous rocks**. Some form inside the Earth. Others reach the surface through volcanoes.

The energy (heat) for driving the internal processes of the rock cycle comes from radioactivity.

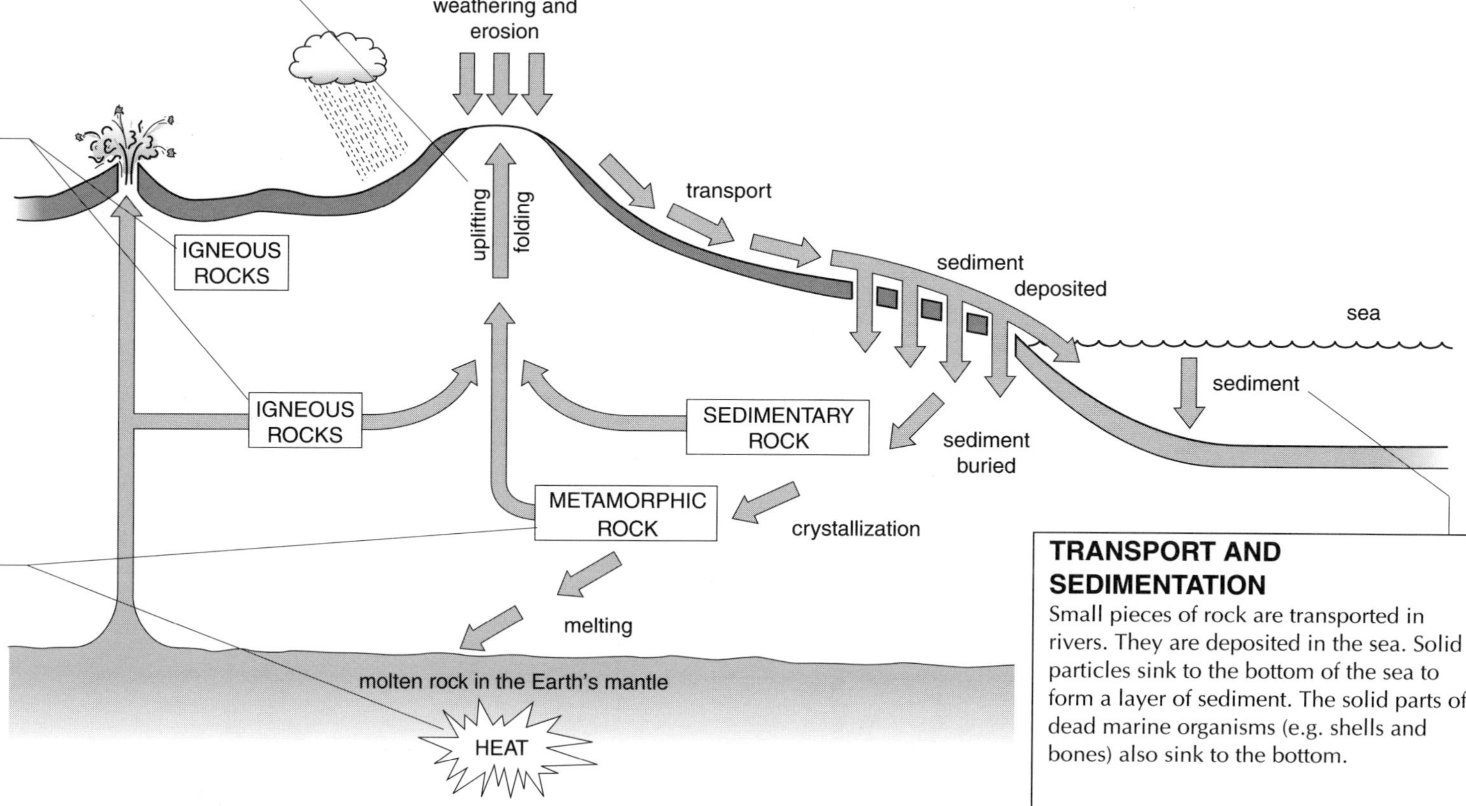

METAMORPHISM AND MELTING
As sedimentary and igneous rocks are buried they are subjected to heat and pressure. Some change into **metamorphic rocks**.

If heated enough, rocks melt and rejoin the magma.

TRANSPORT AND SEDIMENTATION
Small pieces of rock are transported in rivers. They are deposited in the sea. Solid particles sink to the bottom of the sea to form a layer of sediment. The solid parts of dead marine organisms (e.g. shells and bones) also sink to the bottom.

B23 – Types of rock

Different types of rock are formed by different processes and so have different structures.

IGNEOUS ROCKS
(e.g. granite and basalt)

Formed by:
- magma cooling under the Earth's surface (granite)
- magma cooling on the Earth's surface after volcanic activity (basalt)

Evidence:
- rocks contain large crystals formed as liquid (magma) cooled
- some volcanic rocks are glass-like resulting from high temperatures

Uses:
- Igneous rocks often contain 'veins' of ores from which metals can be extracted
- granite – roads, building

SEDIMENTARY ROCKS
(e.g. sandstone, limestone, coal)

Formed by:
- particles of eroded, older rock (mudstone, sandstone)
- precipitation of chemical compounds from solution (limestone, china clay)
- layers of plant remains (coal)

Evidence:
- layers of rocks clearly visible
- rounded grains visible (e.g. in sandstone)
- fossils present (e.g. fern leaves in coal, shells in limestone)

Uses:
- coal – fossil fuel
- sandstone – building
- limestone – building, making lime for neutralizing acid soils, making cement

METAMORPHIC ROCKS
(e.g. marble, slate, quartzite)

Formed by:
- action of high pressure and high temperature on sedimentary and igneous rocks inside the Earth:

  marble formed from limestone

  slate formed from mudstone

  quartzite formed from sandstone

Evidence:
- bands of rock visible
- different crystal size within bands (larger closer to the magma where cooling was slower)

Uses:
- marble – decorative floors, walls, statues
- slate – splits into sheets for roofing

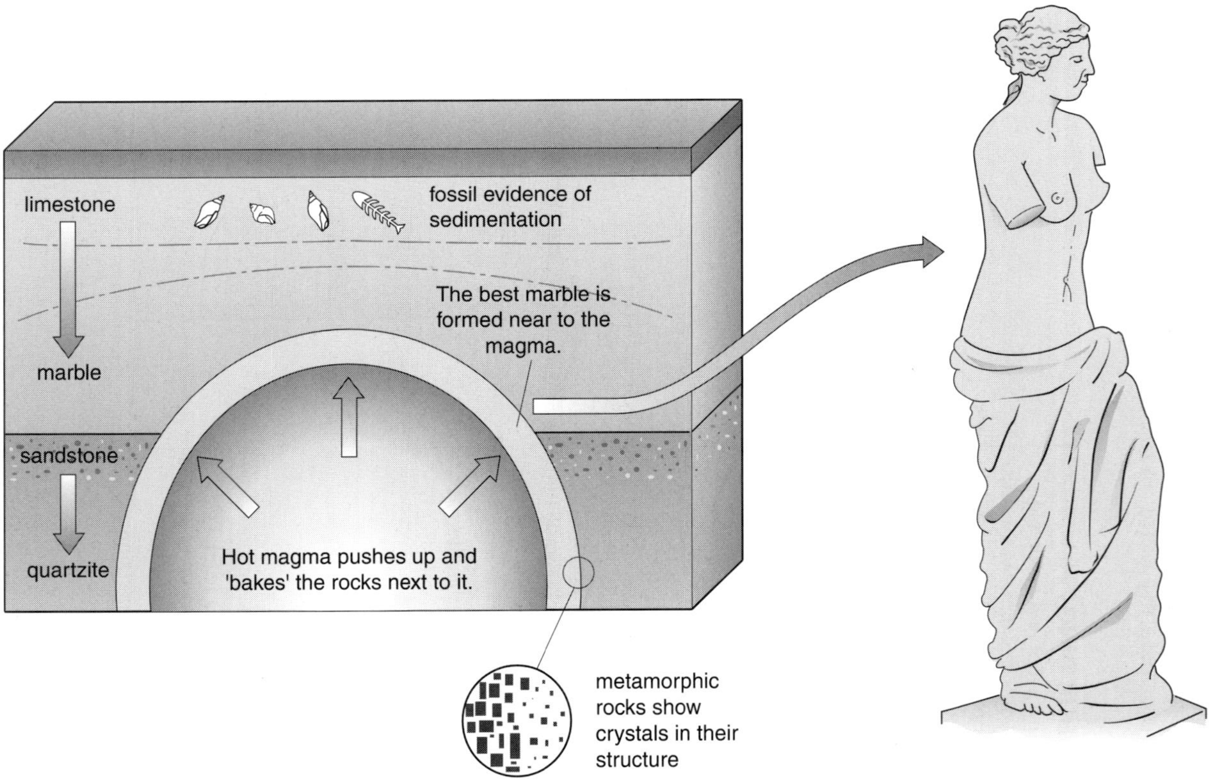

B24 – The Earth's structure and tectonic plates

There is evidence that the Earth's continents are floating on 'plates' of the mantle. These plates are moving – making new rocks and destroying others.

STRUCTURE OF THE EARTH
The pattern of earthquake waves travelling through the Earth suggest that it has a solid core and a hot, liquid outer core.

Volcanoes show that the mantle of the Earth is hot and under pressure.

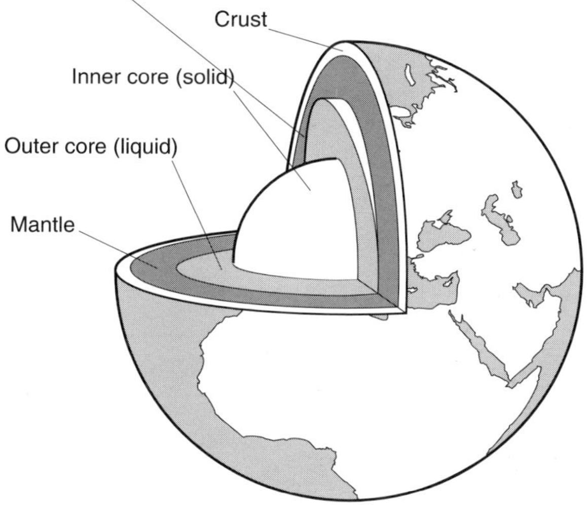

TECTONIC PLATE THEORY
The theory states that the rocks of the Earth's crust which make up the continents are floating on 'plates' within the mantle. Convection currents inside the Earth make the plates move and so the continents 'drift'.

Evidence:
- The layers of rocks on continents separated by great oceans match.
- Mountains and chains of ocean islands occur where tectonic plates meet.
- Earthquake zones and volcanoes occur mainly where plates meet.
- The shapes of the continents seem to fit together suggesting that they were once joined in one huge continent (**pangaea**).

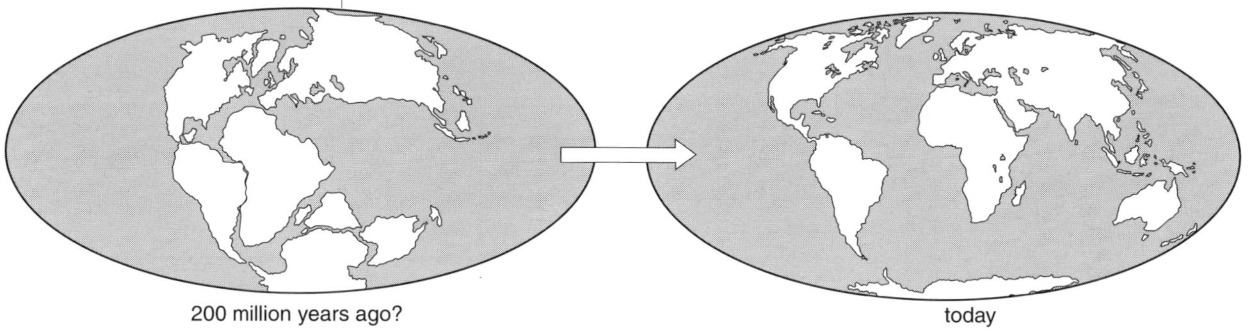

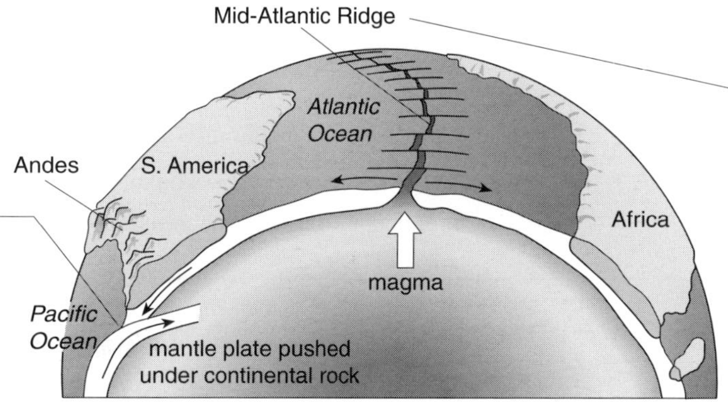

Destructive plate margins
In some places, one plate sinks below another plate. This causes volcanoes and earthquakes. As the lower plate is pushed deeper, the rocks melt. The upper plate is pushed upwards. Its rocks get folded into huge mountain ranges (e.g. the Andes and the Himalayas).

Constructive plate margins
In some deep ocean trenches, magma forces its way to the surface forming new mountains and volcanoes.

Older rocks are pushed aside and the sea floor spreads. This pushes the continents apart.

B25 – The periodic table of elements

The periodic table arranges all known elements according to their atomic numbers.

PERIODS →

- The horizontal rows of elements are called **periods**.
- A period contains elements with different properties.
- Each period (apart from the first) shows a trend from metallic to non-metallic properties.

GROUPS ↓

- The long vertical columns of elements are called **groups**.
- The groups are numbered 0 to 7.
- A group contains elements with similar chemical properties.
- Going down a group, the properties of the elements show trends.
- Hydrogen is unlike any other element – it is not part of a group.

ATOMIC NUMBER

The elements in the periodic table are arranged in order of increasing atomic number. This tells us the number of protons in the nucleus of the element. It also tells us the number of electrons in an atom.

1	2	←				transition elements					→	3	4	5	6	7	0
						1 H 1											4 He 2
7 Li 3	9 Be 4											11 B 5	12 C 6	14 N 7	16 O 8	19 F 9	20 Ne 10
23 Na 11	24 Mg 12											27 Al 13	28 Si 14	31 P 15	32 S 16	35 Cl 17	40 Ar 18
39 K 19	40 Ca 20	45 Sc 21	48 Ti 22	51 V 23	52 Cr 24	55 Mn 25	56 Fe 26	59 Co 27	59 Ni 28	64 Cu 29	65 Zn 30	70 Ga 31	73 Ge 32	75 As 33	79 Se 34	80 Br 35	84 Kr 36
85 Rb 37	88 Sr 38	89 Y 39	91 Zr 40	93 Nb 41	96 Mo 42	99 Tc 43	101 Ru 44	103 Rh 45	106 Pd 46	108 Ag 47	112 Cd 48	115 In 49	119 Sn 50	122 Sb 51	128 Te 52	127 I 53	131 Xe 54
133 Cs 55	137 Ba 56	139 La • 57	178 Hf 72	181 Ta 73	184 W 74	186 Re 75	190 Os 76	192 Ir 77	195 Pt 78	197 Au 79	201 Hg 80	204 Tl 81	207 Pb 82	209 Bi 83	210 Po 84	210 At 85	222 Rn 86
223 Fr 87	226 Ra 88	227 Ac * 89															

Elements not shown:
- • 58-71 Lathanoid series
- * 90-103 Actinoid series

Key

a	
	X
b	

a=relative atomic mass
X=symbol
b=atomic (proton) number

METAL AND NON-METALS

This zig-zag line divides the periodic table into metallic and non-metallic elements. The metals appear on the left and the metals on the right. There are many more metals than non-metals.

Some elements near the line show 'mixed' properties. For example, carbon (graphite) is a non-metal but it is a good conductor of electricity. These elements are called **metalloids**.

TRANSITION METALS

- These metals come between Group 2 and Group 3. They are generally hard metals with high boiling points.
- Many form coloured salts, e.g. copper(II) sulphate is blue, potassium manganate(VII) is purple, iron(II) sulphate is green.
- They form ions with different charges e.g. Cu^+ and Cu^{2+}, Fe^{2+} and Fe^{3+}. This means they can form different compounds with the same element e.g. copper(I) oxide Cu_2O and copper(II) oxide – CuO.
- Some transition metals are useful catalysts for important reactions, e.g. vanadium(V) oxide in making sulphuric acid, iron for making ammonia, nickel for making margarine.

B26 – Electronic structure of atoms

The chemical properties of an element are determined by the way in which electrons are arranged in its atoms.

Atoms are neutral. The number of electrons balances the number of protons in the nucleus.

Electrons are arranged in **shells** or **energy** levels. Each shell can contain a maximum number of electrons.

- first shell: maximum 2 electrons
- second shell: maximum 8 electrons
- third shell: maximum 8 electrons

Electrons fill these shells from the lowest energy upwards. Once a shell is full, the next electron must go into the next, higher level. The electronic structure of an atom tells us how many electrons are in each shell, e.g.

He = 2   C = 2.4   Na = 2.8.1   S = 2.8.6

Electronic structure of chlorine

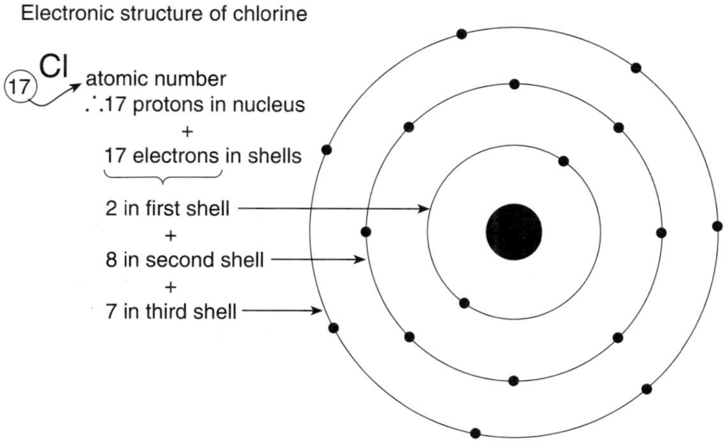

Electronic structure = 2.8.7

ELECTRONIC STRUCTURE AND POSITION IN THE PERIODIC TABLE

The periodic table arranges the elements in order of atomic number. Therefore, the position of an element in the table is also related to the arrangement of electrons. The electronic structures of the first 18 elements are shown below.

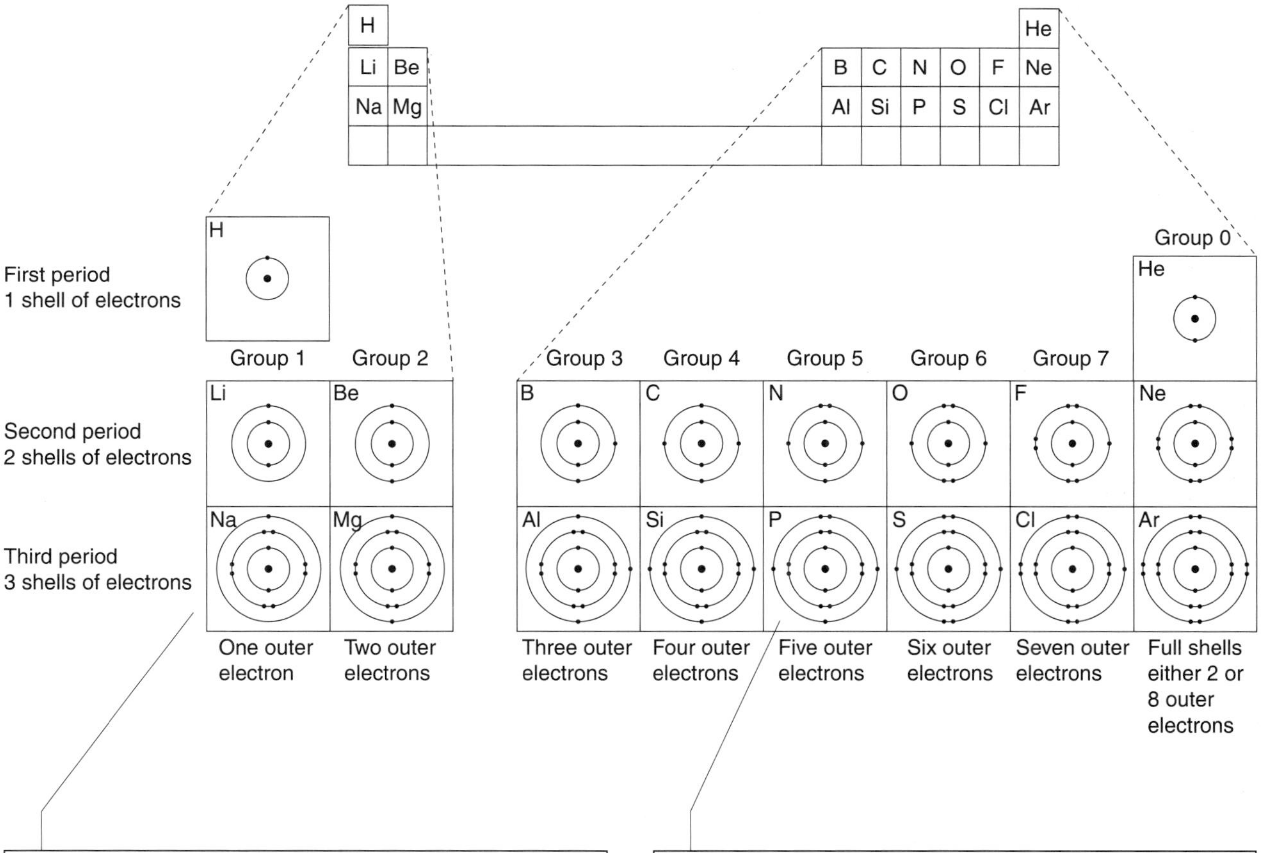

Going across a period ➔ from Group 1 to Group 0, each successive element has one more electron in its outer shell.

Group 0 elements have full outer shells.

In a Group ↓, all the elements have the same number of electrons in the outer shell. This determines the chemical properties of the elements because it is the outer electrons which take part in reactions.

B27 – Group 1: the alkali metals

Group 1 elements have one electron in the outer shell. This makes them reactive metals.

All the elements in Group 1:
- are soft metals – easily cut with a knife
- are shiny when cut but tarnish quickly
- are kept under oil to prevent reaction with air
- have one electron in the outer shell of their atoms
- lose the outer electron easily to form positive ions
- react vigorously with water to produce hydrogen and an alkaline solution
- form ionic compounds which dissolve in water

As we go down Group 1:
- the atoms become larger
- the melting and boiling points (m.p. and b.p.) decrease
- the metals become more reactive

The metals become more reactive as the atom becomes larger because the attraction between the nucleus and the outer electron is weaker.

Metal	Atom	Electronic structure	Ion formed	Increasing reactivity	Decreasing melting point (°C)	Decreasing boiling point (°C)
Lithium	${}^{7}_{3}Li$	2.1	Li^+		181°C	1342°C
Sodium	${}^{23}_{11}Na$	2.8.1	Na^+		98°C	883°C
Potassium	${}^{39}_{19}K$	2.8.8.1	K^+		63°C	760°C

Reactions with water

The alkali metals react vigorously with water. They all produce hydrogen and an alkaline solution.

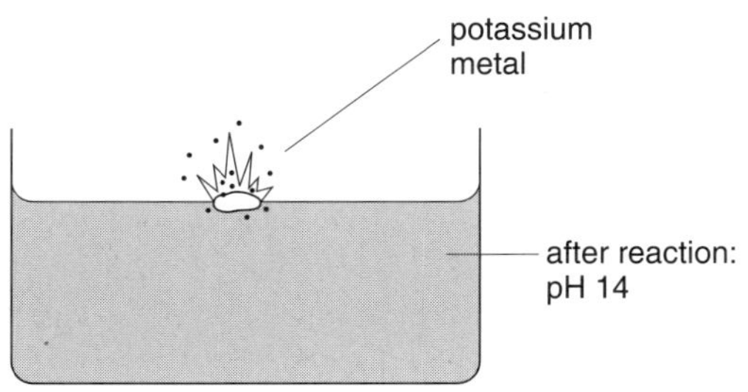

$2K(s) + H_2O(l) \rightarrow H_2(g) + 2KOH(aq)$

potassium + water → hydrogen + potassium hydroxide solution

Reactions with chlorine

The alkali metals all burn in chlorine gas. They produce white, solid chlorides.

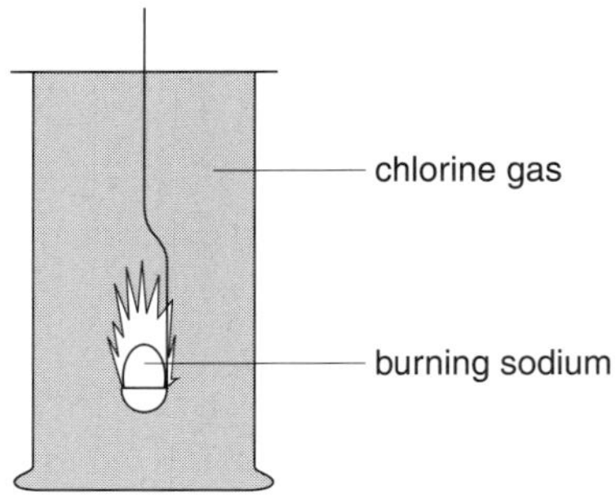

$2Na(s) + Cl_2(g) \rightarrow 2NaCl(s)$

sodium + chlorine → sodium chloride

Making sodium hydroxide solution

Sodium hydroxide is a very important chemical. It is used in making soap, paper, and ceramics. It can be made by the electrolysis of sodium chloride solution (brine). Hydrogen and chlorine are also produced.

The ion-exchange membrane keeps the hydrogen and chlorine apart but allows the sodium ions to move to the cathode.

At the anode:

$2Cl^-(aq) - 2e^- \rightarrow Cl_2(g)$

At the cathode:

$2H_2O(l) + 2e^- \rightarrow 2OH^-(aq) + H_2(g)$

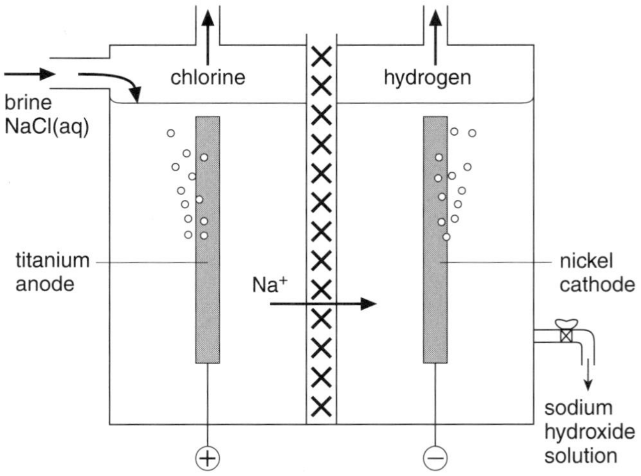

B28 – Group 7: the halogens

Group 7 elements have outer shells which need one more electron to make them full. This makes them reactive non-metals.

All the elements in Group 7:

- are non-metals with characteristic colours
- exist as molecules with two atoms (**diatomic**)
- gain one extra electron easily to form a negative ion
- react with hydrogen to produce hydrogen halides which are acidic in water (HF, HCl, HBr, HI)
- react with metals to form ionic compounds (metal halides)

As we go up Group 7:

- the atoms become smaller
- the melting and boiling points decrease
- the elements become more reactive
- each halogen displaces the ones below it from compounds

Halogens form negatively charged ions. Halogens with smaller atoms are more reactive than those with larger ones because the nucleus attracts more strongly the electron needed to form an ion.

Element	Atom	Electronic structure	Ion formed	Decreasing reactivity	Physical state at r.t.p.	Increasing melting point (°C)	Increasing boiling point (°C)
Fluorine	$^{19}_{9}F$	2.7	F^-		yellow gas	–220	–188
Chlorine	$^{35}_{17}Cl$	2.8.7	Cl^-		green gas	–101	–35
Bromine	$^{80}_{25}Br$	2.8.8.7	Br^-		red-brown liquid	–7	+59
Iodine	$^{127}_{53}I$	2.8.8.18.7	I^-		dark grey solid	+114	+184

Reactions with metals

The halogens react with metals to produce metal halides. The reaction is less vigorous and needs more activation energy (heat) as you go down the Group.

For example, sodium burns in halogen gas to form clouds of white, solid sodium halide.

sodium metal + halogen → sodium halide

$$2Na(s) + Cl_2(g) \rightarrow 2NaCl(s)$$
$$2Na(s) + Br_2(g) \rightarrow 2NaBr(s)$$
$$2Na(s) + I_2(g) \rightarrow 2NaI(s)$$

increasing reactivity

Reactions with silver nitrate

Halide ions react with silver ions to form insoluble precipitates. These have characteristic colours and darken in light. Silver halides are used in photographic films.

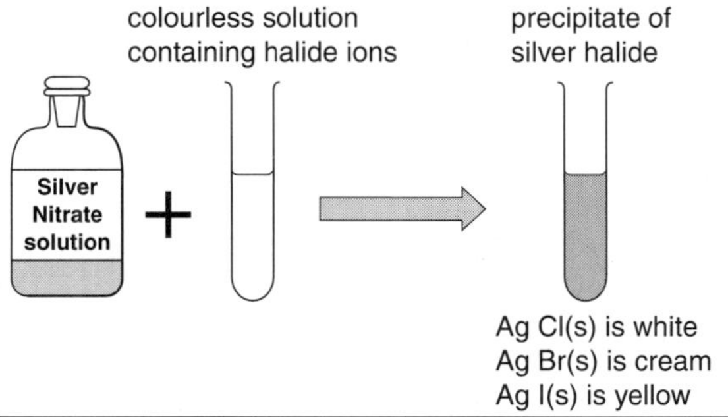

Uses of halogens

A solution of chlorine in water can be used to kill bacteria. It is:

- added to drinking water
- used in domestic cleaning fluids
- added to swimming pools

Iodine (in alcohol solution) is used as an antiseptic on wounds.

Fluoride ions harden tooth enamel and so can help to prevent tooth decay. Fluoride is:

- added to toothpaste
- added to drinking water (in some areas)

B29 – Group 0: the noble gases

Group 0 elements have outer shells which are completely full. This makes them very unreactive.

All the elements in Group 0:

- are non-metals
- are colourless, odourless, tasteless gases
- have 'molecules' with just one atom (**monatomic**)
- occur in small quantities in the air
- have completely full electron shells
- **are extremely unreactive**

As we go down Group 0:

- the atoms become larger
- the melting and boiling points increase
- the gas becomes more dense

Element	Atom	Electronic structure	Increasing density	Increasing melting point (°C)	Increasing boiling point (°C)
Helium	$^{4}_{2}He$	2		*	−269
Neon	$^{20}_{10}Ne$	2.8		−249	−246
Argon	$^{40}_{18}Ar$	2.8.8		−189	−186
Krypton	$^{84}_{36}Kr$	2.8.8.8		−157	−153
Xenon	$^{131}_{54}Xe$	2.8.8.18.8		−112	−108

* cannot be solidified at normal pressures

Uses of the noble gases

The uses of the noble gases are based on:

- the low density of helium
- the unreactive nature of the gases
- the coloured light emitted when an electric current is passed through the gas in a discharge tube

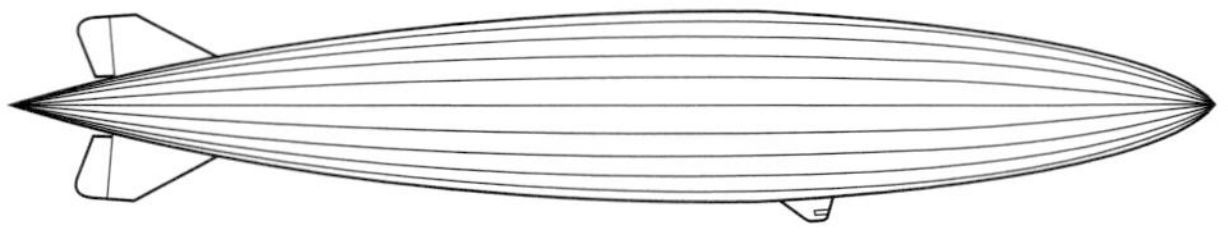

helium - very low density and will not burn

argon - will not react with hot metal filament

xenon filled flash gun - will not react at high temperatures

coloured 'neon' lights - these may contain neon, argon or krypton

B30 – The transition elements

The transition elements occur between Group 2 and Group 3 of the periodic table. They include many important metals.

The transition elements:
- are all metals
- have high melting points (except zinc)
- have high densities (except titanium)
- form coloured salts
- can form ions with different charges (e.g. Cu^+ and Cu^{2+})
- include several metals that are useful catalysts

Iron, cobalt and nickel are strongly magnetic metals. They are used to make magnets.

Copper, gold and silver are very good conductors of electricity. They are used in electrical circuits.

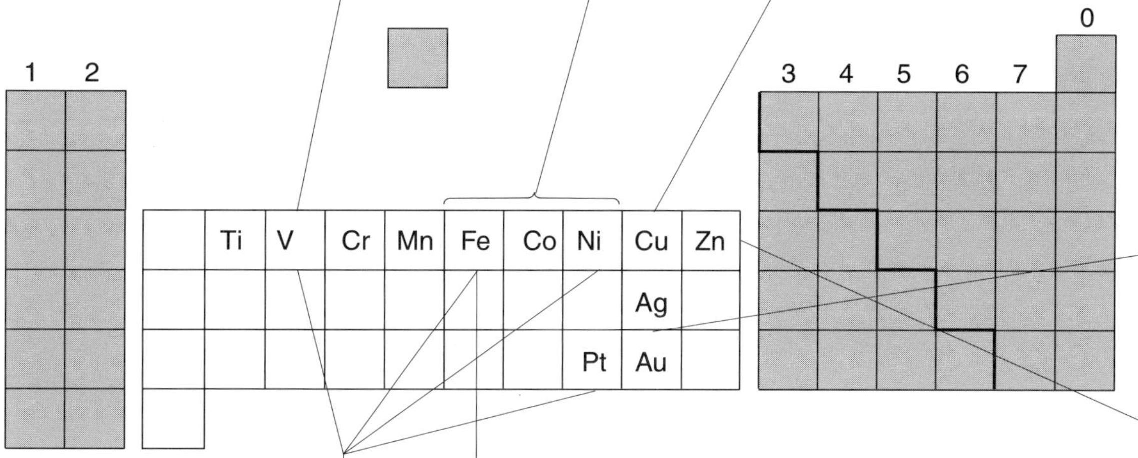

Silver, gold and platinum are used for jewellery. They are attractive, rare and expensive, and can be fashioned into intricate shapes.

Several transition metals are useful catalysts:
- **iron** catalyses the reaction to make ammonia (NH_3) from nitrogen and hydrogen
- **vanadium(V) oxide** catalyses the reaction to make sulphur trioxide from sulphur dioxide and oxygen
- **nickel** is used to make margarine from plant oils
- **platinum** is used in the catalytic converters of cars

Iron is perhaps the most important metal. Pure iron is alloyed with small amounts of carbon to make steel. Other metals may be added to make special steels e.g. chrome and nickel for stainless steel.

Iron and steel rust in the presence of water and oxygen (air).

Rust can be prevented by excluding the air and water (painting, greasing, coating with another metal).

A more reactive metal, usually zinc, can be used to protect the iron or steel.

Zinc, nickel and chromium are used to prevent iron and steel from rusting. They can be used to coat the steel (electroplating). Chrome and nickel can be used to make stainless steel alloy.

B31 – Acids

Acids are very important substances. Some are produced naturally in plants and animals. Others are manufactured for use in industrial processes.

General properties of acids

- 'sour taste', e.g. citric acid in lemon juice
- react with water to make hydrogen ions in solution $H^+(aq)$
- react with metals to release hydrogen gas
- react with carbonates to release carbon dioxide gas
- react with bases to make salts
- make blue litmus go red
- make universal indicator go red

Some common acids

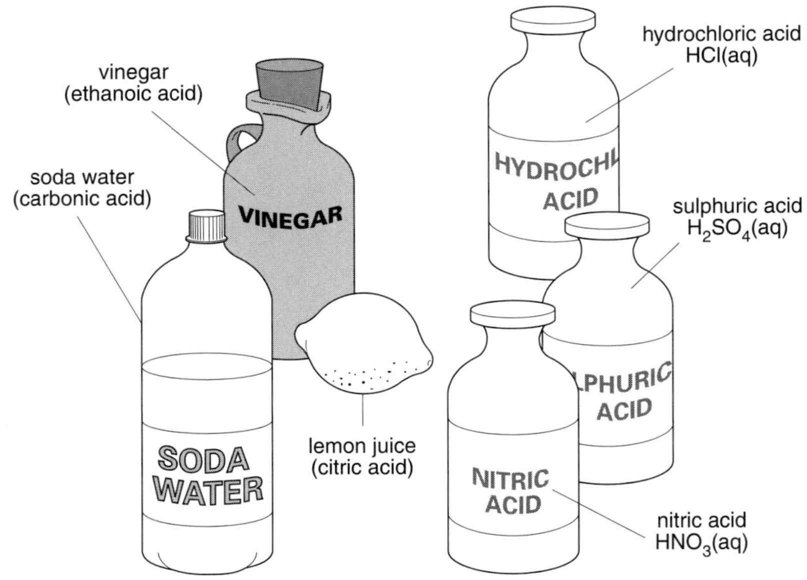

Acids in water

In water, acids react to release hydrogen ions.

$$\mathbf{HCl}(g) + \mathbf{H_2O}(l) \rightarrow \mathbf{H^+}(aq) + \mathbf{Cl^-}(aq)$$

Acids with reactive metals

Reactive metals react with acids. They displace the hydrogen ions to form metal salts.

$$\mathbf{Mg} + \mathbf{2HCl} \rightarrow \mathbf{H_2}(g) + \mathbf{MgCl_2}$$

displaces   to form salt

Acids with bases

A base is a substance which neutralizes an acid. Metal oxides, hydroxides and carbonates are bases.

When bases and acids react, the metal in the base replaces the hydrogen to make a **salt**.

$$\textbf{acid} + \textbf{base} \rightarrow \textbf{salt} + \textbf{water}$$

$$HCl + KOH \rightarrow KCl + H_2O$$

$$H_2SO_4 + MgO \rightarrow MgSO_4 + H_2O$$

displaces   to form salt

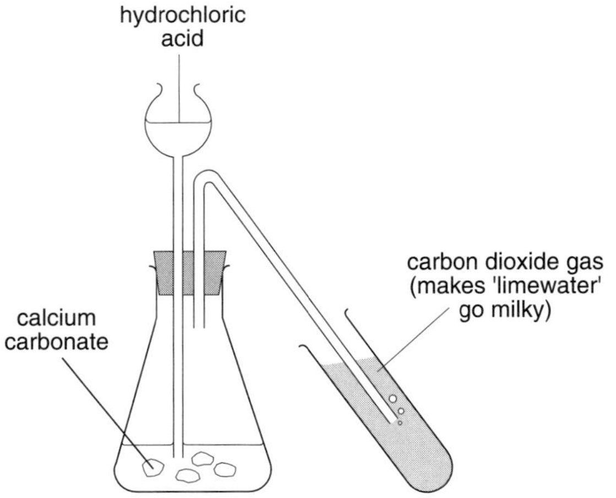

Acids with carbonates and hydrogencarbonates

Carbonates and hydrogencarbonates are bases. When they neutralize acids they release carbon dioxide gas.

$$\textbf{acid} + \textbf{carbonate} \rightarrow \textbf{salt} + \textbf{water} + \textbf{carbon dioxide}$$

$$2HCl + CaCO_3 \rightarrow CaCl_2 + H_2O + CO_2$$

$$\textbf{acid} + \textbf{hydrogencarbonate} \rightarrow \textbf{salt} + \textbf{water} + \textbf{carbon dioxide}$$

$$H_2SO_4 + 2NaHCO_3 \rightarrow Na_2SO_4 + 2H_2O + 2CO_2$$

B32 – Neutralization

Acids are neutralized when they react with bases. Neutralization reactions are important in industry and in agriculture.

ACIDS ARE NEUTRALIZED BY ALKALIS

Acids produce H^+ ions in solution.
$HCl + H_2O \rightarrow H^+ (aq) + Cl^-(aq)$

Some bases are soluble in water. These are called alkalis.
Alkalis produce OH^- ions in solution.
$NaOH + H_2O \rightarrow OH^-(aq) + Na^+(aq)$

When an alkali is added to an acid the products are neutral.

$$\mathbf{H^+}(aq) + \mathbf{OH^-}(aq) \rightarrow \mathbf{H_2O}(l)$$

(The Cl^- and Na^+ ions stay in solution.)

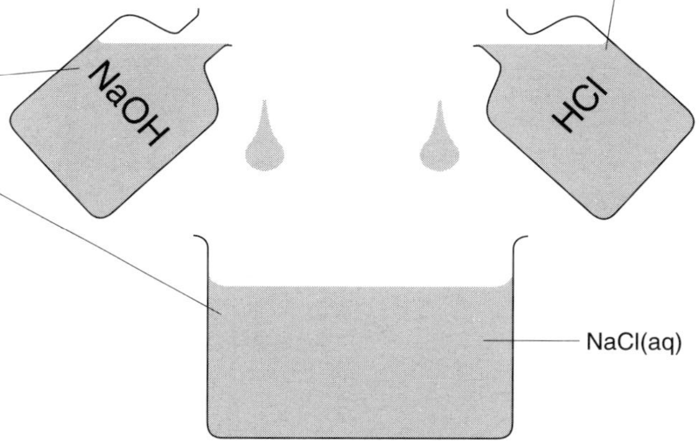

USING NEUTRALIZATION

- Most plants grow better if the soil is neutral or slightly alkaline (pH 6–7). Lime (calcium hydroxide) is used to neutralize acid soils.
- Acid rain has made some lakes too acidic for organisms to live. Lime can be added to neutralize the acid.
- Hydrochloric acid is produced in the stomach. Too much acid can cause indigestion. This can be cured by taking a medicine containing a base such as magnesium carbonate.
- Wasp stings are alkaline. They can be neutralized with an acid, e.g. vinegar.
- Bee stings are acidic. They can be neutralized with sodium hydrogencarbonate (bicarbonate of soda).

The acidity or alkalinity of a solution can be measured on the **pH scale**.

pH scale	**0**	**1**	**2**	**3**	**4**	**5**	**6**	**7**	**8**	**9**	**10**	**11**	**12**	**13**	**14**
Description		strong acid		weak acid				neutral			weak alkali				strong alkali
Examples		HCl HNO_3		H_2CO_3 (carbonic acid)				H_2O NaCl			$NH_3(aq)$				NaOH $Ca(OH)_2$
Colour of litmus indicator		RED						PURPLE							BLUE
Colour of universal indicator		RED		YELLOW				GREEN			BLUE				VIOLET

B33 – Rates of reaction

The rate of reaction tells us how much of a product is made in a given time. The rate of reaction depends on the conditions in which the reactants are brought together.

RATE OF REACTION

The rate of reaction tells us:

- how much product is made in a given time

  or

- how much reactant is used up in a given time

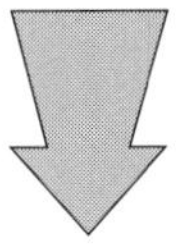

FACTORS AFFECTING RATES OF REACTION

THE PARTICLE MODEL FOR CHEMICAL REACTIONS

A reaction takes place when the reacting particles collide with enough energy to break the existing bonds so that the products can form.

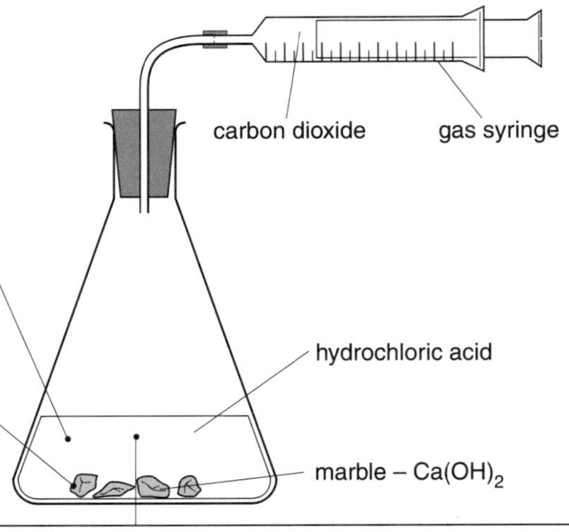

Temperature

Heating the reactants makes their particles move faster. This makes them collide more often and, when they do, more of them have enough energy to **activate** the reaction.

- **In this experiment warming the acid increases the rate of reaction (i.e. the volume of CO_2 gas produced every second).**

Surface area of solid reactants

Collisions take place with the surface of a solid reactant. Breaking the solid into smaller pieces increases the surface area.

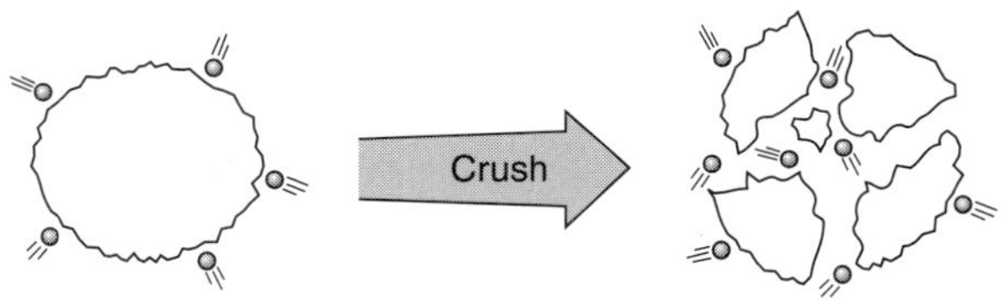

- **In this experiment using calcium carbonate powder rather than large marble chips increases the rate of reaction.**

Concentration

Increasing the concentration of a reactant in solution increases the number of particles and so collisions take place more frequently.

- **In this experiment using hydrochloric acid which is more concentrated (e.g. 2M rather than 1M) increases the rate of reaction.**

CATALYSTS AND RATES OF REACTION

A catalyst does not take part in a reaction. It lowers the activation energy required. This means that more of the colliding particles will have enough energy to activate the reaction.

- **Using a catalyst increases the rate of reaction.**

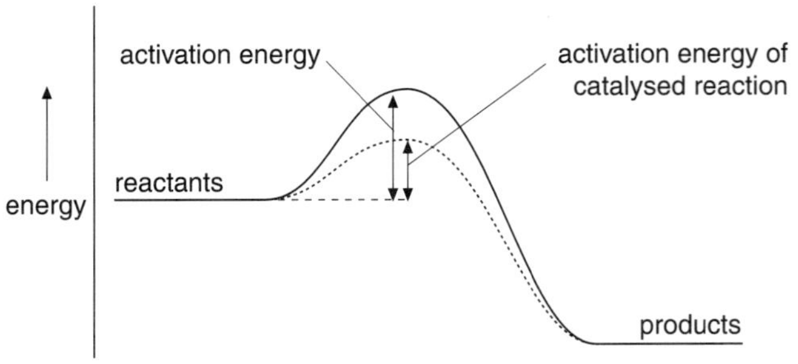

B34 – Enzymes and their uses

Enzymes are complex proteins found in living cells. They act as **catalysts** for a wide range of reactions.

Enzymes

- An **enzyme** is a biological **catalyst**. It increases the rate of a reaction but is not altered by it.
- Each enzyme catalyses one specific reaction.
- Enzymes work best within a small range of temperature. Above 45°C they stop working.
- Each enzyme works best within a small range of pH. Some work best in alkaline conditions, others need an acidic environment.

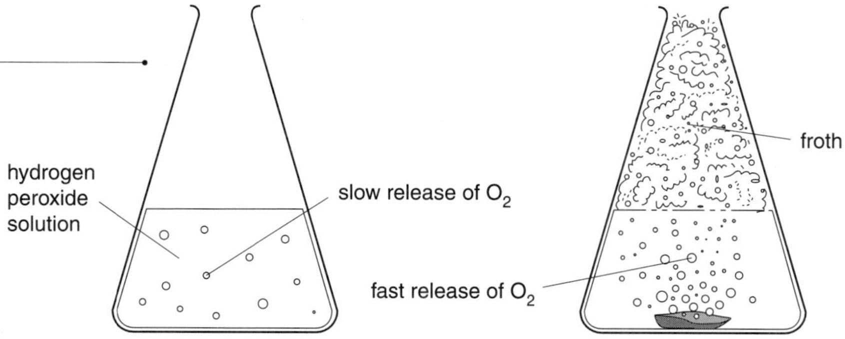

An enzyme in raw liver catalyses the reaction $2H_2O_2 \rightarrow O_2 + 2H_2O$

A model for enzyme action

The enzyme shape provides an **active site** for other molecules to react – provided they have the right shape!

At the active site the reaction can take place at a lower activation energy.

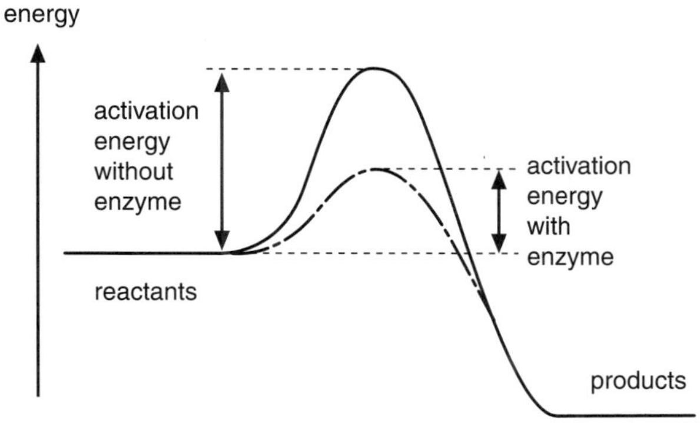

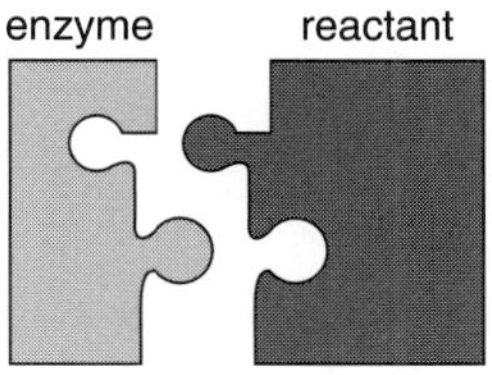

1 Only reactant molecules of the correct shape can fit the enzyme's active site. The enzyme only catalyses this particular reaction.

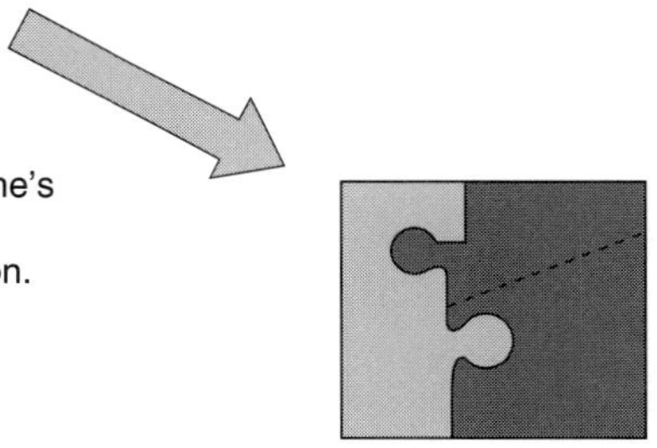

2 Reactant molecule 'locked' in the active site. The reaction can now take place at lower energies.

3 Product molecules leave the active site. The enzyme is left unchanged, ready to accept another reactant molecule.

USES OF ENZYMES

Baking and brewing

Enzymes in yeast catalyse the fermentation reaction which converts sugars into alcohol and carbon dioxide.

When used in making bread, the CO_2 bubbles make the dough rise before baking.

In the brewing industry, fermentation is used to make alcoholic drinks: beer, wine and spirits.

Making yoghurt and cheese

Yoghurt is made by adding bacteria to milk. Enzymes produced by the bacteria convert lactose (sugar) to lactic acid. This makes the milk curdle.

Cheeses are also made by causing milk to curdle. To make firm, long-lasting cheeses an enzyme called **rennet** is added to milk.

'Biological' detergents

Some washing detergents contain enzymes to digest protein stains.

B35 – Reversible reactions

Many chemical reactions can be reversed. Some of the most important industrial processes are based on reversible reactions.

Heating blue copper(II) sulphate crystals produces white anhydrous copper(II) sulphate and water.

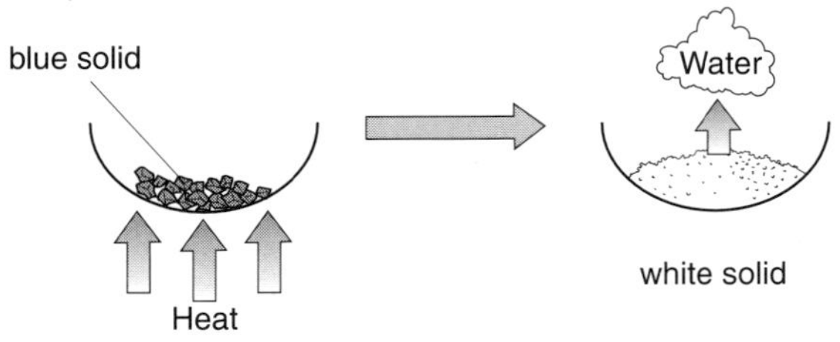

Adding water to white, anhydrous copper(II) sulphate turns it blue. It also gets hot!

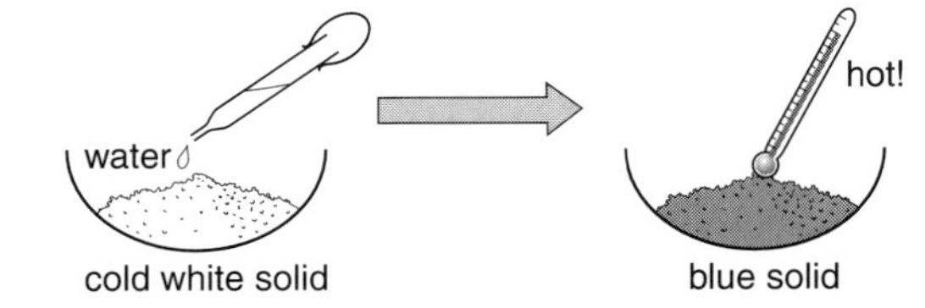

This is a reversible reaction. We use a double arrow to show that the equation can be read in both directions.

$$\mathbf{CuSO_4.5H_2O + heat \rightleftharpoons CuSO_4 + 5H_2O}$$

blue, hydrated copper(II) sulphate; white, anhydrous copper(II) sulphate; water

EQUILIBRIUM IN REVERSIBLE REACTIONS

The Haber process (see B36) for making ammonia is based on the reversible reaction:

$$\mathbf{N_2 + 3H_2 \rightleftharpoons 2NH_3 + heat}$$

Forward reaction → → →
nitrogen and hydrogen combine – ammonia and heat produced

Back reaction ← ← ←
ammonia breaks down when heated – nitrogen and hydrogen produced

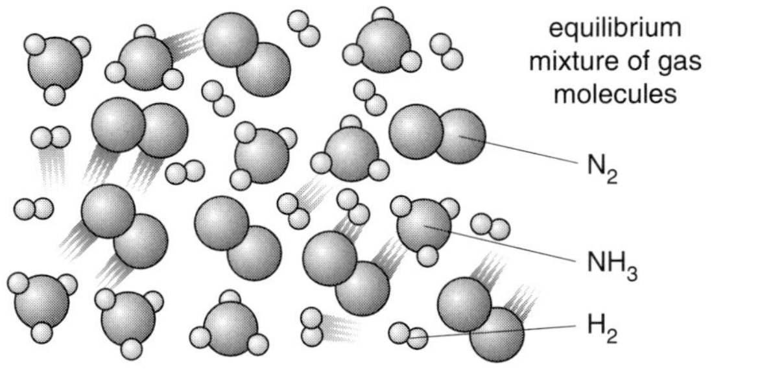

At **equilibrium**, the two reactions will be taking place at the same rate. Ammonia will break down at the same rate as it is formed!

CHANGING THE EQUILIBRIUM POSITION

Changing the pressure
When the reactants and products include gases, changing the pressure may change the equilibrium position.

In this case, four volumes of nitrogen and hydrogen produce just two volumes of ammonia gas. Using a high pressure (200 × atmospheric pressure) makes more ammonia.

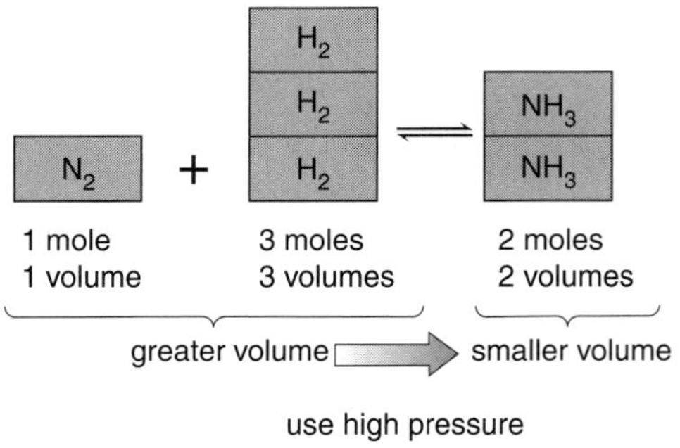

Changing the quantities
Increasing the amount of hydrogen and nitrogen increases the amount of ammonia produced because there are more reactant molecules for the forward reaction. Removing ammonia would have the same effect on the equilibrium position.

Changing the temperature
In this case, the back reaction takes in heat. Raising the temperature increases the rate at which ammonia breaks down.

Unfortunately, the reaction will not start at low energies and so the Haber process uses a temperature of about 500°C as a compromise.

Using a catalyst?
Catalysts do not change the equilibrium position. However, they do speed up the forward reaction so that equilibrium is reached more quickly.

In the Haber process, an iron catalyst is used.

B36 – Making ammonia: the Haber process

Millions of tonnes of ammonia are manufactured every year. Most of it is used to make fertilizers.

THE HABER PROCESS

Ammonia for use in industry is made by the direct combination of nitrogen and hydrogen.

$$N_2(g) + 3H_2(g) \rightleftharpoons 2NH_3(g)$$

The reaction is reversible. Special conditions are used to increase the rate of the forward reaction, i.e. to produce more ammonia.

- **High pressure**: about 200 × atmospheric pressure. This increases the concentration of nitrogen and hydrogen molecules raising the rate of the forward reaction.
- **Iron catalyst**: This increases the rate of the forward reaction.
- **High temperature**: about 500°C.

Even under these conditions, only about 20% of the nitrogen and hydrogen combine. The gases are cooled so that the ammonia liquifies. Unused hydrogen and nitrogen are sent through the reaction chamber again.

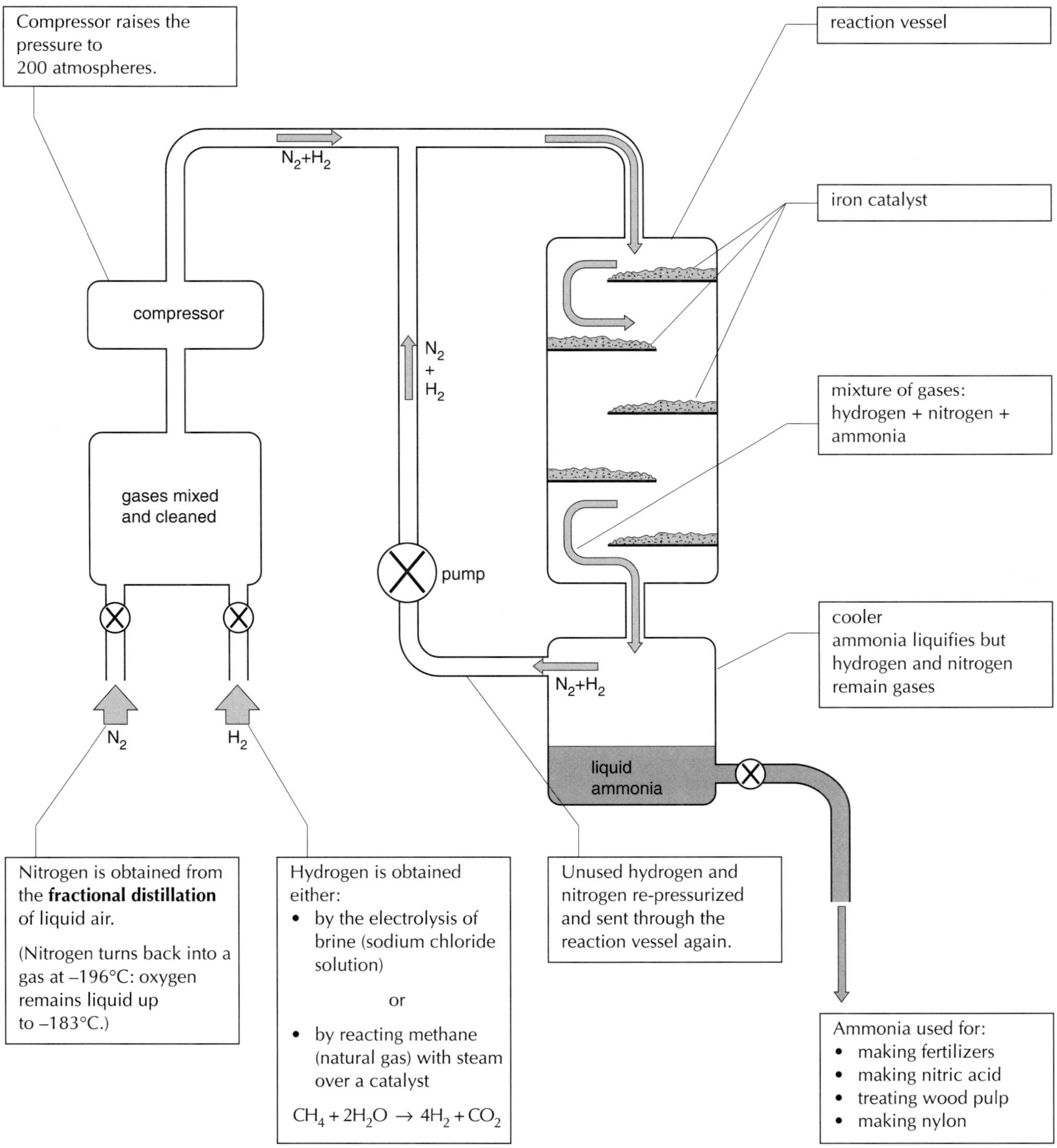

B37 – Fertilizer production

Plants need elements from the soil for healthy growth.
The main ones are nitrogen, potassium and phosphorus.

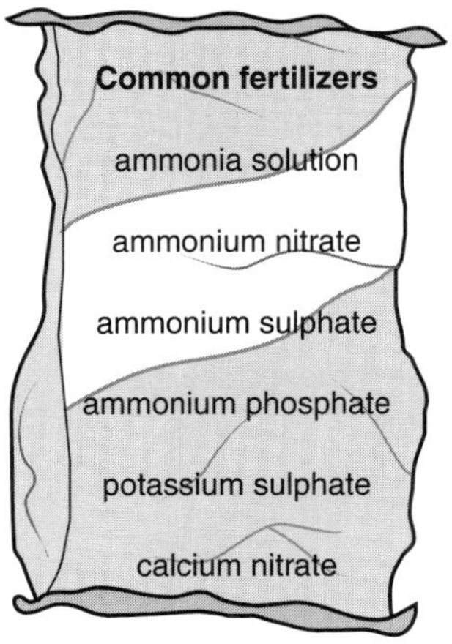

ARTIFICIAL FERTILIZERS

When crops are harvested they remove essential elements from the soil. These need to be replaced either with **natural fertilizers** (e.g. manure and compost) or with **artificial fertilizers** made in factories.

MAKING FERTILIZERS

Most fertilizers are the salts of acids. They are produced by neutralizing the acid with a base.

ACID + BASE → SALT + WATER

- Nitric acid makes nitrates.
- Sulphuric acid makes sulphates.
- Phosphoric acid makes phosphates.

THE HABER PROCESS AND FERTILIZERS

- Some ammonia solution from the Haber process is used directly as a fertilizer.
- A lot of it goes to make nitric acid.
- Nitric acid can then be neutralized by more ammonia solution to make ammonium nitrate fertilizer.

Making nitric acid

① **Reaction chamber**: Ammonia and oxygen react in the presence of a catalyst to give nitrogen monoxide.

$$4NH_3(g) + 5O_2(g) \rightarrow 4NO(g) + 6H_2O(g)$$

② **Oxidizing tower**: The nitrogen monoxide is oxidized by more oxygen to give nitrogen dioxide.

$$2NO(g) + O_2(g) \rightarrow 2NO_2(g)$$

③ **Absorption tower**: Nitrogen dioxide is absorbed by water, in the presence of oxygen, to give nitric acid.

$$4NO_2(g) + O_2(g) + 2H_2O(l) \rightarrow 4HNO_3(aq)$$

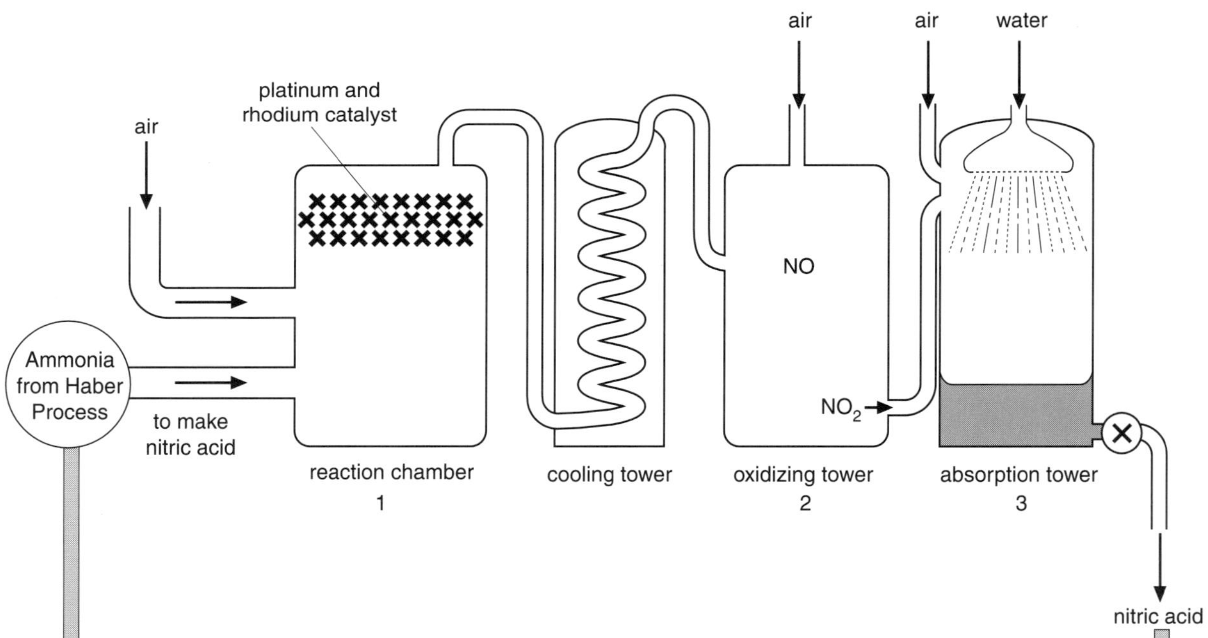

Neutralization

Ammonia solution from the Haber process neutralizes nitric acid:

$$NH_3(aq) + HNO_3(aq) \rightarrow NH_4NO_3(aq)$$

Solid ammonium nitrate is made from solution by evaporating off the water.

B38 – Exothermic and endothermic reactions

Some reactions take in energy from their surroundings; others give out energy.

EXOTHERMIC REACTIONS

In an **exothermic reaction** the reactants give out thermal energy (heat). We usually detect this as a temperature rise.

Combustion reactions are **exothermic**. They may need some energy to get started (**activation energy**) but then they keep going and release energy as heat.

The reaction between calcium metal and water is highly exothermic.

$\mathbf{Ca}(s) + \mathbf{H_2O}(l) \rightarrow \mathbf{Ca(OH)_2}(aq) + \mathbf{H_2}(g) + \mathbf{energy}$

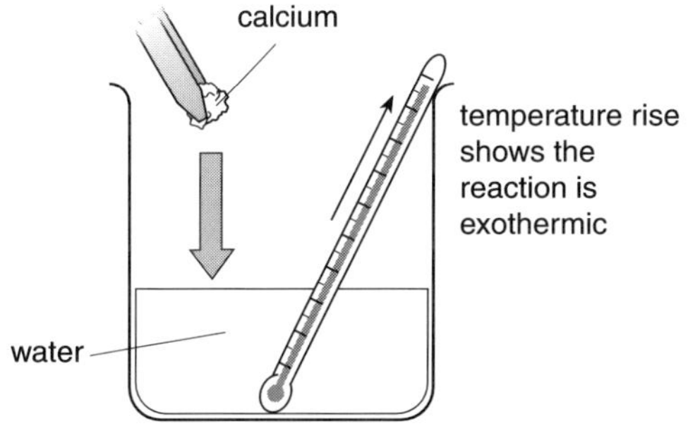

The combustion of methane gas is exothermic. Notice that you have to supply the activation energy in order to start the reaction.

$\mathbf{CH_4}(g) + \mathbf{2O_2}(g) \rightarrow \mathbf{CO_2}(g) + \mathbf{2H_2O}(g) + \mathbf{energy}$

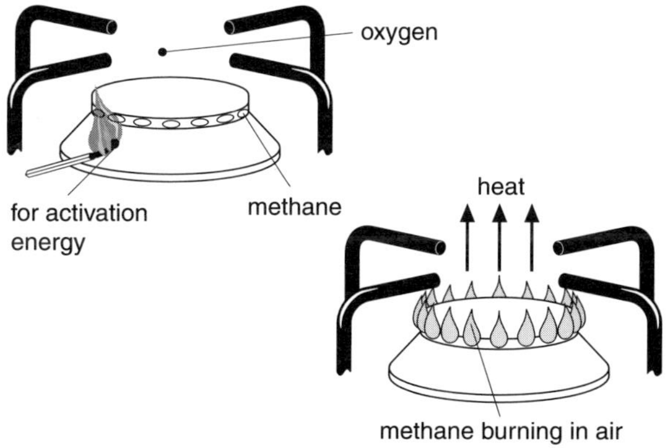

ENDOTHERMIC REACTIONS

In an **endothermic reaction** the reactants take in thermal energy from their surroundings. In some reactions we detect this as a drop in temperature.

Many endothermic reactions have to be heated continuously to keep them going.

Dissolving potassium nitrate in water is an endothermic reaction.

$\mathbf{KNO_3}(s) + \mathbf{H_2O}(l) + \mathbf{energy} \rightarrow \mathbf{K^+}(aq) + \mathbf{NO_3^-}(aq)$

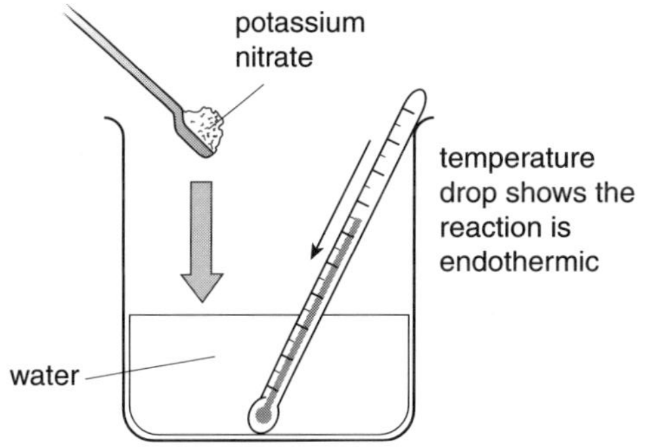

The decomposition of calcium carbonate by heating is endothermic. If you stop heating the reaction stops.

$\mathbf{CaCO_3}(s) + \mathbf{energy} \rightarrow \mathbf{CaO}(s) + \mathbf{CO_2}(g)$

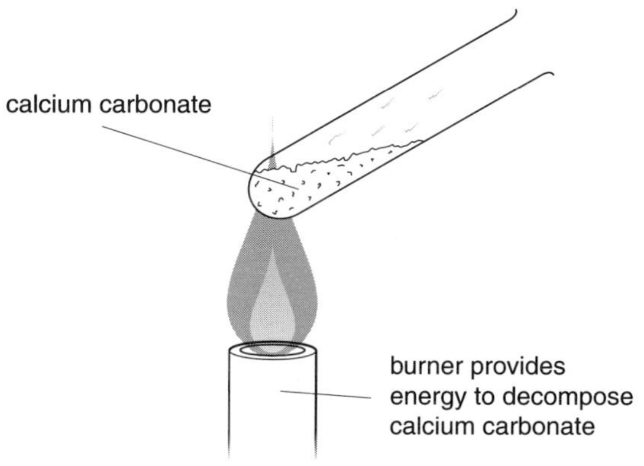

B39 – Breaking and making bonds

Most chemical reactions involve breaking bonds in the reactants and making new bonds to form the products.

In chemical reactions, the bonds in reacting molecules are broken. New bonds are then made to form the products.

- Bond breaking uses energy. Bond making **releases** energy.
- If breaking bonds uses more energy than is released, the reaction is **endothermic**.
- If breaking bonds uses less energy than is released, the reaction is **exothermic**.

Combustion reactions are exothermic. The energy they release was originally stored in the bonds of the fuel. This example uses the burning of methane gas.

Equation	CH_4	+ $2O_2$ →	CO_2	+ $2H_2O$	
Bonds to be broken to start reaction	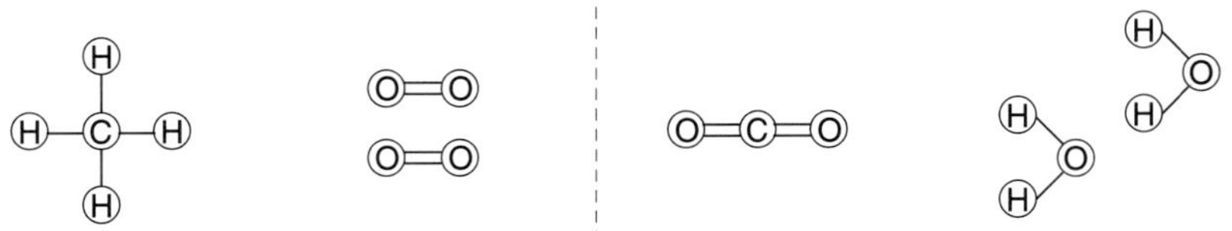				Bonds to be made in forming products
Energy needed to break bonds (for burning 1 mole of methane)	4 lots of C–H 4 × 412 kJ	2 lots of O=O 2 × 496 kJ	2 lots of C=O 2 × 743 kJ	4 lots of O–H 4 × 463 kJ	Energy released by making bonds
Total energy needed	2640 kJ		3338 kJ		Total energy released
Overall difference in energy	**2640 kJ – 3338 kJ = –698 kJ**				

(– means energy is given out)

We can show this on an **energy diagram**:

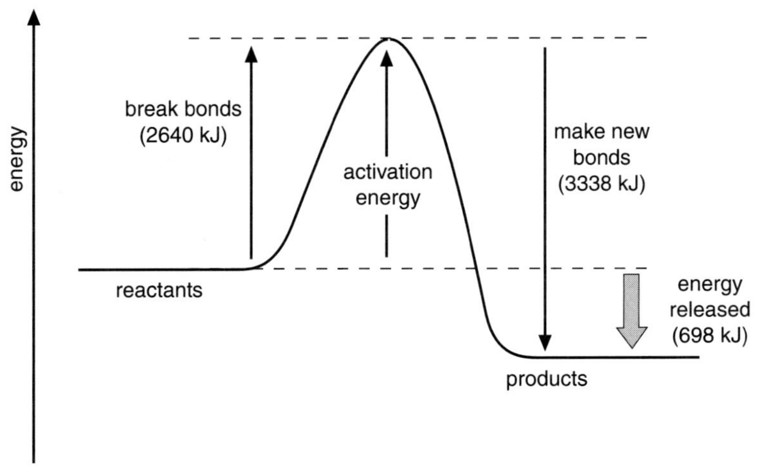

Physics

PHYSICAL PROCESSES

Page	Topic	Revised ✔	See also ...
92	C1 – Static electricity		
93	✗ C2 – Electric currents and circuits		B14
94	✗ C3 – Charge and energy transfer in circuits		
95	✗ C4 – Measuring current, voltage and resistance		
96	C5 – Ohm's law		
97	C6 – Direct and alternating current		
98	✗ C7 – Electrical safety in the home		
99	✗ C8 – Power and the cost of electrical energy		
100	C9 – Magnetism and electromagnetism		
101	C10 – The motor effect		
102	C11 – Electromagnetic induction		
103	C12 – Transformers		
104	C13 – Transmission of electricity		
105	C14 – Forces on materials		
106	C15 – Pressure		
107	C16 – Pressure in liquids		
108	C17 – Pressure in gases		B1
109	C18 – Moments		
110	C19 – Force, work and power		
111	C20 – Work, potential energy and kinetic energy		
112	C21 – Speed, velocity and acceleration		
113	C22 – Laws of motion		
114	C23 – Friction and stopping		
115	✗ C24 – Waves and energy transfer		
116	✗ C25 – Wave properties 1: wave equation and reflection		
117	✗ C26 – Wave properties 2: refraction and diffraction		A12
118	C27 – Total internal reflection of light		
119	C28 – Ultrasound and its uses		
120	C29 – Seismic waves and the Earth's structure		B24
121	C30 – The electromagnetic spectrum		
122	✗ C31 – Conduction, convection and radiation		B10
123	C32 – Energy efficiency		
124	C33 – Nuclei and radioactivity		B2
125	C34 – Types of nuclear radiation		A2, A25
126	C35 – Radioactive half-life		B23
127	C36 – Earth and the Solar System		
128	C37 – Gravitational force		
129	C38 – 'Life cycle' of a star		
130	C39 – Theories of the origins of the universe		

C1 – Static electricity

Some materials can 'hold' electric charges. These exert forces on other charges. This can be useful or can cause problems.

CHARGES IN ATOMS

Materials are made of atoms. Atoms are neutral but if some electrons are removed or added, the material becomes charged.

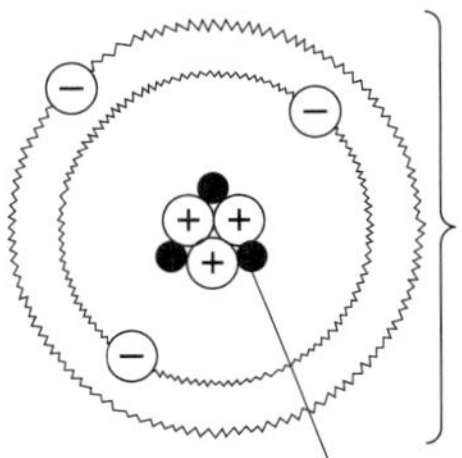

CHARGING BY FRICTION

Some **insulators** become charged when rubbed with a cloth. This is because **electrons** are transferred.

Perspex is positively charged by rubbing.

Polythene is negatively charged by rubbing.

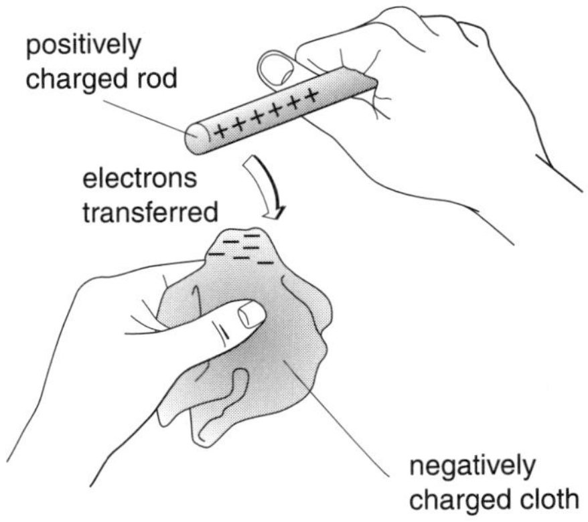

ATTRACTION AND REPULSION: CHARGED OBJECTS EXERT FORCES ON EACH OTHER

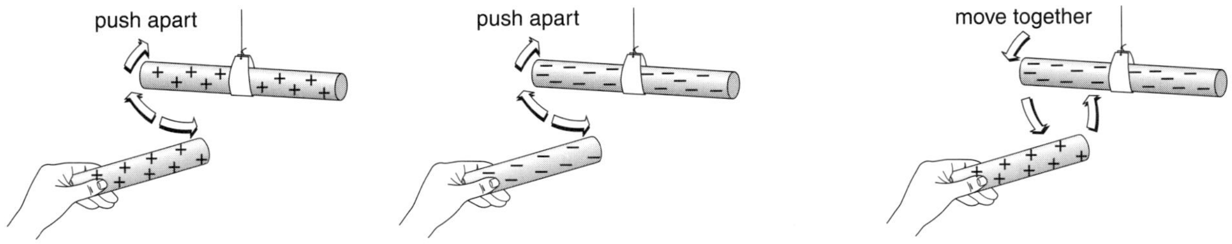

Like charges repel.

Opposite charges attract.

ELECTROSTATIC INDUCTION

- Charged objects **attract** neutral objects.
- Electrons move inside the neutral object, causing a separation of charges.
- An opposite charge is **induced** near to the charged object.

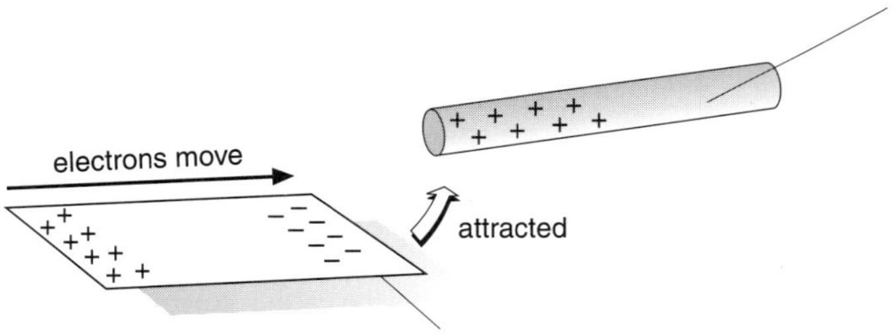

USING STATIC ELECTRICITY

Photocopiers: An electrostatic 'image' of the object to be copied is made on the photocopier drum. Special 'ink' (toner) sticks to the drum only where it is charged. This is transferred to a piece of paper and fixed by heating.

Dust precipitation: In factories, dust and solid particles are removed from smoke by charging them. They stick to plates given the opposite charge inside the chimney rather than being allowed to escape into the air.

Paint spraying: Parts to be painted are charged. Paint droplets are given the opposite charge so that they are attracted to the unpainted parts. This gives a smooth coating and reduces wasted paint.

DANGERS OF STATIC ELECTRICITY

Refuelling aircraft: If too much static electricity builds up in one place it can cause a spark. When refuelling an aircraft, all static charge must be allowed to flow to Earth through a metal strap to avoid an explosion.

Cleaning oil tanks: Oil tankers are cleaned with high pressure water jets. These can cause a build up of charge which could cause a spark. Earthing allows excess charge to flow away, reducing the chance of an explosion.

Working with chips: Static electricity can destroy computer chips and other components. Workers building computers are connected to Earth by a metal strap.

C2 – Electric currents and circuits

Charge flows in an electrical conductor when a potential difference (voltage) is applied across it. The flow of charge is an electrical current.

ELECTRIC CURRENT

Metals and other good conductors have electrons which are free to move. When a cell is attached to a metal wire, negatively charged electrons move towards the positive terminal. A current flows in the wire.

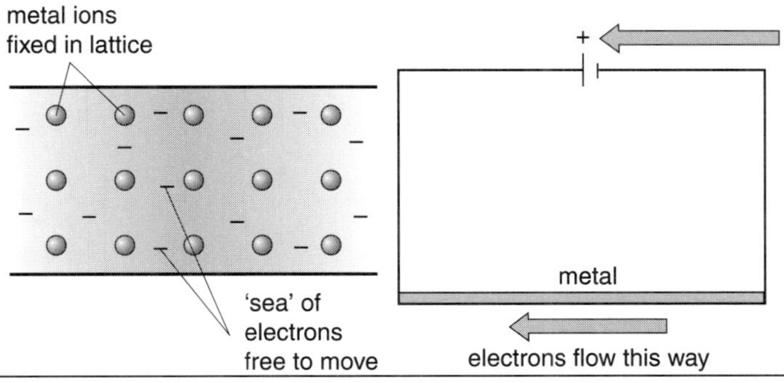

The cell supplies electrons with energy and 'forces' them to move. We say the cell has applied a **voltage** or **potential difference** (**pd**).

SERIES CIRCUITS

An electric current will only flow when there is a complete 'path' of wire and/or components which conduct electricity. This is a **circuit**.

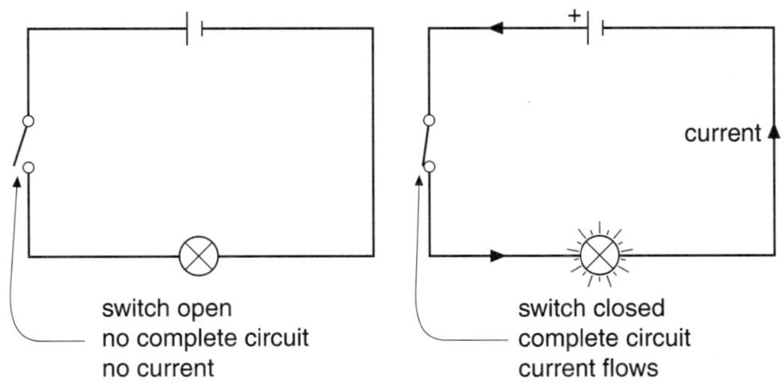

Notice that we draw conventional current from + to –. Electron flow is in the opposite direction.

In a **series** circuit, all the components are linked in one path; there is no branching. The current is the same at all points in the circuit.

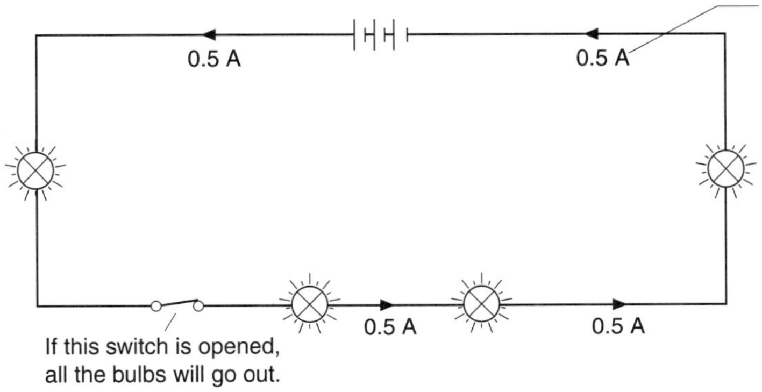

We measure electric charge in **coulombs** (**C**) and electric current in **amps** (**A**). A current of 1A means that 1C of charge is flowing every second (1A=1C/s).

PARALLEL CIRCUITS

In a parallel circuit there are branches where the current 'splits'.

The current may be different in each parallel path but the current flowing into the network is always exactly the same as the total current flowing out.

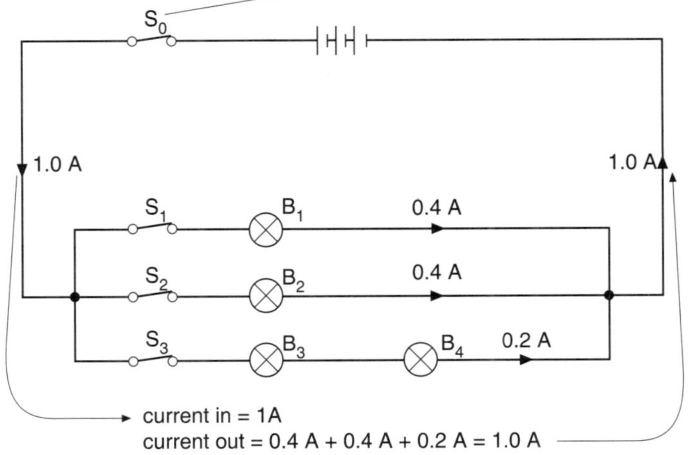

Switch S_0 controls all four bulbs.

S_1 only controls B_1.

S_2 only controls B_2.

S_3 controls B_3 and B_4 only.

C3 – Charge and energy transfer in circuits

When a current flows in an electrical component energy is converted. Cells energize the charge carriers.

CHARGE AND CURRENT

- Current is the flow of charged particles (electrons or ions).
- Current is measured using an **ammeter**:

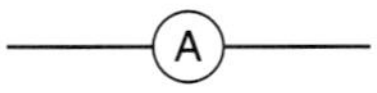

- The size of a current tells us how much charge flows in 1 second.
- Charge is measured in coulombs (C).
- Current is measured in amperes (A).
- 1 amp = 1 coulomb per second.

Charge = current × time

($Q = I \times t$)

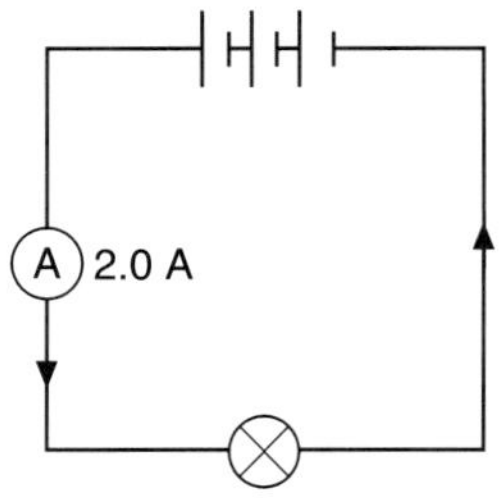

The current is 2.0 A.

In each second, 2 C of charge passes any point in the circuit.

In 10 seconds, 20 C (2 A × 10 s) of charge would pass.

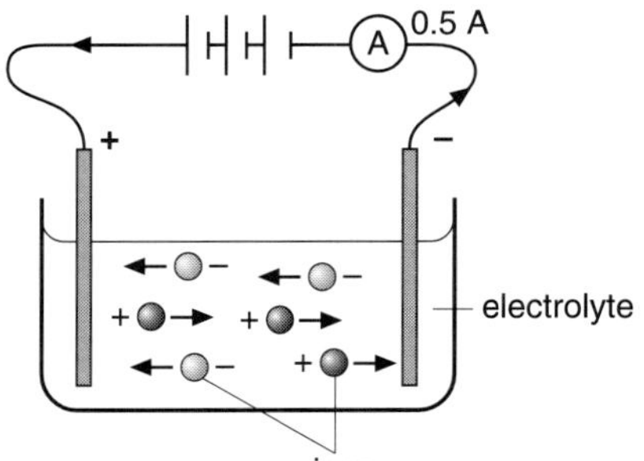

The current is 0.5 A. In each second, ions carrying 0.5 C of charge arrive at each electrode.

In 60 seconds, the charge arriving at the anode is 0.5 A × 60 s = 30 C.

ENERGY TRANSFER IN CIRCUITS

The cell or battery gives energy to the electrons.

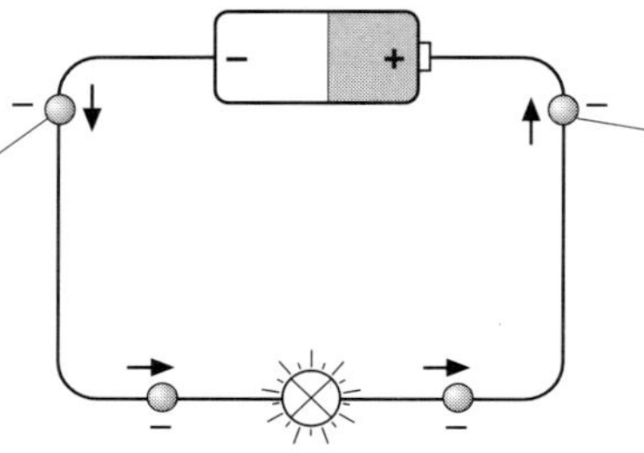

Electrons leaving the battery have maximum energy.

Electrons entering the battery have little energy. The chemical reaction in the cells re-energizes them.

As electrons pass through the bulb, most of their energy is converted into heat and light.

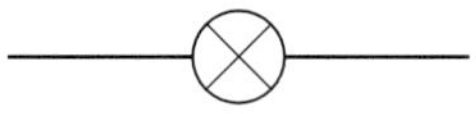

In lamps, energy is transferred as heat and light.

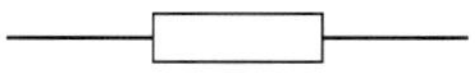

In resistors, energy is transferred as heat.

In bells and buzzers, energy is transferred as sound.

ENERGY AND VOLTAGE

- The amount of energy a battery or power supply gives to charged particles is called the **voltage** or **potential difference** (pd).
- A 1 volt supply will give 1 joule of energy to every 1 coulomb of charge that passes through it.

Energy = voltage × charge

(Energy = $V \times Q$)

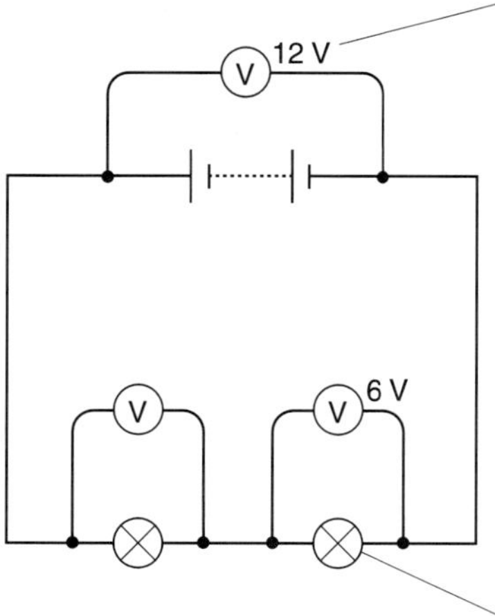

The battery gives a voltage (pd) of 12 V across its terminals. It gives 12 J of energy to each coulomb of charge.

Voltage (pd) across this bulb is 6 V. Each coulomb of charge that passes through the bulb converts 6 J of energy.

C4 – Measuring current, voltage and resistance

Meters are used to measure current and voltage in circuits. However, they must be connected correctly.

MEASURING CURRENT

Current is measured using an **ammeter**.

The ammeter is connected **in series** with the component or part of the circuit being investigated.

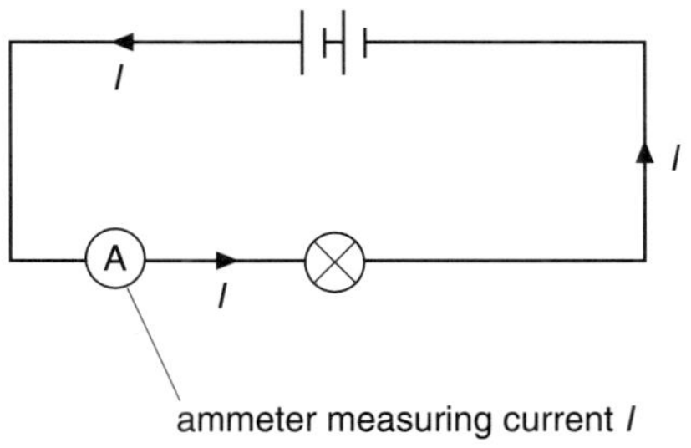

In a series circuit the current is the same at all points. In a parallel circuit the current may be different in each path of the network.

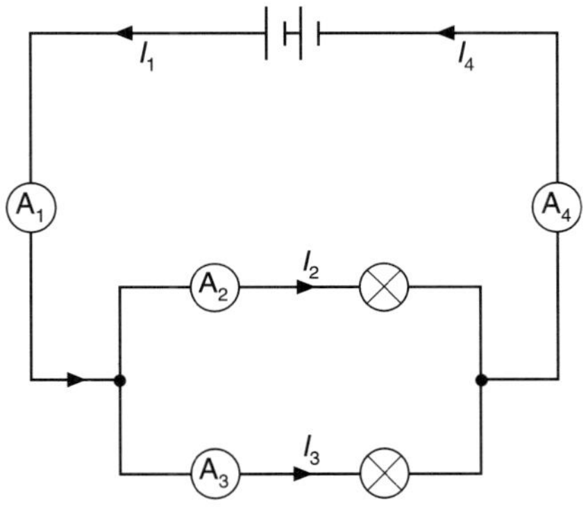

$I_1 = (I_2 + I_3) = I_4$

MEASURING VOLTAGE

Voltage is measured using a **voltmeter**.

The voltmeter is connected **in parallel** with the component being investigated. This is to measure the potential difference (voltage) **between** two points in the circuit.

In a series circuit, the pds across the components add up to the pd across the power supply.

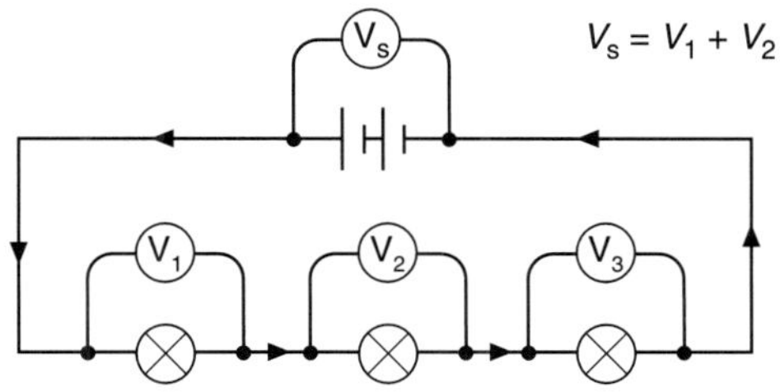

$V_s = V_1 + V_2 + V_3$

In a parallel circuit, the total pd across each pathway is the same.

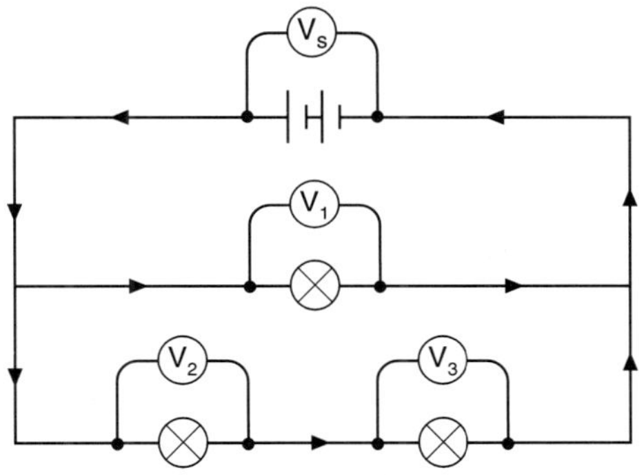

$V_s = V_1 = (V_2 + V_3)$

MEASURING RESISTANCE

Resistance tells us the pd needed to make a current of 1A flow through a circuit or a component.

Larger resistances need greater voltages for the same current.

Resistance can be measured using an **ohmmeter**. It can also be measured using an ammeter (for current) and a voltmeter (for pd).

Note that the ammeter is in series and the voltmeter is in parallel.

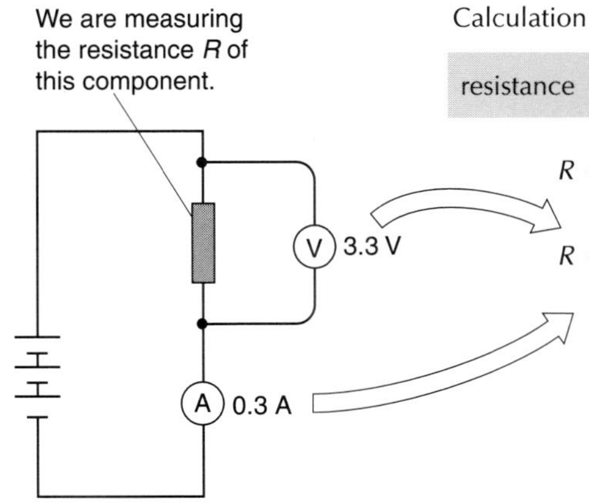

Calculation:

$$\text{resistance} = \frac{\text{voltage}}{\text{current}}$$

$$R = \frac{V}{I}$$

$$R = \frac{3.3\text{ V}}{0.3\text{ A}} = 11\ \Omega$$

(Ω = ohms)

C5 – Ohm's law

Ohm's law tells us about the relationship between current and applied potential difference in a conductor. Many components obey Ohm's law – others do not!

VOLTAGE AND CURRENT IN A CONDUCTOR

This circuit is used to investigate the relationship between the current in a conductor and the voltage (pd) applied across it.

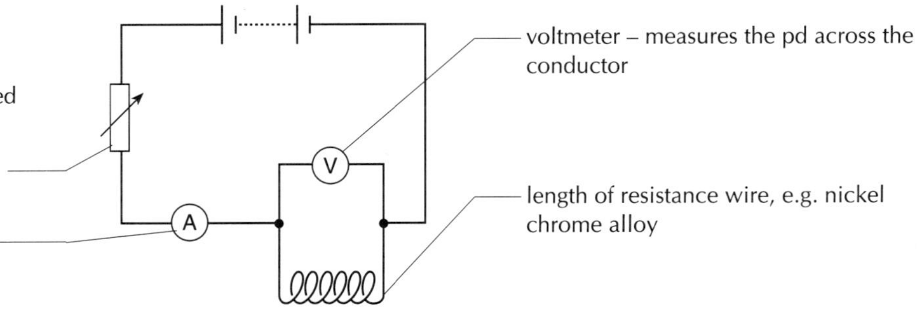

Typical Results:

pd (volts)	current (amps)
0.0	0.0
1.0	0.2
2.0	0.4
3.0	0.6
4.0	0.8
5.0	1.0

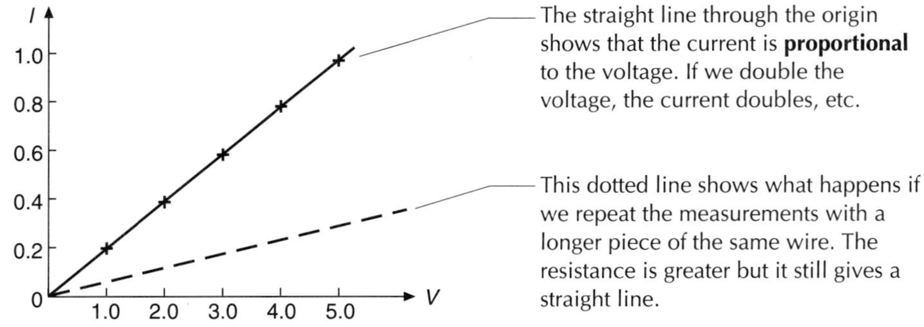

Ohm's law: the current in a conductor is proportional to the voltage applied provided that the temperature does not change.

COMPONENTS THAT DO NOT OBEY OHM'S LAW

Filament lamps: The filament in a bulb is a metal. However, it is designed to get hotter as the current through it increases. The filament has a much higher resistance when it is hot than when it is cold. This is its characteristic current/voltage graph:

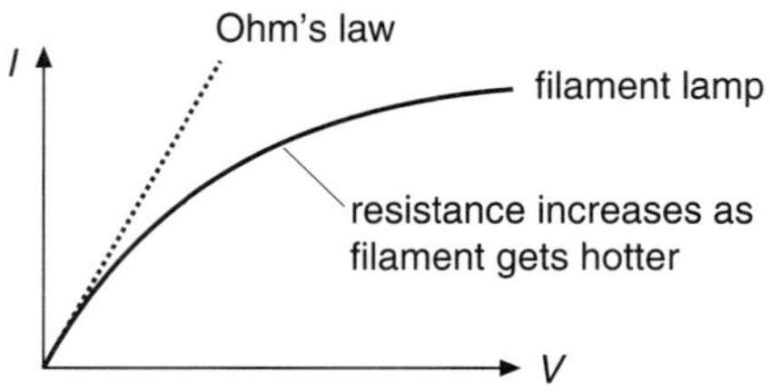

Semi-conductor devices: Electrical components that contain semi-conductors (e.g. silicon or germanium) do not behave like metals. For example, the **diode** only conducts electricity in one direction. This is its characteristic current/voltage graph:

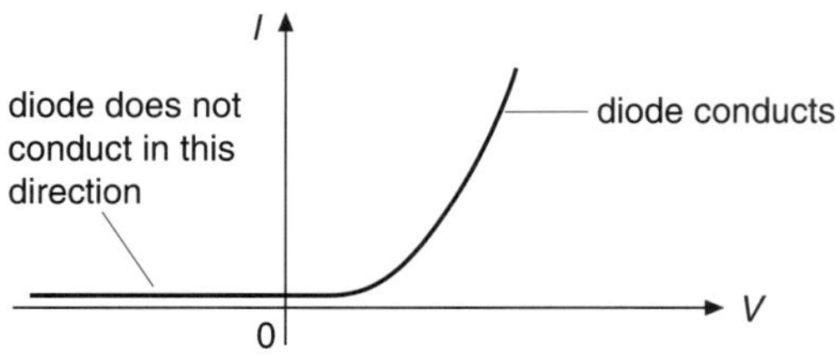

Thermistor: 

The resistance of a thermistor changes with temperature. Most thermistors are made to have a resistance which falls as the temperature rises.

Light dependent resistor (LDR): 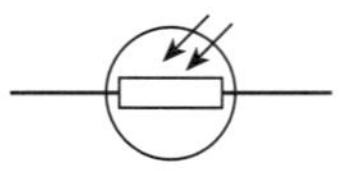

The resistance of an LDR changes with light intensity. When bright light falls on an LDR, its resistance decreases.

C6 – Direct and alternating current

The voltage supplied by a battery is very different from that supplied to our homes.

DIRECT CURRENT (DC)

A cell or battery gives a steady voltage. The + terminal is always positive and the – terminal is always negative. When connected to a circuit, the current always flows in the same direction.

This is **direct current** (**DC**).

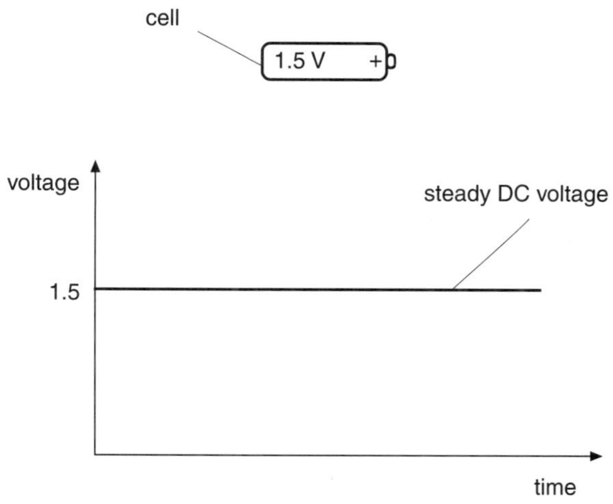

ALTERNATING CURRENT (AC)

The generators which supply mains electricity to our homes give a voltage which changes in size and direction. When we connect a light bulb to the mains supply, the current in it flows forwards and backwards 50 times a second.

This is **alternating current** (**AC**).

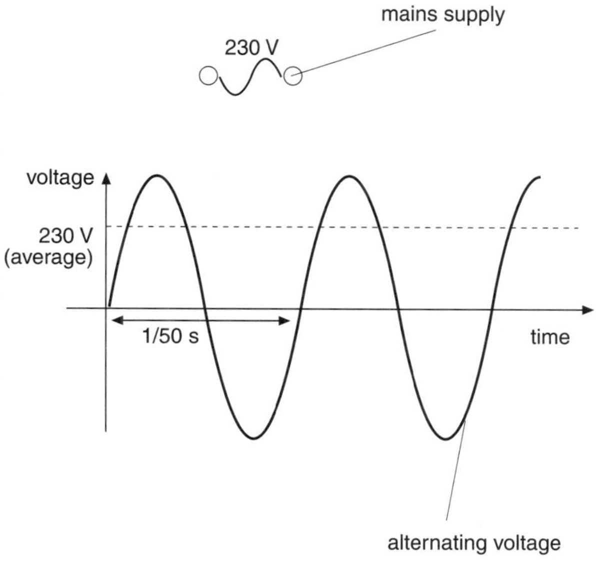

MAINS ELECTRICITY IN THE HOME

In the UK homes are supplied with electricity at about **230 V**. The supply alternates at a frequency of **50 Hz** (50 hertz = 50 cycles per second). There are three wires in the house circuit:

Live: The voltage here alternates at 50 Hz. On average it is at 230 V. It is very dangerous to touch this wire. You will get a shock if you do.

Neutral: This wire does carry current but it is earthed by the electricity company so it stays at about 0 V.

Earth: This wire does not normally carry any current. It is there for safety. If a fault occurs, a large current flows to earth and blows the fuse.

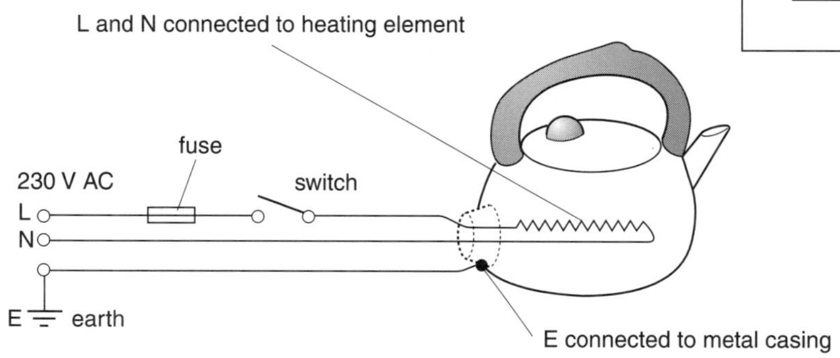

WHY USE AC?

- Generators at power stations are turned by steam or water. As they spin it is easy to produce an alternating voltage.
- Heating elements and light bulbs work perfectly well on DC or AC supplies.
- Alternating voltages can be easily stepped up or down to the desired voltage using transformers.
- Some electrical components only work on DC. However, AC is easily turned into DC using diode circuits called **rectifiers**.

C7 – Electrical safety in the home

Electricity is potentially dangerous. Domestic circuits contain several safety measures.

SWITCHES

Switches (and fuses) are fitted in the live wire of the circuit. When the switch is open, the appliance is disconnected from the 230 V supply.

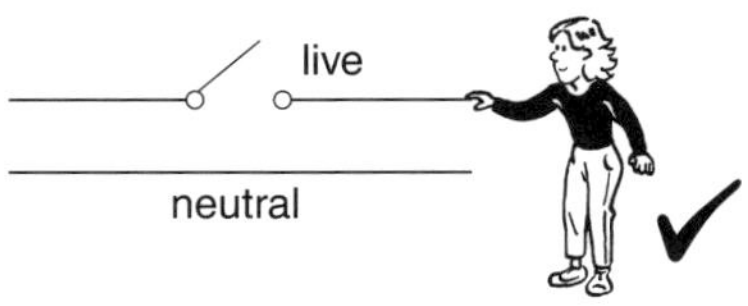

If a switch is incorrectly fitted in the neutral wire, it will still turn the appliance on and off, but the 230 V live wire will still be connected. Touching this will give a shock.

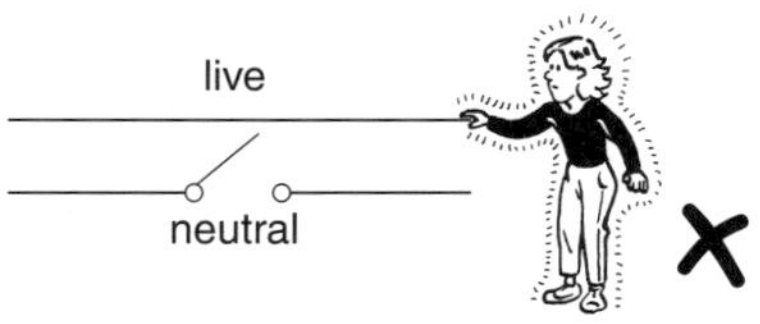

EARTHING

Here the live wire has broken and is touching the casing of the appliance. This connects it to the 230 V supply. When someone touches it, a current flows through the person to earth, giving a shock.

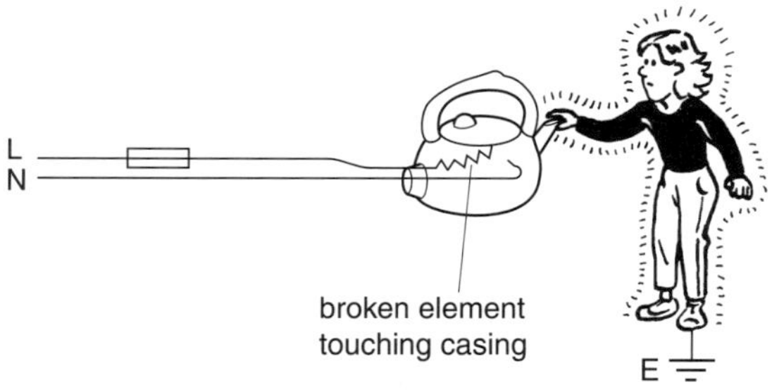

Here an earth wire is connected. Now when the live wire touches the casing a large current immediately flows through the earth wire. This blows the fuse and disconnects the appliance from the supply.

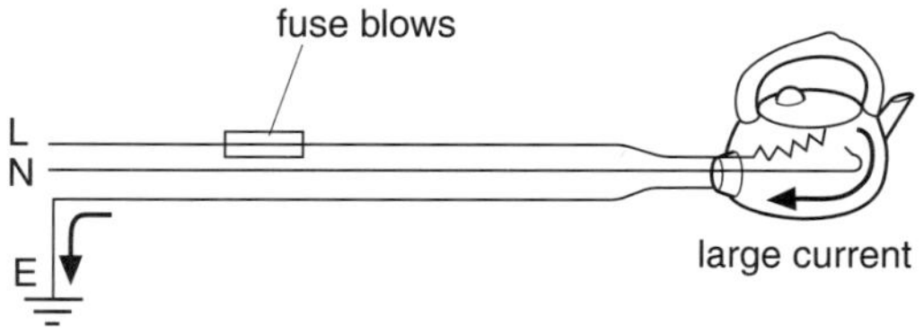

DOUBLE INSULATION

Some appliances do not have an earth wire but are double insulated. All the parts that the user can touch are plastic or are coated in plastic. Now if a fault occurs and the live wire touches the casing, the user cannot get a shock.

FUSES AND CIRCUIT BREAKERS

If a fault occurs, causing a large current to flow, the appliance and the house wiring could be damaged. Overheating could start a fire.

The wiring in a house has several parts – lighting, downstairs sockets, upstairs sockets, cooker, etc. Each circuit is protected by a fuse or circuit breaker. A fuse melts if the current gets too high. This breaks the circuit. A circuit breaker is an electromagnetic switch which breaks the circuit if the current goes above a certain level. If a fuse 'blows' it must be replaced. If a circuit breaker 'trips' it can be reset by pushing a button.

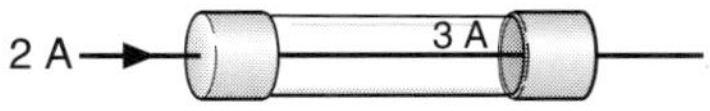

This fuse will conduct currents up to 3 A only.

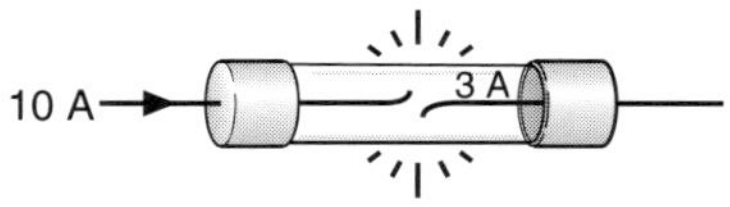

If the current exceeds 3 A, the fuse wire quickly melts.

A plug has a fuse inside. The fuse rating should be just large enough to let the appliance work properly.

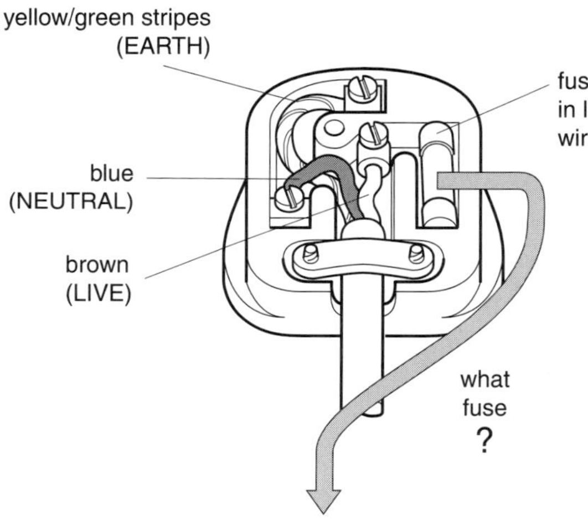

appliance	operating current	fuse rating
lamp	0.25 A	1A or 3 A
TV	1.5 A	3 A
kettle	4 A	13 A
2 kW heater	8 A	13 A

RESIDUAL CURRENT CIRCUIT BREAKERS (RCCB)

Fuses and circuit breakers will allow some current to flow to earth before they break the circuit. This can be dangerous when using, for example, garden equipment. An RCCB constantly monitors the current in the live and neutral wires. These should always be the same but if a fault develops and the RCCB detects a difference, it breaks the circuit.

C8 – Power and the cost of electrical energy

Electricity companies charge for the energy 'used' in homes and factories.

ELECTRICAL POWER

- Appliances convert electrical energy into different forms.
- The power rating of an appliance tells us how quickly the appliance converts energy.
- The unit of power is the **watt** (**W**).
- 1 W means that 1 joule of energy is converted in 1 second. 1 W = 1 J/s.
- 1 kilowatt = 1000 W = 1000 J/s

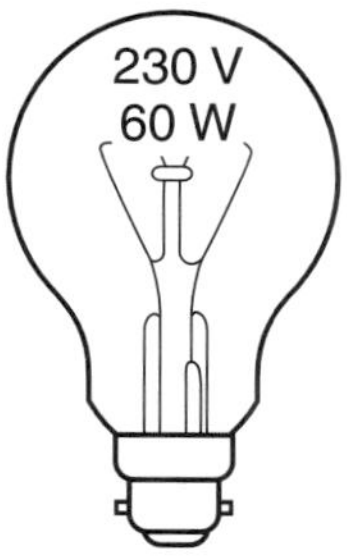

When connected to a 230 V supply, this bulb converts 60 J of electrical energy to light and heat in each second. Its power is 60 W.

Typical power ratings

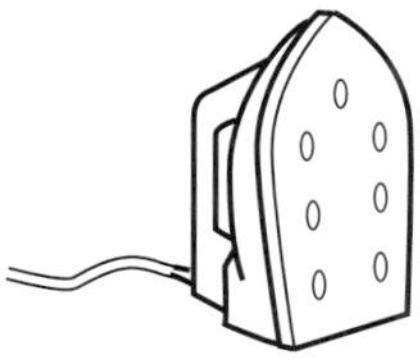

500 W iron

650 W television

1250 W hair dryer

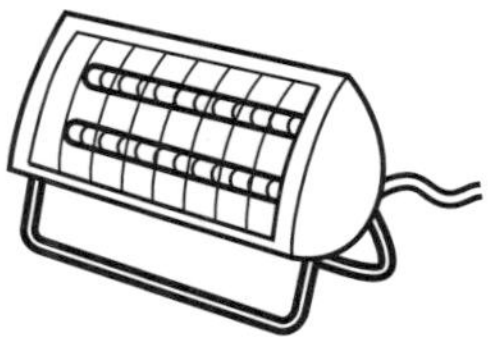

2000 W electric fire

POWER, VOLTAGE AND CURRENT

The power of an appliance is related to the voltage across it and the current flowing.

power = voltage × current

$P = V \times I$

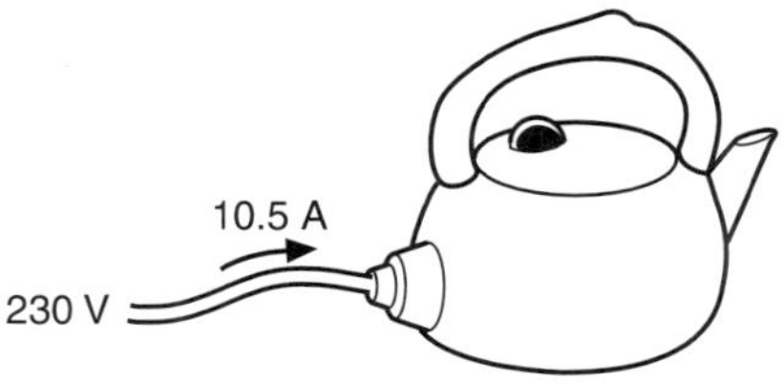

Example:
An electric kettle is connected to the 230 V mains supply. It draws a current of 10.5 A. What is its power?

$P = V \times I$

P = 230 V × 10.5 A = 2415 W

PAYING FOR ELECTRICAL ENERGY

Electricity companies charge for energy in '**units**'. Each unit is the amount of energy converted by a 1 kW appliance in 1 hour. A unit is also called a **kilowatt hour**.

The cost of electrical energy varies but is about 8p for each unit.

Examples:
A 2 kW heater is used for 6 hours.

Energy used = 2 kW × 6 h = 12 kWh

Cost = 12 kWh x 8p = 96p

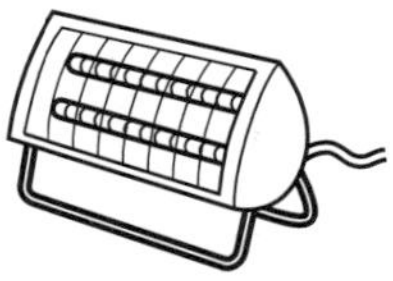

2 kW

for

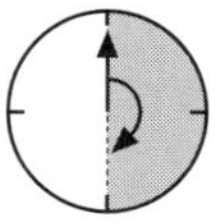

6 hours

= 12 kWh (12 units)

A 100 W light bulb is left on for 9 hours.

Energy used = 0.1 kW × 9 h = 0.9 kWh

Cost = 0.9 kWh × 8p = 7.2p

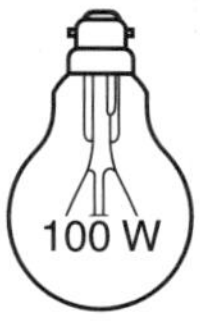

0.1 kW

for

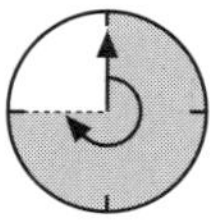

9 hours

= 0.9 kWh (0.9 units)

C9 – Magnetism and electromagnetism

Permanent magnets attract some materials but not others. Electric currents also produce magnetic fields.

MAGNETISM

Magnets attract materials containing the elements iron, nickel and cobalt. Iron and steel are strongly magnetic. Aluminium, copper, plastic and glass are examples of non-magnetic materials.

The area around a magnet where it will affect magnetic materials is called a **magnetic field**. The strongest parts of a magnetic field are called **poles**.

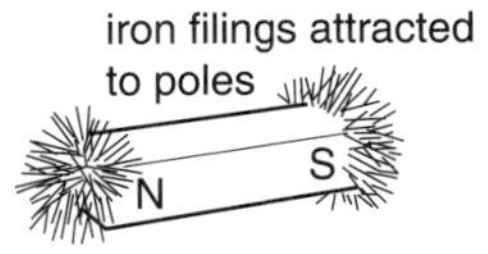

If a magnet is suspended it will settle down in a north–south direction just like a magnetized compass needle. We call the poles 'north-seeking' (**N**) and 'south-seeking' (**S**).

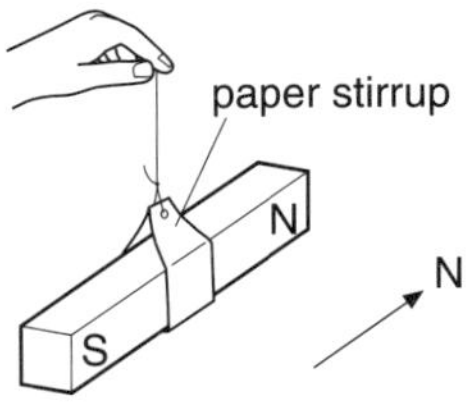

Similar magnetic poles repel each other.

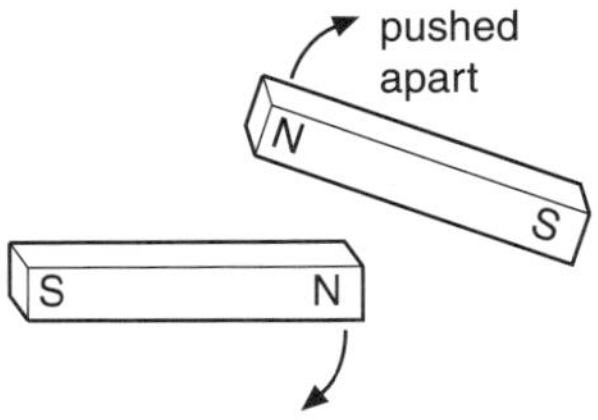

Opposite magnetic poles attract each other.

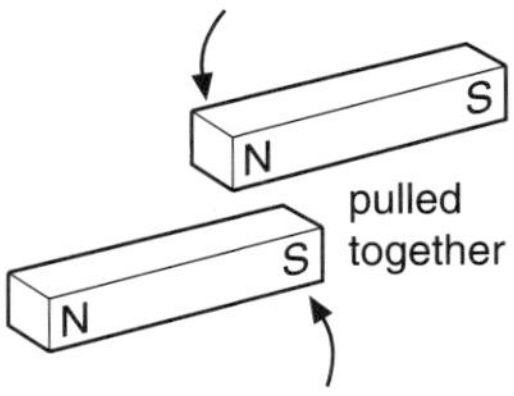

Magnetic fields

The direction and shape of a magnetic field can be found using plotting compasses and iron filings.

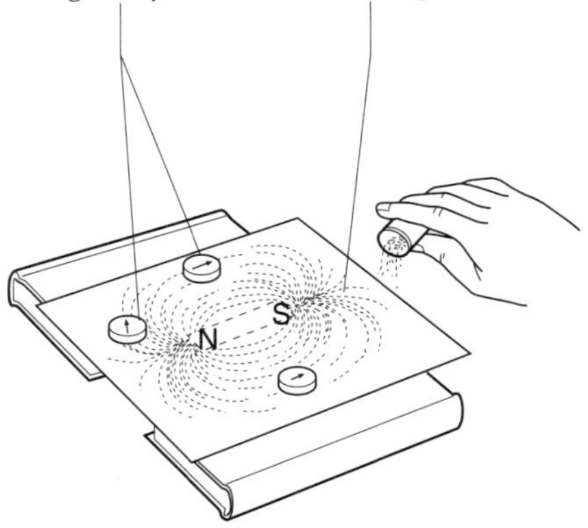

- The magnetic field lines are closer together where the field is stronger.
- Their direction is from the N pole to the S pole.

These show the fields between two magnets.

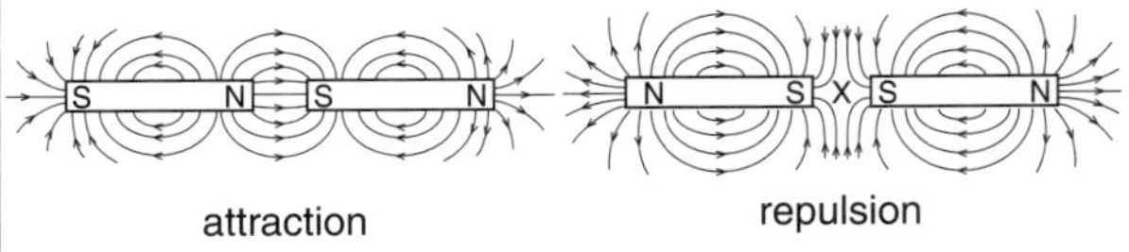

ELECTROMAGNETISM

A magnetic field can be detected around a wire carrying a current. When the current is turned off, the magnetic field disappears. When the current is reversed, the magnetic field reverses. This is **electromagnetism**.

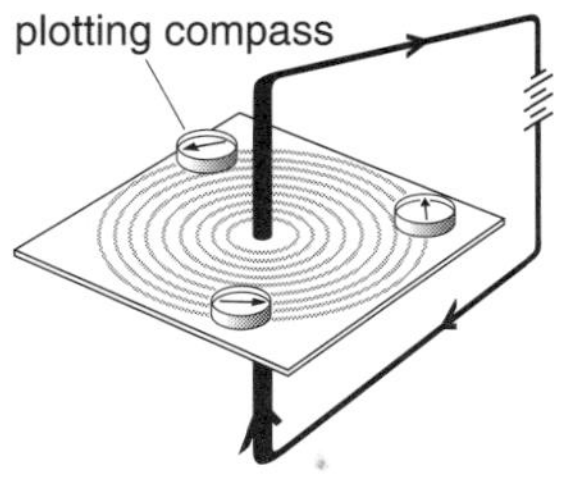

The field is made stronger by winding the wire into a coil. The field around the coil looks like the field of a bar magnet.

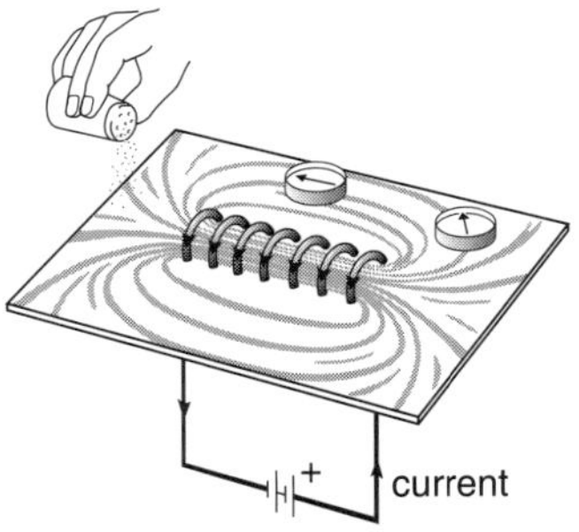

The strength of an electromagnet depends on:

- the current in the coil
- the number of turns in the coil
- the cross-sectional area of the coil
- the material inside the coil (an iron or steel core makes the field much stronger)

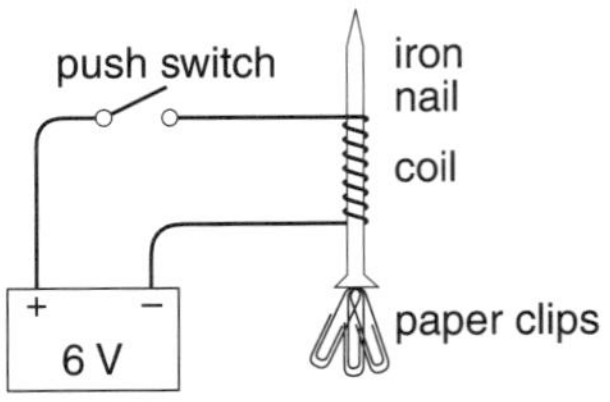

A simple electromagnet

C10 – The motor effect

A current-carrying wire in a magnetic field experiences a force. This effect is used in motors and speakers.

THE MOTOR EFFECT

This wire is in a magnetic field. When the switch is closed, a current flows.

The interaction of the magnetic field due to the current and that of the magnets produces a force on the wire.

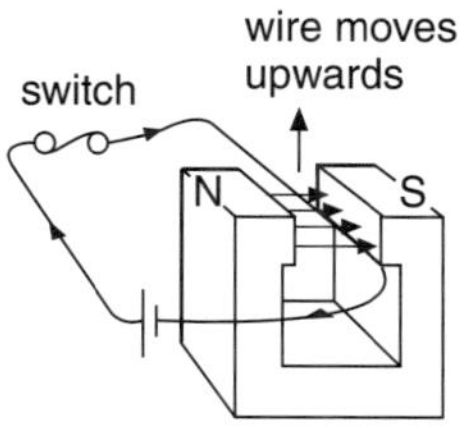

The **size** of the force on the wire can be increased by:

- increasing the current
- increasing the strength of the magnetic field
- increasing the length of wire in the magnetic field

The direction of the force can be reversed either by reversing the current or by reversing the magnetic field.

FLEMING'S LEFT HAND RULE

The direction of the force on the wire (and its motion) can be predicted using this rule:

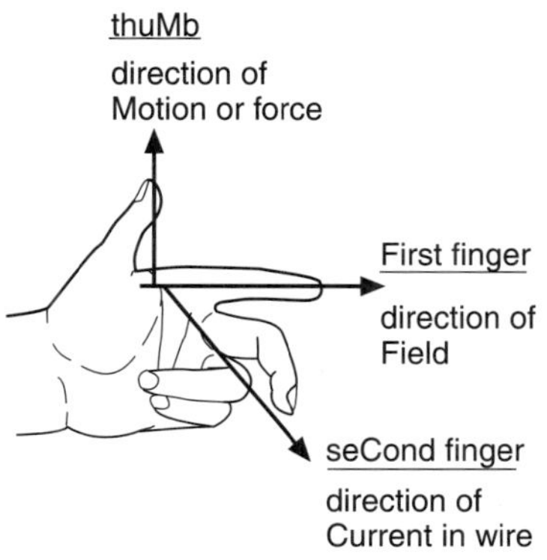

LOUDSPEAKER

The alternating current signals sent from the amplifier of a television or CD player pass through a coil inside the speaker. The coil is between the poles of a strong magnet. As the current changes size and direction, the moving coil makes the cone of the loudspeaker move in and out very rapidly. This vibrates the air, giving the sound we hear.

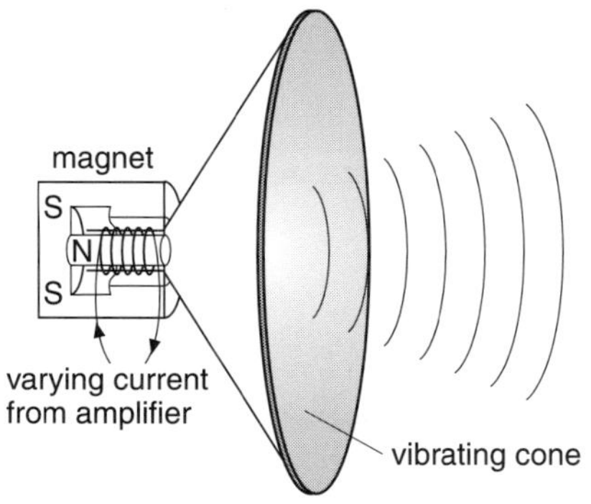

SIMPLE DC MOTOR

The simple DC motor is a coil mounted on an axle so that it can spin between two magnets. The ends of the coil are connected to a split ring or commutator. Connections to the battery are made through carbon brushes which rub against the commutator.

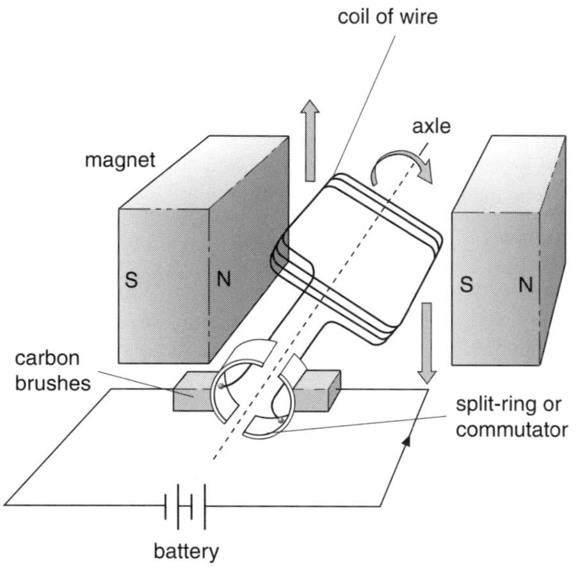

The commutator swaps the connections to the battery at the top of each revolution so that the current is always flowing the same way. This keeps the coil spinning in the same direction.

End view of motor

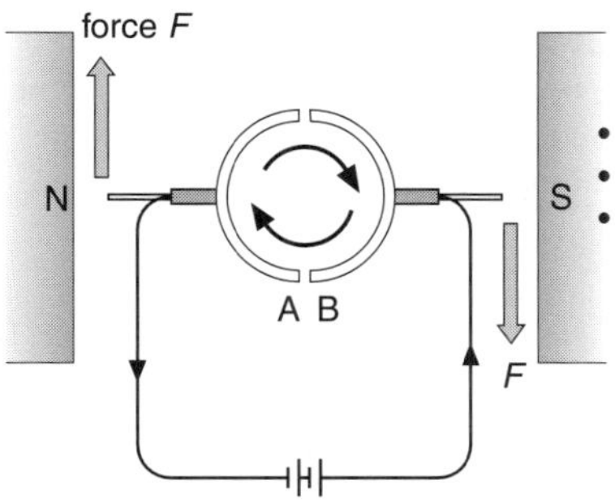

- coil flat
- forces are opposite
- coil turns

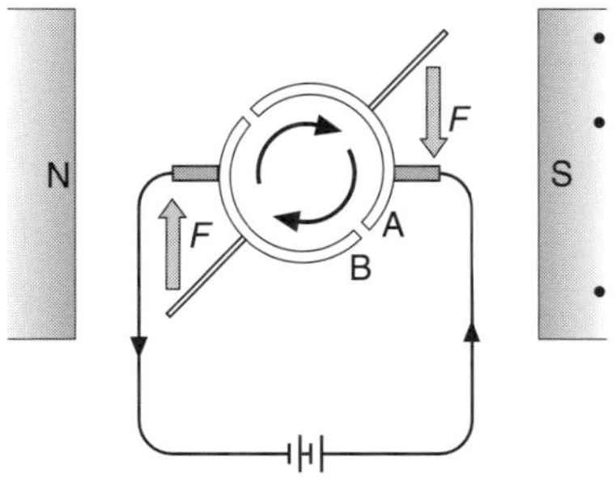

- just past the top
- each brush is now touching the other half of the split ring
- coil keeps turning in same direction

C11 – Electromagnetic induction

Generating electricity using electromagnetic induction is of vital importance in the modern world.

ELECTROMAGNETIC INDUCTION

When a conductor (e.g. a wire) moves across a magnetic field, it cuts through field lines. This **induces** (generates) a voltage across the ends of the wire. If the wire is part of a circuit a current flows.

It does not matter whether the wire moves or the magnet moves as long as one moves **relative** to the other.

For a higher induced voltage:

- move the wire faster
- use a stronger magnetic field

The induced voltage can be reversed by:

- reversing the magnetic field
- reversing the direction of motion

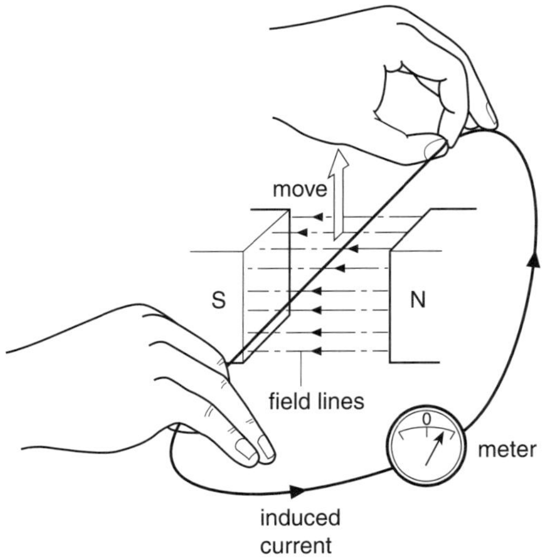

A current can also be generated by moving a magnet into a coil of wire. As the magnet moves, field lines are cut.

For a higher induced voltage:

- move the magnet faster
- use a stronger magnet

The induced voltage can be reversed by:

- reversing the magnetic field (i.e. turning the magnet round)
- reversing the direction of motion (i.e. pulling the magnet out of the coil)

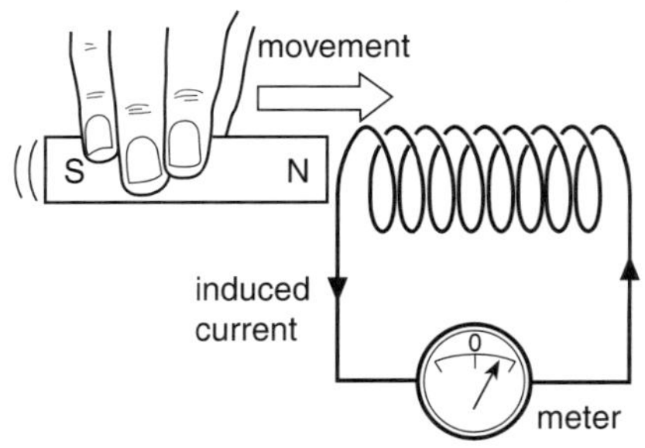

SIMPLE AC GENERATOR

A coil of wire is turned in a magnetic field. Each side of the coil cuts through the field lines – first in one direction and then in the other. An alternating current is induced.

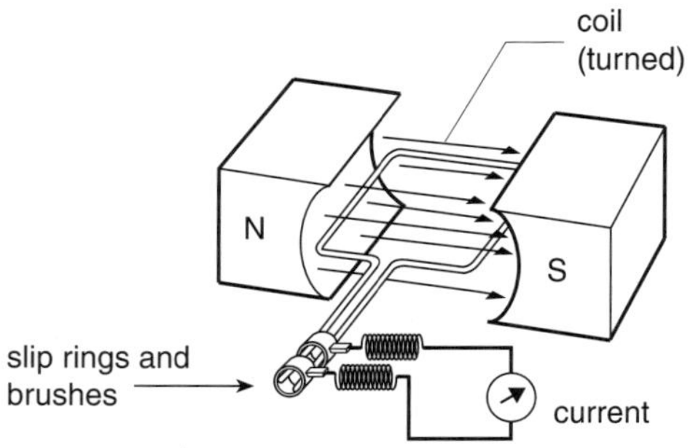

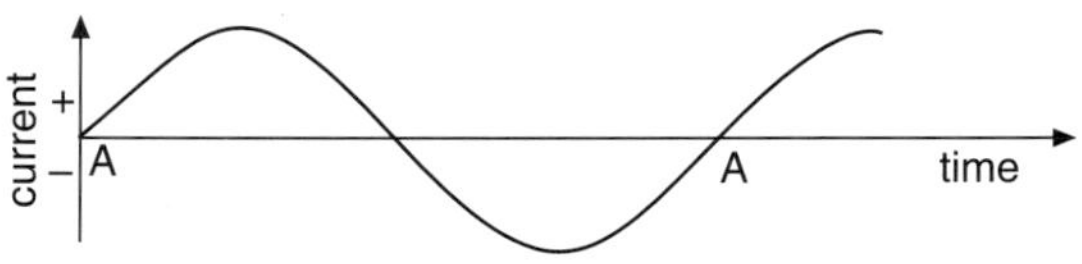

A to A = one complete rotation of coil

REVOLVING MAGNET DYNAMO

In a bicycle dynamo a magnet revolves so that the magnetic field through the coil keeps changing. An alternating current flows in the cycle lamps.

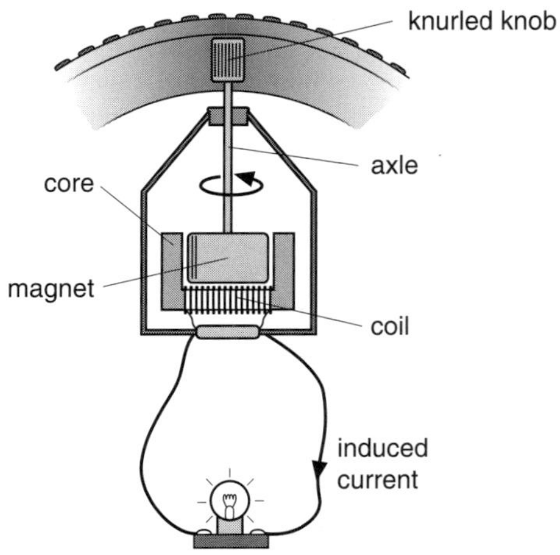

C12 – Transformers

Transformers are very important electrical 'machines'. They allow us to change the voltage of alternating supplies. They are used inside electrical devices and for transmitting electrical power.

A transformer has two separate coils of wire wound on an iron core. When a current flows in the primary coil it produces a magnetic field. This passes through the secondary coil 'guided' by the iron core. If the field changes, a voltage will be induced in the secondary coil. (This is just like moving a magnet into or out of a coil.)

- When the switch is closed, a magnetic field suddenly passes through the secondary coil. A current is induced.
- When the switch is opened again, the magnetic field in the core suddenly disappears. This change induces a current in the secondary coil but in the opposite direction.
- Notice that a current is only induced when the current in the primary circuit is changing. A steady current produces no current in the secondary circuit.

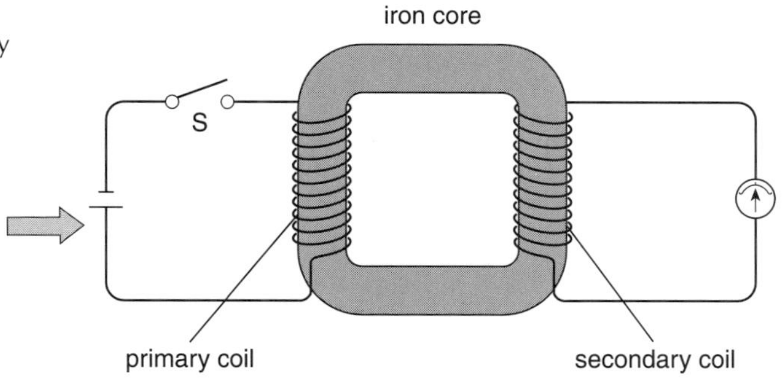

When an AC supply is connected to the primary side, an alternating voltage is induced in the secondary coil.

Transformers work on AC.

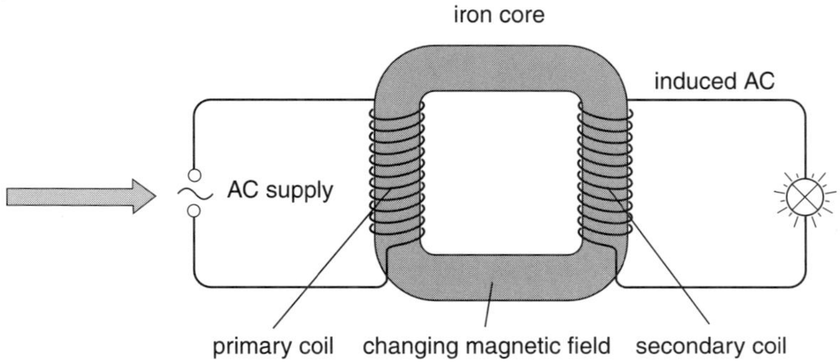

CHANGING VOLTAGES

Transformers are used for changing voltages. The output voltage is connected to the input voltage by this equation:

$$\frac{N_p}{N_s} = \frac{V_p}{V_s}$$

N_p = number of turns in primary coil

N_s = number of turns in secondary coil

V_p = input voltage (across primary)

V_s = output voltage (across secondary)

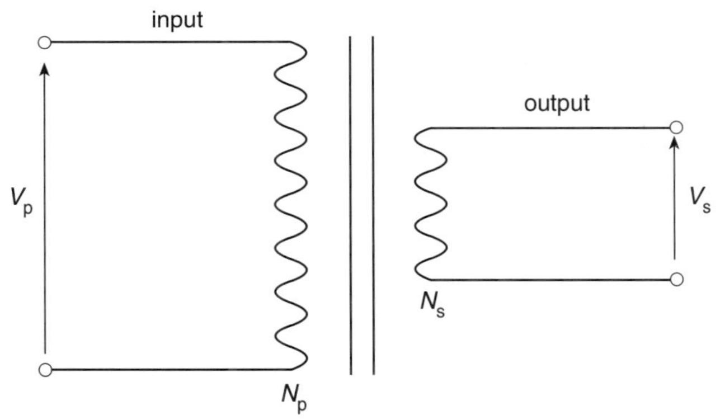

STEP-UP TRANSFORMERS

To increase or step up the voltage we need more turns in the secondary coil than in the primary coil.

Example: A transformer has 100 turns on the primary coil and 2000 on the secondary coil. It is connected to a 2 V alternating supply.

The output voltage is given by: $\frac{N_p}{N_s} = \frac{V_p}{V_s}$

$\frac{100}{2000} = \frac{2\text{ V}}{V_s}$ rearranging $V_s = \frac{2\text{ V} \times 2000}{100}$

$$\mathbf{V_s = 40\text{ V}}$$

(2 V stepped up to 40 V)

STEP-DOWN TRANSFORMERS

To decrease or step down the voltage we need more turns in the primary coil than in the secondary coil.

Example: A transformer has 2300 turns on the primary coil and 60 on the secondary coil. It is connected to the 230 V mains supply.

The output voltage is given by: $\frac{N_p}{N_s} = \frac{V_p}{V_s}$

$\frac{2300}{60} = \frac{230\text{ V}}{V_s}$ rearranging $V_s = \frac{230\text{ V} \times 60}{2300}$

$$\mathbf{V_s = 6\text{ V}}$$

(230 V stepped down to 6 V)

C13 – Transmission of electricity

Electricity is generated at power stations. It is then distributed around the country via a vast network or grid of transformers and cables.

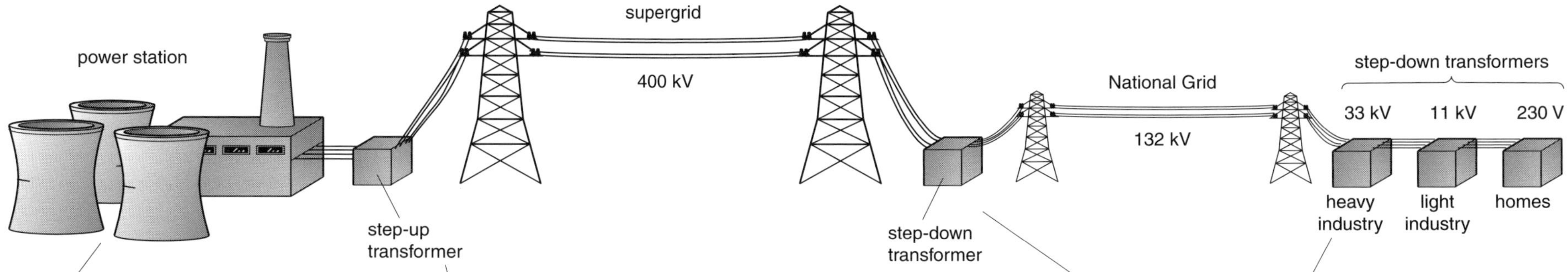

Power stations

Oil, gas, coal or nuclear fuel is used to heat water and turn it into steam.

The steam turns turbines connected to generators.

A 400 megawatt generator produces currents of about 20 000 A at about 20 000 V.

(Remember: **power** = **current** × **voltage**)

(Other generation sources include: solar, wind, hydro.)

Step-up transformers

When a transformer steps up voltage, the current is stepped down. The power in the secondary circuit is (almost) the same as the power in the primary circuit.

$$I_p \times V_p = I_s \times V_s$$

By using a very high voltage, power can be transmitted at a much lower current. This means that less energy is lost as heat in the power lines.

The supergrid is at 400 kV. At this voltage a power of 400 MW can be transmitted at a current of just 1000 A. (400 000 V × 1000 A = 400 MW)

Step-down transformers

Step-down transformers reduce the voltage to suitable levels for use in factories. The voltage is stepped down to 230 V for use in the home.

Notice that it is much more convenient to transmit electricity as AC because transformers only work on alternating supplies.

C14 – Forces on materials

Understanding how forces change the shape of materials helps us to use them effectively in the construction and manufacturing industries.

FORCES ON MATERIALS

Forces cause materials to **deform**. 'Pulling' forces cause **tension**. 'Pushing' forces cause **compression**.

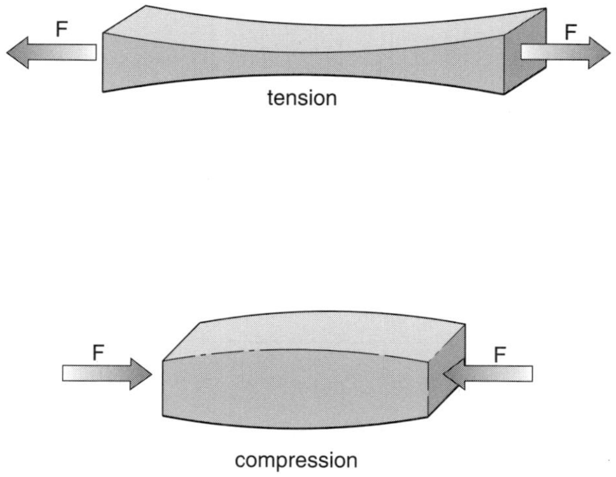

When the forces are removed, the material may spring back to its original shape. This is **elastic** behaviour.

Some materials remain stretched or compressed when the forces are removed. This is **plastic** behaviour.

Stretching wires and springs

A metal wire or spring behaves according to Hooke's Law for small loads. When the load is removed it goes back to its original length. It is **elastic**.

After the elastic limit has been reached, the metal or spring starts to deform **plastically**. When the load is removed, it does not go back to the original length. It is left permanently deformed.

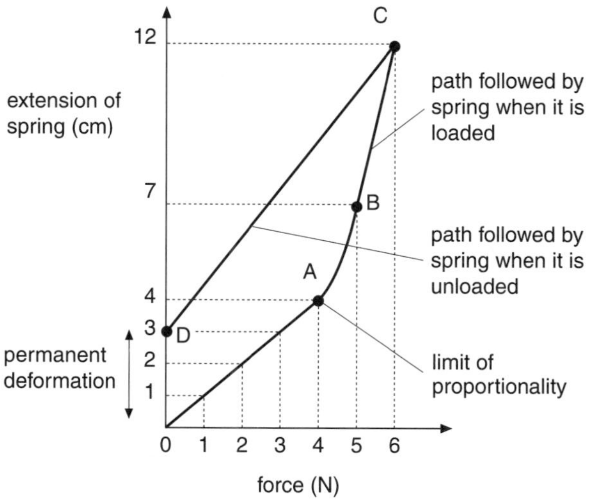

Hooke's law

Springs and many other materials obey Hooke's law when they are compressed or stretched. This states that:

up to a certain limit, the extension is proportional to the load applied.

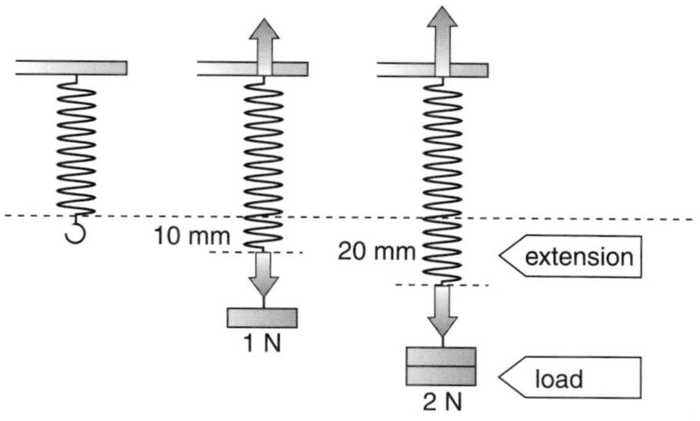

Load in N	0	1	2	3	4	5
Extension in mm	0	10	20	30	40	58

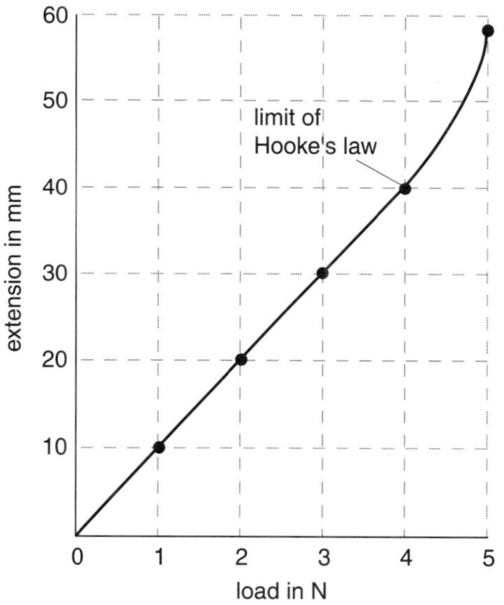

Stretching rubber

Rubber is a very useful material. It can be stretched to several times its original size but it will still spring back. It has a very large elastic limit.

At first the rubber is very easy to stretch but after it reaches a certain length it needs a large force to stretch any further. This is because rubber is made up of very long twisted molecules. As a load is applied, these molecules are straightened. Once they are straight, it becomes very difficult to make them any longer.

C15 – Pressure

Pressure depends on the size of the force applied and the area of the surface it acts on.

- When a force is applied to a surface it applies pressure.
- The pressure depends on the size of the force and the area on which it acts.

$$\textbf{pressure} = \frac{\textbf{force}}{\textbf{area}}$$

(Note that we use the force acting at 90° to the surface, i.e. the force is at a normal to the area.)

The unit of pressure is the **pascal**.

The pressure is one pascal when a force of 1 N acts (at 90°) on an area of 1 m^2.

1 Pa = 1 N/m^2

Calculation:

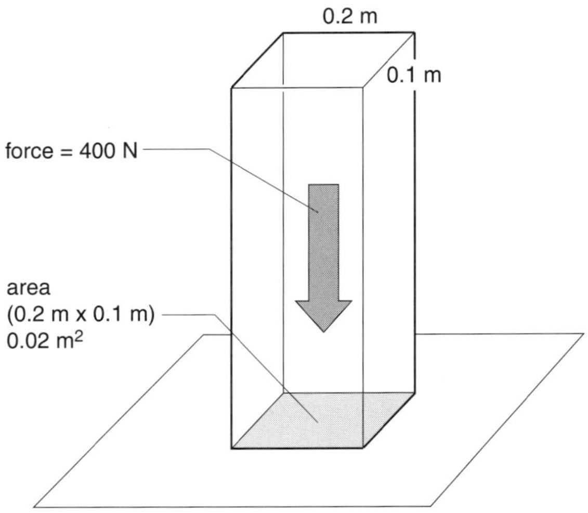

The block has a weight of **400 N**.

It is resting on an area of **0.02 m^2**.

$$\text{Pressure} = \frac{400\ \text{N}}{0.02\ \text{m}^2} = \mathbf{20000\ Pa}$$

USES OF HIGH PRESSURE

(concentrating the force)

Drawing pin

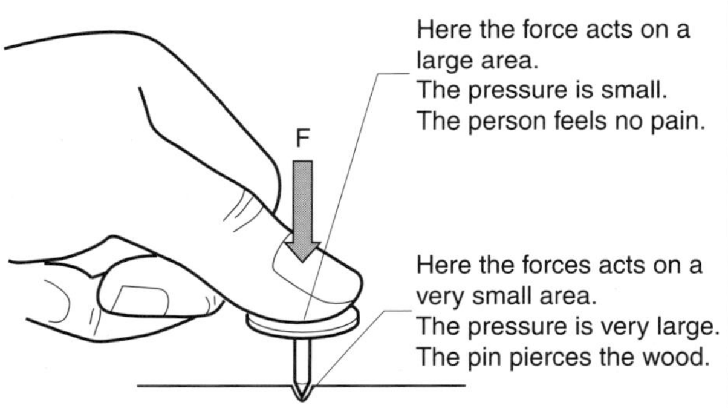

Studs on hockey boots

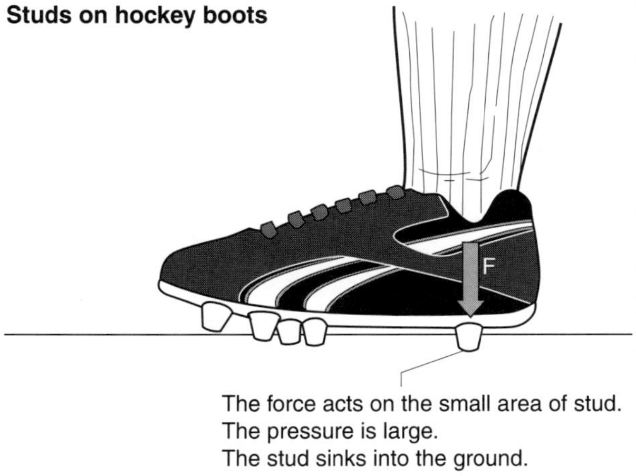

USES OF LOW PRESSURE

(spreading the force)

Washer

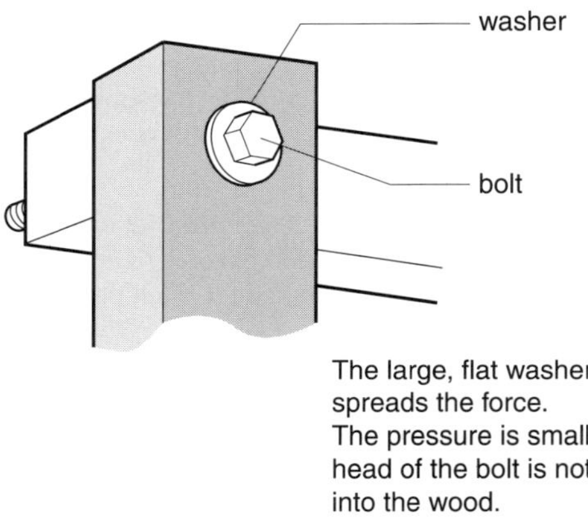

Snow shoes

The weight of the person is spread over a large area by the snow shoes.
The pressure is small so the person does not sink far into the snow.

C16 – Pressure in liquids

Hydraulic machines use incompressible liquids to transmit pressure through pipes.

Beneath the surface of a liquid there is a pressure due to the weight of the liquid above. The pressure increases the deeper you go.

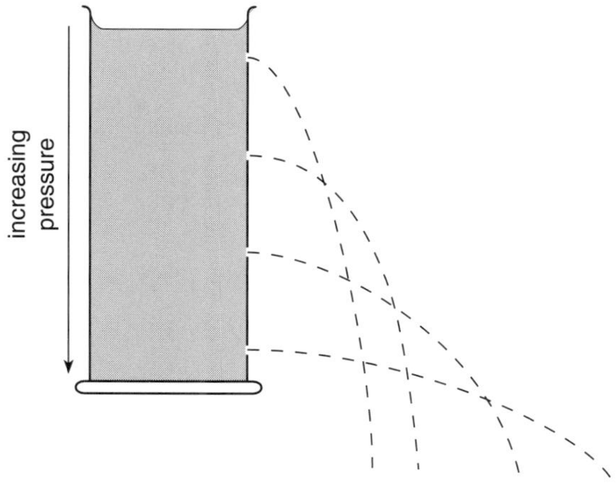

The pressure also depends on the density of the liquid. Denser liquids exert greater pressures.

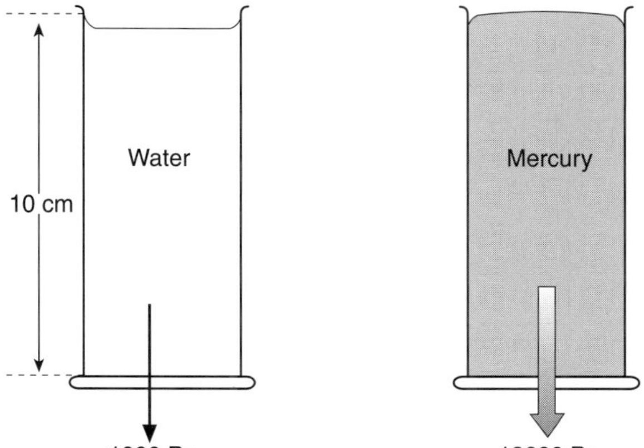

The pressure in a liquid acts in all directions.

HYDRAULIC MACHINES

Liquids are difficult to compress because their molecules are close together. This makes them suitable for transmitting pressure through tubes. Hydraulic machines use liquid under pressure to transmit pressure. If the liquid presses on a large surface area it can exert a very great force. The examples below show hydraulic machines as **force multipliers**.

Hydraulic jack

A force is applied to a small **master cylinder** of liquid. The pressure is high.

The pressure is transmitted to a **slave cylinder** with a greater area. This can now exert a large force to lift the car.

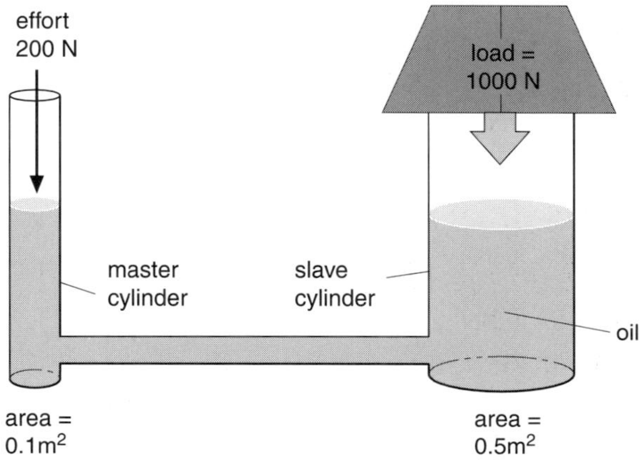

Principle of an hydraulic jack

Car braking system

Pressing on the brake pedal exerts a force on the liquid in the small master cylinder. The pressure is high.

The pressure is transmitted to the brakes where it presses on pistons in the slave cylinders. This exerts a large force which presses the brake pads on to the discs to stop the car.

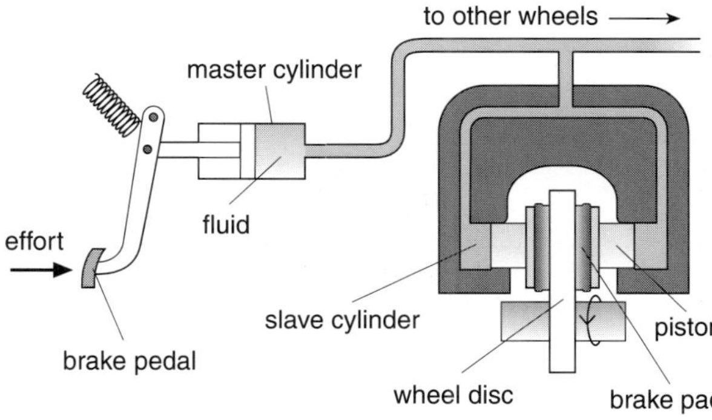

Hydraulic braking system

C17 – Pressure in gases

Gas molecules are constantly in motion. As they collide with surfaces they exert pressure.

PRESSURE AND VOLUME OF A GAS

This apparatus is used for investigating the relationship between pressure and volume for a gas at a constant temperature.

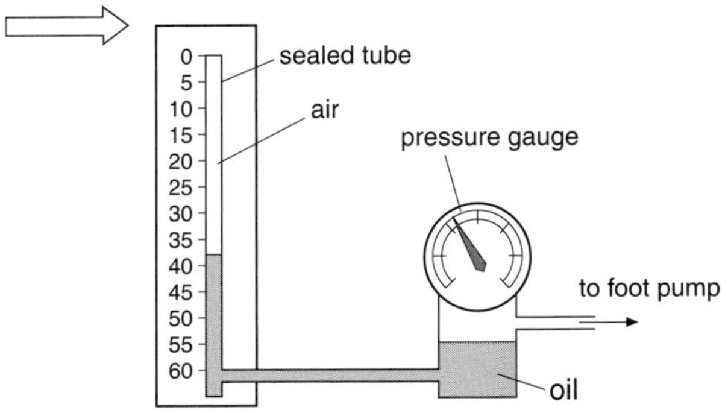

A fixed mass of gas is trapped in the tube. A pump is used to increase the pressure on the gas.

The volume of the gas decreases until the gas pressure equals the pressure compressing it.

The experiment is repeated several times. Each time the pressure and the volume are recorded in a table.

The results table shows that the pressure multiplied by the volume always gives the same value. In other words, if we double the pressure on the gas, the volume halves.

The results confirm **Boyle's law**:

If a fixed mass of gas is kept at a constant temperature, pressure × volume remains the same.

$P \times V$ = constant

Typical results

Pressure/Pa	Volume/cm^3	$P \times V$
110 000	50	5 500 000
137 500	40	5 500 000
220 000	25	5 500 000
275 000	20	5 500 000
550 000	10	5 500 000

Kinetic theory explanation

As the volume is decreased, the molecules have less space to move around. They are moving at the same speed (temperature unchanged) and so they have more collisions with the container walls in each second. This raises the pressure.

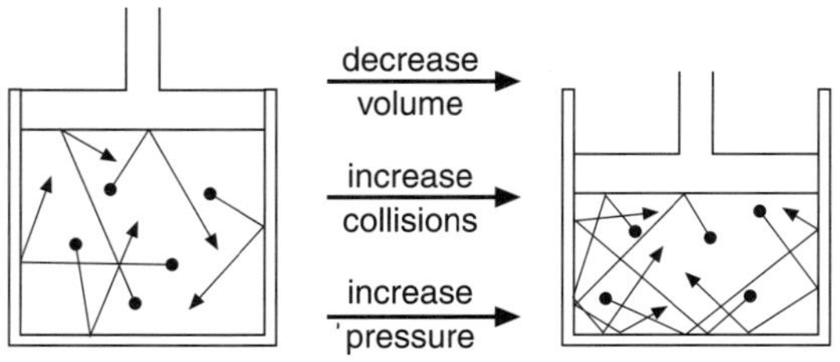

Example calculation

500 cm^3 of air is trapped at a pressure of 100000 Pa.

The pressure is increased to 250000 Pa at the same temperature. What is the new volume (V_2) of the gas?

$$\text{pressure} \times \text{volume} = \text{constant}$$

$$P_1 \times V_1 = P_2 \times V_2$$

$$100000 \times 500 = 250000 \times V_2$$

$$V_2 = \frac{100000 \times 500}{250000} = 200\ cm^3$$

(The pressure increases 2.5 times: the volume decreases 2.5 times.)

C18 – Moments

Levers are perhaps the most ancient of machines. They use the principle of moments.

MOMENT OF A FORCE

When a force acts at a distance from a pivot, it has a **turning effect**. The size of the turning effect is called the moment of the force.

moment = force × distance from pivot

(The distance must be measured at 90° to the force. This is the **perpendicular** distance.)

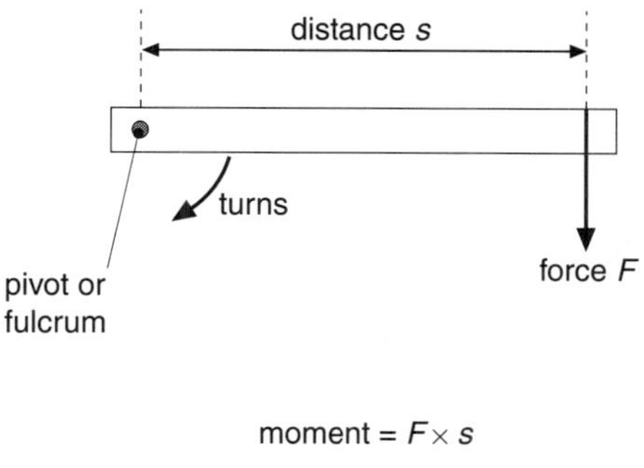

BALANCING MOMENTS

If two forces act on an object mounted on a pivot, it will turn unless the moments are **balanced**.

In this case the see saw is balanced because the moment on the right-hand side trying to turn it clockwise is the same size as the moment on the left-hand side trying to turn it anti-clockwise.

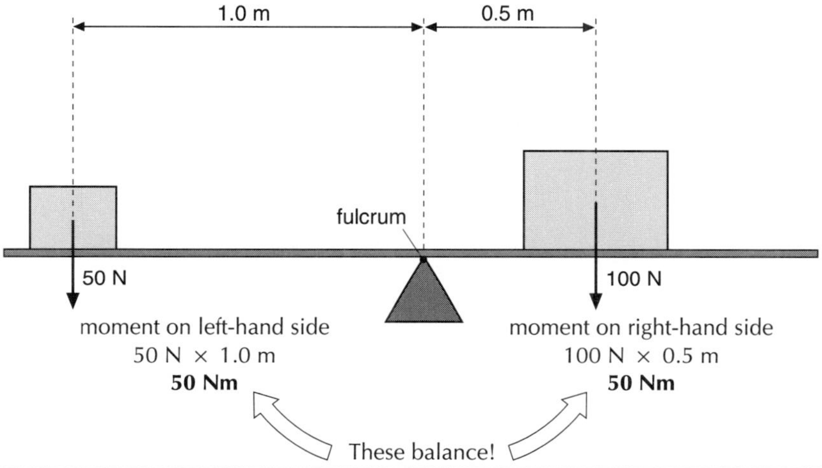

USING MOMENTS

The principle of moments can be used in simple machines called levers.

In these examples, the load (force) is close to the pivot. The effort is much further away. This allows a small effort to overcome the moment of a large load.

Levers like these are force multipliers.

Claw hammer

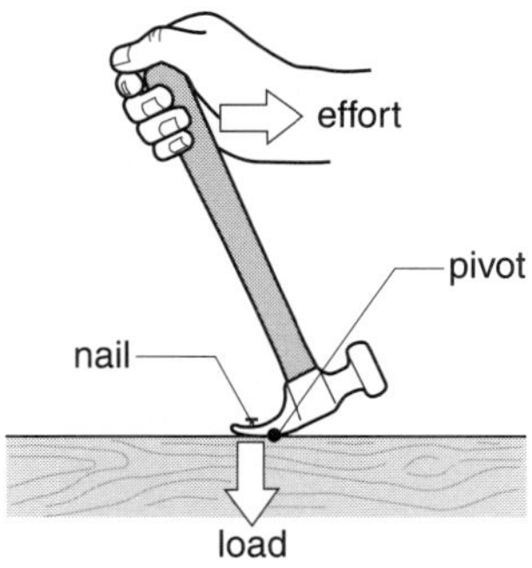

The long handle of the hammer allows a small force to overcome the large force between the nail and the wood.

Spanner

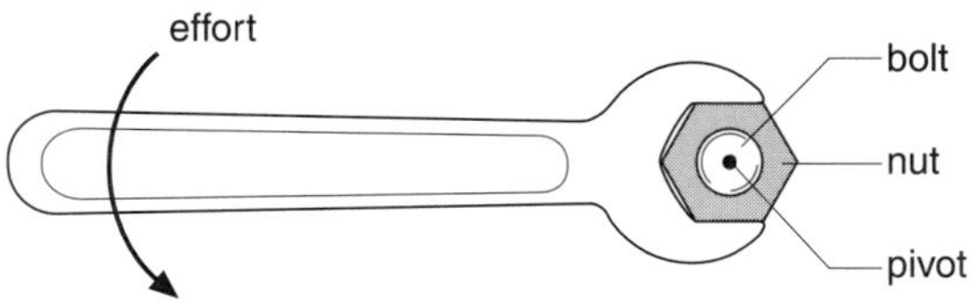

A long spanner allows a small force to overcome the large forces between the nut and the bolt.

C19 – Force, work and power

In science, the word 'work' refers specifically to the action of a force making an object move.

WORK

Work is done when a force makes an object move.

The amount of work done is defined by:

work done = force × distance moved

(The distance must be measured in the direction of the force.)

1 J of work is done when a force of 1 N moves through a distance of 1 m.

Notice that the unit of work is the same as the unit of energy. This is because energy must be transferred when work is done.

Example 1

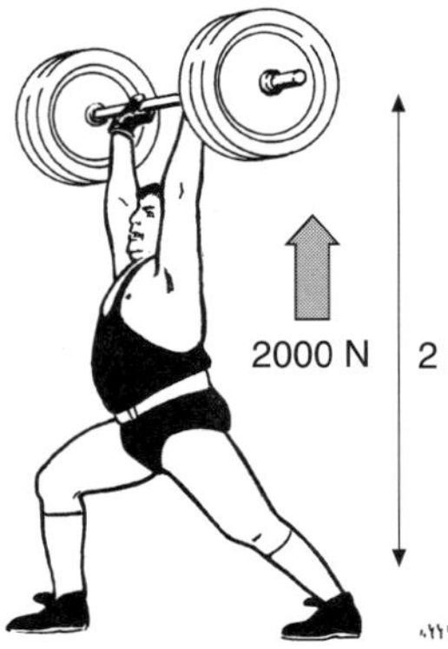

The athlete uses a force of 2000 N to lift the weights.

He raises the bar through 2 m.

work done = force × distance

work done = 2000 N × 2 m

work done = **4000 J**

Example 2

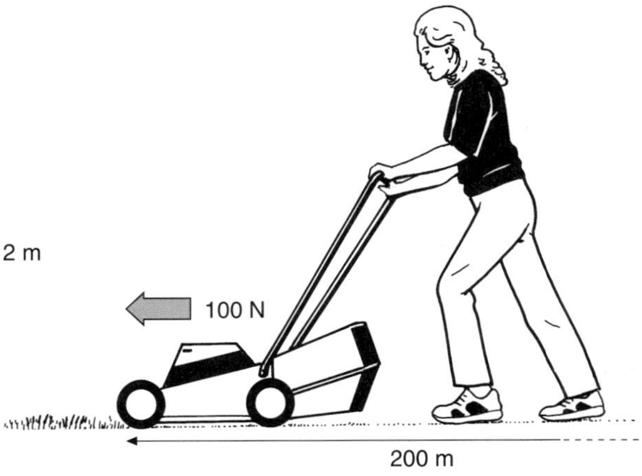

A force of 100 N is being used to push the lawnmower.

She pushes it a total of 200 m.

work done = force × distance

work done = 100 N × 200 m

work done = **2000 J**

POWER

Power tells us how quickly work is being done (and how rapidly energy is being transferred).

$$\textbf{power} = \frac{\textbf{work done}}{\textbf{time taken}}$$

The unit of power is the **watt** (**W**). A power of 1 W means that 1 J of work is being done in 1 second.

1 kilowatt (kW) = 1000 W

Example

A crane takes 240 s to lift a concrete block which weighs 10 000 N from the ground to the top of a 30 m building.

work done = 10000 N × 30 m
= 300 000 J

$$\text{power} = \frac{\text{work}}{\text{time}} = \frac{300\,000\text{ J}}{240\text{ s}}$$

power = **1250 W**

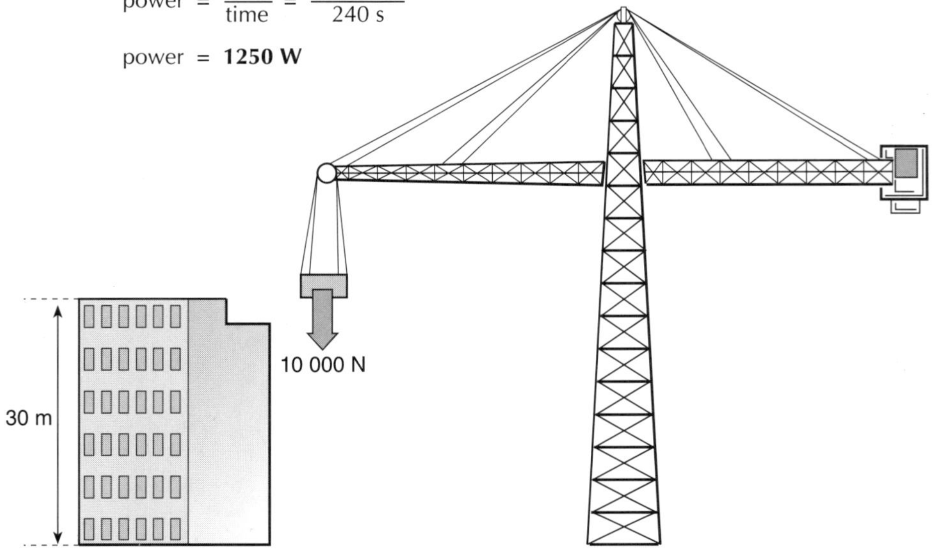

C20 – Work, potential energy and kinetic energy

When objects are lifted they gain potential energy: when they fall they gain kinetic energy.

WORK AND POTENTIAL ENERGY

To lift an object we need to do work against gravity. We can calculate the work done using the equation:

work done = force × vertical distance object is raised

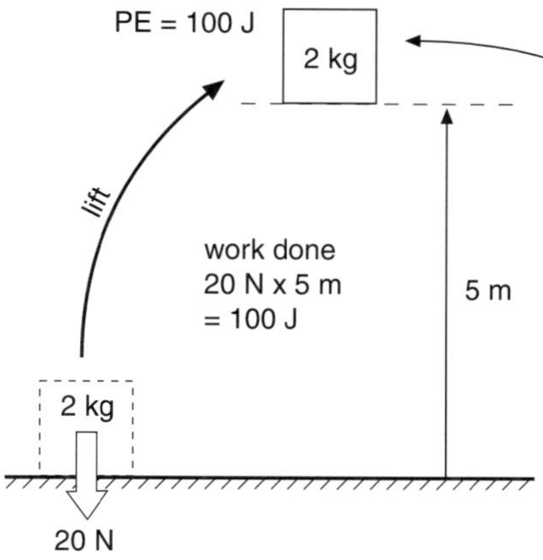

Now that the object has been lifted from the ground it has gravitational potential energy (PE). The amount of PE is exactly the same as the amount of work done in lifting it.

PE = mgh

m = mass
g = gravitational strength (10 N/kg)
h = vertical height

KINETIC ENERGY

A moving object possesses kinetic energy (KE). The amount of KE depends on the mass of the object and its velocity.

KE = $\frac{1}{2}mv^2$

m = mass
v = velocity
(v^2 = velocity × velocity)

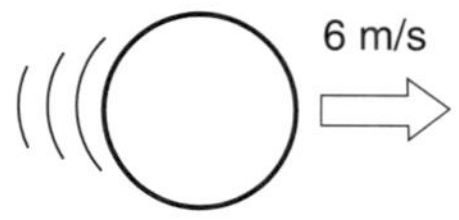

m = 0.5 kg

KE = $\frac{1}{2}mv^2$ = $\frac{1}{2}$ x 0.5 x 6 x 6 J

KE = 9 J

WORK, POTENTIAL ENERGY AND KINETIC ENERGY

- Work is needed to increase the PE of an object.
- As the object falls, its PE is converted into KE.
- Just as it hits the ground, all the PE has been converted into KE.
- The total energy (PE + KE) remains the same.

Object on ground

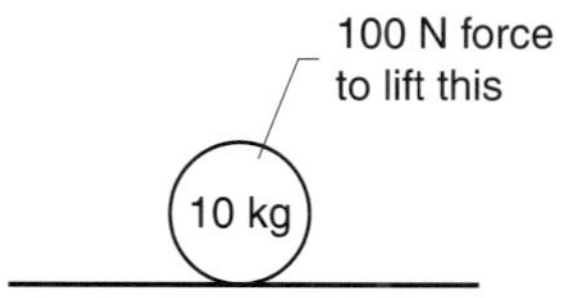

PE = 0

KE = 0

Someone lifts the object

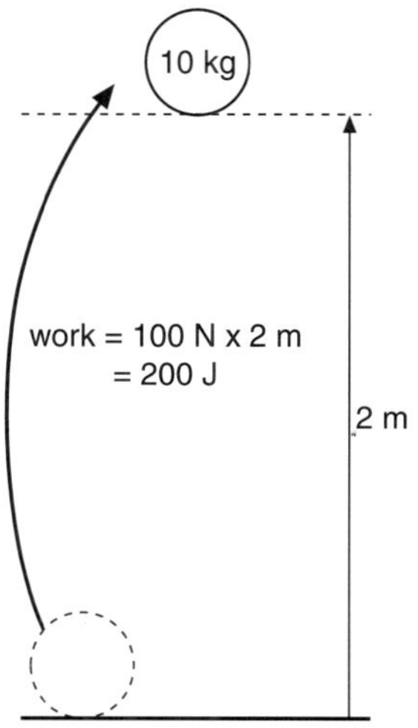

PE = 200 J

KE = 0

Total energy = 200 J

Object falling

(halfway down)

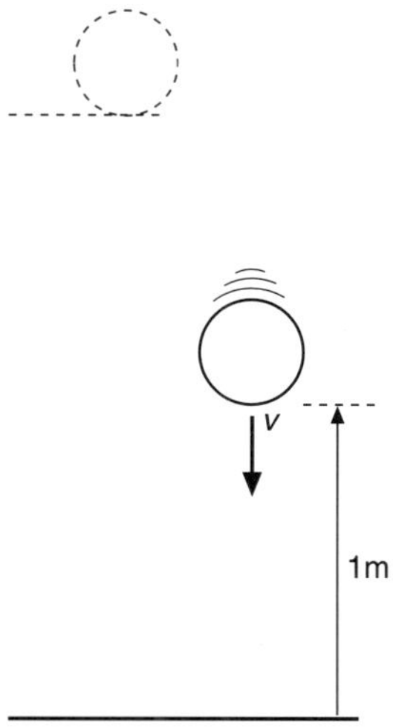

PE = 100 J

KE = 100 J

Total energy = 200 J

Object just about to hit ground

PE = 0 (almost)

KE = 200 J (almost)

Total energy = 200 J

C21 – Speed, velocity and acceleration

Understanding the motion of everyday objects also helps us understand the movement of atoms and of galaxies.

SPEED

The speed of an object tells us how far it travels in a given time.

$$\text{speed} = \frac{\text{distance}}{\text{time}}$$

If we know the speed of an object we can calculate how far it will travel in any given time.

We can plot the distance moved by an object on a **distance–time** graph.

The slope of the graph tells us the speed of the object.

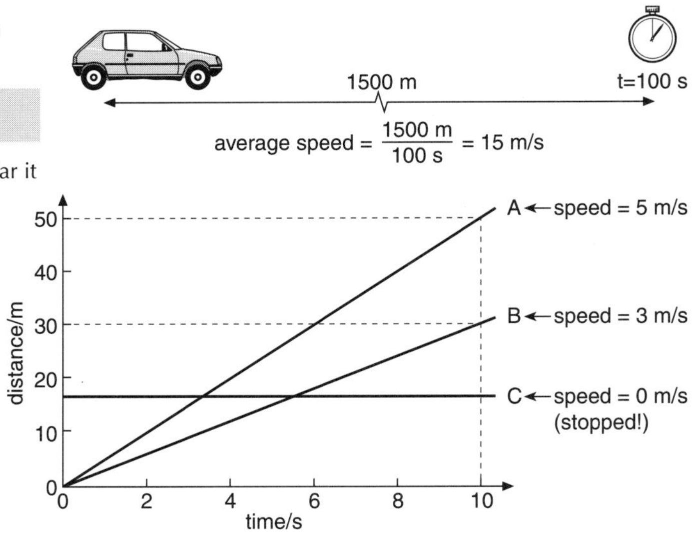

VELOCITY

- Velocity tells us the speed of an object **and its direction**.
- Quantities with size and direction (e.g. velocity, acceleration and force) are called **vectors**. Vectors are shown as arrows.
- Quantities which only have size (e.g. speed and energy) are called **scalars**.

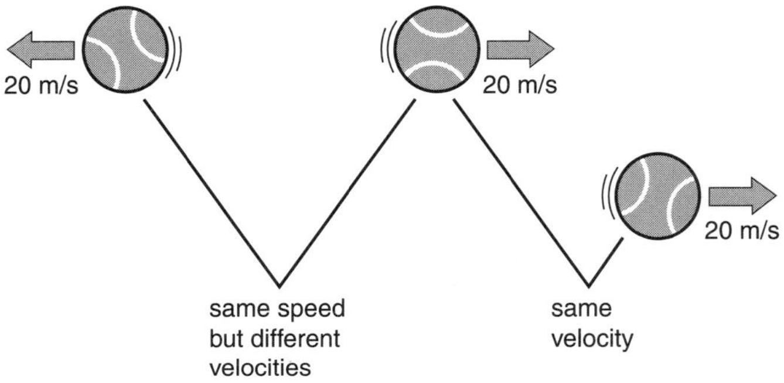

ACCELERATION

An object is accelerating if its velocity (i.e. the speed and/or direction) is changing.

The acceleration tells us how quickly the velocity is changing.

$$\text{acceleration} = \frac{\text{change of velocity}}{\text{time}}$$

The unit of acceleration is m/s/s ('metres per second per second'). This can also be written as **m/s²** ('metres per second squared').

We can see if an object is accelerating by looking at a **speed–time** graph of its motion. The slope of the line gives the acceleration.

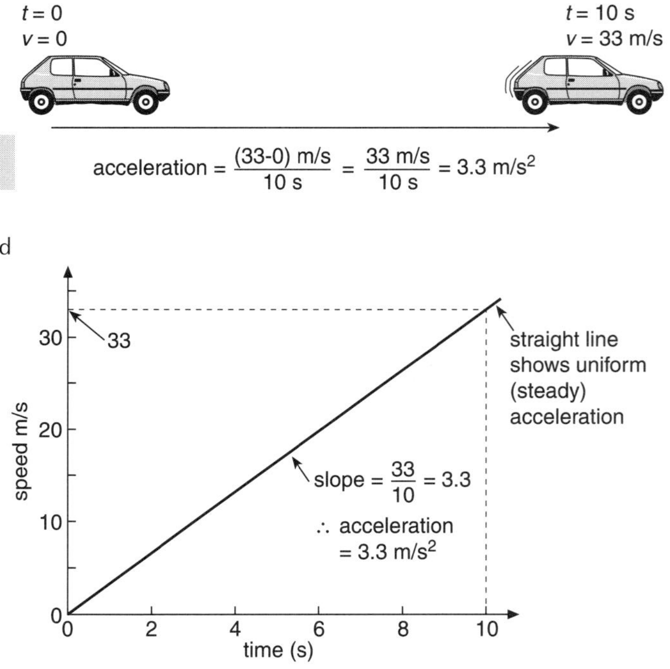

C23 – Friction and stopping

Friction is a problem when it 'wastes' energy but in some applications it is extremely useful.

FRICTION IN FALLING

Objects moving through air generate a frictional force called air **resistance**. The faster the object is moving, the greater the friction it experiences.

When a free-fall parachutist jumps from a plane the initial acceleration is about 10 m/s^2. As the parachutist accelerates towards the ground, the air resistance increases.

Eventually the frictional resistance increases to a point where it balances the weight of the parachutist. Because the forces are now balanced there is no acceleration.

This maximum speed downwards is called the **terminal velocity**. It can be seen on this graph.

Parachutist just after jumping from the plane

downwards force = weight

air resistance = zero

acceleration (g) ≈ 10 m/s^2

Parachutist after reaching terminal velocity

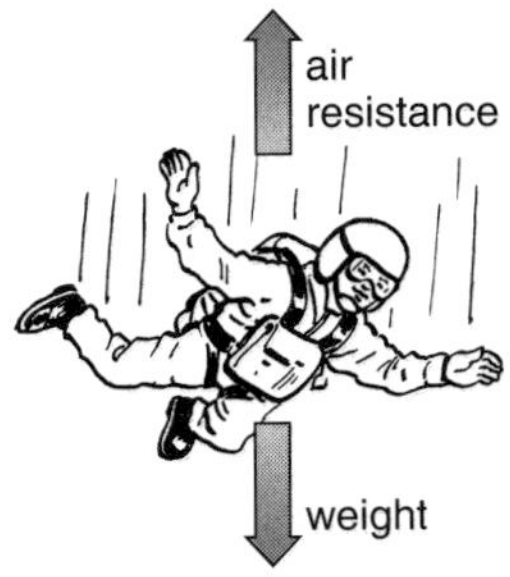

air resistance (up) balances the weight (down)

acceleration = zero

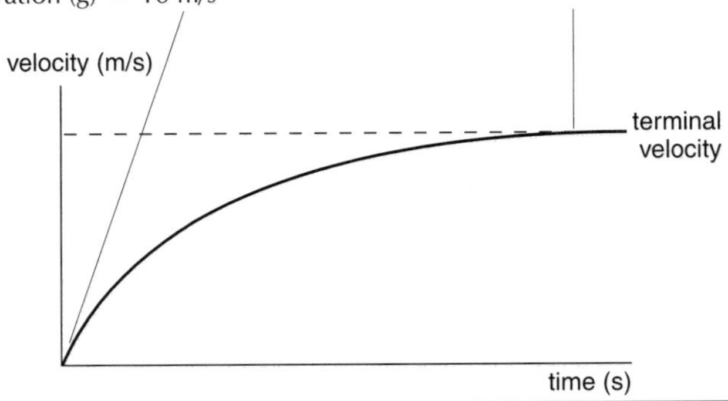

BRAKING IN A CAR

When a driver presses on the brake pedal, brake pads are pressed against the discs attached to the wheels. This increases the friction and slows the car down.

When an incident occurs which needs 'emergency braking' the driver takes time to react and so the car travels for some distance before the driver starts to brake. This is called the **thinking distance**.

Once the brake has been applied, it takes time for the car to decelerate to rest (0 m/s).The distance that the car takes to come to rest is called the **braking distance**.

Adding the thinking and braking distances gives the **total stopping distance**.

Factors affecting stopping distances

- **speed** of the car (higher speeds mean longer stopping distances)
- **mass** of the car (bigger mass means less deceleration for the same braking force)
- **efficiency of the brakes** (worn brake pads or low brake pressure mean less friction)
- **tyre conditions** (smooth tyres mean less friction)
- **road conditions** (wet roads, ice or snow mean less friction)
- **alertness of the driver** (tiredness, alcohol, some illegal drugs and some medicines increase reaction times).

Typical stopping distances
(ordinary car on dry roads)

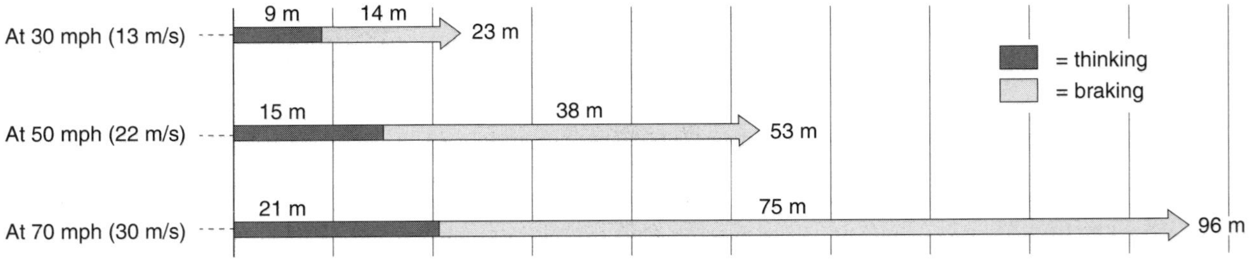

C24 – Waves and energy transfer

Waves transfer energy without transferring matter. Energy from the Sun reaches us via waves.

Waves transfer energy from place to place without moving any matter. Indeed, electromagnetic waves can transfer energy across a vacuum. There are two types of wave, **transverse** and **longitudinal**.

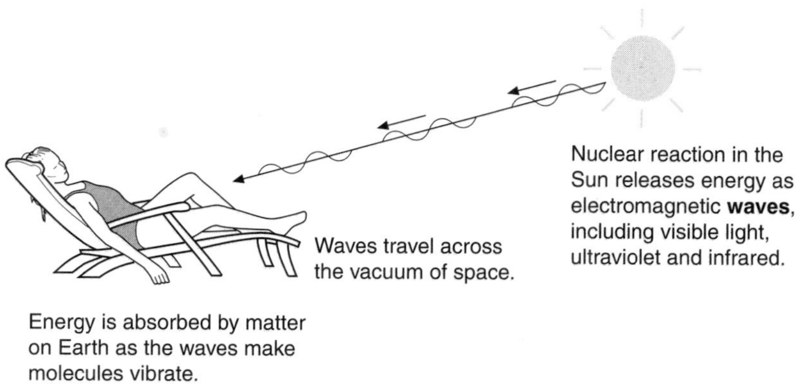

TRANSVERSE WAVES

A transverse wave moves at right angles to the vibration causing it. Waves on ropes, waves on the surface of water, and electromagnetic waves are all transverse.

If the vibration causing the wave is regular in time, the wave has this shape.

- The distance between two successive 'peaks' is the **wavelength** (λ).
- The number of complete waves in one second is the **frequency**.
- The maximum displacement is the **amplitude**.

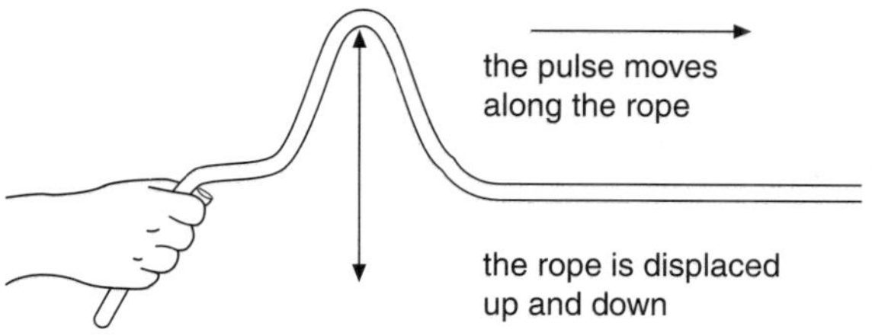

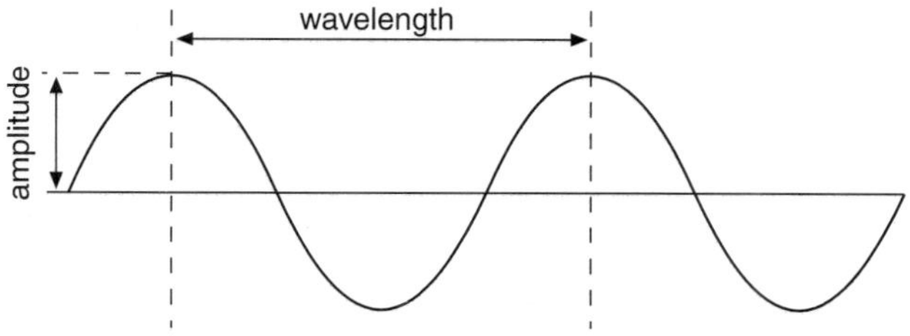

LONGITUDINAL WAVES

A longitudinal wave moves in the same direction as the vibration causing it. Sound waves and compression waves in springs are examples of longitudinal waves.

If the vibration causing the wave is **regular** in time, the wave has this structure. The distance between two successive compressions is the **wavelength** (λ).

Sound waves cannot pass through a vacuum. The source (loudspeaker cone) compresses air molecules. When the sound wave arrives at the ear, the changing pressure makes the eardrum vibrate.

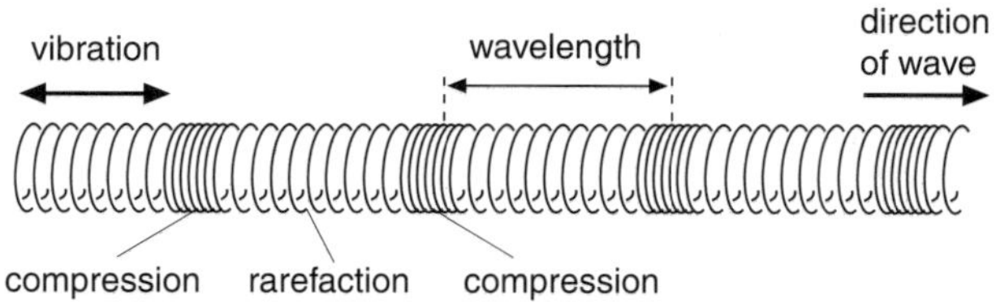

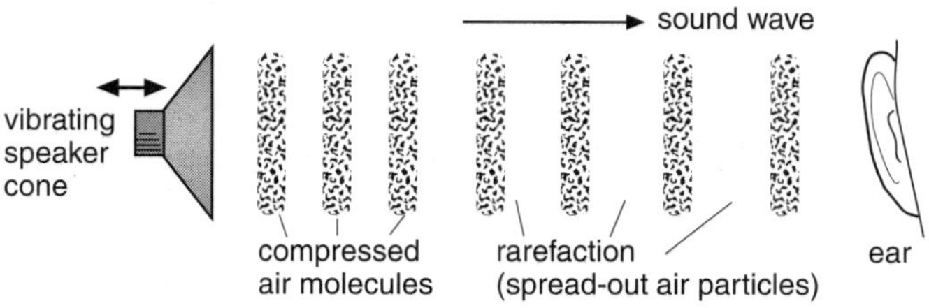

C27 – Total internal reflection of light

Light can pass through very long, thin fibres of glass with little loss of energy. Coded information can be sent through fibre optic cables using this effect.

INTERNAL REFLECTION IN GLASS

When light crosses from one medium to another some of it is reflected. At small angles of incidence the reflected ray is very weak but as the angle increases it gets stronger. Beyond a certain **critical angle** all the light gets reflected. The critical angle for a glass/air boundary is about 42°.

angle of incidence 35°

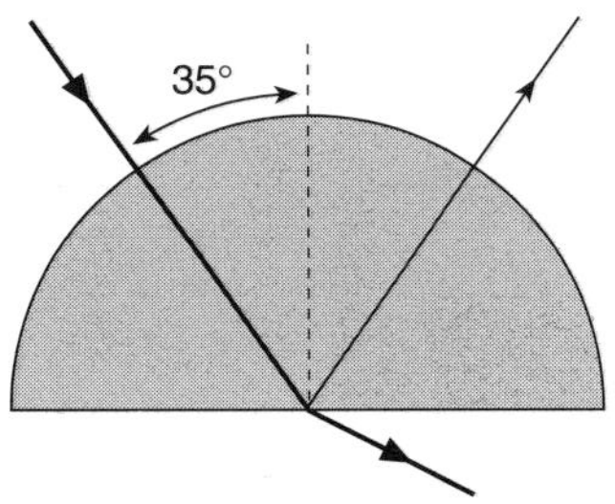

Nearly all light gets out as refracted ray.

angle of incidence = 42°

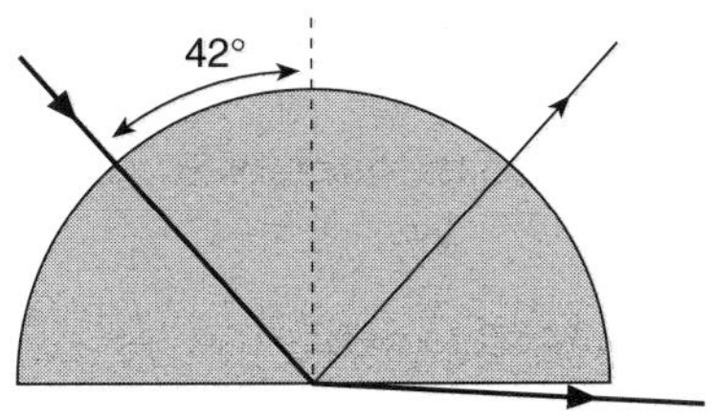

Refracted ray *just* gets out.

angle of incidence = 50°

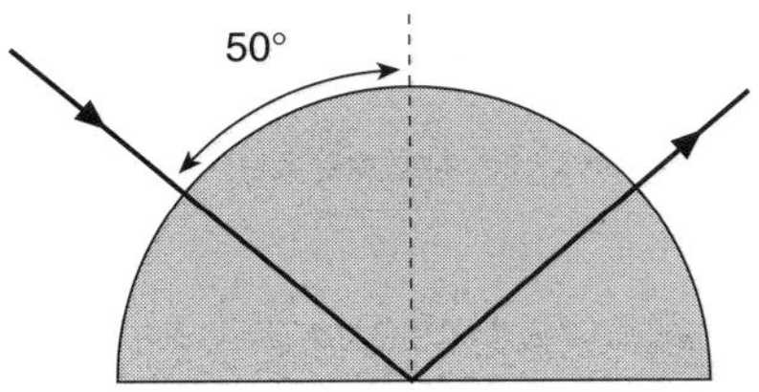

Total internal reflection

USING TOTAL INTERNAL REFLECTION

Triangular prisms

A triangular prism with angles 90°, 45° and 45° can be used as a mirror. Light enters without deviating and then hits the next boundary at 45°. This is greater than the critical angle so the light is reflected.

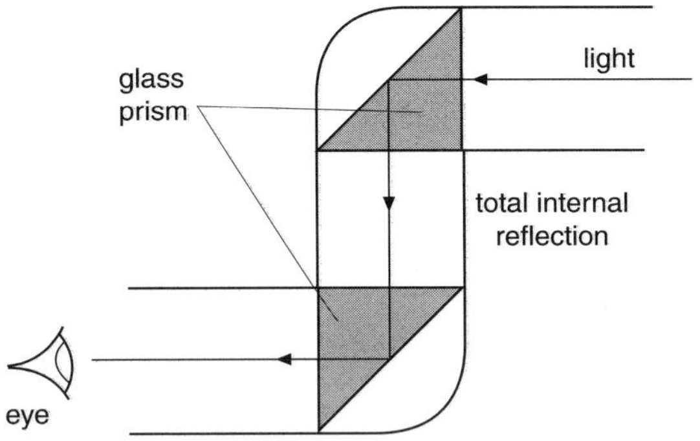

This periscope uses total internal reflection inside triangular prisms. Binoculars and some cameras also use prisms in this way.

Fibre optics

Light entering an optical fibre always hits the walls at an angle greater than the critical angle so it is all reflected. The light emerges from the other end almost as bright as it went in.

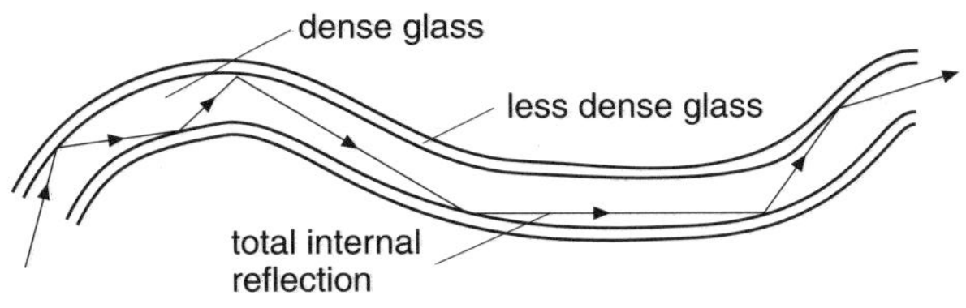

Surgeons can use fibre optics when performing 'keyhole surgery'. A bundle of fibres carries light to illuminate an area inside the body. Reflected light then travels back up other fibres to a microscope so the surgeon can see what is happening.

Fibre optics are important in the rapid, efficient transfer of data. Telephone messages, video pictures and computer data can all be transmitted through optical fibres.

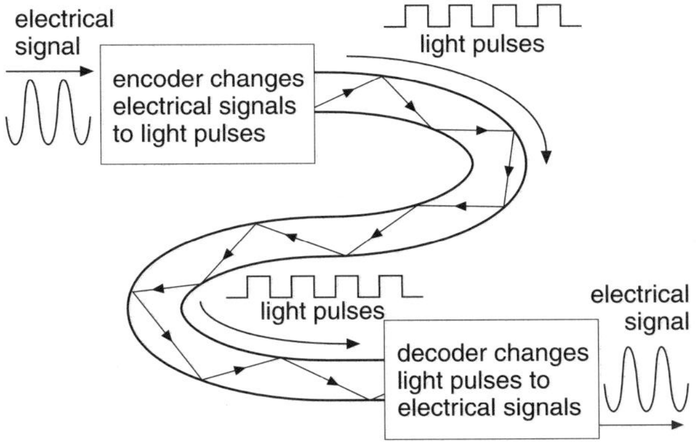

C28 – Ultrasound and its uses

Humans can hear sounds with frequencies of about 15 Hz to 20 000 Hz. Some animals can hear much higher frequencies. Bats, for example, can detect frequencies up to 100 kHz.

ULTRASOUND

Sound waves can be generated with frequencies much higher than 20 kHz. They are beyond the normal human hearing range and so are called **ultrasound**.

Ultrasound has many uses.

Industrial uses of ultrasound

1 Detecting cracks and flaws in metals

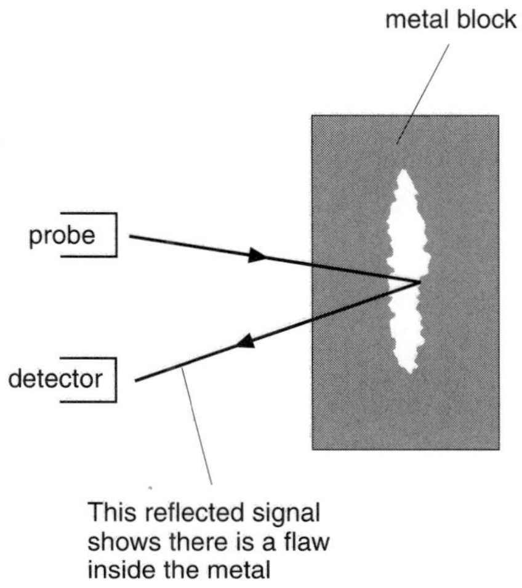

2 Controlling production processes

This machine is rolling steel sheet. The thickness must be carefully controlled. If the sheet is too thin, more ultrasound gets through to the detector. A signal is sent to the control unit which increases the gap between the rollers. If the sheet is too thick, less ultrasound gets through. A signal tells the control unit to move the rollers closer together.

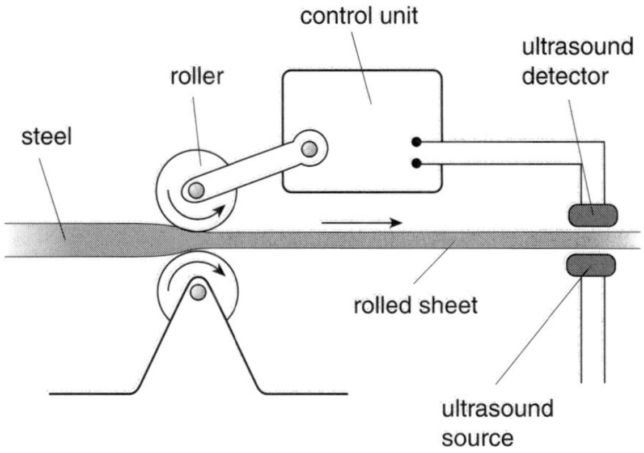

3 Cleaning delicate objects

High frequency ultrasound makes the object vibrate at very high frequency. This 'shakes' the dirt from the surface.

Depth finding

Ships can use ultrasound to find the depth of water below them. A transmitter sends out a pulse of ultrasound. A microphone picks up the echo reflected from the sea bed. The time between the original pulse being sent out and the echo being received can be used to calculate the depth.

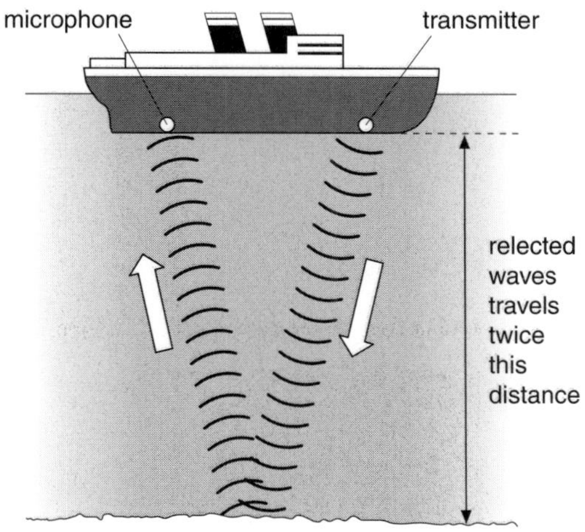

$$\text{speed of sound in water} = \frac{2 \times \text{depth of water}}{\text{time taken}}$$

Scanning embryos in the womb

An ultrasonic scanner can be used to check on the condition of an unborn baby. Pulses of ultrasound are sent into the body. The waves are reflected where different tissues meet. The **echoes** are detected and then turned into a picture by a computer.

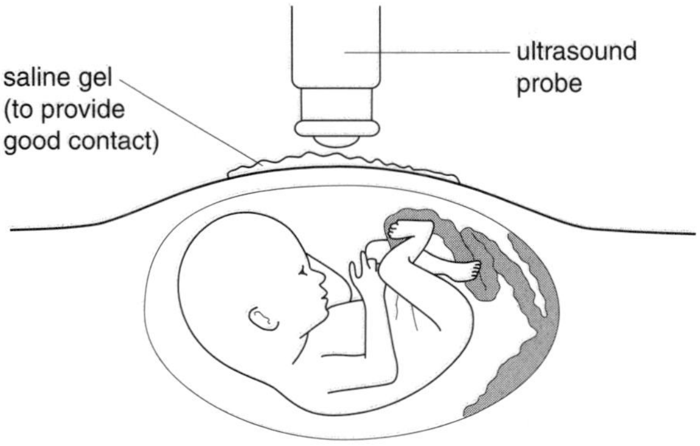

Ultrasonic scanning

Ultrasound is safe. X-rays cannot be used as they could harm the baby.

C31 – Conduction, convection and radiation

Understanding the ways in which thermal energy (heat) is transferred helps us to design heating and cooling systems.

TEMPERATURE DIFFERENCE AND ENERGY TRANSFER

Thermal energy ('heat') flows from places where the temperature is high to places where it is low.

Hot bodies transfer energy to cooler objects.

The three main mechanisms for the transfer of heat are: **conduction**, **convection**, and **radiation**.

CONDUCTION

Heat is **conducted** in solids when high energy particles pass some of their energy to neighbouring particles.

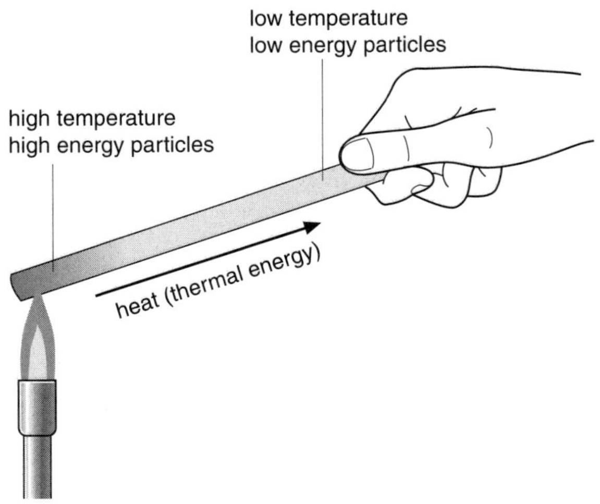

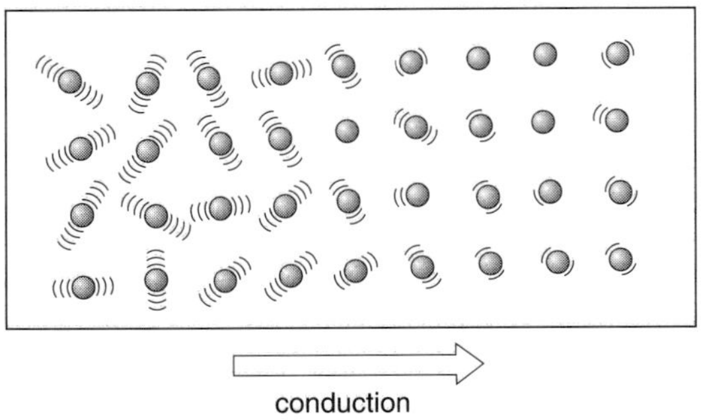

Vibrating particles transfer energy but they do not move along the lattice.

Metals are good conductors of heat. Some energy is passed from ion to ion. In addition, conduction electrons can transfer energy as they move freely through the lattice. Non-metals such as wood, glass and plastic are poor conductors because they do not have free electrons.

Liquids are poor conductors of heat. Gases are very poor conductors because their particles are not closely bound. Poor conductors are good **insulators**.

CONVECTION

Fluids (liquids and gases) can flow. As warm regions of liquid or gas move, they transfer energy.

When a fluid is heated it expands and becomes less dense. It rises as cooler, denser fluid moves down to displace it. This sets up a **convection current**.

Winds in the atmosphere are convection currents.

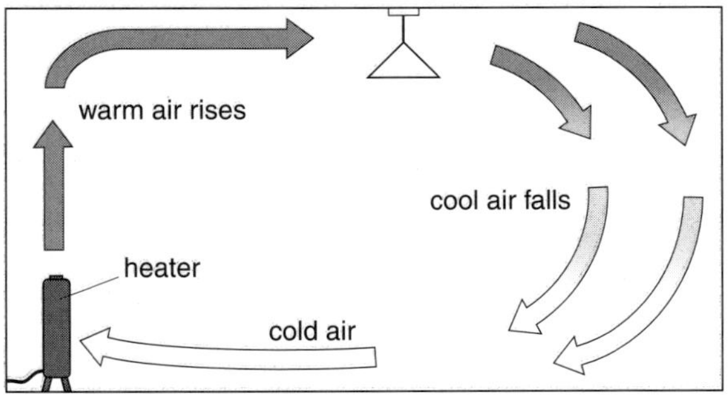

Warm air circulates in a room by convection.

RADIATION

Hot objects radiate heat. As charged particles in the object vibrate they set up electromagnetic waves. These transfer energy even across a vacuum. Heat is mainly transmitted as **infra red** radiation.

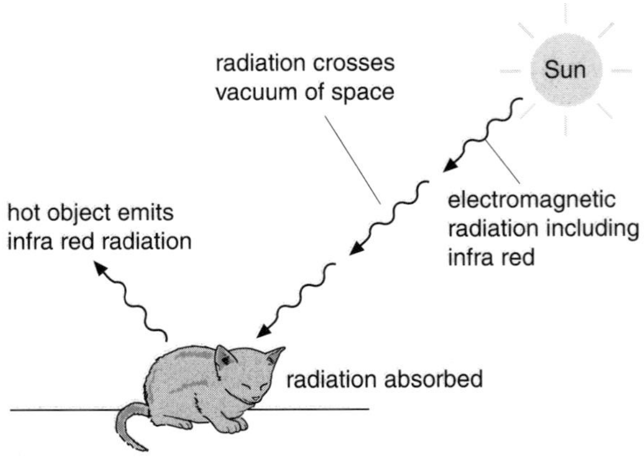

- The higher the temperature of an object the more energy it radiates.
- Black, dull surfaces radiate more energy (at the same temperature) than shiny surfaces.
- Black, dull surfaces absorb more radiated energy than white or shiny surfaces. Shiny surfaces **reflect** the radiation.

C32 – Energy efficiency

The production of electrical energy uses up our limited stocks of fossil fuels and creates environmental problems. We need to make the best use possible of our energy.

EFFICIENCY

We put energy in to machines and electrical appliances to get them to do useful work. However, some energy is 'wasted'. The efficiency tells us how much useful work or energy is produced.

$$\textbf{efficiency} = \frac{\textbf{'useful' energy out}}{\textbf{energy in}} \times 100\%$$

Example:

A light bulb is rated at 60 W. In each second it converts 60 J of energy into 20 J of light energy and 40 J of thermal energy. What is its efficiency?

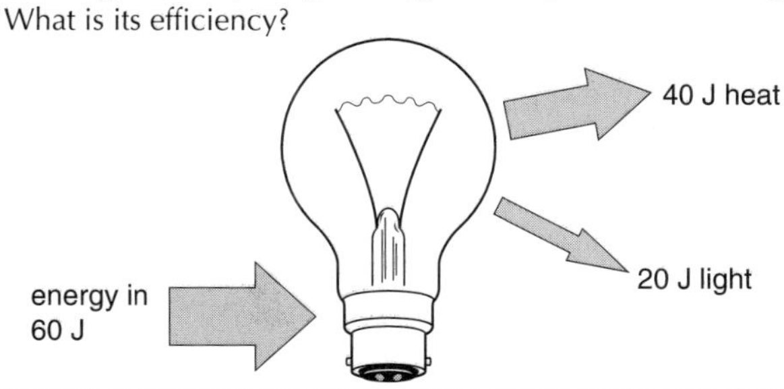

$$\textbf{efficiency} = \frac{20}{60} \times 100\% = 33\%$$

Notice that only 33% of the electrical energy has been turned into light. The other 67% is 'wasted' as heat.

Fluorescent tubes and bulbs are much more efficient than filament bulbs because they do not get so hot.

Efficiency in the home

We buy energy to heat our homes. Much of this is 'lost'. It goes to heat up the air outside. As the energy gets spread between more and more particles, it becomes more difficult to use.

We can use energy more efficiently by using better (more efficient) appliances and by using thermostats and electronic control systems. However, the best way is to **insulate**.

- insulate roof space with mineral wool
- double glaze windows
- fit draft excluders to doors and windows
- hang heavy curtains at windows
- use fitted carpets on floors
- fill cavity walls with foam (stops convection across the cavity)

These are typical energy losses without insulation.

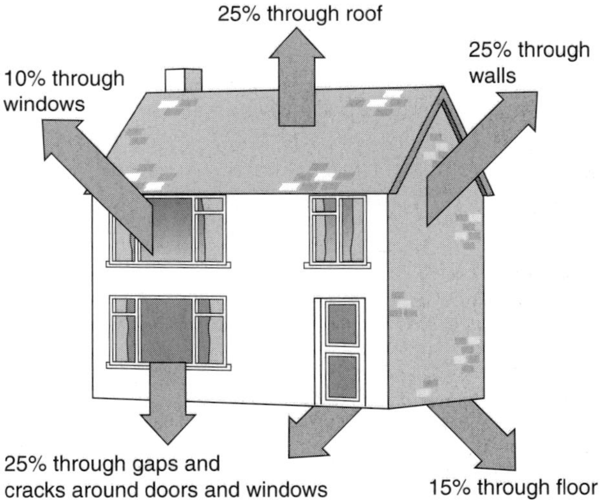

Why be efficient?

Most of our energy comes from **non-renewable** sources, e.g. coal, oil and gas. Reserves of these are limited. The more efficient we are in using energy, the longer our reserves will last.

All forms of power generation cause some environmental problems. If we use energy more efficiently, we will need fewer power stations.

We could generate energy from renewable sources, e.g. solar power, wind power and tidal power, but we do not yet have the capacity to replace our fossil fuel power stations.

C35 – Radioactive half-life

We cannot control radioactive processes but we can monitor how fast isotopes decay.

HALF-LIFE

Radioactive decay takes place in the nucleus of an atom. It is not affected by changes in temperature or pressure. The rate at which a radio-isotope decays is constant.

The half-life is the time taken for half the atoms in a sample of radioactive isotope to decay.

Example:

The half-life of cobalt-60 is about 5 years. If we start with 16 g of cobalt-60, it will change like this.

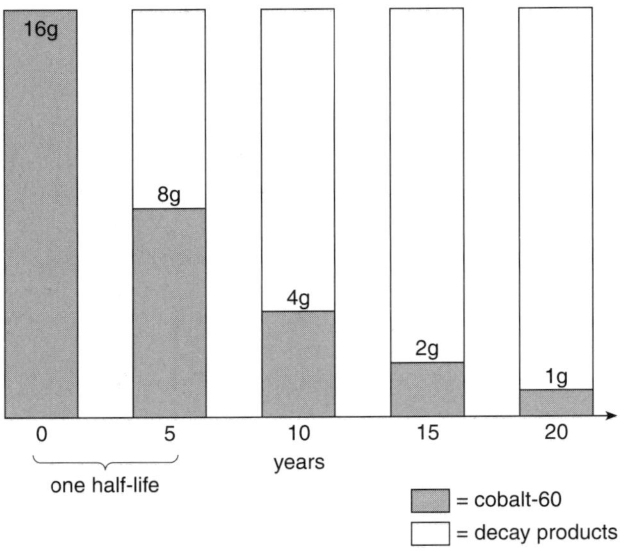

Each radio-isotope has its own half-life. We can measure half-life by putting a Geiger counter close to a radioactive sample and then plotting the count-rate against time.

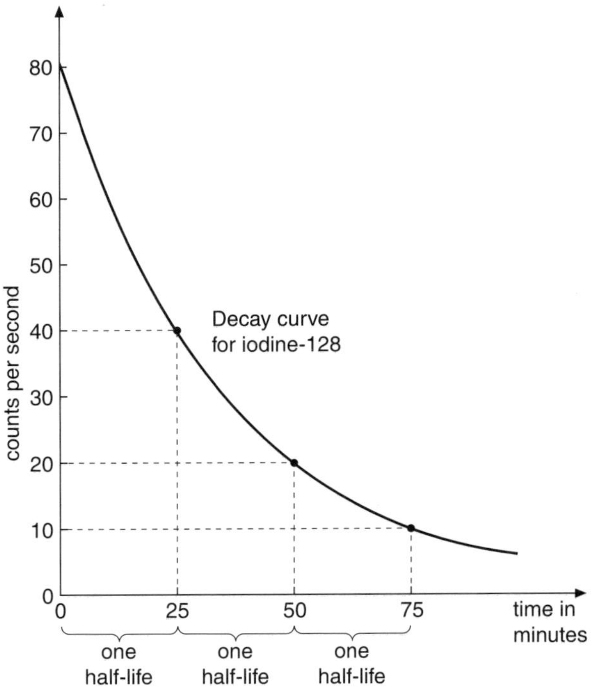

Dating rocks

When rocks are formed they contain radioactive isotopes. For example, some igneous rocks contain potassium-40. This decays to give argon, which is trapped in the rock. By measuring the proportions of potassium-40 and argon in the rock we can estimate how long ago the rock was formed. The older the rock, the less potassium-40 and the more argon there will be.

A similar method compares the amount of uranium in a rock with the amount of lead. This is because uranium isotopes decay, through a long series of changes, into stable lead. Older rocks have less uranium and more lead.

Both methods give the age of the oldest rocks on Earth to be about 4600 million years.

BACKGROUND RADIATION

There is radiation all around us. The main sources are:

- radioactive gases emitted from rocks, e.g. thoron
- rocks, e.g. granite
- space (cosmic radiation)
- human activities (medical activities, generation of nuclear power and processing radioactive materials)

Radioactive tracers

Radioactive isotopes can be used to 'mark' liquids; they can then be traced using a detector. The isotope used must have a half-life which is long enough to let the measurements be carried out but short enough to decay without any long-term damage.

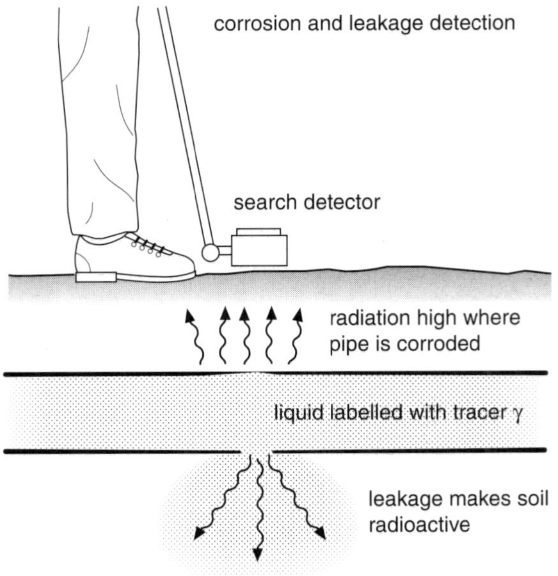

C36 – Earth and the Solar System

The Earth is just one of nine planets in our Solar System. Our Sun is just one of billions of stars in the galaxy.

THE SOLAR SYSTEM

- The Earth is the third planet from the Sun.
- It is about 150 million km from the Sun.
- Comets are bodies of rocks and ice which orbit the Sun. Halley's comet is visible from Earth every 76 years.

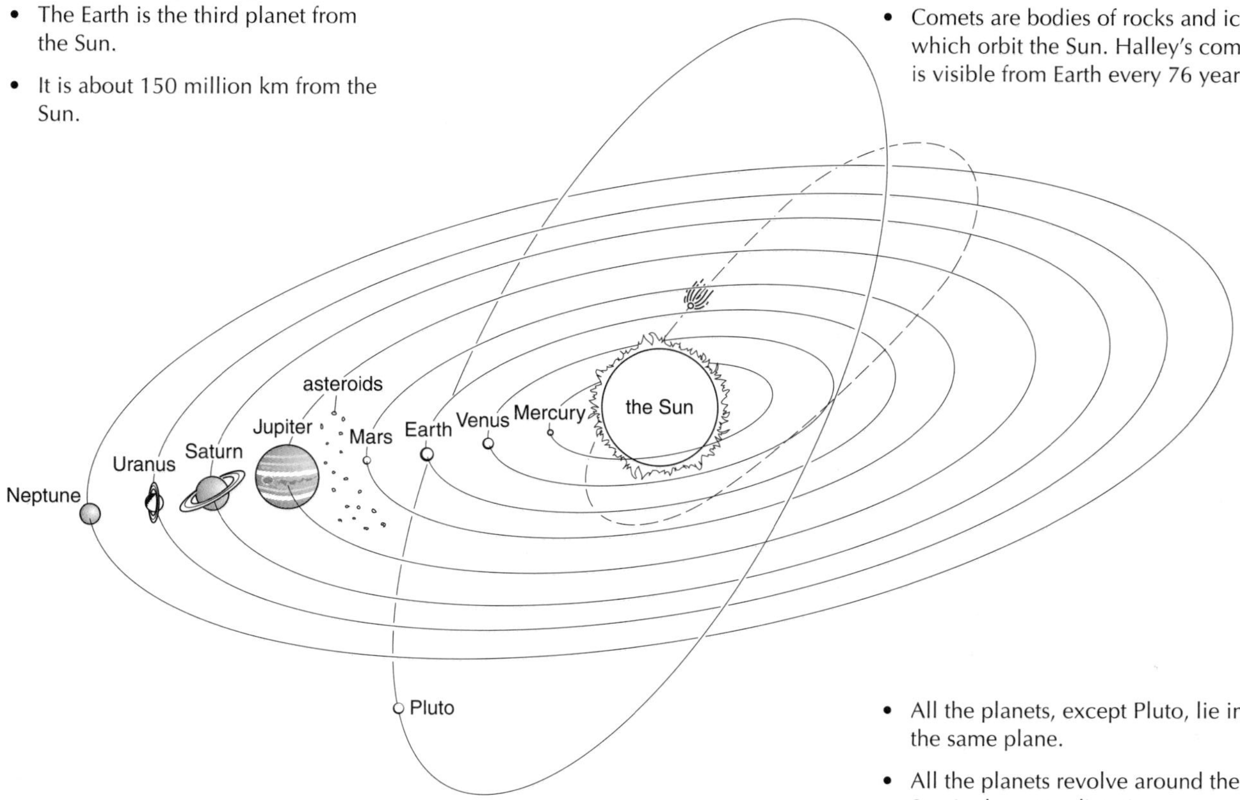

- All the planets, except Pluto, lie in the same plane.
- All the planets revolve around the Sun in the same direction.

THE EARTH

Day and night

The Earth takes 24 hours to rotate once on its axis. This is one day. As the Earth spins, the side facing the sun has **daylight**. It is night on the opposite side.

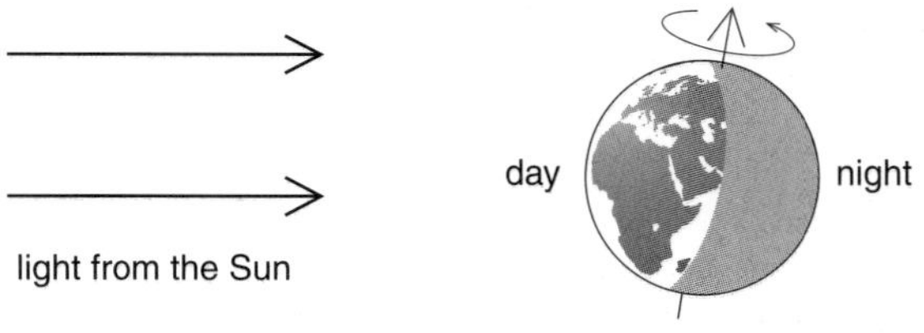

Seasons of the year

The Earth takes just over 365 days to orbit the Sun. This is one **year**.

The Earth is tilted on its axis (at 23.5°) so we have **seasons**.

During the winter, places receive less energy per square metre and so temperatures are lower. Also the Sun is above the horizon for a shorter period of time so the number of daylight hours is reduced. At the same time the other hemisphere experiences summer: higher temperatures and longer periods of daylight.

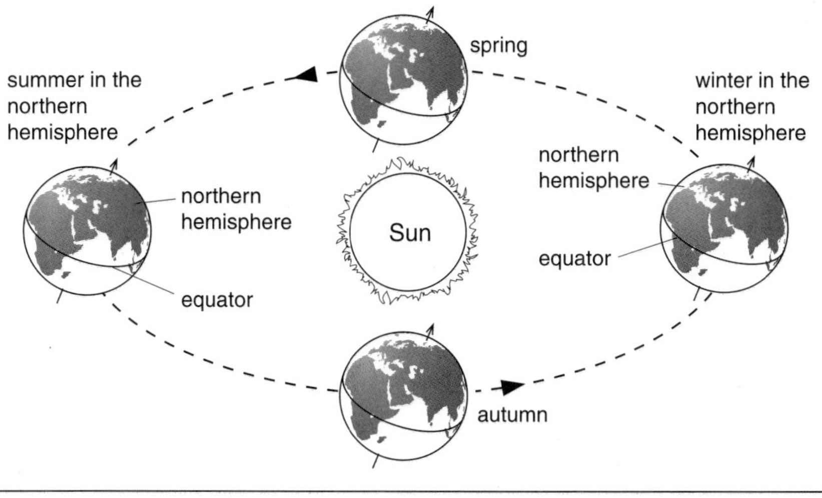

C38 – 'Life cycle' of a star

Stars are celestial bodies which emit light and other forms of radiation from nuclear reactions. Our Sun is just one of the billions of stars in our galaxy.

'BIRTH' OF A STAR

Stars form in the huge clouds of dust and hydrogen gas (**nebulae**) found on the edges of galaxies.

Hydrogen particles are attracted to each other by gravity. As they are forced together, their energy is converted into heat. If they get hot enough, a nuclear reaction starts. Hydrogen particles collide and 'fuse' together to form helium nuclei. This **nuclear fusion** releases a huge amount of energy.

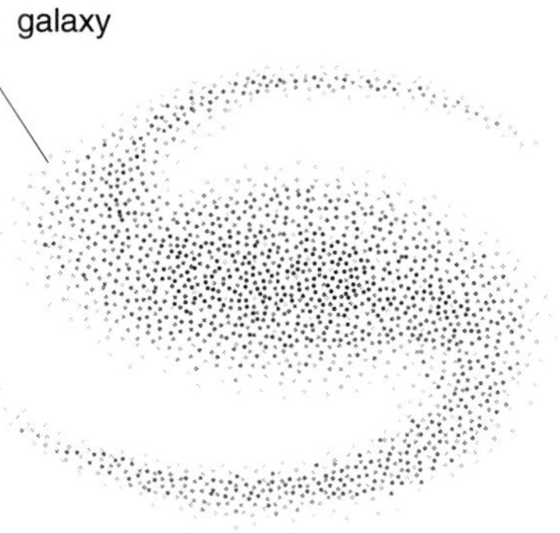

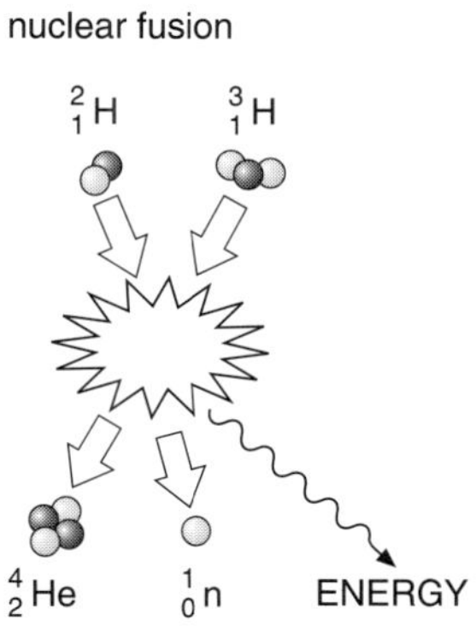

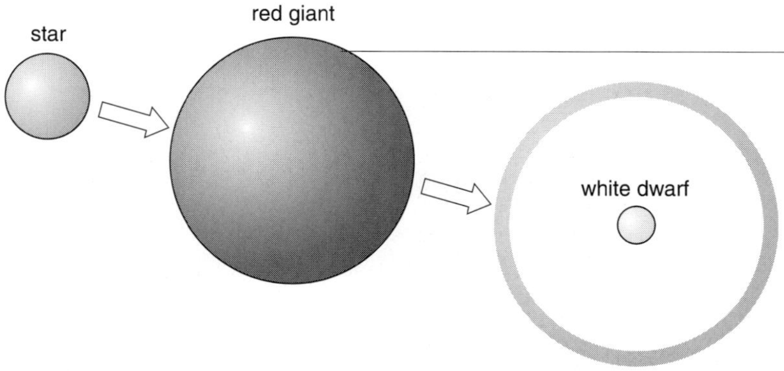

'DEATH' OF A STAR

When a star has used up most of its nuclear fuel it gets cooler and expands to form a huge star called a **red giant**. Our Sun will turn into a red giant in about 5000 million years! It will be several hundred times larger than it is now.

When the outer layers drift away, a small cool star called a **white dwarf** is left.

Very big stars may die in a much more spectacular way. As the massive red giant shrinks, it gets hot enough for new nuclear reactions to start. This may cause a huge explosion called a **supernova**.

The supernova leaves a small, dense star called a **neutron star**.

Large neutron stars can collapse even further. The particles become so compressed and dense that nothing, not even light, can escape from their gravitational pull. This is a **black hole**.

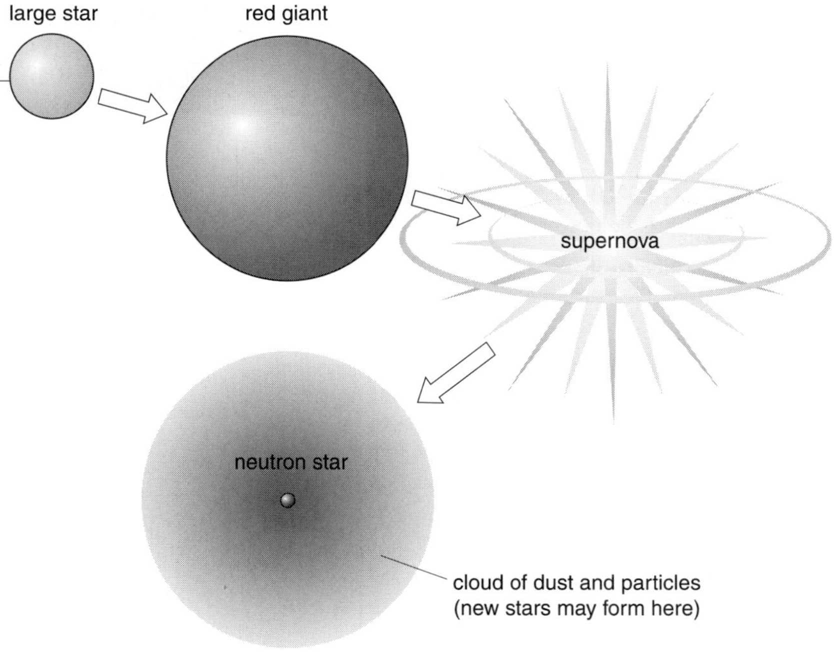

C39 – Theories of the origin of the universe

We do not know how the universe began. However, observations of outer space allow us to form theories which we can then test.

RED SHIFT

When scientists looked at light emitted by stars in distant galaxies they found that the wavelengths were longer than expected. The spectrum of light was 'shifted' towards the **red end**. This red shift shows that distant galaxies are moving away from the Earth at great speed.

Scientists also found that light from galaxies that are further from the Earth showed greater red shift, so they must be travelling at greater speeds.

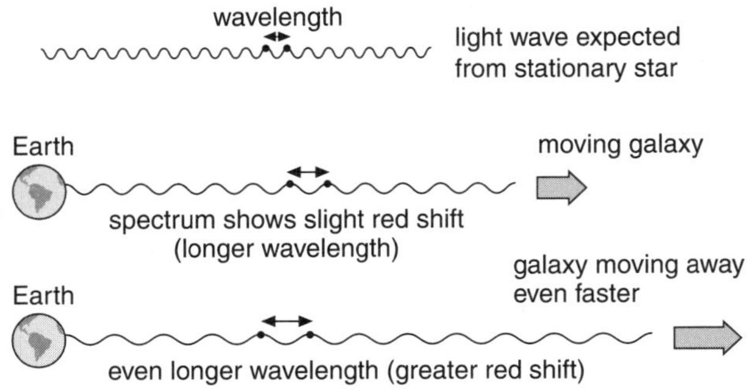

THE BIG BANG THEORY

The Big Bang Theory suggests that all the matter in the universe started as one large mass in one place. This then exploded. The galaxies are moving apart because of that explosion.

Using the speed of the galaxies it is estimated that the Big Bang took place between 10 and 20 billion years ago!

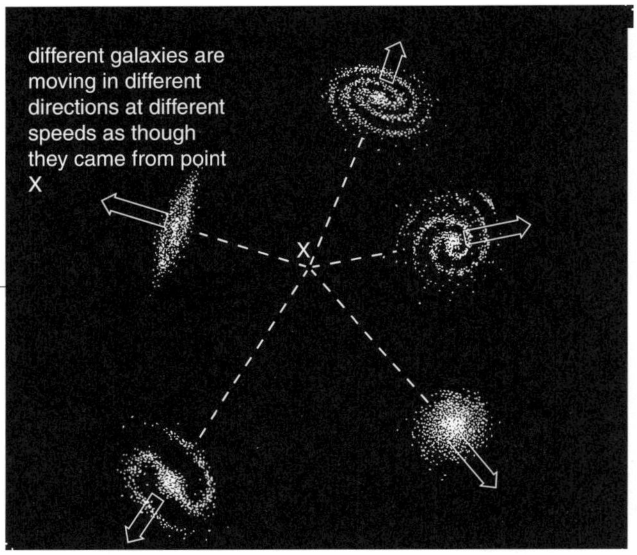

EXPANDING OR PULSATING UNIVERSE?

What will happen to the universe in the future?

The **Expanding Universe Theory** suggests that the galaxies will continue to move apart for ever and that there was only ever one Big Bang.

The **Pulsating or Oscillating Universe Theory** suggests that gravitational forces are slowing down the expansion of the universe and that eventually the galaxies will start to move together again. If this happens, all the matter in the universe will be compressed until there is another Big Bang and the whole process will begin again.

The future of the universe depends on the total amount of matter in it. If there is enough mass, gravity will cause the universe to collapse. If there is not enough, gravity will be too weak and the universe will keep on expanding.

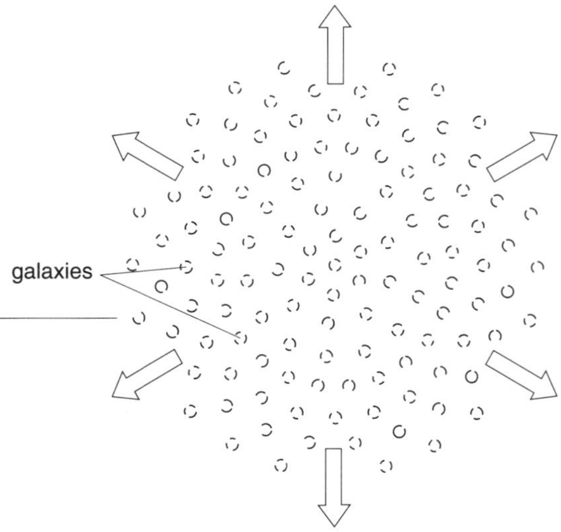

We live in an expanding universe. Does it contain enough matter to make it collapse or will it go on expanding?

Questions

The **Multiple choice** and the **Short answer/Structured questions** are arranged and numbered according to the Contents listings: A - biology, B - chemistry, C - physics (GCSE Attainment Targets Sc2, Sc3, Sc4):

Questions A1, A2 ... biology:
(Sc2 - *Life Processes and Living Things*)
Questions B1, B2 ... chemistry:
(Sc3 - *Materials and Their Properties*)
Questions C1, C2 ... physics:
(Sc4 - *Physical Processes*)

There are no **Free response/Long questions.**

ANSWER SPACES: the answer spaces have generally been omitted from the **Short answer/Structured questions** section.

EXAMINATION TIER: references are provided underneath all question numbers:

F - ***foundation*** (GCSE grades G-C)
H - ***higher*** (GCSE grades D-A*)

QUESTION COVERAGE: no attempt has been made to cover every aspect of every syllabus. The selection of questions has been made to reasonably represent the syllabuses available and to enable you to assess your own subject strengths and weaknesses.

ANSWERS: All answers are provided by the author.

Multiple Choice:
Part A: A1-B, A2-D, A3-A, A4-B, A5-C, A6-B, A7-D, A8-C, A9-A, A10-A, A11-D, A12-C, A13-B, A14-B, A15-D, A16-B, A17-B, A18-B, A19-A.
Part B: B1-B, B2-C, B3-A, B4-D, B5-B, B6-A, B7-A, B8-A, B9-C, B10- C, B11-B, B12-A, B13-B, B14-C, B15-D.
Part C: C1-A, C2-B, C3-C, C4-D, C5-D, C6-D, C7-C, C8-D, C9-D, C10-D, C11-C, C12-C, C13-D, C14-C, C15-A, C16-A.
Short answer/Structured questions:
Part C: C1 800 J, C3(a) 50 km/h, C3(b) 5 s, C7(a) 2.4 units, C7(b) 84p

Multiple choice questions

(All **Multiple choice** questions are provided by London Examinations (Edexcel).)

A1. (F) Here is a diagram of some organs in the body.

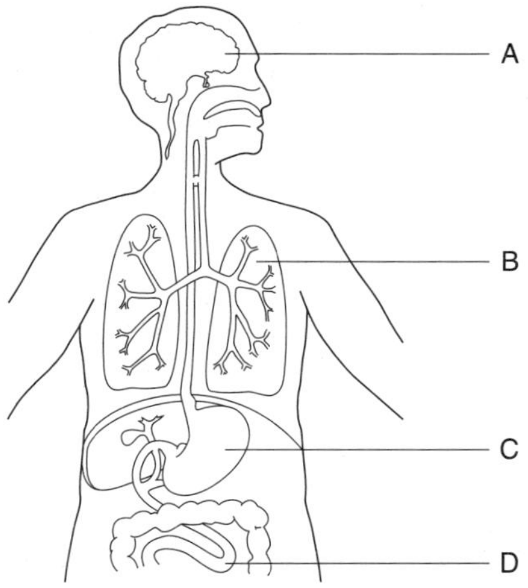

Which organ (**A**, **B**, **C**, or **D**) is a lung?

A2. (F) Urine is produced by the
A liver
B intestines
C stomach
D kidneys

Use the diagram of the eye to answer questions 3 and 4.

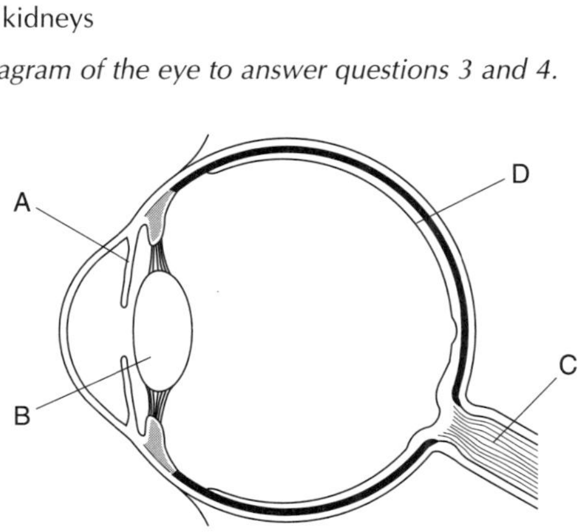

A3. (F) Which part of the eye (**A**, **B**, **C** or **D**) is the iris?

A4. (F) Which part of the eye (**A**, **B**, **C** or **D**) is used to focus light?

A5. (F) The list shows some effects of alcohol.
Which effect (**A**, **B**, **C** or **D**) is most dangerous in a driver?
A it changes a person's mood
B it can lead to increased weight
C it slows reaction times
D it increases blood flow to the skin

A6. (H) Urea is a waste product from excess protein in the diet.
Urea is produced from
A protein in the kidney
B amino acids in the liver
C amino acids in the kidney
D protein in the liver

A7. (H) Amphetamines are stimulants. This means they
A are pain killers
B increase self awareness
C make the body relax
D give feelings of energy and self confidence

A8. (H) Which statement (A, B, C or D) about sweating and shivering is true?
A sweating and shivering both help to cool the body
B sweating and shivering both help to heat the body
C sweating helps to cool the body, shivering helps to heat it up
D shivering helps to cool the body, sweating helps to heat it up

A9. (H) 'Homeostasis' means keeping conditions inside the body constant.
Which one of these (A, B, C or D) is an example of homeostasis?
A controlling the temperature of the body
B controlling the emptying of the bladder
C controlling hand movement when touching a hot object
D controlling the amount of light entering the eye

A10. (F) A group of tissues working together make
- **A** an organ
- **B** an organism
- **C** a system
- **D** a cell

A11. (F) During intercourse, millions of sperm cells are released into the woman's vagina.
How many sperm cells fertilize the egg cell (ovum)?
- **A** millions
- **B** four
- **C** two
- **D** one

A12. (H) Equal numbers of brown mice and white mice were released into a wood. More brown mice survived. This is because white mice
- **A** eat less than brown mice
- **B** breed more quickly than brown mice
- **C** are easier to see than brown mice
- **D** move more quickly than brown mice

A13. (H) The sex of a baby is decided by the X and Y chromosomes
If the baby is female, each body cell contains
- **A** one X and one Y chromosome
- **B** two X chromosomes
- **C** two Y and two X chromosomes
- **D** two Y chromosomes

A14. (H) These lists shows three structures in cells. Which list (**A**, **B**, **C** or **D**) shows them in order from smallest to largest?
- **A** chromosome, gene, nucleus
- **B** gene, chromosome, nucleus
- **C** gene, nucleus, chromosome
- **D** nucleus, gene, chromosome

A15. (H) Over a long period of time, some animals have changed and adapted to suit new environments.
This has happened by
- **A** artificial selection
- **B** cloning
- **C** a lack of predators
- **D** natural selection

A16. (F) The roots of a plant absorb
- **A** oxygen
- **B** water
- **C** light
- **D** carbon dioxide

A17. (F) The leaves of a plant make
- **A** nitrogen
- **B** food
- **C** water
- **D** light

A18. (H) Farmers make soil conditions unsuitable for growth of denitrifying bacteria because these bacteria
- **A** break down dead plants and animals
- **B** use up nitrates and nitrites
- **C** live in the roots of plants
- **D** fix atmospheric nitrogen

A19. (H) The 'greenhouse effect' is caused by changed levels of carbon dioxide in the atmosphere.
Deforestation and the burning of plants affect carbon dioxide levels because
- **A** plants use carbon dioxide in photosynthesis and release it when they are burnt
- **B** plants use carbon dioxide in photosynthesis and also when they are burnt
- **C** plants produce carbon dioxide during photosynthesis and release it when they are burnt
- **D** plants produce carbon dioxide during photosynthesis and also when they are burnt

B1. (F) Granite and basalt are both examples of
- **A** fossils
- **B** igneous rocks
- **C** minerals
- **D** sedimentary rocks

B2. (F) Aluminium is a good choice of material for making a frying pan for use on an electric cooker because it
- **A** is shiny
- **B** is malleable
- **C** conducts heat well
- **D** conducts electricity well

B3. (F) Which of these substances combines with hydrogen to form ammonia?
- **A** nitrogen
- **B** oxygen
- **C** sulphuric acid
- **D** water

B4. (H) Scientists believe the Earth's surface is made up of massive plates moving slowly in different directions.
This theory is called
- **A** plate dynamics
- **B** continental plates
- **C** plate drifts
- **D** plate tectonics

B5. (H) In the blast furnace, iron is extracted by roasting iron ore with
- **A** aluminium
- **B** carbon
- **C** copper
- **D** hydrogen

B6. (H) A soft rock contains layers of tiny fossils. The rock is most likely to be
- **A** sedimentary
- **B** metamorphic
- **C** igneous
- **D** basalt

B7. (F) Which of these (A, B, C or D) is a mixture of substances?
- **A** air
- **B** oxygen
- **C** iron
- **D** water

B8. (F) Which of these methods (A, B, C or D) will NOT separate sand from water?
- **A** chromatography
- **B** decanting
- **C** evaporation
- **D** filtering

B9. Which of these is the smallest particle?
(F)
A atom
B molecule
C electron
D nucleus

B10. An atom can become a positive ion by
(H)
A losing a neutron
B gaining a neutron
C losing an electron
D gaining an electron

B11. Which of these (**A**, **B**, **C** or **D**) shows the correct charge for a calcium ion?
(H)
A Ca^{1+}
B Ca^{2+}
C Cl^{1+}
D Cl^{2+}

B12. A calcium atom has an atomic number of 20 and a mass number of 40.
(H)
Which of these (**A**, **B**, **C** or **D**) shows the number of particles present in a calcium atom?

	electrons	neutrons	protons
A	20	20	20
B	20	40	20
C	40	20	40
D	40	40	20

The information below is for questions 13, 14 and 15.

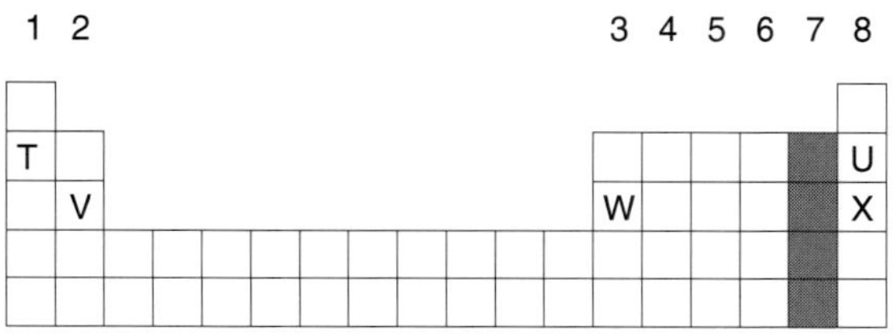

B13. The shaded region shows
(F)
A alkali metals
B halogens
C noble gases
D semi-metals

B14. Which elements are in the same period?
(F)
A T and V
B U and X
C V, W and X
D U, W and X

B15. Which element is the most chemically inert?
(F)
A T
B V
C W
D X

C1. A car is travelling on a level road. The driver has to stop quickly.
(F)
Which of these (**A**, **B**, **C** or **D**) has the greatest effect on the stopping distance?
A the kinetic energy of the car
B the potential energy of the car
C the straightness of the road
D how far the driver can see

C2. A skier is sliding down a slope at a steady speed.
(F)
Which of the following is true?

A there are no forces on the skier
B the forces on the skier are balanced
C there is an unbalanced force downwards
D there is an unbalanced force along the slope

C3. The diagram shows a crane lifting a load of 30 000 N through a distance of 10 metres.
(F)

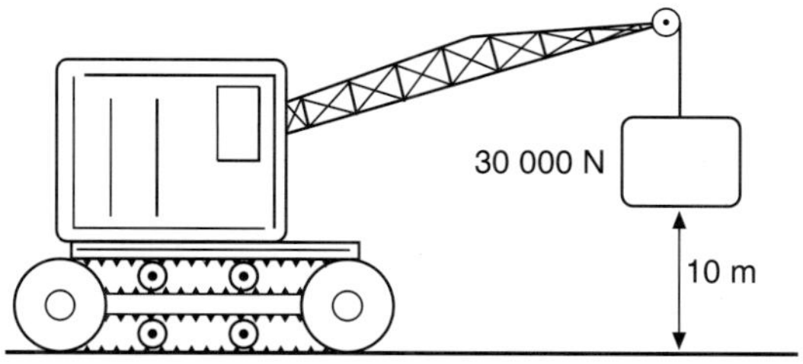

How much useful work does the crane do on the load?
A 3 000 J
B 3 000 N/m
C 300 000 J
D 300 000 N

C4. A constant force acts on an object. If there is no friction, which of these velocity (v) – time (t) graphs (**A**, **B**, **C** or **D**) shows the motion of the object?
(H)

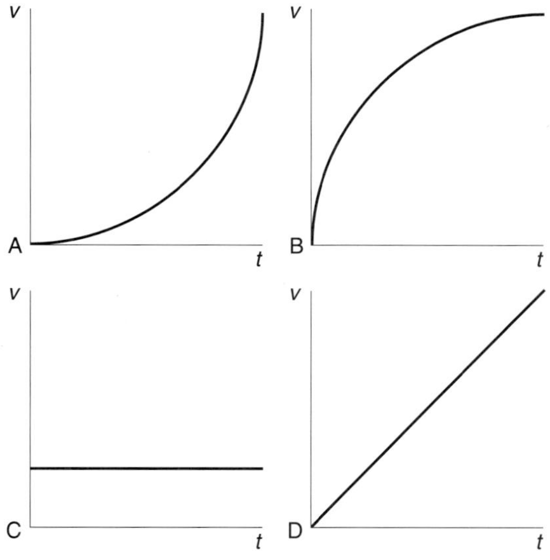

C5. (H) Which of these (**A**, **B**, **C** or **D**) involves most power?
- **A** a force of 10 N moving 10 m in 10 s
- **B** a force of 20 N moving 5 m in 10 s
- **C** a force of 10 N moving 5 m in 5 s
- **D** a force of 10 N moving 10 m in 5 s

C6. (F) Here is a diagram of a wave.

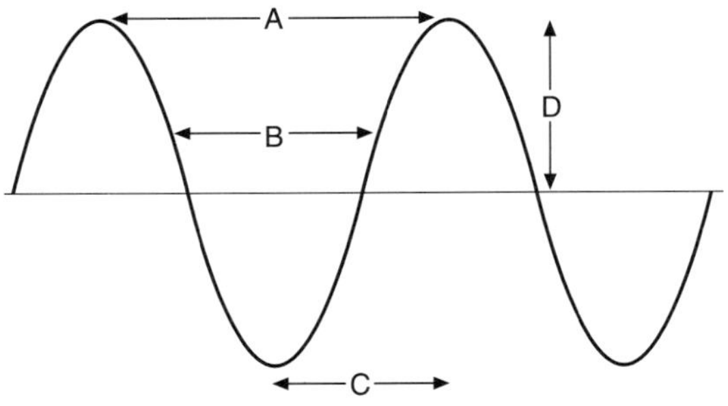

Which letter (**A**, **B**, **C** or **D**) shows the amplitude?

C7. (F) One of these diagrams (**A**, **B**, **C** or **D**) shows what happens when a vertical ray of light is reflected by a mirror. Which one is it?

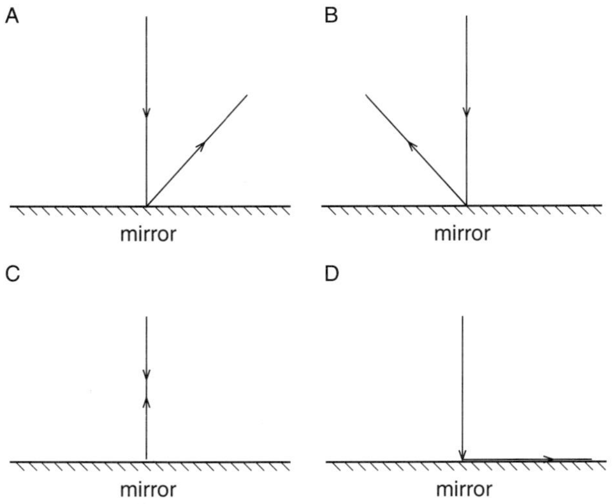

C8. (H) The ray diagrams show a ray of light passing through a block of glass. The block is in air.

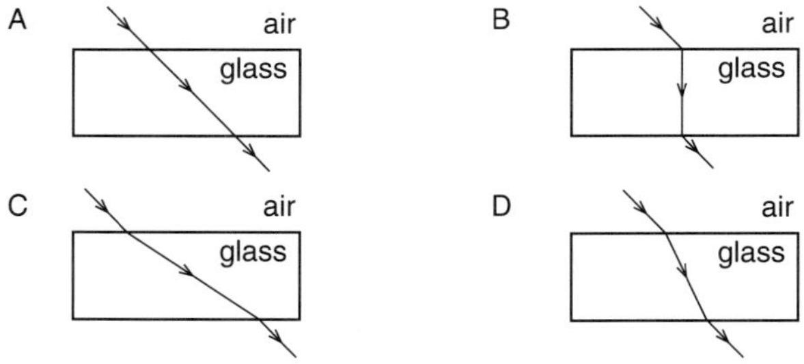

Which of these (**A**, **B**, **C** or **D**) is correct?

C9. (H) Here are some statements about electromagnetic waves.
1. they all travel through a vacuum
2. they all travel with the same velocity in any one medium
3. they all carry energy from one place to another

Which of these statements (choose **A**, **B**, **C** or **D**) is correct?
- **A** 1 only
- **B** 1 and 2 only
- **C** 2 and 3 only
- **D** 1, 2 and 3

C10. (H) Which of these statements (**A**, **B**, **C** or **D**) about ultraviolet light (UV) is **NOT** true?
- **A** it makes some materials fluoresce
- **B** it can cause tanning of the skin
- **C** it is emitted by the Sun
- **D** it travels faster than visible light

C11. (F) Giles has a 2 kW electric fire. The meter shows that there is only 3 kWh of electricity left.
How long can Giles have his fire on? Is it
- **A** 40 minutes
- **B** 1 hour
- **C** 1 hour 30 minutes
- **D** 6 hours

C12. (F) Which of these (**A**, **B**, **C** or **D**) shows a correctly wired ammeter and voltmeter?

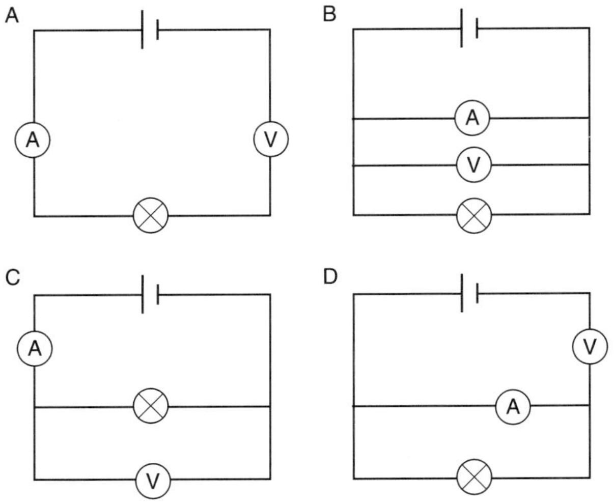

C13. (H) A material is used to make electrical fuses. Which property is essential for its use?
- **A** bad conductor of electricity
- **B** high boiling point
- **C** high density
- **D** low melting point

C14. (H) A coil of wire is rotated in a permanent magnetic field. Which of these (**A**, **B**, **C** or **D**) will happen?
- **A** the coil starts to rotate on its own
- **B** the magnetic field reduces to zero
- **C** an electric current is produced
- **D** the magnet starts to rotate

C15. (H) Wayne is designing a control system for a tropical fish tank heater. The system uses a 240 V (volt) supply and has an internal resistance of 240 Ω (ohms). Which of these fuses should he fit into the system?
- **A** 3 amp fuse
- **B** 5 amp fuse
- **C** 10 amp fuse
- **D** 13 amp fuse

C16. (H) When viewing a total eclipse of the Sun, an observer on the Earth passes into the shadow of the Moon. At this instant the observer can deduce that
- **A** heat (IR) and light travel at the same speed
- **B** light waves can be diffracted
- **C** light waves can interfere to give darkness
- **D** white light is made up of different colours

Short answer/Structured questions

A1. (F)

(a) Choose words from this list to complete the sentences that follow. Each word may be used once or not at all.

cells chloroplasts chromosomes genes
organs organisms nucleus tissues

Each body cell contains a .... which controls the cell's activities and characteristics. This contains pairs of ...., which are made up of a number of small units of inheritance called ....
Collections of similar cells working together are called ....
These make up .... which work together as systems allowing .... to survive. [6]

(b) Cells are surrounded by a cell membrane. Give two jobs carried out by a cell membrane. [2]

(SEG 98Sp)

A2. (H)

(a) The diagram shows the human female and male sex organs.

(i) Describe the functions of part B, C, E and G in the processes which lead up to fertilization. [4]

(ii) Name the structure where implantation of the embryo normally takes place. [1]

(b) Sometimes a minor infection can block tube B. Explain how this may affect the woman's chances of getting pregnant. [2]

(c) The diagram shows a mammalian sperm and egg.

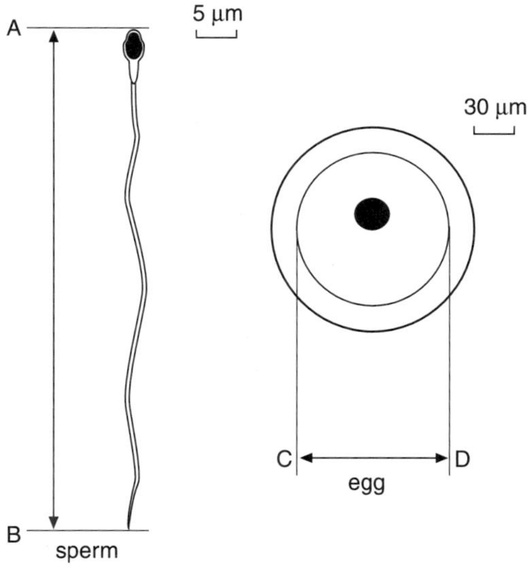

(i) Using the scales provided, work out the actual size of the gametes.
Show your working. [2]

(ii) Explain how the structure of the sperm enables it to carry out its function. [1]

A3. (F)

Robert set up this experiment (above right) to find out how light affects the rate at which plants make their own food by photosynthesis.

Robert put the lamp 100 cm away from the plant and counted the number of bubbles made by the plant in one minute. He then moved the lamp nearer to the beaker and counted the number of bubbles again.

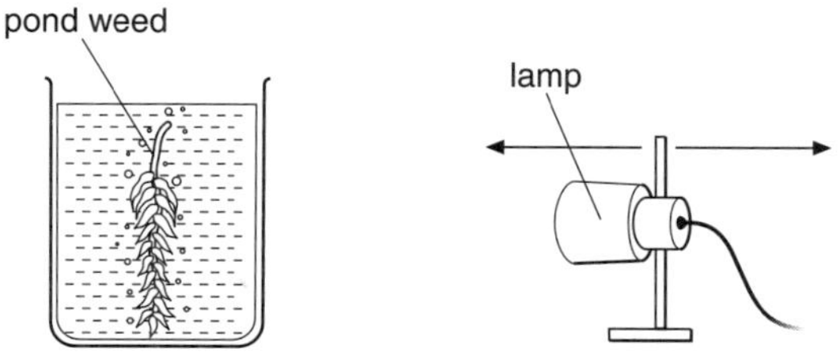

The table shows his results.

distance from lamp in cm	*number of bubbles per* minute
100	10
80	20
60	32
40	37
20	37

[2]

(a) Plot the points on a piece of graph paper.

(b) Draw the line of best fit on your grid. [1]

(c) Predict the number of bubbles per minute if the lamp is placed 10 cm from the plant. [1]

(d) Use these results to finish this sentence:

As the distance from the lamp ____________ ,
the rate of photosynthesis _____________ . [2]

(MEG Sp)

A4. (H)

(a) Domestic animals and cultivated plants can be improved by selective breeding.

(i) Describe the process of selective breeding. [3]

(ii) State **two** characteristics a farmer could improve in his wheat crop by selective breeding. [2]

(b) Tall, high-yielding tomato plants are deliberately crossed with short, disease-resistant tomato plants.

The genotype of the tall plant is **HH** and that of the short plant is **hh**. The dominant allele is **H**.

(i) Write the genotype of the F_1 generation plants. [1]

(ii) What proportion of the F_1 generation plants would be tall? [1]

(iii) The F_1 generation plants are allowed to self-pollinate. The seeds from this cross are grown. State and explain the probable proportions of tall and short plants in the offspring. [2]

(c) Genetic engineers can be successful in changing characteristics of some plants and animals. Scientists are trying to transfer the nitrogen-fixing ability associated with plants such as peas into crops such as cereals.

(i) Describe how the characteristics of an organism can be changed by genetic engineering. [3]

(ii) In developing new varieties of plants by genetic engineering, what danger should scientists be aware of and what precautions should they take? [3]

(MEG Sp)

A5. (H) **(a)** Microorganisms have important roles to play in the recycling of wastes and in food production.

The diagram shows a nitrogen cycle in grassland.

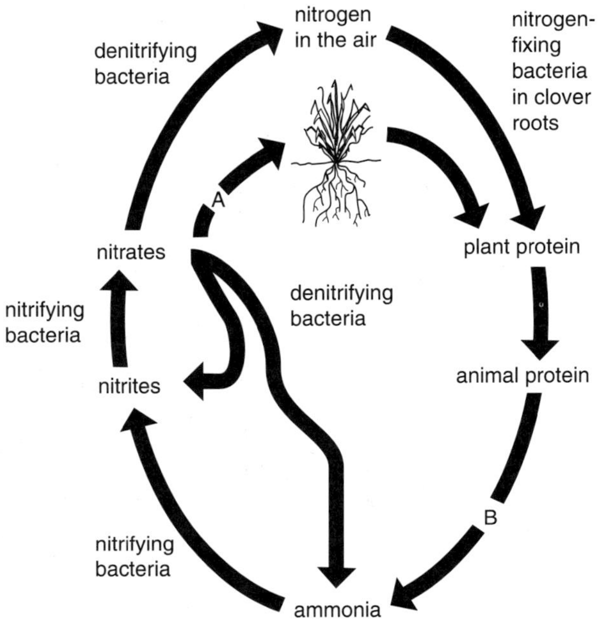

(i) Why do plants need nitrogen? [1]

(ii) What processes are represented by arrows A and B? [2]

(iii) What is the importance of nitrifying bacteria in the cycle? [2]

(iv) Knowing that nitrifying and nitrogen-fixing bacteria both require oxygen while denitrifying bacteria do not, what advice would you give to farmers relating to care of the soil? [2]

(v) Sundew is a plant which has leaves adapted to trap and digest insects.
Suggest why sundew can grow well in soils lacking nitrogen. [2]

(NICCEA)

A6. (F) A group of students studied the feeding pattern in a pond. The food web (above right) shows their results.

(a) What information is given by the arrows in this food web? [2]

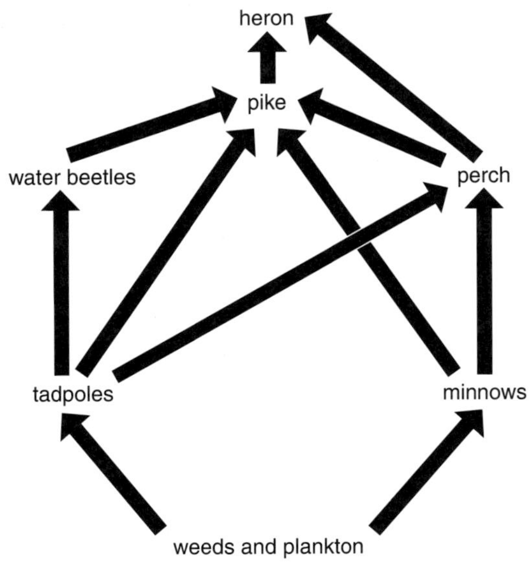

(b) A disease killed most of the minnows. Describe and explain the likely effects of this on the following organisms in the pond: perch; tadpoles; plankton. [6]

(SEG 98Sp)

A7. (H) The diagram shows a piece of food moving through the intestine.

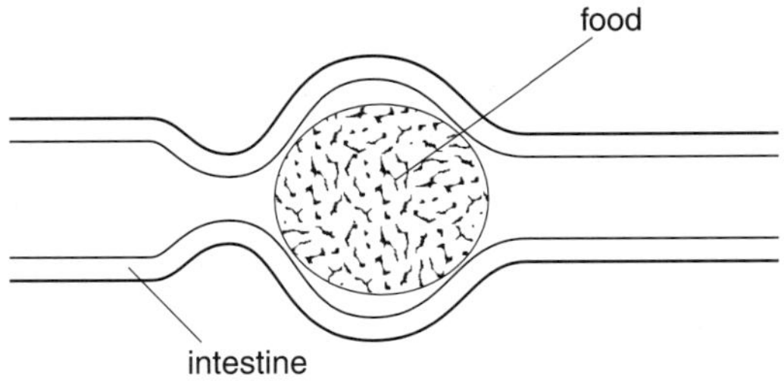

(a) Describe how the food is moved and how fibre in the diet may make this process more effective. [3]

(b) (i) Bread contains:

starch sugar protein fat calcium

Which of these food types stains blue-black when iodine solution is added to it? [1]

(ii) Describe how you would test the bread for protein and state the result you would expect if protein is present. [2]

(iii) Describe a practical procedure you could do to find out how much heat energy you could get out of a piece of food e.g. a peanut. [3]

(c) Explain why a sample of human saliva could change a 1% starch solution into maltose, but a sample of digestive juice from the stomach would not have this effect. [2]

(d) 'Undigested food is egested and not excreted.' Explain what is meant by this statement. [2]

(MEG 98Sp)

B1. (H) The element magnesium (atomic number 12) reacts with chlorine (atomic number 17) to form the compound magnesium chloride, $MgCl_2$

(a) Give the meaning of each of the following words: element; compound. [2]

(b) Sketch and complete the diagrams to show the arrangements of electrons in a magnesium atom and in a chlorine atom. [2]

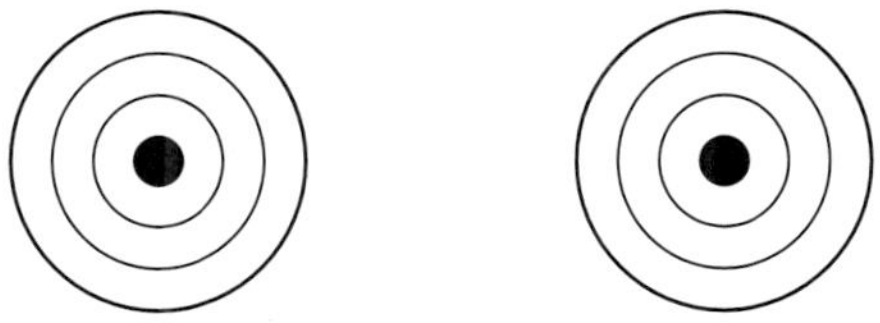

(c) What happens to these electron arrangements when magnesium reacts with chlorine to form magnesium chloride, $MgCl_2$? [4]

(d) The compound magnesium chloride has ionic bonding. Explain what this means. [2]

(SEG 98Sp)

B2 (H) Organic chemistry is the chemistry of carbon compounds.

(a) (i) What is the main source of organic chemicals? [1]

(ii) Draw the structural formula for ethane, the second member of the alkane series of saturated hydrocarbons. [1]

(iii) Alkenes are unsaturated hydrocarbons. Describe a simple chemical test which can be used to distinguish between the gases ethene and ethane. What result would you expect for **ethane**? [3]

(iv) Ethene can be used to make ethanol. Complete the formula equation for this reaction.

C_2H_4 + → [2]

(b) A diagram of the cell used in the electrolysis of aluminium oxide (Al_2O_3) is shown below.

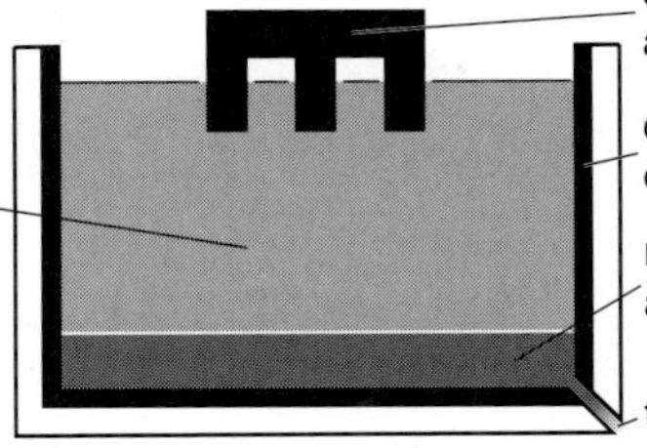

(i) Why must the aluminium oxide be molten? [1]

(ii) What is the purpose of the cryolite? [1]

(iii) Explain clearly what happens to the aluminium ions during this electrolysis. [3]

(iv) Explain how carbon dioxide can also be formed during the extraction of aluminium. [1]

(c) Draw a diagram to show the arrangement of the electrons in a molecule of oxygen gas, O_2. [2]

(NICCEA)

B3 (H) The diagram represents the arrangement of electrons in a magnesium atom.

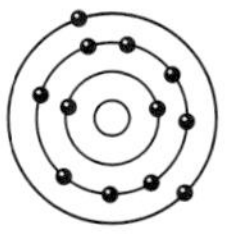

(a) Complete the table.

	number of protons	number of neutrons	number of electrons	electron arrangement
magnesium-24				2,8,2
oxygen-16		8	8	

[3]

(b) Magnesium oxide contains ionic bonding. Explain fully, in terms of transfer of electrons and the formation of ions, the changes which occur when magnesium oxide is formed from magnesium and oxygen atoms. [4]

(c) Sodium chloride and magnesium oxide have similar crystal structures and both contain ionic bonding. The melting points of sodium chloride and magnesium oxide are 800°C and 2800°C respectively.

Suggest why the melting point of magnesium oxide is much higher than the melting point of sodium chloride.

(Sodium chloride contains Na^+ and Cl^- ions.) [3]

(MEG 98Sp)

B4. (F) Crude oil is a mixture of different chemicals called hydrocarbons. Crude oil can be separated by heating it up and then collecting fractions at different temperatures.

This apparatus can be used to do it.

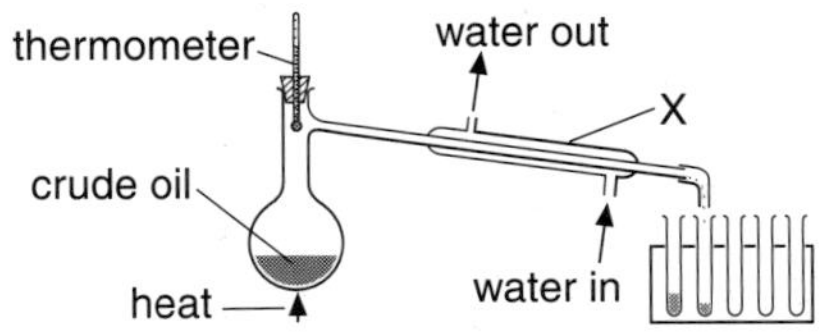

(a) Write down the name of the method used to separate the crude oil. [2]

(b) What is the job of part X? [1]

(c) The table shows some of the properties of the fractions.

fraction	temperature in °C	how runny?	colour	how it burns
A	up to 70	very	clear	easily, clean flame
B	70 to 150	fairly	pale yellow	fairly easy, a bit smoky
C	150 to 230	not very	yellow	difficult to light, a smoky flame

(i) Another fraction was collected between 230°C and 300°C. What would it be like? [3]

(ii) Fraction **A** is used as a fuel in a car engine. Suggest reasons why fraction **C** would be unsuitable for use in a car engine. [3]

(MEG)

B5 (H) This question is about the Periodic Table and some of its elements.

(a) (i) Give two features of the Periodic Table developed by Mendeleev. [2]

(ii) Predict which is the most reactive non-metal element. [1]

(b) Calcium is a reactive Group II metal.

(i) Describe **three** different **observations** from the reaction between calcium and water. [3]

(ii) Suggest **one** similarity and **one** difference you would expect to observe if barium, another Group II, element, rather than calcium, was placed in water. [2]

(iii) Predict the formula of the **compound** formed from the reaction of barium with water. [1]

(c) Fluorine is the lightest element in Group VII. Use your knowledge and understanding of trends within the halogens and properties of chlorine to answer this part of the question.

(i) What physical state would you expect for fluorine at room temperature and pressure? [1]

(ii) Explain why would you expect fluorine to be a non-metal. [1]

(iii) Predict the formula of aluminium fluoride. [1]

(iv) Write a balanced formula equation for the reaction of fluorine with potassium bromide. [2]

(v) Which halogen would you expect to be most reactive? [1]

(NICCEA)

B6 (F) Using indicators it is possible to classify everyday substances as acidic, alkaline or neutral. The table below gives the pH values for several 'household' substances:

substance	pH value
battery acid	1.0
vinegar	3.5
orange juice	4.0
milk	6.5
water	7.0
baking soda	8.5
washing soda	11.5
oven spray	13.0

(a) (i) Name a suitable indicator to measure the above pH values. [1]

(ii) What colour would this indicator turn in

an alkaline solution? [1]

an acidic solution? [1]

(b) From the above table name a substance which is

(i) a weak alkali [1]

(ii) a strong acid [1]

(iii) a neutral substance [1]

(c) (i) Grapes contain a weak acid. What pH value would you expect for pure grape juice? [1]

(ii) Nettle stings contain a weak acid called methanoic acid. Name a **suitable** substance from the table which would be used to neutralize this acid. [1]

(d) "Milk of Magnesia" contains the base magnesium hydroxide.

(i) Name the salt formed when "Milk of Magnesia" reacts with hydrochloric acid in the stomach. [1]

(ii) Why is magnesium hydroxide described as a base but not an alkali? [2]

(e) Complete the following word equations for the following neutralization reactions:-

(i) zinc + sulphuric acid →

(ii) calcium carbonate + hydrochloric acid →

(iii) sodium hydroxide + hydrochloric acid →

[4]

(NICCEA)

B7 (H) **(a)** Convection currents occur in the molten mantle of the Earth. The diagram represents the structure of the inside of the Earth.

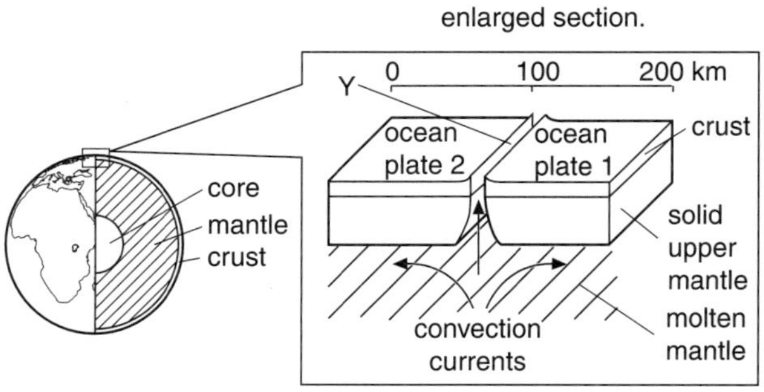

(i) Describe what you might expect to find at **Y**. [1]

(ii) Suggest **two** effects that the convection currents would have on the ocean plates. [2]

(b) The diagrams show how the map of the Earth has changed over the past 200 million years.

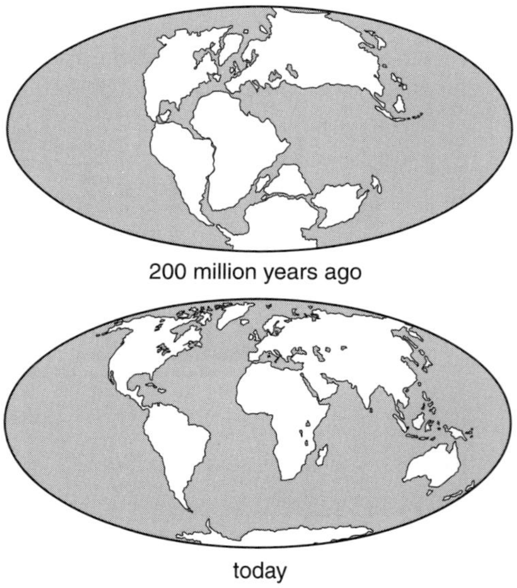

Suggest how this change could have happened, and what might happen to the continents during the next 200 million years. [4]

(MEG)

B8 (H) Ammonia is made by combining nitrogen with hydrogen.

(a) (i) What are the two sources of hydrogen in this diagram? [1]

(ii) Carbon dioxide can be removed by reacting the gas with an alkaline solution.
Explain why. [1]

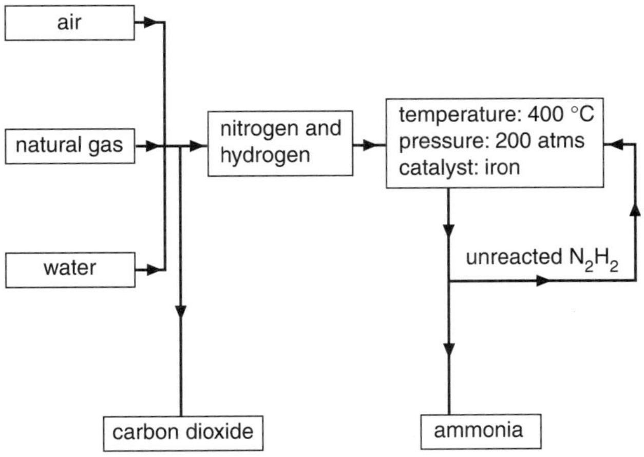

(b) (i) Balance the equation for the formation of ammonia.

..... N_2 + ... H_2 $\rightleftharpoons$ ..... NH_3 [1]

(ii) In this equation what does $\rightleftharpoons$ represent? [1]

(iii) The rate of reaction to form ammonia is increased by increasing the pressure. Explain why, in terms of the collision theory. [2]

(iv) A catalyst is used in this reaction. The use of the catalyst makes the process more economical. Explain why. [2]

(c) Some of the ammonia is used to make the fertilizer ammonium nitrate.

$$\underset{\text{ammonia}}{NH_3} + \underset{\text{nitric acid}}{HNO_3} \rightarrow \underset{\text{ammonium nitrate}}{NH_4NO_3}$$

(i) Calculate the relative formula mass of ammonium nitrate.
(Relative atomic masses are:
H 1; N 14; O 16.) [1]

(ii) How many tonnes of ammonium nitrate can be made from 340 tonnes of ammonia? [3]

(iii) Explain one environmental problem caused by the excessive use of a fertilizer such as ammonium nitrate. [2]

(SEG 98Sp)

C1
(F)

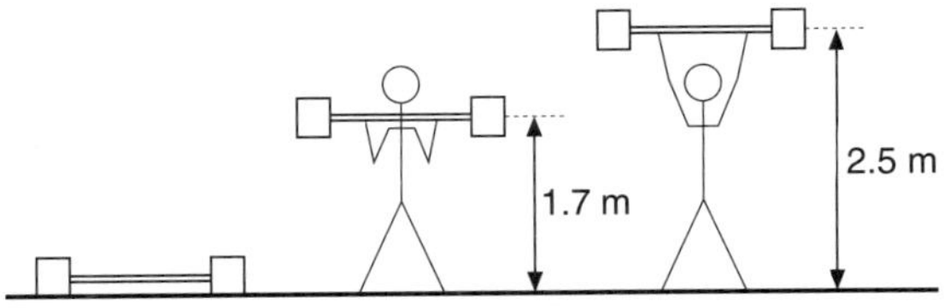

In the 'clean and jerk' a weightlifter lifts a bar cleanly to his chest and pauses before jerking the bar above his head. The weight of the bar is 1000 N.

Calculate the work done in the 'jerk' part of the lift. [2]

(WJEC)

C2
(F)

Mr. Singh has read a leaflet about how houses can lose heat.
He decides to reduce the heat loss through the roof of his house.

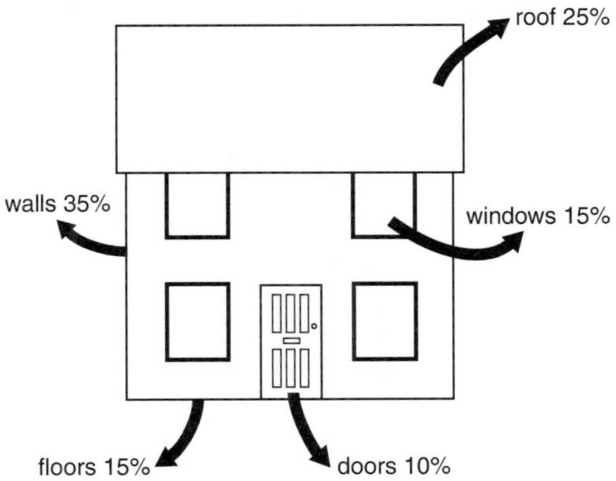

(a) Suggest how Mr. Singh can reduce the amount of heat lost through the roof of his house. [1]

(b) Explain how the method you have suggested reduces heat loss. [2]

(c) Mr. Singh would like to use renewable energy to heat the water in his house.
He fits a solar panel to the roof.

(i) Explain what renewable means. [1]

(ii) Explain how a solar panel can be used to heat water. [2]

(MEG)

C3
(F)

A van travels at a steady speed. After 10 seconds the brakes are put on until the van stops. The speed–time graph shows this motion.

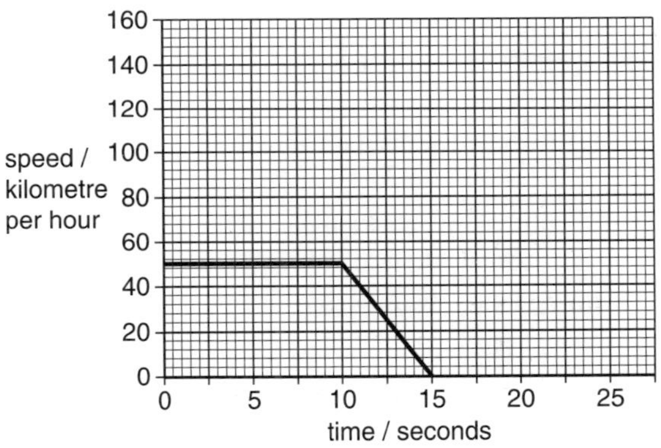

(a) What is the van's speed (km/h) when the brakes are first put on? [1]

(b) How long, in seconds, does the van take to come to rest after the brakes come on? [1]

A car travels at 80 km/h. The brakes are put on after 10 seconds. The car slows down at the same rate as the van.

(c) On a sketch of the grid draw the graph for the speed of the car. [3]

(d) Explain why the car travels further during braking. [1]

(e) Why are motorists advised to leave a large gap between them and the car in front when travelling at high speed on a motorway? [2]

(MEG)

C4
(F)

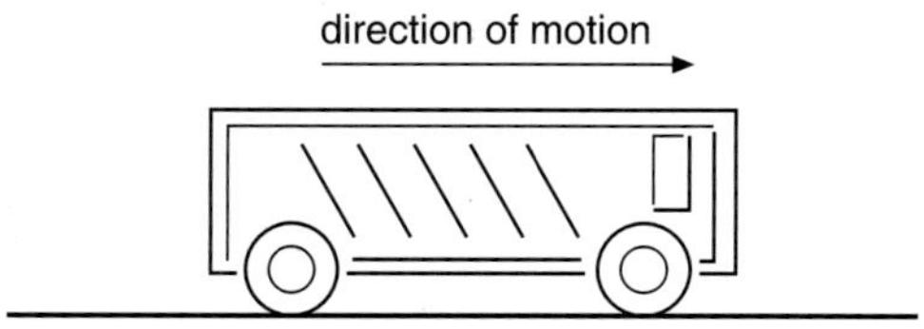

A truck, moving at constant speed, is acted upon by a constant force.

(a) Describe, as fully as you can, how the motion of the truck is affected

(i) when the force is in the direction of motion, [1]

(ii) when the force is in the opposite direction to the motion. [2]

(b) If the size of the force were bigger, how would this affect your answers to parts (**a**)(**i**) and (**a**)(**ii**)? [2]

(WJEC)

C5 The diagram shows the eclipse of the Sun – a solar eclipse.
(F)

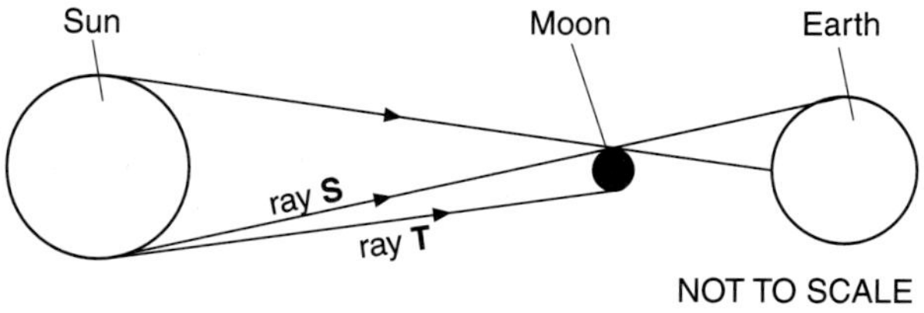

(a) Redraw the diagram and on it:

(i) finish ray **T**. [1]

(ii) clearly label the part of the Earth that is in total darkness with a **U**. [1]

(b) Ray **S** has been drawn.

(i) Draw the other ray which shows the limit of the part of the Earth where there is partial darkness. [1]

(ii) Clearly label the area where there is partial darkness with a **P**. [1]

(MEG 98Sp)

C6 **(a)** In a recycling plant, an electromagnet separates scrap iron from household rubbish.
(F)

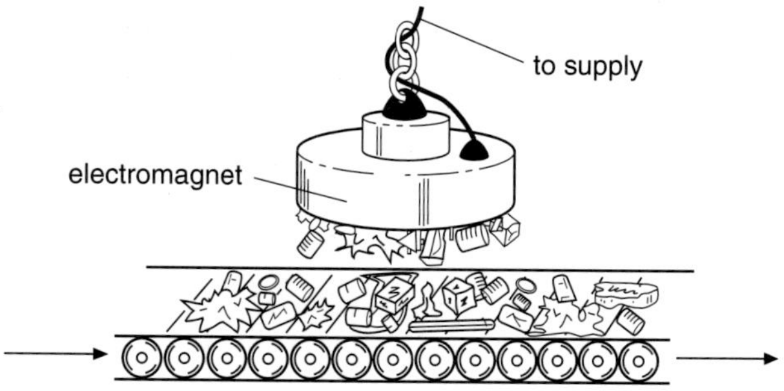

Items containing iron are attracted to the electromagnet. The electromagnet is then placed over a skip.

(i) What must the operator do to drop the scrap iron into the skip? [1]

(ii) Why can't this electromagnet be used to separate aluminium cans from the rubbish? [1]

(b) This shows a simple electromagnet used in a laboratory.

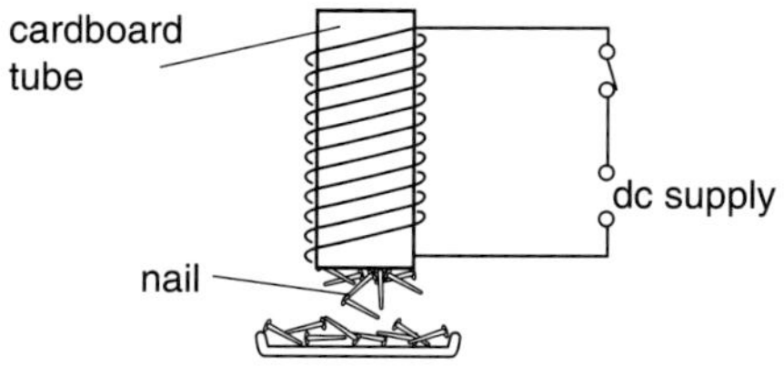

Suggest two ways in which the electromagnet can be made to pick up more nails. [2]

(MEG 98Sp)

C7 **(a)** Annie's hairdryer has a power rating of 1.6 kW.
(F) She uses it for a total time of 1.5 hours each week.

Use energy = power × time to calculate how many **units** of electrical energy she uses in one week. Write down the name of the **unit**. [3]

(b) One 'unit' costs 7 pence.
Calculate the total cost (pence) of drying her hair over a period of five weeks. [2]

(MEG Sp)

C8 A microscope is used to look at some smoke particles in a glass container.
(F)

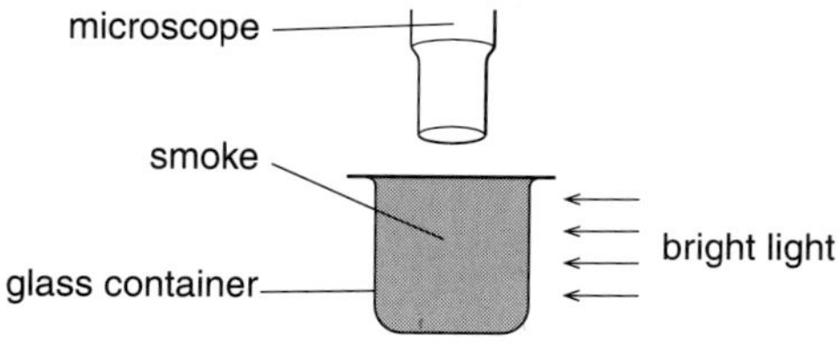

The smoke is illuminated by a bright light.

The movement of the smoke particles is called Brownian Motion.

(a) Describe the motion of the smoke particles. [2]

(b) Explain why the smoke particles move like this. [2]

(c) How would the motion change if smaller smoke particles are used? [1]

(MEG 98Sp)

C9 **(a)** Nuclear power station workers may be exposed to alpha, beta and gamma radiations.
(F)

type of radiation	*What is it?*	*What type of charge does it carry?*
alpha		
beta	electron	negative
gamma		

(b) A film badge is used to check their exposure to radiation.
The badge has three sections.

Section X has no absorber.
Section Y has a plastic absorber.
Section Z has both a plastic and an aluminium absorber which is 4 mm thick.

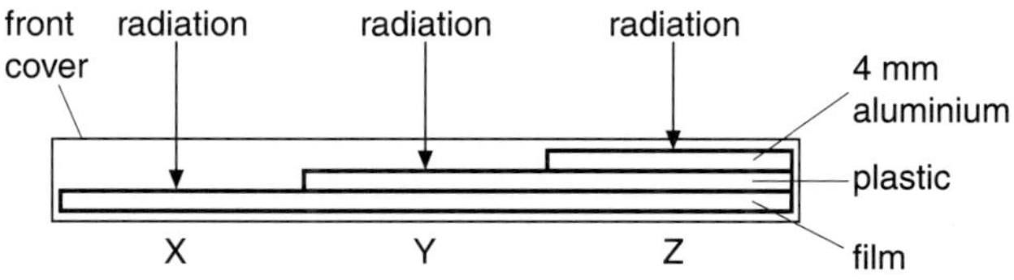

When the film is developed it turns black where it has been exposed to radiation.

Complete the table to show whether the film in section Y and Z will be black after exposure to alpha, beta, or gamma radiations.
Write 'black' or 'not black'.

type of radiation	*section X*	*section Y*	*section Z*
alpha	black		
beta	black		
gamma	black		

(*MEG*)

C10 **(a)** What words complete the following sentences.

(F) **(i)** The Earth travels around the Sun once every ....? [1]

(ii) The Moon travels around the Earth once every ....? [1]

(iii) The Earth spins on its axis once every ....? [1]

(b) The following diagram shows the Solar System. It is **not** drawn to scale.

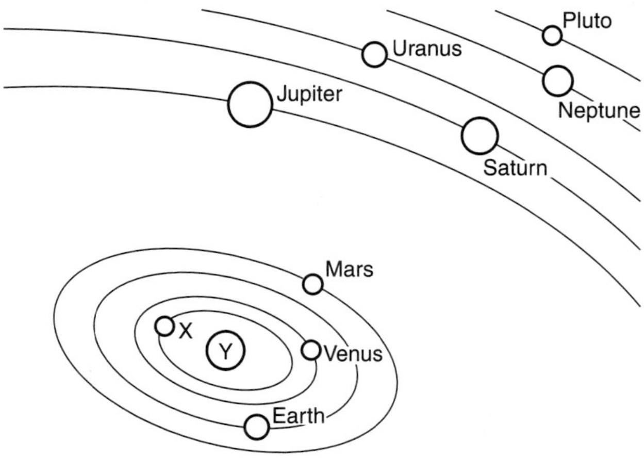

(i) Name **X** and **Y**. [2]

(ii) Name one planet that takes longer than Mars to complete one orbit of the Sun.

Give a reason for your choice. [2]

(c) Arrange the following parts of the Universe in increasing order of size.

galaxy Moon planet Solar System star [3]

(*SEG 98Sp*)

INDEX